THE GLOBAL EXPERIENCE

Readings in World History Since 1500

VOLUME II

Second Edition

THE GLOBAL EXPERIENCE

Readings in World History Since 1500

VOLUME II

Edited by
PHILIP F. RILEY
FRANK A. GEROME
HENRY A. MYERS
CHONG K. YOON
James Madison University

Special Contributor
MARY LOUISE LOE

Prentice Hall
Englewood Cliffs, New Jersey 07632

Library of Congress Cataloging-in-Publication Data

The Global experience / edited by Philip F. Riley . . . [et al.] ;
    special contributor, Mary Louise Loe.
        p.   cm.
    Contents: v. 1. Readings in world history to 1500 — v.
2. Readings in world history since 1500.
    ISBN 0-13-356981-0 (v. 1). — ISBN 0-13-356999-3 (v. 2)
    1. World history. I. Riley, Philip F.
D20.G56 1992
909—dc20   91-22738
                                                    CIP

Acquisitions editor: Steve Dalphin
Production editor: Linda B. Pawelchak
Supervisory editor: Joan L. Stone
Copy editor: Linda B. Pawelchak
Cover design: Ray Lundgren Graphics, Ltd.
Prepress buyer: Kelly Behr
Manufacturing buyer: Mary Ann Gloriande
Editorial assistant: Caffie Risher

© 1992, 1987 by Prentice-Hall, Inc.
a Simon & Schuster Company
Englewood Cliffs, New Jersey 07632

Printed in the United States of America

10 9 8 7 6 5 4 3

ISBN 0-13-356999-3

Prentice-Hall International (UK) Limited, *London*
Prentice-Hall of Australia Pty. Limited, *Sydney*
Prentice-Hall Canada Inc., *Toronto*
Prentice-Hall Hispanoamericana, S.A., *Mexico*
Prentice-Hall of India Private Limited, *New Delhi*
Prentice-Hall of Japan, Inc., *Tokyo*
Simon & Schuster Asia Pte. Ltd., *Singapore*
Editora Prentice-Hall do Brasil, Ltda., *Rio de Janeiro*

For
Raymond C. Dingledine, Jr.
1919–1990
Teacher, Scholar, Friend

CONTENTS

An Era of Global Violence   *168*

China, Russia, and Mexico in Upheaval   *168*

World War I: Battle   *180*

World War I: Diplomacy   *186*

Stalin's Revolution   *194*

Soviet Industrialization   *203*

Fascism: Three Faces   *207*

PREFACE

This anthology is a brief, balanced collection of primary materials, organized chronologically and focused on global themes.

In preparing this collection, we have been mindful of three concerns. First, any informed understanding of the world in the late twentieth century must begin with history. We believe the most useful mode of historical study — particularly for college students — is world history. Because men and women make history, the documents we have chosen depict the variety of their experiences over time on a global scale. To help students study and appreciate these experiences, we have selected excerpts from both classic texts and less familiar but equally important readings. This material illustrates patterns of global change and exchange, as well as the distinct achievements of the major civilizations.

Second, to encourage the comparative study of world history and to reinforce the underlying links between civilizations, we have organized the readings into chronological sections. By doing so we hope to underscore global patterns of development and, at the same time, permit our readers to study documents of special interest selectively.

Third, to help clarify our selections, particularly those readings that may be unfamiliar to students, we have included introductory comments as well as questions to consider. We hope this material will help students gain a better understanding of the text and connect their historical study to contemporary issues and problems.

Our students, particularly in their questions and criticisms, have shaped our work more than they know. Our colleagues at James Madison University have also helped immeasurably. Michael J. Galgano, Head, Department of History, has assisted us at every turn; he enthusiastically found us the means and time to complete this project. Martha B. Caldwell, William H. Ingham, Caroline Marshall, Daniel McFarland, and Jacqueline Walker provided insights and suggestions to make this a better book. Mary Louise Loe not only contributed the sections on Russian and Soviet history but helped us throughout our work.

Sheila Riley aided with the final editing. Debra Ryman and Gordon Miller skillfully assisted us in securing materials through interlibrary loan.

The second edition of *The Global Experience: Readings in World History* contains a number of new sections, new selections, and new translations, as well as changes in the selections published in our first edition. Among the new selections in Volume I are: A Japanese Creation Epic: *Nihongi*; A Mayan Creation Story: *Popol Vuh*; Papyrus Lansing: A Schoolbook; The Banquet of Ashurnasirpal; Widow Burning: Two Views of Sati; Guanyin: Compassion of the Bodhisattva; The Free Will: "The Burning House"; The Writings of St. Paul on Women; Tacitus, *The Annals*; Pliny the Younger, *Letters to Emperor Trajan*; M. Minucius Felix, *Octavius*; Commentaries on Islamic Law and Culture; Muslim Culture in Baghdad; The *Nibelungenlied*; Ibn Fadlan's Account of Vikings in Early Russia; Liutprand, Bishop of Cremona, *A Mission to Constantinople*; Memoirs of Usamah Ibn-Munqidh; The Rule of Saint Francis; A Father's Letter to His Sons Studying at Toulouse; Imperial Examination System; Emperor T'ai-tsung, "On the Art of Government"; Chinese Footbinding; John Pian del Carpini, *The Tartars*; Kuyuk Khan, Letter to Pope Innocent IV; The Yuan Code: Homicide; Tsunetomo Yamamoto, *Hagakure*; The Forty-Seven Ronin; Konstantin Mihailvic, *Memoirs of a Janissary*; Martin Luther at the Diet of Worms; Pero Vaz de Caminha and the Brazilian Indians; Antonio Pigafetta, *Magellan's Voyage*; and Bernal Díaz del Castillo, The Conquest of Mexico.

Among the new additions to Volume II are: Lady Mary Wortley Montague, Embassy to Constantinople; Anthony Monseratte, S.J., *Journey to the Court of Akbar*; Léonhard Euler, "Newton's Discovery of the Principle of Gravity"; Ceremonial for Visitors: Court Tribute; The Laws for the Military House (Buke Shohatto), 1615; Andrew Carnegie, *Triumphant Democracy*; "Women Miners in the English Coal Pits"; Robert Southey, "The Battle of Blenheim"; Heinrich von Treitschke, Conquest and National Greatness; Otto von Bismarck, Making German Patriotism Effective; Gandhi: Facing the British in India; First Japanese Embassy to the United States; Geisha: *Glimpse of Unfamiliar Japan*; "World War I: A Frenchman's Recollections"; Stalin, "Socialism in One Country; Stalin *On the Draft Constitution of the U.S.S.R.*; Rudolf Hoess, "Eyewitness to Hitler's Genocide"; "Tojo Makes Plea of Self Defense"; Thomas and Margaret Melady, Statement of African Unity; Mikhail Gorbachev and *Perestroika*; Václav Havel, Address to Congress; Richard von Weizsäcker, "The Day of German Unity"; William F. Buckley, "Human Rights and American Foreign Policy"; Gustavo Gutiérrez, *A Theology of Liberation*; The Second "Maekawa" Report.

In making these revisions, we were guided by the advice and criticism of our colleagues, J. Chris Arndt, Gordon M. Fisher, Steven W. Guerrier, Raymond M. Hyser, and David Owusu-Ansah; as well as Robert C. Figueira, of Saint Mary's

College, Winona, Minnesota ; Donald C. Holsinger of Seattle Pacific University ; and John O. Hunwick of Northwestern University; and the following reviewers— Norman R. Bennett, Boston University; Charles Gruber, Marshall University; and Loyd E. Lee, SUNY–New Paltz. We are very grateful for all their criticism and we would appreciate your comments as well. Send your comments to Philip F. Riley, Department of History, James Madison University, Harrisonburg, VA 22807.

GLOBAL CONTACTS

Age of Exploration and Expansion

Almost a century before Portuguese captain Vasco da Gama successfully rounded the Cape of Good Hope and reached the Malabar coast of India in 1498, in 1405, Emperor Yung-lo (1403–1424) of the Ming dynasty (1308–1644) had launched the first of a series of grand-scale maritime expeditions. Over the next 28 years, the Chinese court dispatched six more large-scale naval expeditions to Southeast Asia, India, Persia, and the east coast of Africa. These gigantic expeditions involved more than 70,000 men and hundreds of vessels, and covered thousands of nautical miles. In contrast with the goals of the European adventurers who came to Asia several decades later, the main purpose of these grand undertakings was neither conquest nor trade. The Ming government was mainly interested in spreading and enhancing its dynastic prestige and power as well as winning for China the nominal control of those distant regions. By 1415, 19 kingdoms had sent tributes to the Ming court; however, after nearly three decades of naval expeditions, not a single permanent overseas Ming colony was established.

Then, in 1433, the great Ming naval expeditions suddenly ceased, never to resume. Although scholars do not know the precise reasons why China refused to embark on her own Age of Exploration, possible explanations might include: the high cost of the naval expeditions; China's long-held tradition of anti-commercialism; and the ruling Confucian scholars' and officials' prejudice toward the seafaring people, who neglected to observe two important Confucian virtues — namely, filial piety and ancestor worship. Had those Chinese seafarers sustained support from a leader like Portugal's Prince Henry, the course of world history might have been quite different; certainly China would have "discovered" such distant lands as Spain, England, and France. A little more than six decades after the last Ming naval expedition of 1433, Vasco da Gama opened an era of European domination of the Asian waters. The compass and gunpowder, two important gifts of China to the West, permitted the Europeans to develop empires in Asia.

As the demand for Oriental products increased in Western Europe in the fifteenth century, merchants and monarchs, hoping to break the Italian monopoly of that trade, began their search for an all-water route to the East. Another powerful impetus was a strong sense of Christian duty to convert pagans and infidels. For centuries, Portuguese and Spaniards had struggled to expel the Muslims who occupied their land. That effort generated a religious fervor and missionary zeal and also helped establish a sense of national

1

identity. By the early fifteenth century, Portugal had become a unified state, separate from the expanding Spanish kingdoms of Leon and Castile. The Iberians, with their strategic location facing the Atlantic and with new knowledge of navigation and shipbuilding gained from Italian seafarers on the Mediterranean, initiated the age of European exploration and expansion.

One of the most important explorers the Spanish monarchs sponsored was Christopher Columbus. As a youth, he had served as a seaman on various ships in the Mediterranean and eventually settled in Portugal where he developed his idea of reaching Asia by sailing west. He was not successful in gaining financial support from the Portuguese monarchs who favored opening the sea route to India by way of Africa but he continued his search for a sponsor in Spain. After the fall of the Muslim stronghold of Granada on January 2, 1492, Queen Isabella finally agreed to his terms. Columbus's four expeditions to the Caribbean and the coastline of Central America established the beginning of Spain's empire in the Western Hemisphere. The final reading in this section describes the conquest of Mexico.

1

Cheng Ho [Zheng He][1]: Ming Maritime Expeditions

Most of the large naval expeditions of the Ming dynasty were led by a Muslim court eunuch named Cheng Ho (1371–1433). The following selection describes China's Columbus and the maritime explorations that he led.

QUESTIONS TO CONSIDER

1. What does the size, organization, and nature of the Ming maritime fleet indicate about China's capabilities in the early fifteenth century?
2. What do the Ming Emperor's bans on imperial naval explorations suggest about Chinese views of the world?
3. Compare and contrast the Ming maritime expeditions with the Age of Discovery in Western history. What motives inspired Cheng Ho and Columbus?

Cheng Ho (1371–1433), eunuch and commander-in-chief of the Ming expeditionary fleets in the early years of the 15th century, was born into a family named Ma at K'un-yang in central Yunnan [Kunyang]. His great-grandfather was named

1. See note on Chinese spelling on page 30.

From Carrington Goodrich, ed., *Dictionary of Ming Biography, 1368–1644*, vol. 1, A–L (New York: Columbia University Press, 1976), pp. 194–198, passim. Copyright © 1976 Columbia University Press. Reprinted by permission.

Bayan, and his grandfather and father were both named Ḥājjī, which suggests that the two probably visited Mecca and that the family had a long tradition of Islamic faith and may have been of Mongol-Arab origin. At the beginning of the Ming dynasty, a number of generals who fought on the frontier were in charge of recruiting eunuchs for the court. In 1381, when Yunnan was pacified by an army under Fu Yu-de, Cheng Ho, at that time about ten years old, was one of the children selected to be castrated. As a trainee for eunuch service, he was assigned to the retinue of Chu Ti [Zhu Di] [Emperor Yung-lo]. In his early twenties, he accompanied Chu Ti on a series of military campaigns and in the course of them took up a career in the army. As his family records relate, "when he entered adulthood, he reportedly became seven feet tall and had a waist about five feet in circumference. His cheeks and forehead were high but his nose was small. He had glaring eyes and a voice as loud as a huge bell. He knew a great deal about warfare and was well accustomed to battle.". . .

Cheng Ho first achieved official prominence early in 1404 when he was promoted to the position of director of eunuch affairs and granted the surname of Cheng [Zheng]. Shortly afterward he received the appointment of commander-in-chief of the first expedition. Meanwhile local officials of the eastern coastal regions were ordered to build ocean-going vessels. By July, 1405, some 1,180 ships of various sizes and types had been constructed. The large or treasure ships were, according to measures of that time, as much as 440 feet long and 186.2 wide, and those of medium size, or horse ships, 370 feet long and 150 wide. There were supply ships which measured 280 feet in length and 120 in breadth, and billet ships measuring 240 feet by 94. The battleships equipped with cannon were much smaller, measuring only 180 feet by 68. Most of the treasure ships were the product of the Lung-chiang [Long Jiang] shipyard near Nanking [Nanjing]. None of these has survived, but near the site of the shipyard was recently discovered (1957) a large wooden rudder (length 11 meters) thought to have been fashioned for one of the bigger vessels. It is now preserved in the Kiangsu [Jiangsu] provincial museum.

The first voyage began in the summer of 1405 with a 27,800 man crew and 62 (or 63) large and 255 smaller vessels. . . . [In the second voyage, which was launched in late autumn of 1407, the expedition sailed into the Indian Ocean.]

. . . In the summer of 1409 Cheng Ho returned to Nanking to report on his mission to the emperor. Here he built a temple in honor of T'ien-fei [Tianfei], the goddess of the sea, to whose virtue and power he attributed the safe voyages of his fleets. The inscription on the stele erected later (May 3, 1416) has been partly translated into French by Claudine Lombard-Salmon ; the complete Chinese text may be found in the book by Louis Gaillard.

After a brief stay in the capital, Cheng Ho was again sent overseas, accompanied by Wang Ching-hung [Wang Jinghong] and Hou Hsien [Hou Xian]. His third voyage was comparable to the first and second in the number of men but with only 48 vessels ; it lasted from September, 1409, to June, 1411. This expedition reached the same destination on the Malabar coast of India, but along the way several excursions were made, including brief visits to Siam, Malacca, Sumatra, and Ceylon. It also undertook lumbering operations and gathered fragrant herbs in the Sembilan Islands. . . .

It was the fourth voyage, which began in 1413 and ended in August, 1415, that took the expedition far beyond its earlier destinations. Under the same command but with a crew of 27,670 men and some 63 large vessels, the expedition touched at a number of new places, including the Maldives, Hormuz, the Hadramaut coast, and Aden. In Sumatra the expedition became involved in a local power struggle at Ch'iao-shan [Qiaoshan] (Samudra-Pasai). A usurper by the name of Su-wa-la, after murdering the king, directed his forces against the expedition, but was subsequently defeated and pursued as far as Lambri, where he and his family were captured. The prisoners were taken to Nanking on the return of the fleet. As a result of this voyage, nineteen countries sent envoys and tribute to the Ming court. Chu Ti was so pleased with the results that he rewarded all participants in the expedition according to their ranks.

In December, 1416, Cheng Ho was commissioned to escort home the envoys of the nineteen states, and embarked, possibly in the autumn of 1417, on his fifth voyage, which lasted up to August, 1419. The returning envoys, who had witnessed the delight of the Ming emperor at his first sight of a giraffe, spread the news to other countries. Hence an impressive collection of strange animals, among them lions, leopards, single-humped camels, ostriches, zebras, rhinoceroses, antelopes, and giraffes offered by rulers of several states highlighted this journey.

The spring of 1421 saw the launching of the sixth voyage, but Cheng may not have joined the fleet until later. It returned on September 3, 1422, accompanied by a large number of envoys from such states as Hormuz, Aden, Djofar, La-sa (Al-shsā?), Brawa, Mogadishu, Calicut, Cochin, Cail, Ceylon, the Maldive Islands, Lambri, Sumatra, Aru, Malacca, Kan-pa-li (Coyampadi?), Sulu, Bengal, Borneo, Ku-ma-la (-lang, Cabarruyan Islands?), and Ts'eng-pa (Zanzibar). The number of countries visited on this trip has not been listed, but the expedition reached at least as far as Aden, near the mouth of the Red Sea, and Mogadishu and Brawa on the coast of east Africa. . . .

In the meanwhile Chu Ti had died (August 12, 1424), and almost at once the idea of another maritime expedition came under attack. The emperor designate, Chu Kao-chih [Zhu Gaozhi], promptly (August 28) released from prison Hsia Yüan-chi [Xia Yuanji], perhaps the most outspoken critic of the treasure fleets, and on September 7, the very day of Chu's accession to the throne as the fourth Ming emperor, other voices joined Hsia's in recommending their abolition. This protest seems to have settled the matter, for in the following February Cheng Ho received an appointment as garrison commander of the Nanking district, and was told to maintain order in his own expeditionary forces, and consult with Wang Ching-hung and two other eunuchs. . . .

Only a few months later the fourth emperor died and for several years the plan to launch another expedition lay dormant. Finally in June, 1430, his successor, the fifth emperor, Chu Chan-chi [Zhu Zhanji], issued an order for the seventh (and what proved to be the last) voyage, but it was not to leave the Fukien [Fujian] coast until a year and a half later. It returned in July, 1433. The mission was intended to regenerate the tributary relationships once maintained under Chu Ti, which had significantly weakened since his death. A score of states were revisited, including those along the coasts of the Arabian peninsula and eastern Africa. In this instance too ambassadors returned with the fleet, bringing such gifts as giraffes, elephants, and horses. Cheng Ho, who was already in his sixties, did not perhaps visit all of them in person, and some of the side missions were conducted by his aides. . . .

. . . What happened to Cheng Ho from this point is not clear. It has customarily been said that he died in 1435 or 1436 at the age of sixty-five, no specific date or site of burial being indicated in contemporary sources. A later source, the *T'ung-chih Shang Chiang liang-hsien chih* [*Tongzhi Shang Jiang liangxian Zhi*] (preface of 1874), 3/39a, however, maintains that Cheng Ho died at Calicut and was buried at Niushou-shan outside Nanking. If this be true, he must have passed away early in 1433.

2

Christopher Columbus, *Journal of First Voyage to America*

Columbus and his crew of 90 sailed from Spain on August 3, 1492, arriving at San Salvador in the Bahamas in October. After three additional voyages exploring the Yucatan peninsula and Central America, he died in poverty and neglect, still believing he had discovered the coast of Asia.

QUESTIONS TO CONSIDER

1. What did Columbus tell his crew in order to pacify and encourage them when they complained and became impatient with the length of the voyage?
2. What was the nature of this initial encounter between Spaniards and the natives? What were the reactions of each?
3. In what ways do these journal notes reveal some of Spain's motives for exploration, conquest, and colonization?

Monday, Oct. 8th. Steered W.S.W. and sailed day and night eleven or twelve leagues; at times during the night, fifteen miles an hour, if the account can be depended upon. Found the sea like the river at Seville, *"thanks to God,"* says the Admiral. The air soft as that of Seville in April, and so fragrant that it was delicious to breathe it. The weeds appeared very fresh. Many land birds, one of which they took, flying towards the S.W.; also *grajaos*, ducks, and a pelican were seen.

Tuesday, Oct. 9th. Sailed S.W. five leagues, when the wind changed, and they stood W. by N. four leagues. Sailed in the whole day and night, twenty leagues and a half; reckoned to the crew seventeen. All night heard birds passing.

Wednesday, Oct. 10th. Steered W.S.W. and sailed at time ten miles an hour, at others twelve, and at others, seven; day and night made fifty-nine leagues'

From Christopher Columbus, *Journal of First Voyage to America* (New York : A. & C. Boni, 1924), pp. 20–26, passim.

progress ; reckoned to the crew but forty-four. Here the men lost all patience, and complained of the length of the voyage, but the Admiral encouraged them in the best manner he could, representing the profits they were about to acquire, and adding that it was to no purpose to complain, having come so far, they had nothing to do but continue on to the Indies, till with the help of our Lord, they should arrive there.

Thursday, Oct. 11th. Steered W.S.W. ; and encountered a heavier sea than they had met with before in the whole voyage. Saw pardelas and a green rush near the vessel. The crew of the Pinta saw a cane and a log ; they also picked up a stick which appeared to have been carved with an iron tool, a piece of cane, a plant which grows on land, and a board. The crew of the Niña saw other signs of land, and a stalk loaded with roseberries. These signs encouraged them, and they all grew cheerful. Sailed this day till sunset, twenty-seven leagues.

After sunset steered their original course W. and sailed twelve miles an hour till two hours after midnight, going ninety miles, which are twenty-two leagues and a half ; and as the Pinta was the swiftest sailer, and kept ahead of the Admiral, she discovered land and made the signals which had been ordered. . . . At two o'clock in the morning the land was discovered, at two leagues' distance ; they took in sail and remained under the squaresail lying to till day, which was Friday, when they found themselves near a small island, one of the Lucayos, called in the Indian language Guanahani. Presently they descried people, naked, and the Admiral landed in the boat, which was armed, along with Martin Alonzo Pinzon, and Vincent Yañez his brother, captain of the Niña. The Admiral bore the royal standard, and the two captains each a banner of the Green Cross, which all the ships had carried ; this contained the initials of the names of the King and Queen each side of the cross, and a crown over each letter. Arrived on shore, they saw trees very green, many streams of water, and divers sorts of fruits. The Admiral called upon the two Captains, and the rest of the crew who landed, as also to Rodrigo de Escovedo, notary of the fleet, and Rodrigo Sánchez, of Segovia, to bear witness that he before all others took possession (as in fact he did) of that island for the King and Queen his sovereigns, making the requisite declarations, which are more at large set down here in writing. Numbers of the people of the island straightway collected together. Here follow the precise words of the Admiral : "As I saw that they were very friendly to us, and perceived that they could be much more easily converted to our holy faith by gentle means than by force, I presented them with some red caps, and strings of beads to wear upon the neck, and many other trifles of small value, wherewith they were much delighted, and became wonderfully attached to us. Afterwards they came swimming to the boats, bringing parrots, balls of cotton thread, javelins and many other things which they exchanged for articles we gave them, such as glass beads, and hawk's bells ; which trade was carried on with the utmost good will. But they seemed on the whole to me, to be a very poor people. They all go completely naked, even the women, though I saw but one girl. All whom I saw were young, not above thirty years of age, well made, with fine shapes and faces ; their hair short, and coarse like that of a horse's tail, combed toward the forehead, except a small portion which they suffer to hang down behind, and never cut. . . . It appears to me, that the people are ingenious, and would be good servants ; and I am of opinion that they would very readily become Christians, as they appear to have no religion. They very quickly learn such words as are spoken to them. If it please our Lord, I intend at my return to carry home six of them to your Highnesses, that they may learn our language. I saw no beasts in the island, nor any sort of animals except parrots." These are the words of the Admiral.

3

Bernal Díaz del Castillo, The Conquest of Mexico

Bernal Díaz del Castillo, one of the soldiers who fought with Cortés in the conquest of Mexico, wrote a vivid account of that event. In the selection that follows, he describes the battle with the Tlascalan Indians who were traditional enemies of the Aztecs and who, after their defeat by the Spaniards, became their allies after witnessing the superiority of their weapons and fighting ability. This alliance was a major factor in the success of the Spanish conquest.

QUESTIONS TO CONSIDER

1. Why did the Spaniards bury their dead in the underground houses that the Indians had built? Why were so few Spaniards killed?
2. What did Spaniards use to attempt to cure their wounded?
3. Why were so few conquistadors able to defeat considerably larger numbers of Indians?

The next morning, the 5th September, 1519, we mustered the horses. There was not one of the wounded men who did not come forward to join the ranks and give as much help as he could. The crossbowmen were warned to use the store of darts very cautiously, some of them loading while the others were shooting, and the musketeers were to act in the same way, and the men with sword and shield were instructed to aim their cuts and thrusts at the bowels [of their enemies] so that they would not dare to come as close to us as they did before. With our banner unfurled, and four of our comrades guarding the standard-bearer, Corral, we set out from our camp. We had not marched half a quarter of a league before we began to see the fields crowded with warriors with great feather crests and distinguishing devices, and to hear the blare of horns and trumpets.

All the plain was swarming with warriors and we stood four hundred men in number, and of those many sick and wounded. And we knew for certain that this

Bernal Díaz del Castillo, *The True History of the Conquest of New Spain,* trans. and ed. by A. P. Maudslay (London : The Hakluyt Society, 1908–1916), 5 vols., I, pp. 237–240, passim.

time our foe came with the determination to leave none of us alive excepting those who would be sacrificed to their idols.

How they began to charge on us! What a hail of stones sped from their slings! As for their bowmen, the javelins lay like corn on the threshing floor ; all of them barbed and fire-hardened, which would pierce any armour and would reach the vitals where there is no protection ; the men with swords and shields and other arms larger than swords, such as broadswords, and lances, how they pressed on us and with what mighty shouts and yells they charged upon us! The steady bearing of our artillery, musketeers, and crossbowmen, was indeed a help to us, and we did the enemy much damage, and those of them who came close to us with their swords and broadswords met with such sword play from us that they were forced back and they did not close in on us so often as in the last battle. The horsemen were so skillful and bore themselves so valiantly that, after God who protected us, they were our bulwark. However, I saw that our troops were in considerable confusion, so that neither the shouts of Cortés nor the other captains availed to make them close up their ranks, and so many Indians charged down on us that it was only by a miracle of sword play that we could make them give way so that our ranks could be reformed. One thing only saved our lives, and that was that the enemy were so numerous and so crowded one on another that the shots wrought havoc among them, and in addition to this they were not well commanded, for all the captains with their forces could not come into action and from what we knew, since the last battle had been fought, there had been disputes and quarrels between the Captain Xicotenga and another captain the son of Chichimecatecle, over what the one had said to the other, that he had not fought well in the previous battle ; to this the son of Chichimecatecle replied that he had fought better than Xicotenga, and was ready to prove it by personal combat. So in this battle Chichimecatecle and his men would not help Xicotenga, and we knew for a certainty that he had also called on the company of Huexotzinco to abstain from fighting. Besides this, ever since the last battle they were afraid of the horses and the musketry, and the swords and crossbows, and our hard fighting ; above all was the mercy of God which gave us strength to endure. So Xicotenga was not obeyed by two of the commanders, and we were doing great damage to his men, for we were killing many of them, and this they tried to conceal ; for as they were so numerous, whenever one of their men was wounded, they immediately bound him up and carried him off on their shoulders, so that in this battle, as in the last, we never saw a dead man.

The enemy was already losing heart, and knowing that the followers of the other two captains whom I have already named, would not come to their assistance, they began to give way. It seems that in that battle we had killed one very important captain, and the enemy began to retreat in good order, our horsemen following them at a hard gallop for a short distance, for they could not sit their horses for fatigue, and when we found ourselves free from that multitude of warriors, we gave thanks to God.

In this engagement, one soldier was killed, and sixty were wounded, and all the horses were wounded as well. They gave me two wounds, one in the head with a stone, and one in the thigh with an arrow ; but this did not prevent me from fighting, and keeping watch, and helping our soldiers, and all the soldiers who were wounded did the same ; for if the wounds were not very dangerous, we had to fight and keep guard, wounded as we were, for few of us remained unwounded.

Then we returned to our camp, well contented, and giving thanks to God. We buried the dead in one of those houses which the Indians had built underground, so that the enemy should not see that we were mortals, but should believe that, as they said, we were Teules. We threw much earth over the top of the house, so that they should not smell the bodies, then we doctored all the wounded with the fat of an Indian. It was cold comfort to be even without salt or oil with which to cure the wounded. There was another want from which we suffered, and it was a severe one — and that was clothes with which to cover ourselves, for such a cold wind came from the snow mountains, that it made us shiver, for our lances and muskets and crossbows made a poor covering.

WEST COMES TO EAST

Driven by the love for gold, God, and glory, hardy and adventurous European traders, dedicated missionaries, and daring explorers took to the open seas and reached the shores of Asia in the last decade of the fifteenth and early decades of the sixteenth centuries. But while these Europeans were looking beyond the European horizon and venturing out on the stormy seas, Asian empires were generally turning inward, overwhelmed by internal decay, civil war, and dynastic transition. When Portuguese captain Vasco da Gama successfully led three small ships around the Cape of Good Hope and reached the western shores of the Indian subcontinent in 1498, the last ruling dynasty of the Delhi Sultanate (1206–1526) was in its final stages of disintegration. In 1549, Japan was at the tail end of a century-long series of civil wars when a founding member of the Society of Jesus, St. Francis Xavier, arrived in western Japan and introduced Christianity to that country. In China, by the time Portuguese explorers reached an off-shore island near Canton in 1514, the once powerful Ming dynasty had begun to enter a long drawn-out period of dynastic decline. Such fluid circumstances created favorable opportunities for European adventurers to establish their footholds on Asian shores.

The most dedicated and successful pioneers were the Jesuit missionaries. During the span of about two centuries — from St. Francis Xavier's first unsuccessful attempt to enter China in 1547 to the dissolution of the Jesuit order in 1773 — several hundred "soldiers of the cross" were dispatched to China. Among the early Jesuit pioneers, the single most successful and important figure was Matteo Ricci, an Italian Jesuit (1551–1610). Besides his skillful approach to proselytism, Ricci's contributions to the bridging of East and West were invaluable and enduring.

Early Europeans in Asian ports brought not only Bibles but also firearms. Among the items that Portuguese traders first brought to Japan in 1543 was the arquebus, an early portable gun, which greatly fascinated the Japanese who had long held a tradition of glorifying warriors and were in the midst of feudal wars. The "barbarian" firearms became avidly sought by Japanese feudal lords, and Japanese blacksmiths reproduced them in large quantities. Cannons appeared in Japan about 1558. In 1575, by employing 3000 musketeers, Oda Nobunaga (1534–1582), a powerful warlord during the warring state period, won a decisive victory at the Battle of Nagashino over his enemies, who were armed with swords, bows, arrows, and pikes (long spears). After a century of disruption and disunity in the land, this victory paved the way for the unification of Japan. Thus, Japanese feudal lords with greater resources were now able to arm their soldiers with modern firearms and build larger, improved castles that could withstand musket and cannon attacks.

In addition, the European missionaries had phenomenal success in converting the Japanese to Christianity. Within a half century after St. Francis Xavier had first begun preaching in Japan in 1549, 75 Jesuit missionaries had won some 300,000 converts and established over 200 churches. This was the Jesuit missionaries' greatest success story in Asia. But a reversal of fortunes soon followed. In 1587, the new military master of Japan, Toyotomi Hideyoshi, became suspicious of the loyalty of the Japanese converts, and although the order was not rigorously enforced, he ordered all missionaries deported from Japan. The persecution of Christians was intensified when a new military government under Tokugawa Ieyasu was established in 1603. The early rulers of Tokugawa Japan regarded Christianity as subversive and ideologically incompatible with Tokugawa feudal principles. The Tokugawa paranoia about a secret collusion between the restless Japanese dissidents and the European powers resulted in a ban on travel by Japanese nationals to and from foreign lands. The Spanish and Portuguese missionaries were suspected to be the vanguard of aggression. For these reasons, the Tokugawa government closed the country to the outside world. This self-imposed isolation of Japan was to last more than two centuries until 1854, when American Commodore Matthew C. Perry signed the Treaty of Kanagawa.

Matteo Ricci and China

Ricci reached Macao in 1582. He had to overcome seemingly insuperable difficulties before gaining a foothold in China, which was rigidly Confucian and xenophobic. Ricci was quick to realize that the Jesuits could not hope to succeed in China if they adopted the same proselytizing approach that other missionaries had used. Immediately he set out to work from the top down : He began to penetrate the Chinese ruling class, not so much as a Christian missionary but rather as a learned friend and scientist. To dispel suspicion on the part of Chinese scholars and officials, he at first wore the robes of the Buddhist monk and then changed to those of the Confucian scholar-official class. Besides his mastery of the Chinese language and the classics, he made an intense study of Chinese history, customs, geography, philosophy, and government. He also knew how to arouse the curiosity and fancy of Chinese officials and scholars by presenting them with gifts previously unknown to them, such as clocks, sundials, clavichords, and astrolabes. As a result, Ricci won the respect, admiration, and friendship of the Chinese scholar-officials. At last, in 1601, after 18 strenuous years, Ricci was allowed by the Chinese emperor to establish his residence at the imperial capital, where he stayed until his death in 1610. Ricci was buried in a plot donated by the emperor.

For a period of 28 years, with patience, keen intellect, tact, and dedication, Ricci laid a permanent foundation for Christianity in China. Hundreds of fellow Jesuits followed in his footsteps to China and won thousands of Chinese converts. At the same time, Ricci and many of the Jesuits who later came to China developed a respect and fascination for Chinese civilization. Because of this scholarly interest, many of these Jesuits, starting with Ricci, emerged as pioneers in Sinology in the West. They built a bridge between the two worlds. They introduced Confucius to Europe, and the Bible, Copernicus, and Euclid to China. Their letters and writings on Chinese history, government, society, philosophy, geography, and customs became the chief reference sources on China for the Europeans.

In particular, Ricci's diary, *De Propagatone Christiana apud Sinas* (On the Propagation of Christianity Among the Chinese), contributed greatly to Europe's understanding of China. The diary was posthumously published in 1615 by Ricci's co-worker, the Belgian Jesuit Nicholas Trigault, who edited and translated the original Italian into Latin. This diary was widely read in seventeenth-century Europe and appeared in several European languages. Ricci described various aspects of Chinese life and institutions such as Confucian philosophy, the imperial examination system, the bureaucracy, the arts and sciences, customs, and religions. Thus, Ricci's journal reopened China to Europe three centuries after Marco Polo had first bridged the gap through his famous travelogue. The following selection is Ricci's description, as presented by Father Trigault, of China's pacifistic tradition and the triennial rotation system of the imperial government.

4

Matteo Ricci, *Journals*

QUESTIONS TO CONSIDER

1. How do you compare the people and society of China described by Ricci with those of Europe in the sixteenth century?
2. How did Ricci describe China's pacifistic tradition? Do you agree or disagree with Ricci's assessment? Why?

Before closing this chapter on Chinese public administration, it would seem to be quite worth while recording a few more things in which this people differ from Europeans. To begin with, it seems to be quite remarkable when we stop to consider it, that in a kingdom of almost limitless expanse and innumerable popula-

From *China in the Sixteenth Century: The Journals of Matthew Ricci, 1583–1610*, by Matthew Ricci, translated by Louis J. Gallagher, S.J. (New York: Random House, 1953), pp. 54–56, 58–59. Copyright 1942 and renewed 1970 by Louis J. Gallagher, S.J. Reprinted by permission of Random House, Inc.

tion, and abounding in copious supplies of every description, though they have a well-equipped army and navy that could easily conquer the neighboring nations, neither the King nor his people ever think of waging a war of aggression. They are quite content with what they have and are not ambitious of conquest. In this respect they are much different from the people of Europe, who are frequently discontent with their own governments and covetous of what others enjoy. While the nations of the West seem to be entirely consumed with the idea of supreme domination, they cannot even preserve what their ancestors have bequeathed them, as the Chinese have done through a period of some thousands of years. This assertion seems to have some bearing upon what many of our writers maintain relative to the initial founding of the empire, when they assert that the Chinese not only subjugated the neighboring nations but extended their sway even as far as India. After diligent study of the history of China, covering a period of more than four thousand years, I must admit that I have never seen any mention of such conquest, nor have I ever heard of them extending the boundaries of their empire. On the contrary, in frequent inquiry among learned Chinese historians, relative to this assertion, their answer has always been the same; that it was not so and could not possibly be so. Not to question the reputation of the writers who have recorded the error, the mistake may have arisen from the fact that certain evidences of the presence of the Chinese have been discovered beyond the confines of the kingdom. For example, one might cite the Philippine Islands, to which they found their way in private enterprise rather than on any official commission by their government.

Another remarkable fact and quite worthy of note as marking a difference from the West, is that the entire kingdom is administered by the Order of the Learned, commonly known as The Philosophers. The responsibility for orderly management of the entire realm is wholly and completely committed to their charge and care. The army, both officers and soldiers, hold them in high respect and show them the promptest obedience and deference, and not infrequently the military are disciplined by them as a schoolboy might be punished by his master. Policies of war are formulated and military questions are decided by the Philosophers only, and their advice and counsel has more weight with the King than that of the military leaders. In fact very few of these, and only on rare occasions, are admitted to war consultations. Hence it follows that those who aspire to be cultured frown upon war and would prefer the lowest rank in the philosophical order to the highest in the military, realizing that the Philosophers far excel military leaders in the good will and the respect of the people and in opportunities of acquiring wealth. What is still more surprising to strangers is that these same Philosophers, as they are called, with respect to nobility of sentiment and in contempt of danger and death, where fidelity to King and country is concerned, surpass even those whose particular profession is the defense of the fatherland. Perhaps this sentiment has its origin in the fact that the mind of man is ennobled by the study of letters. Or again, it may have developed from the fact that from the beginning and foundation of this empire the study of letters was always more acceptable to the people than the profession of arms, as being more suitable to a people who had little or no interest in the extension of the empire.

The order and harmony that prevails among magistrates, both high and low, in the provinces and in the regal Curia is also worthy of admiration. Their attitude toward the King, in exact obedience and in external ceremony, is a cause of wonderment to a foreigner. The literati would never think of omitting certain customary formal visits to one another or the regular practice of freely offering gifts. In the courts and elsewhere, inferiors always bend the knee when speaking to a superior, and address him in the most dignified language. The same is true of the people toward their prefects and toward the mayor of the city, even though these officers may have arisen from the lowest state in life before attaining their literary degrees and admittance to the magistracy. The term of office of all the dignitaries we have been discussing is three years, unless one be confirmed in his position or promoted by order of the crown. Usually they are promoted but not for the same locality, lest they should develop friendships and become lenient in the administration of justice, or develop a following in the province in which they are so influential. The experience of past ages has taught them that a magistrate burdened with favors is likely to incline toward the introduction of novelties and away from the rigor of the law.

. . . No one is permitted to carry arms within city limits, not even soldiers or officers, military prefects or magistrates, unless one be en route to war or on the way to drill or to a military school. Certain of the higher magistrates, however, may be accompanied by an armed guard. Such is their dislike for arms that no one is allowed to have them in his home, except perhaps a metal dagger which might be needed on a journey as protection against robbers. Fighting and violence among the people are practically unheard of, save what might be concluded by hair pulling and scratching, and there is no requiting of injuries by wounds and death. On the contrary, one who will not fight and restrains himself from returning a blow is praised for his prudence and bravery.

5

Introduction of Firearms to Japan

The following selection is an eyewitness account of the fascination displayed by the local samurai on an off-shore island of southern Kyushu for the firearms introduced by Portuguese traders.

QUESTIONS TO CONSIDER

1. Compare the impact of firearms on the political development of feudal Japan with that on medieval and early modern Europe.
2. Why did swordsmanship continue to be held basic and honored by the Japanese feudal warrior class down to the nineteenth century, despite the fascination with firearms?

On August 25,[1] 1543, a large unidentified ship with a crew of more than one hundred appeared in the port of Tanegashima. The crew's appearance was without parallel and their language was unintelligible. They looked strange. . . . Many of them carried an object which was about two or three feet long.[2] The object had a straight, hollow, and heavy barrel which was closed on the bottom end. It had a hole in its side, through which fire was put. It had a unique shape. They filled the object with magical powder and added a small lead ball. Then they set a target on the edge of the beach, held the object, positioned themselves, aimed with squinted eye, and blasted fire from the end. It hit the target squarely without exception. Its blast resembled lightning and its sound was like roaring thunder. Everyone there covered his ears. . . . Without questioning the price or difficulty in obtaining the object, Tokitaka, the lord of Tanegashima, bought two barbarian firearms and treasured them as family heirlooms.

6

Seclusion Edict of 1636

Of the five seclusion edicts issued by the Tokugawa government over a period of 27 years, from 1612 to 1639, the edict reproduced below, issued on May 19, 1636, contained all essential aspects of the national seclusion.

QUESTIONS TO CONSIDER

1. What were the reasons for the self-imposed isolation of Japan under Tokugawa rule?
2. What were some of the short- and long-term effects of the Tokugawa seclusion policy?

1. Japanese ships shall by no means be sent abroad.
2. No Japanese shall be sent abroad. Anyone violating this prohibition shall suffer the penalty of death, and the shipowner and crew shall be held up together with the ship.
3. All Japanese residing abroad shall be put to death when they return home.
4. All Christians shall be examined by official examiners.

From "Teppoki," in Kasahara Kazuo and Inoue Mitsusada, eds., *Seisen Nihonshi Shiryoshu* (Tokyo: Yamakawa Shuppansha, 1968), p. 102. Reprinted by permission of Yamakawa Shuppansha. Translated by C. K. Yoon.
  1. The date and month were based on the lunar calendar.
  2. Japanese foot (1 Japanese foot = 0.995 U.S. foot).
From Yosoburo Takekoshi, *The Economic Aspects of the History of the Civilization of Japan*, vol. 2 (New York: Macmillan, 1930), pp. 128–129. Reproduced by the kind permission of Unwin Hyman Ltd.

5. Informers against Christians shall be rewarded.
6. The arrival of foreign ships must be reported to Edo, and watch kept over them.
7. The Namban people (Spaniards or Portuguese) and any other people with evil titles propagating Christianity shall be incarcerated in the Omura prison as before.
8. Even ships shall not be left untouched in the matter of exterminating Christians.
9. Everything shall be done in order to see that no Christian is survived by descendants, and anyone disregarding this injunction shall be put to death, while proper punishment shall be meted out to the other members of his family according to their deeds.
10. Children born of the Namban people (Spaniards or Portuguese) in Nagasaki and people adopting these Namban children into their family shall be put to death; capital punishment shall also be meted out to those Namban descendants if they return to Japan, and their relatives in Japan, who may communicate with them, shall receive suitable punishment.
11. The samurai shall not purchase goods on board foreign ships directly from foreigners.
12. The white yarns (raw silk) sent on foreign ships shall be allotted to the five privileged cities and other quarters as stipulated after establishing their prices.
13. After the settling of the price of raw silk, the sale of any goods other than raw silk may be freely carried on between the dealers concerned. It is to be added that, as Chinese ships are small and cannot, therefore, bring large consignments, the authorities may issue orders for sale at their discretion. The delivery of goods other than raw silk shall be effected within twenty days after the settling of their prices.
14. The date of departure homeward of foreign ships shall not be later than September 20th. Any ships arriving in Japan later than usual shall sail for home within fifty days after their arrival. No date is fixed for departure of Chinese ships. They shall be caused to set sail a little later than Portuguese or Spanish ships at the discretion of the authorities concerned.
15. Foreign ships shall take back with them all they are unable to sell of their cargo.
16. The arrival in Nagasaki of representatives of the five cities (representatives of the privileged silk merchants of Kyoto, Sakai, Edo, Nagasaki, and Osaka) shall not be later than July 5th. Any of them arriving at the destination later than this date shall lose the privilege of the sale of raw silk.
17. Ships arriving at Hirado shall not transact business pending the establishment of prices at Nagasaki.

African Slavery

Certainly one of the most lucrative items in the mercantile world of the Atlantic trader was African slavery. From the end of the fifteenth century to the end of the nineteenth century, slavers pillaged Africa for cheap labor to work the plantations of the New World. Twelve million Africans were sold into slavery and crossed the Atlantic, but it is estimated that perhaps 20 to 25 million died in the turmoil and warfare that accompanied this passage to the New World.

One African who survived the journey was Olaudah Equiano (c. 1745–1797), an Ibo born in eastern Nigeria near Benin. When Equiano was 10 years old, he and his sister were captured from their home by local robbers who quickly sold the children to slavers. Equiano served a series of masters, first in the Barbados and later in Virginia; he was finally bought by a British naval officer who took him to Canada, England, and then back to the West Indies. This owner gave Equiano the new name of Gustavus Vassa. In 1766, by luck and frugal trading, Equiano had saved the hefty sum of 40 pounds sterling, which was enough money to buy his freedom. As a freeman, he returned to England, where he worked as a barber, a domestic servant, and a sailor.

In 1789, he published a two-volume set of memoirs in English, describing his life in Africa and his experiences as a slave. His account, excerpted in the following reading, became a best seller in England and soon enabled Equiano to become active in the English anti-slavery movement.

7

A Slave's Memoir: *Equiano's Travels*

QUESTIONS TO CONSIDER

1. What does this memoir tell us about the organization and extent of slavery in the eighteenth-century Atlantic world?
2. What does this selection indicate about Equiano's African home and African culture?
3. What does the memoir, particularly its subtitle (*The Interesting Narrative of the Life of Olaudah Equiano or Gustavus Vassa the African*), tell us about the cultural effects of slavery upon Africans in the eighteenth century?

One day, when all our people were gone out to their works as usual and only I and my dear sister were left to mind the house, two men and a woman got over our walls, and in a moment seized us both, and without giving us time to cry out or make resistance they stopped our mouths and ran off with us into the nearest wood. Here they tied our hands and continued to carry us as far as they could till night came on, when we reached a small house where the robbers halted for refreshment and spent the night. . . .

The first object which saluted my eyes when I arrived on the coast was the sea, and a slave ship which was then riding at anchor and waiting for its cargo. These filled me with astonishment, which was soon converted into terror when I was carried on board. I was immediately handled and tossed up to see if I were sound by some of the crew, and I was now persuaded that I had gotten into a world of bad spirits and that they were going to kill me. Their complexions too differing so much from ours, their long hair and the language they spoke (which was very different from any I had ever heard) united to confirm me in this belief. Indeed such were the horrors of my views and fears at the moment that, if ten thousand worlds had been my own, I would have freely parted with them all to have exchanged my condition with that of the meanest slave in my own country. When I looked round the ship too and saw a large furnace or copper boiling and a multitude of black people of every description chained together, every one of their countenances expressing dejection and sorrow, I no longer doubted of my fate; and quite overpowered with horror and anguish, I fell motionless on the deck and fainted. When I recovered a little I found some black people about me, who I believed were some of those who had brought me on board and had been receiving their pay; they talked to me in order to cheer me, but all in vain. I asked them if we were not to be eaten by those white men with horrible looks, red faces, and loose hair. They told me I was not, and one of the crew brought me a small portion of spirituous liquor in a wine glass, but being afraid of him I would not take it out of his hand. One of the blacks there took it from him and gave it to me, and I took a little down my palate, which instead of reviving me, as they thought it would, threw me into the greatest consternation at the strange feeling it produced, having never tasted such any liquor before. Soon after this the blacks who brought me on board went off, and left me abandoned to despair. . . .

The stench of the hold while we were on the coast was so intolerably loathsome that it was dangerous to remain there for any time, and some of us had been permitted to stay on the deck for the fresh air; but now that the whole ship's cargo were confined together it became absolutely pestilential. The closeness of the place and the heat of the climate, added to the number in the ship, which was so crowded that each had scarcely room to run himself, almost suffocated us. This produced copious perspirations, so that the air soon became unfit for respiration from a variety of loathsome smells, and brought on a sickness among the slaves, of which many died, thus falling victims to the improvident avarice, as I may call it, of their purchasers. This wretched situation was again aggravated by the galling of

From Paul Edwards, ed., *Equiano's Travels: His Autobiography. The Interesting Narrative of the Life of Olaudah Equiano or Gustavus Vassa the African* (London: Heinemann Educational Books, 1967), pp. 16–32, passim. This abridgement © Paul Edwards 1967. Reprinted by permission.

the chains, now become insupportable, and the filth of the necessary tubs, into which the children often fell and were almost suffocated. The shrieks of the women and the groans of the dying rendered the whole a scene of horror almost inconceivable. Happily perhaps for myself I was soon reduced so low here that it was thought necessary to keep me almost always on deck, and from my extreme youth I was not put in fetters. . . .

At last we came in sight of the island of Barbados, at which the whites on board gave a great shout and made many signs of joy to us. We did not know what to think of this, but as the vessel drew nearer we plainly saw the harbour and other ships of different kinds and sizes, and we soon anchored amongst them off Bridgetown. Many merchants and planters now came on board, though it was in the evening. They put us in separate parcels and examined us attentively. They also made us jump, and pointed to the land, signifying we were to go there. We thought by this we should be eaten by these ugly men, as they appeared to us ; and when soon after we were all put down under the deck again, there was much dread and trembling among us, and nothing but bitter cries to be heard all the night from these apprehensions, insomuch that at last the white people got some old slaves from the land to pacify us. They told us we were not to be eaten but to work, and were soon to go on land where we should see many of our country people. This report eased us much ; and sure enough soon after we were landed there came to us Africans of all languages. We were conducted immediately to the merchant's yard, where we were all pent up together like so many sheep in a fold without regard to sex or age. As every object was new to me everything I saw filled me with surprise. What struck me first was that the houses were built with storeys, and in every other respect different from those in Africa : but I was still more astonished on seeing people on horseback. I did not know what this could mean, and indeed I thought these people were full of nothing but magical arts. While I was in this astonishment one of my fellow prisoners spoke to a countryman of his about the horses, who said they were the same kind they had in their country. I understood them though they were from a distant part of Africa, and I thought it odd I had not seen any horses there ; but afterwards when I came to converse with different Africans I found they had many horses amongst them, and much larger than those I then saw. We were not many days in the merchant's custody before we were sold after their usual manner, which is this : On a signal given, (as the beat of a drum) the buyers rush at once into the yard where the slaves are confined, and make choice of that parcel they like best. The noise and clamour with which this is attended and the eagerness visible in the countenances of the buyers serve not a little to increase the apprehensions of the terrified Africans, who may well be supposed to consider them as the ministers of that destruction to which they think themselves devoted. In this matter, without scruple, are relations and friends separated, most of them never to see each other again. I remember in the vessel in which I was brought over, in the men's apartment there were several brothers who, in the sale, were sold in different lots ; and it was very moving on this occasion to see and hear their cries at parting. O, ye nominal Christians ! might not an African ask you, Do unto all men as you would men should do unto you ? Is it not enough that we are torn from our country and friends to toil for your luxury and lust of gain ? Must every tender feeling be likewise sacrificed to your avarice ? Are the dearest friends and relations, now rendered more dear by their separation from their kindred, still to be parted from each other and thus prevented from cheering the gloom of slavery with the small comfort of being together and mingling their sufferings and sorrows? Why are parents to lose their children, brothers their sisters, or husbands their wives? Surely this is a new refinement in cruelty which, while it has no advantage to atone for it, thus aggravates distress and adds fresh horrors even to the wretchedness of slavery.

GLOBAL PATTERNS OF POLITICS AND CULTURE

Ottoman Culture

8

Lady Mary Wortley Montagu, Embassy to Constantinople

A unique vista on Ottoman culture is contained in the "Embassy Letters" of Lady Mary Wortley Montague (1689–1762), who lived in Constantinople in 1717–1718 with her husband, Edward Wortley Montagu, the English Ambassador to Turkey. Her Embassy Letters differ from those of many of her contemporaries in at least two respects. First, unlike many eighteenth-century writers, Lady Mary made a serious effort to learn Turkish and to study Ottoman culture firsthand. Second, she did not accept the trite eighteenth-century notions of "Oriental-Despotism" or "Turkish sensuality." Instead she found Constantinople to be a wonderful city and in many ways more advanced than Europe. Two of these ways, described in the letters below, involved the condition of women and the use of inoculations against the dread disease of smallpox. Stricken with this disease at the age of 26, Lady Mary not only lost all of her eyelashes but her face remained permanently disfigured. Despite strong objections from the medical and religious authorities, Lady Mary introduced the practice to England, inoculated her son, and persuaded other English notables, including Princess Caroline, to use the Turkish system of "engrafting" on their children.

QUESTIONS TO CONSIDER

1. In theory, Islamic women enjoyed fewer liberties than Christian women, but Lady Mary finds that the "subjugation" of Turkish women actually gave them greater freedom than their European counterparts. Are her arguments valid?
2. According to Lady Mary, what were the special advantages enjoyed by Turkish women?
3. Why would the English establishment condemn Lady Mary's efforts to bring inoculation to England even though it had proved successful?
4. What do these letters (along with Reading 19) suggest about the role of women in the European Enlightenment?

To Lady Mar, 1 April 1717

. . . I never saw in my life so many fine heads of hair. I have counted one hundred and ten of these tresses of one lady's, all natural ; but it must be owned that every beauty is more common here than with us. It is surprising to see a young woman that is not very handsome. They have naturally the most beautiful complexions in the world and generally large black eyes. I can assure you with great truth that the Court of England (though I believe it the fairest in Christendom) cannot show so many beauties as are under our protection here. They generally shape their eye-brows, and the Greeks and Turks have a custom of putting round their eyes on the inside a black tincture that, at a distance or by candlelight, adds very much to the blackness of them. I fancy many of our ladies would be overjoyed to know this se-cret, but it is too visible by day. They dye their nails rose color ; I own I cannot enough accustom myself to this fashion to find any beauty in it.

As to their morality or good conduct, I can say like Arlequin,[1] "It is just as it is with you", and the Turkish ladies don't commit one sin the less for not being Christians. Now I am a little acquainted with their ways, I cannot forbear admir-ing either the exemplary discretion or extreme stupidity of all the writers that have given accounts of them. It is very easy to see they have more liberty than we have, no woman of what rank so ever being permitted to go in the streets without two muslins, one that covers her face all but her eyes and another that hides the whole dress of her head and hangs half way down her back ; and their shapes are wholly concealed by a thing they call a *Ferigée,* which no woman of any sort ap-pears without. This has strait sleeves that reaches to their fingers' ends and it laps all round them, not unlike a riding hood. In winter it is of cloth and in summer, plain stuff or silk. You may guess how effectually this disguises them, that there is no distinguishing the great lady from her slave, and it is impossible for the most jealous husband to know his wife when he meets her, and no man dare either touch or follow a woman in the street.

This perpetual masquerade gives them entire liberty of following their incli-nations without danger of discovery. The most usual method of intrigue is to send an appointment to the lover to meet the lady at a Jew's shop, which are as notori-ously convenient as our Indian houses, and yet even those that don't make that use of them do not scruple to go to buy a penny's-worth and tumble over rich goods, which are chiefly to be found amongst that sort of people. The great ladies seldom let their gallants know who they are, and it is so difficult to find it out that they can very seldom guess at her name they have corresponded with above half a year to-gether. You may easily imagine that the number of faithful wives very small in a country where they have nothing to fear from their lover's indiscretion, since we see so many that have the courage to expose themselves to that in this world and all the threatened punishment of the next, which is never preached to the Turkish damsels. Neither have they much to apprehend from the resentment of their hus-bands, those ladies that are rich having all their money in their own hands, which they take with them upon a divorce with an addition which he is obliged to give

From Lord Wharncliffe, ed., *The Letters and Works of Lady Mary Wortley Montagu* (London : Henry G. Bohn, 1861), I, pp. 298–300, 307–309. Spelling and punctuation slightly modified.

1. Arlequin was a character in the well-known play, *The Emperor of the Moon,* who announces that morality on the moon is no different from morality on earth.

them. Upon the whole, I look upon the Turkish women as the only free people in the empire. The very Divan[2] pays a respect to them, and the Grand Signor[3] himself, when a Pasha[4] is executed, never violates the privileges of the harem (or women's apartment) which remains unsearched entire to the widow. They are queens of their slaves, which the husband has no permission so much as to look upon, except it be an old woman or two that his lady chooses. It is true their law permits them four wives, but there is no instance of a man of quality that makes use of this liberty, or of a woman of rank that would suffer it. When a husband happens to be inconstant (as those things will happen) he keeps his mistress in a house apart and visits her as privately as he can, just as it is with you. Among all the great men here I only know the *Defterdar* (i.e. treasurer) that keeps a number of she slaves for his own use (that is, on his own side of the house, for a slave once given to serve a lady is entirely at her disposal), and he is spoke of as a libertine, or what we should call a rake, and his wife won't see him, though she continues to live in his house.

Thus you see, dear sister, the manners of mankind do not differ so widely as our voyage writers would make us believe. Perhaps it would be more entertaining to add a few surprising customs of my own invention, but nothing seems to me so agreeable as truth, and I believe nothing so acceptable to you.

To Sarah Chiswell, 1 April 1717

Those dreadful stories you have heard of the plague have very little foundation in truth. I own I have much ado to reconcile myself to the sound of a word which has always given me such terrible ideas, though I am convinced there is little more in it than a fever, as a proof of which we passed through two or three towns most violently infected. In the very next house where we lay, in one of them, two persons died of it. Luckily for me I was so well deceived that I knew nothing of the matter, and I was made believe that our second cook who fell ill there had only a great cold. However, we left our doctor to take care of him, and yesterday they both arrived here in good health and I am now let into the secret that he has had the plague. There are many that escape of it, neither is the air ever infected. I am persuaded it would be as easy to root it out here as out of Italy and France, but it does so little mischief, they are not very solicitous about it and are content to suffer this distemper instead of our variety, which they are utterly unacquainted with.

Apropos of distempers, I am going to tell you a thing that I am sure will make you wish yourself here. The smallpox, so fatal and so general amongst us, is here entirely harmless by the invention of engrafting (which is the term they give it). There is a set of old women who make it their business to perform the operation. Every autumn, in the month of September, when the great heat is abated, people send to one another to know if any of their family has a mind to have the smallpox. They make parties for this purpose, and when they are met (commonly fifteen or sixteen together) the old woman comes with a nutshell full of the matter of the best sort of smallpox and asks what veins you please to have opened. She im-

2. This was the privy council of the Turkish government, presided over by the Grand Vizier.
3. The Sultan.
4. An officer of rank.

mediately rips open that you offer to her with a large needle (which gives you no more pain than a common scratch) and puts into the vein as much venom as can lie upon the head of her needle, and after binds up the little wound with a hollow bit of shell, and in this manner opens four or five veins. The Grecians have commonly the superstition of opening one in the middle of the forehead, in each arm, and on the breast to mark the sign of the cross, but this has a very ill effect, all these wounds leaving little scars, and is not done by those that are not superstitious, who choose to have them in the legs or that part of the arm that is concealed. The children or young patients play together all the rest of the day and are in perfect health till the eighth. Then the fever begins to seize them and they keep their beds two days, very seldom three. They have very rarely above twenty or thirty in their faces, which never mark, and in eight days time they are as well as before their illness. Where they are wounded there remains running sores during the distemper, which I don't doubt is a great relief to it. Every year thousands undergo this operation and the French Ambassador says pleasantly that they take the smallpox here by way of diversion as they take the waters in other countries. There is no example of anyone that has died in it, and you may believe I am very well satisfied of the safety of the experiment since I intend to try it on my dear little son. I am patriot enough to take pains to bring this useful invention into fashion England, and I should not fail to write to some of our doctors very particularly about it if I knew anyone of them that I thought had virtue enough to destroy such a considerable branch of their revenue for the good of mankind, but that distemper is too beneficial to them not to expose to all their resentment the hardy wight [strength] that should undertake to put an end to it. Perhaps if I live to return I may, however, have courage to war with them.

Four Early Modern Rulers

Four of the most powerful rulers of the early modern era were Akbar, Emperor of Mogul India (1556–1605),[1] Louis XIV, King of France (1643–1715), K'ang-hsi [Kangxi], Emperor of China (1661–1722), and Peter I (known as Peter the Great), Emperor of Russia (1682–1725). Each of these rulers overcame the challenge of domestic revolt and threats of foreign invasion to build a durable model of absolutism in the early modern world.

By successful military conquests, Akbar, the third ruler of Mogul India, expanded the relatively small kingdom that he had inherited into a vast empire extending from Bengal in the east to Afghanistan in the west, and from Kashmir in the north to the Deccan plateau in the south. He also ended centuries of political fragmentation and social instability by skillfully winning over the unruly and recalcitrant Rajputs (Hindu warriors) to his side, and by effecting religious reconciliation between Muslims and Hindus. Through administrative innovations, he achieved a much greater degree of centralized

---

1. Mogul is also spelled Mughul, Mughal, and Mongol.

power than any previous dynasties in Indian history. Although he could neither read nor write, Akbar was a great patron of art and architecture and promoted scholarship.

At the age of 18, K'ang-hsi faced the prospect of revolt in the bitter San Fan civil war (1673–1681). By emerging victorious from this war and later by crushing further rebellion on the island of Taiwan, K'ang-hsi skillfully laid the essential foundation of his dynasty's rule of China until 1911.

When Louis XIV was barely 10 years of age, he had to flee Paris to escape the civil wars of the Fronde (1648–1653). Upon the defeat of his enemies, Louis set about perfecting a model of French absolutism that lasted until 1789. Similarly, Peter the Great, at the age of 26, cut short his western tour to crush the revolt of his palace guard in 1698. Peter then inaugurated a sweeping series of economic, military, and political reforms that set the course for Russian absolutism until 1917.

Each of these men was keenly interested in war and in improving the bureaucratic efficiency of the government. K'ang-hsi took his role as emperor very seriously, noting that "one act of negligence may result in trouble for hundreds and thousands of generations."[2] His careful performance of official duty was eloquently evidenced in his handling of cases involving the death penalty. Every case of capital punishment in the Chinese Empire was reviewed by K'ang-hsi personally.

Though Louis XIV loved pleasure and ceremony, he prided himself on working regularly each day for at least two or three hours at a time. Unlike his predecessors, he never appointed a first minister but considered himself solely responsible for high policy.

K'ang-hsi personally led his troops in the field against the Mongols. Certainly Louis and Peter both loved war, and Peter, like K'ang-hsi, actively commanded his armies in the field. Peter's wars against Sweden, Ottoman Turkey, and the Crimean Tatars signaled Russia's emergence as a European power. More important, Peter's comprehensive military and administrative reforms ensured a strong military tradition — thereby enabling his successors to make Russia a first-rank world power.

9

Anthony Monseratte, S.J., *Journey to the Court of Akbar*

The following excerpts are from the oldest account of the life and government of Akbar and his empire in the West. It was written by a Portuguese Jesuit priest, Anthony Monserrate, during the 1580s.

---

2. Immanuel C. Y. Hsu, *The Rise of Modern China,* 3rd ed. (New York : Oxford University Press, 1983), p. 30.

QUESTIONS TO CONSIDER

1. How do you compare the life and government of Akbar with those of Emperor K'ang-hsi of Manchu China, Louis XIV of France, and Peter the Great of Russia?
2. Why is Akbar considered to be one of the most extraordinary rulers in all of Indian history?

Characteristics of Akbar

He has broad shoulders, somewhat bandy legs well-suited for horsemanship, and a light-brown complexion. He carries his head bent towards the right shoulder. His forehead is broad and open, his eyes so bright and flashing that they seem like a sea shimmering in the sunlight. His eyelashes are very long, as also are those of the Sauromates,[1] Sinae,[2] Niphones,[3] and most other north-Asiatic races. His eyebrows are not strongly marked. His nose is straight and small, though not insignificant. His nostrils are widely opened, as though in derision. Between the left nostril and the upper lip there is a mole. He shaves his beard, but wears a moustache like that of a Turkish youth who has not yet attained to manhood (for on reaching manhood they begin to affect a beard). Contrary to the custom of his race he does not cut his hair; nor does he wear a hat, but a turban, into which he gathers up his hair. He does this, they say, as a concession to Indian usages, and to please his Indian subjects. He limps in his left leg, though indeed he has never received any injury there. His body is exceedingly well-built and is neither too thin nor too stout. He is sturdy, hearty and robust. When he laughs, his face becomes almost distorted. His expression is tranquil, serene and open, full also of dignity, and when he is angry, of awful majesty. When the priests first saw him he was thirty-eight years of age. It is hard to exaggerate how accessible he makes himself to all who wish audience of him. For he creates an opportunity almost every day for any of the common people or of the nobles to see him and converse with him; and he endeavours to show himself pleasant-spoken and affable rather than severe toward all who come to speak with him. It is very remarkable how great an effect this courtesy and affability has in attaching to him the minds of his subjects. For in spite of his very heterodox attitude towards the religion of Muhammad, and in spite also of the fact that Musalmans[4] regard such an attitude as an unforgivable offence, Zelaldinus[5] has not yet been assassinated. He has an acute insight, and shows much wise foresight both in avoiding dangers and in seizing favourable opportunities for carrying out his designs. Yet all these fine qualities both of body and mind lose the greater part of their splendour because the lustre of the True Faith is lacking.

Zelaldinus is greatly devoted to hunting, though not equally so to hawking. As he is of a somewhat morose disposition, he amuses himself with various games.

S. N. Banerjee, annot., and J. S. Hoyland, trans., *Commentary of Father Monserrate, S.J. On His Journey to the Court of Akbar* (London : Oxford University Press, 1922), pp. 196–202.

1. A Scythian tribe in habited lands above the Danube, the Black Sea, and north of the Caucasus.
2. Chinese.
3. Japanese.
4. Muslims.
5. Akbar.

These games afford also a public spectacle to the nobility and the common people, who indeed are very fond of such spectacles. They are the following : — Polo, elephant-fighting, buffalo-fighting, stag-fighting and cock-fighting, boxing contests, battles of gladiators, and the flying of tumbler-pigeons. He is also very fond of strange birds, and indeed of any novel object. He amuses himself with singing, concerts, dances, conjurer's tricks, and the jokes of his jesters, of whom he makes much. However, although he may seem at such times to be at leisure and to have laid aside public affairs, he does not cease to revolve in his mind the heavy cares of state. He is especially remarkable for his love of keeping great crowds of people around him and in his sight ; and thus it comes about that his court is always thronged with multitudes of men of every type, though especially with the nobles, whom he commands to come from their provinces and reside at court for a certain period each year. When he goes outside the palace, he is surrounded and followed by these nobles and a strong body-guard. They have to go on foot until he gives them a nod to indicate that they may mount. All this adds greatly to the wonderful majesty and greatness of the royal court. . . .

His table is very sumptuous, generally consisting of more than forty courses served in great dishes. These are brought into the royal dining-hall covered and wrapped in linen cloths, which are tied up and sealed by the cook, for fear of poison. They are carried by youths to the door of the dining-hall, other servants walking ahead and the master-of-the-household following. Here they are taken over by eunuchs, who hand them to the serving girls who wait on the royal table. He is accustomed to dine in private, except on the occasion of a public banquet. He rarely drinks wine, but quenches his thirst with 'post' or water. When he has drunk immoderately of 'post,' he sinks back stupefied and shaking. He dines alone, reclining on an ordinary couch, which is covered with silken rugs and cushions stuffed with the fine down of some foreign plant.

The splendour of his palaces approaches closely to that of the royal dwellings of Europe. They are magnificently built, from foundation to cornice, of hewn stone, and are decorated both with painting and carving. Unlike the palaces built by other Indian kings, they are lofty ; for an Indian palace is generally as low and humble as an idol-temple. Their total circuit is so large that it easily embraces four great royal dwellings, of which the King's own palace is the largest and the finest. The second palace belongs to the queens, and the third to the royal princes, whilst the fourth is used as a store house and magazine. The roofs of these palaces are not tiled, but are dome-shaped, being protected from the weather on the outside by solid plaster covering the stone slabs. This forms a roof absolutely impervious to moisture. The palaces are decorated also with many pinnacles, supported on four columns, each of which forms a small covered portico. Not a little is added to the beauty of the palaces by charming pigeon-cotes, partly covered with roughcast, and partly showing walls built of small blue and white bricks. The pigeons[6] are cared for by eunuchs and servant-maids. Their evolutions are controlled at will, when they are flying, by means of certain signals, just as those of well-trained soldiery are controlled by a competent general by means of bugles and drums. It will seem little short of miraculous when I affirm that when sent out, they dance, turn somersaults all together in the air, fly in orderly rhythm, and return to their

---

6. Akbar was a great pigeon-fancier. More than 20,000 pigeons, divided into 10 classes, were kept at court.

starting point, all at the sound of a whistle. They are bidden to perch on the roof, to conceal themselves within their nesting-places, or to dart out of them again; and they do everything just as they are told. . . .

He is a great patron of learning, and always keeps around him erudite men, who are directed to discuss before him philosophy, theology, and religion, and to recount to him the history of great kings and glorious deeds of the past. He has an excellent judgment and a good memory, and has attained to a considerable knowledge of many subjects by means of constant and patient listening to such discussions. Thus he not only makes up for his ignorance of letters (for he is entirely unable either to read or write), but he has also become able clearly and lucidly to expound difficult matters. He can give his opinion on any question so shrewdly and keenly, that no one who did not know that he is illiterate would suppose him to be anything but very learned and erudite. And so indeed he is, for in addition to his keen intellect, of which I have already spoken, he excels many of his most learned subjects in eloquence, as well as in that authority and dignity which befits a King. The wise men are wont every day to hold disputations on literary subjects before him. He listens with delight, not to actors, but to mimics and jesters, thinking their style of speaking to have a literary flavour. For the lawgiver (Muhammad) forbade all kinds of plays, both tragic and comic, and all acting, being such an impostor that, in order to gain a reputation for goodness and sanctity, he forbade things which are not in themselves wrong. And having once gained this reputation he found the way easy to a position from which he could issue those precepts of his which are alien not only to the innate dignity of human nature but also to the general conscience of mankind. For, to draw attention to one or two such points, he allowed incestuous unions with closely-related women, excepting only the mother and the sister. He also invented and introduced amongst the Musalmans two forms of marriage, first that with regular consorts, who may number four: and second that with those who are merely called wives, and who may be as numerous as a man's resources allow. Musalman kings employ this sanction and licence of the foulest immorality in order to ratify peace and to create friendly relationships with their vassal princes or neighbouring monarchs. For they marry the daughters and sisters of such rulers. Hence Zelaldinus has more than 300 wives, dwelling in separate suites of rooms in a very large palace. Yet when the priests were at the court he had only three sons and two daughters.

10

Louis XIV, *Mémoires for the Instruction of the Dauphin*

Louis XIV (1643–1715) ruled France during that country's most splendid century. Ever mindful of how quickly death could strike him, Louis dictated the following instructions for his only son. He hoped to ensure that, even if he should die before completing his son's education, the Dauphin would rule wisely.

QUESTIONS TO CONSIDER

1. Why did Louis XIV believe his son should study history?
2. Compare Louis XIV's and K'ang-hsi's views on justice and punishment (see Reading 11).
3. Evaluate Louis XIV's counsel to his son with respect to secrecy when working with government officials.

I would not speak to you in this way, my son, if I had seen in you the least tendency toward cruelty, for a bloody and ferocious temper is despicable in a man, and beneath the dignity of a king. On the contrary, I will endeavor to acquaint you with the charm of clemency, the most regal of all virtues since it can only belong to kings; for clemency is one duty for which we can never be repaid. . . .

Whoever pardons too often punishes uselessly the rest of time, for in the terror which restrains men from evil, the hope of pardon lessens the effect of pardon itself. You will not finish the reading of these *Mémoires*, my son, without finding places where I have conquered myself and pardoned offenses that I could justly never forget. But on that occasion when it was a question of state, of the most pernicious examples, and of the most contagious disorder for all my subjects, of a revolt that attacked the very foundations of my authority, I knew that I should overcome my scruples and punish these scoundrels rather than pardoning them. . . .

Whoever is poorly informed cannot avoid poor thinking; and if you search past centuries for all the errors attributed to sovereigns, hardly one can be excused for not knowing something that he should have known, for so it is generally among men that one says "I did not know," or "I did not think."

Frequently after finishing an affair we learn something new and lament that if only we had known this sooner we would have acted differently; in short I believe if a man is fully informed he will always do what he should. Thus it is necessary that a sovereign take the greatest care to be informed of his own times.

But for me, I extended this reflection, for I was convinced that it was not enough to be informed of current affairs but also of ancient times. I consider that a knowledge of these great events, assimilated by a mature mind, can serve to fortify one's reasoning in all important deliberations; for the example of illustrious men and their unique deeds provides very useful perspectives for war and peace, so that a naturally great and generous soul, contemplating these actions, would be inspired by them and ensure that the lessons of history can inspire others as well.

I have heard it said that all the great heroes of the past were conversant with literature and that part of their greatness was due to their literary study. Particularly I found the study of the past to be very useful in becoming wise in the art of war. . . .

But kings must learn not to permit their servants to become too powerful because, if they are promoted too quickly, they are obliged to constantly support

From Charles Dreyss, ed., *Mémoires de Louis XIV Pour L'Instruction du Dauphin*, vol. 2 (Paris: Didier, 1860), pp. 95–97, 266–269, 516–517. Translated by Philip F. Riley. (Dauphin is the title of the eldest son of a French King.)

them or painfully suffer them; usually only weak or clumsy princes tolerate these monstrous promotions.

I am not saying that we should not for our own interest and grandeur wish that our greatness is shared by those in our good graces, but we must carefully guard against their excess. My advice to guarantee this consists of three principal observations.

The first is that you know your affairs completely, because a king who does not know them is always dependent on those who serve him and cannot defend himself from their wiles.

The second, that you divide your confidence among many, so that each of those you have entrusted will check the elevation of his rival, ensuring that the jealousy of one will bridle the ambition of the other.

And the third, that even though you admit a small number of persons into your secret affairs or into your casual conversations, never permit anyone to imagine that they have the power to speak as they please of their good or bad impressions of the others; but, on the contrary, you must expressly maintain a type of association with all who hold important state posts, and give to everyone the same liberty to propose whatever they believe for your service; so that none of them would believe that they could not turn to you for their needs and they think only of your good graces; and lastly the most distant and the most familiar should be persuaded that they are totally dependent upon you.

But you should know that this independence upon which I insist so strongly raises more than anything the authority of the master, and that it alone shows that he is governing them instead of being governed by them: As to the contrary when it ceases, invariably intrigues, liaisons, and cabals enlarge the power of the court and weaken the reputation of the prince.

11

Emperor of China: Self-Portrait of K'ang-hsi [Kangxi][1]

In the exercise of his nearly omnipotent power, Emperor K'ang-hsi seldom failed to show diligence, compassion, and sagacity. The following excerpts represent some of his views on capital punishment and good government.

---

1. There are at least two ways to transcribe Chinese in the English-speaking world: the Wade-Giles system and the Pinyin system. The Wade-Giles system was first developed by an English Sinologist, Thomas F. Wade, in 1867 and was later modified by Herbert Giles in 1912. It became the standard way of transcribing Chinese. But this system has now either been replaced or is in the process of being replaced by Pinyin, the official transcription system of the People's Republic of China. Hereafter, the Pinyin transcriptions will be provided in brackets on the first occurrence of Chinese terms in each reading where they occur. If no transcription appears, the term is the same in both systems.

QUESTIONS TO CONSIDER

1. Why were executions weighed so carefully by K'ang-hsi?
2. How would you characterize K'ang-hsi's prescriptions for good government?

On Capital Punishment

Giving life to people and killing people — those are the powers that the emperor has. He knows that administrative errors in government bureaus can be rectified, but that a criminal who has been executed cannot be brought back to life any more than a chopped string can be joined together again. He knows, too, that sometimes people have to be persuaded into morality by the example of an execution. In 1683, after Taiwan had been captured, the court lecturers and I discussed the image of the fifty-sixth hexagram in the *Book of Changes,* "Fire on the Mountain": the calm of the mountain signifies the care that must be used in imposing penalties; the fire moves rapidly on, burning up the grass, like lawsuits that should be settled speedily. My reading of this was that the ruler needs both clarity and care in punishing: his intent must be to punish in order to avoid the need for further punishing. . . .

In times of war there must be executions for cowardice or disobedience. When the city of K'uch'enghsien [Kucheng Xian] fell to the rebels in the Hupeh [Hubei] campaign of 1675, the commander-in-chief reported that Colonel Malangga had fled; and after Prince Cani verified this in his secret report, I had Malangga beheaded. A few months later two more senior officers fled in the face of the enemy in Shensi, and I had them beheaded in front of their troops. Sekse was beheaded in 1697 for openly disobeying the imperial order that he inform Danjin Ombu of Galdan's death (though I did not order his head exposed as the judges had recommended).

The final penalty of lingering death must be given in cases of treason, as the Legal Code requires. Chu Yung-tso [Zhu Yongzuo] was arrested, and condemned for following the treacherous monk I-nien [Yinian], for writing wild poems and deceiving the people, and for adopting false Ming reign-titles. The Board of Punishments recommended that he be beheaded, but I ordered that the death be lingering. I had awarded the same punishment to the rebel Wang Shih-yüan [Wang Shiyuan], who had claimed to be Chu San T'ai-tzu [Zhu San Taizi], the surviving Ming claimant to the throne, so that the Ming prince's name should be invoked no more as a rallying point for rebels, as had been done too many times before. When Ilaguksan Khutuktu, who had had his spies in the lamas' residences so that they would welcome Galdan's army into China, and had plotted with Galdan and encouraged him in his rebellion, was finally caught, I had him brought to Peking and

From *Emperor of China : Self-Portrait of K'ang-hsi,* by Jonathan Spence (New York: Knopf, 1975), pp. 29–33, 55–56, 143–144, passim. Copyright © 1974 by Jonathan Spence. Reprinted by permission of Alfred A. Knopf, Inc.

cut to death in the Yellow Temple, in the presence of all the Manchu and Mongol princes, and the senior officials, both civil and military. All that was left of Galdan were the ashes, but these we exposed to the public outside the Forbidden City. The corpse of Wu San-kuei [Wu Sangui] I ordered scattered across the provinces of China and decreed the lingering death for Keng Ching-chung [Geng Jingzhong] and ten other generals who had fought for him or Wu San-kuei.

But apart from such treason cases, when there are men who have to be executed immediately (even if it's spring, when executions should not be carried out), or when one is dealing with men like those who plotted against me in the Heir-Apparent crisis and had to be killed immediately and secretly without trial, I have been merciful where possible. For the ruler must always check carefully before executions, and leave room for the hope that men will get better if they are given the time. In the hunt one can kill all the animals caught inside the circle, but one can't always bear to shoot them as they stand there, trapped and exhausted.

As the "San-fan War" began in the South, Yang Ch'i-lung [Yang Qilung] and his men rose in Peking, and the Manchu troops were so stern in reprisal that the people fled in panic to the hills outside the walls. I not only ordered the city gates closed, to stop the city emptying, but promised amnesty to all save the ringleaders, since Yang had misled so many of the common people that we would never be able to clean up all those involved in the case. As the war spread, and reports came in of over one hundred alleged "bandits" beheaded after a single engagement, I sent an edict to the Board of War ordering commanders to use more compassion : . . .

Of all the things that I find distasteful, none is more so than giving a final verdict on the death sentences that are sent to me for ratification after the autumn assizes. The trial reports should all have been checked through by the Board of Punishments and reviewed by the Grand Secretaries during the autumn months, yet still one finds errors of calligraphy — and even whole passages miswritten. This is inexcusable when we are dealing with life and death. Though naturally I could not go through every case in detail, I nevertheless got in the habit of reading through the lists in the palace each year, checking the name and registration and status of each man condemned to death, and the reason for which the death penalty had been given. Then I would check through the list again with the Grand Secretaries and their staff in the audience hall, and we would decide who might be spared.

On Good Government

In the winter of 1672, when I was young, I had told the lecturers in the Maoch'in [Maoqin] Palace that good government seemed to depend on letting the people live at rest, that the way of good government was in not hurting them : having a whole lot of trouble was not as good as stopping trouble from occurring. Likewise I rejected the suggestion that I might let the censors report to me on the basis of hearsay, because dishonest people might use this means to harm the worthy and stir up trouble. Thirty-two years later, when Ts'ao Yin [Zao Yin] suggested rooting out all excess fees in the salt monopoly, working down from the governor-general to the local magistrates, I combined these phrases from the past in my warning to him : "Stirring up trouble is not as good as preventing trouble from occurring. If you just concentrate on matters of immediate concern, I'm afraid that you'll get more than you bargained for." And I used the same caution to others, to military governor Shih I'te [Shi Yide] in 1710 and to General Chang Ku-chen [Chang Guzhen] in 1711.

... "There's an old saying that if the civilian officials don't seek money and the military officials aren't afraid of death, we need never fear that the country won't have Great Peace." How true that is! And again I told him : "The Tao [Dao] of being an official lies in nothing else than this : Be sincere in your heart, and sincere in your administration, don't stir up too much trouble, and have officials and people love you as a mother. That is being a good official." ...

The rulers of the past all took reverence for Heaven and observance of ancestral precepts as the fundamental way in ruling the country. To be sincere in reverence for Heaven and ancestors entails the following : Be kind to men from afar and keep the able ones near, nourish the people, think of the profit of all as being the real profit and the mind of the whole country as being the real mind, be considerate to officials and act as a father to the people, protect the state before danger comes and govern well before there is any disturbance, be always diligent and always careful, and maintain the balance between leniency and strictness, between principle and expediency, so that long-range plans can be made for the country. That's all there is to it.

12

Peter the Great, Correspondence with His Son

Peter I, Emperor of Russia (1682–1725), was never pleased with his son Alexei's behavior. In 1715, Peter forced Alexei to renounce his right of succession. Without his father's permission, Alexei fled Russia in 1716 and returned in 1718. Peter ordered him tried for treason, and as a consequence of judicial torture, Alexei died in the summer of 1718 in the fortress of Peter and Paul. The following selections reveal Peter's determination to defend Russia from all enemies — even if that meant the death of his own son.

QUESTIONS TO CONSIDER

1. What does Peter's letter to Alexei reveal about Peter's attitude toward war and his views on Alexei's right of succession?
2. How would you compare K'ang-hsi's, Louis XIV's, and Peter the Great's approach to absolutist rule? What were their perceptions of "good government,"

the role of violence in statecraft, education, and the use of royal ministers and servants?

3. What type of relationship did Peter and Alexei have?

4. Suppose you were living in early modern times. Which of the four rulers — Akbar, Louis XIV, K'ang-hsi, or Peter the Great would you prefer to live under (see Readings 9, 10, and 11)?

A Letter to Alexei

October 11, 1715

Declaration to My Son,

You cannot be ignorant of what is known to all the world, to what degree our people groaned under the oppression of the Swedes before the beginning of the present war.

By the usurpation of so many maritime places so necessary to our state, they had cut us off from all commerce with the rest of the world, and we saw with regret that besides they had cast a thick veil before the eyes of the clear-sighted. You know what it has cost us in the beginning of this war (in which God alone has led us, as it were, by the hand, and still guides us) to make ourselves experienced in the art of war, and to put a stop to those advantages which our implacable enemies obtained over us.

We submitted to this with a resignation to the will of God, making no doubt but it was he who put us to that trial, till he might lead us into the right way, and we might render ourselves worthy to experience, that the same enemy who at first made others tremble, now in his turn trembles before us, perhaps in a much greater degree. These are the fruits which, next to the assistance of God, we owe to our own toil and to the labour of our faithful and affectionate children, our Russian subjects.

But at the time that I am viewing the prosperity which God has heaped on our native country, if I cast an eye upon the posterity that is to succeed me, my heart is much more penetrated with grief on account of what is to happen, then I rejoice at those blessings that are past, seeing that you, my son, reject all means of making yourself capable of well-governing after me. I say your incapacity is voluntary, because you cannot excuse yourself with want of natural parts and strength of body, as if God had not given you a sufficient share of either; and though your constitution is none of the strongest, yet it cannot be said that it is altogether weak.

But you even will not so much as hear warlike exercises mentioned; though it is by them that we broke through that obscurity in which we were involved, and that we made ourselves known to nations, whose esteem we share at present.

I do not exhort you to make war without lawful reasons; I only desire you to apply yourself to learn the art of it; for it is impossible well to govern without knowing the rules and discipline of it, was it for no other end than for the defense of the country.

I could place before your eyes many instances of what I am proposing to you. I will only mention to you the Greeks, with whom we are united by the same pro-

From Friedrich C. Weber, *The Present State of Russia*, vol. 2 (London, 1722), pp. 97–105.

fession of faith. What occasioned their decay but that they neglected arms? Idleness and repose weakened them, made them submit to tyrants, and brought them to that slavery to which they are now so long since reduced. You mistake, if you think it is enough for a prince to have good generals to act under his order. Everyone looks upon the head; they study his inclinations and conform themselves to them: all the world owns this. My brother during his reign loved magnificence in dress, and great equipages of horses. The nation were not much inclined that way, but the prince's delight soon became that of his subjects, for they are inclined to imitate him in liking a thing as well as disliking it.

If the people so easily break themselves of things which only regard pleasure, will they not forget in time, or will they not more easily give over the practice of arms, the exercise of which is the more painful to them, the less they are kept to it?

You have no inclination to learn war, you do not apply yourself to it, and consequently you will never learn it: And how then can you command others, and judge of the reward which those deserve who do their duty, or punish others who fail of it? You will do nothing, nor judge of anything but by the eyes and help of others, like a young bird that holds up his bill to be fed.

You say that the weak state of your health will not permit you to undergo the fatigues of war: This is an excuse which is no better than the rest. I desire no fatigues, but only inclination, which even sickness itself cannot hinder. Ask those who remember the time of my brother. He was of a constitution weaker by far than yours. He was not able to manage a horse of the least mettle, nor could he hardly mount it: Yet he loved horses, hence it came, that there never was, nor perhaps is there actually now in the nation a finer stable than his was.

By this you see that good success does not always depend on pain, but on the will.

If you think there are some, whose affairs do not fail of success, though they do not go to war themselves; it is true: But if they do not go themselves, yet they have an inclination for it, and understand it.

For instance, the late King of France did not always take the field in person; but it is known to what degree he loved war, and what glorious exploits he performed in it, which made his campaigns to be called the theatre and school of the world. His inclinations were not confined solely to military affairs, he also loved mechanics, manufactures and other establishments, which rendered his kingdom more flourishing than any other whatsoever.

After having made to you all those remonstrances, I return to my former subject which regards you.

I am a man and consequently I must die. To whom shall I leave after me to finish what by the grace of God I have begun, and to preserve what I have partly recovered? To a man, who like the slothful servant hides his talent in the earth, that is to say, who neglects making the best of what God has entrusted to him?

Remember your obstinacy and ill-nature, how often I reproached you with it, and even chastised you for it, and for how many years I almost have not spoke to you; but all this has availed nothing, has effected nothing. It was but losing my time; it was striking the air. You do not make the least endeavors, and all your pleasure seems to consist in staying idle and lazy at home: Things of which you ought to be ashamed (forasmuch as they make you miserable) seem to make up your dearest delight, nor do you foresee the dangerous consequences of it for yourself and for the whole state. St. Paul has left us a great truth when he wrote : If a man know not how to rule his own house, how shall he take of the church of God ?

After having considered all those great inconveniences and reflected upon them, and seeing I cannot bring you to good by any inducement, I have thought fit to give you in writing this act of my last will, with this resolution however to wait still a little longer before I put it in execution, to see if you will mend. If not, I will have you to know that I will deprive you of the succession, as one may cut off a useless member.

Do not fancy, that, because I have no other child but you, I only write this to terrify you. I will certainly put it in execution, if it please God ; for whereas I do not spare my own life for my country and the welfare of my people, why should I spare you who do not render yourself worthy of either ? I would rather choose to transmit them to a worthy stranger, than to my own unworthy son.

Peter

Alexei's Reply

Most Clement Lord and Father,

I have read the paper your Majesty gave me on the 27th of October, 1715, after the funeral of my late consort.

I have nothing to reply to it, but, that if your Majesty will deprive me of the succession to the Crown of Russia by reason of my incapacity, your will be done ; I even most instantly beg it of you, because I do not think myself fit for the government. My memory is very much weakened, and yet it is necessary in affairs. The strength of my mind and of my body is much decayed by the sicknesses which I have undergone, and which have rendered me incapable of governing so many nations ; this requires a more vigorous man than I am.

Therefore I do not aspire after you (whom God preserve many years) to the succession of the Russian Crown, even if I had no brother as I have one at present, whom I pray God preserve. Neither will I pretend for the future to that succession, of which I take God to witness, and swear it upon my soul, in testimony whereof I write and sign this present with my own hand.

I put my children into your hands, and as for myself, I desire nothing of you but a bare maintenance during my life, leaving the whole to your consideration and to your will.

Your most humble servant and son,
Alexei

Degrees of Religious Toleration

From the fourth century, when Christianity was established as the Roman state religion, well into the seventeenth century, religious toleration made no sense to the great majority of Europeans. For them, believing the right things would gain them salvation; believing the wrong things would send them to hell. Heresy, the crime of harboring and spreading false doctrine, was often compared with counterfeiting coins or with spreading a disease worse than leprosy.

The kingdom of Poland experimented briefly and unsuccessfully with religious toleration in the sixteenth century, but it was only in the English North American colonies, Prussia, and the Netherlands that religious toleration made headway in the seventeenth century. Then, with the Enlightenment of the eighteenth century, religious toleration gained widespread acceptance in many parts of Europe.

The following three selections illustrate this change. In his Act Concerning Religion (1649), now usually called the Maryland Toleration Act, Lord Baltimore — himself a member of the Catholic minority in England — granted toleration to what we now call "mainline" Christian denominations. At the same time, he established ferocious punishments for what he construed as blasphemy. Even though these punishments were seldom implemented, they reveal how even a farsighted and relatively tolerant seventeenth-century statesman was unwilling to risk the stability of his government by granting too much religious freedom. On the other hand, Gotthold Ephraim Lessing, a leading German poet and playwright, and Thomas Paine, an influential figure in both the American and French Revolutions, spoke for the eighteenth-century Enlightenment. For them, complete religious toleration was the only rational approach for policy-makers to adopt. Paine's statement appears in *The Rights of Man* (1792), a defense of the French Revolution. Lessing's statement is made by the Jewish title character in his play *Nathan the Wise Man* (1779), as he defends the right of Jews to remain faithful to their religion.

13

The Maryland Toleration Act

In 1632, Charles I issued a charter to Cecilius Calvert, second Baron of Baltimore, as lord proprietor of the territory that is now Maryland. The Calverts were among the few active and politically prominent Catholic families of the time, and Maryland became the only seventeenth-century British colony in

North America where Catholics were particularly welcome. The following selection reveals Lord Baltimore's attitude toward religious toleration.

QUESTIONS TO CONSIDER

1. What sort of dissent was Lord Baltimore willing to tolerate? What limits did he put on religious dissent?
2. What punishments did Lord Baltimore establish for those who exceeded the limits of religious toleration? Why were the punishments so severe?
3. Compare this view of religious freedom with that of the English experience in India (see Reading 41).

An Act concerning Religion: Forasmuch as in a well-governed and Christian commonwealth matters concerning religion and the honor of God ought in the first place to be taken into serious consideration and endeavored to be settled, be it therefore ordered and enacted by the Right Honorable Cecilius Lord Baron of Baltimore, absolute Lord and Proprietary of this province, with the advice and consent of this General Assembly that:

Whatsoever person or persons within this province and the islands thereunto belonging shall from henceforth blaspheme God, that is, curse Him, or deny our Saviour, Jesus Christ, to be the Son of God, or shall deny the Holy Trinity — the Father, Son, and Holy Ghost — or the godhead of any of the said three persons of the Trinity, or the unity of the Godhead, or shall use or utter any reproachful speeches, words or language concerning the said Holy Trinity, or any of the said three persons thereof, shall be punished with death and confiscation or forfeiture of all his or her lands to the Lord Proprietary and his heirs. . . .

Whatsoever person or persons shall from henceforth use or utter any reproachful words or speeches concerning the blessed Virgin Mary, the Mother of our Saviour, or the Holy Apostles or Evangelists, or any of them, shall in such case for the first offense forfeit to the Lord Proprietary . . . the sum of five pounds sterling or the value thereof. . . . But, in case such offender or offenders shall not then have goods and chattels sufficient for the satisfying of such forfeiture, or that the same be not otherwise speedily satisfied, . . . then such offender shall be publicly whipped and be imprisoned during the pleasure of the Lord Proprietary or the . . . chief Governor of this province for the time being. . . . Every such offender or offenders for every second offense shall forfeit ten pounds sterling or the value thereof . . . or, in case such offender or offenders shall not then have goods and chattels within this province sufficient for that purpose, . . . be publicly and severely whipped and imprisoned as before is expressed. . . . Every person . . . offending herein the third time shall . . . forfeit all his lands and goods and be forever banished and expelled out of this province. . . .

From Assembly Proceedings, April 2–21, 1649, in *The Archives of Maryland,* vol. 1, ed. W. H. Browne (Baltimore : Maryland Historical Society, 1883), pp. 244–247. Reprinted by permission of the Maryland Historical Society.

Whatsoever person or persons shall from henceforth upon any occasion of offense or otherwise in a reproachful manner or way declare, call, or denominate any person or persons whatsoever inhabiting, residing, trafficking, trading, or commercing within this province . . . "a heretic," "schismatic," "idolator," "Puritan," "Independent," "Presbyterian," "popish priest," "Jesuit," "Jesuited papist," "Lutheran," "Calvinist," "Anabaptist," "Brownist," "Antinomian," "Barrowist," "Roundhead," "Separatist," or any other name or term in a reproachful manner relating to a matter of religion, shall for every offense forfeit and lose the sum of ten shillings sterling . . . , the one half thereof to be forfeited and paid unto the person and persons of whom such reproachful words are or shall be spoken or uttered, and the other half to the Lord Proprietary. . . .

Every person and persons within this province that shall at any time profane the Sabbath or Lord's Day, called "Sunday," by frequent swearing, drunkenness, or by any uncivil or disorderly recreation, or by working on that day when absolute necessity doth not require it, shall for every first offense forfeit 2 shillings, 6 pence, sterling or the value thereof, and for the second offense 5 shillings . . . and for every time he shall offend in like manner afterwards 10 shillings. . . . In case such offender shall not have sufficient goods . . . , the party so offending shall for the first and second offense . . . be imprisoned till he or she shall publicly in open court before the chief commander, judge, or magistrate of that county, town, or precinct where such offense shall be committed, acknowledge the scandal and offense he hath in that respect given against God and the good and civil government of this province, and . . . for every time afterwards be publicly whipped.

And whereas the enforcing of the conscience in matters of religion hath frequently fallen out to be of dangerous consequence in those commonwealths where it hath been practiced, and for the more quiet and peaceful government of this province, and the better to preserve mutual love and amity among the inhabitants thereof, be it therefore also by the Lord Proprietary with the advice and consent of this Assembly ordained and enacted (except as in this present Act is before declared and set forth) that :

No person or persons whatsoever within this province . . . professing to believe in Jesus Christ shall from henceforth be in any way troubled, molested, or discountenanced for or in respect of his or her religion nor in the free exercise thereof within this province or the islands thereunto belonging nor any way compelled to the belief or exercise of any other religion against his or her consent, so as they be not unfaithful to the Lord Proprietary, or molest or conspire against the civil government established or to be established under him or his heirs. And that all . . . persons that shall presume contrary to this Act and the true intent and meaning thereof directly or indirectly either in person or estate willfully to wrong, disturb, trouble or molest any person whatsoever within this province professing to believe in Jesus Christ for or in respect of his or her religion or the free exercise thereof . . . other than is provided for in this Act : that such person or persons so offending shall be compelled to pay treble damages to the party so wronged or molested and for every such offense shall also forfeit 20 shillings sterling in money or the value thereof. . . . Or if the party so offending shall refuse or be unable to recompense the party so wronged, or to satisfy such fine or forfeiture, then such offender shall be severely punished by public whipping and imprisonment during the pleasure of the Lord Proprietary or his . . . chief Governor of this province for the time being without bail.

14

Thomas Paine, *The Rights of Man*

Thomas Paine (1739–1809), an Englishman who became a leading propagandist on the American side in the War for Independence, subsequently went to France and supported the early stages of the French Revolution. But when the French revolutionaries announced that they would tolerate religious diversity, Paine felt that they were arrogating power to themselves without justification. For Paine, the right to worship according to the dictates of conscience was so fundamental that no government should act as if that right could be granted or denied by the state.

QUESTIONS TO CONSIDER

1. What is the meaning and significance of Paine's statement that ". . . before any human institutions of government were known in the world, there existed . . . a compact between God and man"? Compare and contrast this with Rousseau's concept of the "social contract" (see Reading 20).
2. Why does Paine believe that a variety of religious denominations is healthy and should be tolerated?
3. Why does Paine believe that state enforcement of religious beliefs would be detrimental to both the state and religion?

There is a single idea, which if it strikes rightly upon the mind, either in a legal or a religious sense, will prevent any man, or any body of men, or any government, from going wrong on the subject of religion; which is, that before any human institutions of government were known in the world, there existed, if I may so express it, a compact between God and man, from the beginning of time; and that as the relation and condition which man in his *individual person* stands in toward his Maker cannot be changed, or in any ways altered by any human laws or human authority, that religious devotion, which is a part of this compact, cannot so much as be made a subject of human laws; and that all laws must conform themselves to this prior existing compact, and not assume to make the compact conform to the laws, which, besides being human, are subsequent thereto. The first act of man, when he looked around and saw himself a creature which he did not make, and a world furnished for his reception, must have been devotion; and devotion must ever continue sacred to every individual man, *as it appears right to him*; and governments do mischief by interfering. . . .

   With respect to what are called denominations of religion, if everyone is left to judge of his own religion, there is no such thing as a religion that is wrong; but

From *Writings of Thomas Paine,* edited by Moncure D. Conway (New York: G. P. Putnam's Sons, 1894), pp. 354 n. 10, 326, 515–516.

if they are to judge of each other's religion, there is no such thing as a religion that is right ; and therefore all the world is right, or all the world is wrong. But with respect to religion itself, without regard to names, and as directing itself from the universal family of mankind to the divine object of all adoration, *it is man bringing to his Maker the fruits of his heart;* and though these fruits may differ from each other like the fruits of the earth, the grateful tribute of every one is accepted. . . .

But as religion is very improperly made a political machine, and the reality of it is thereby destroyed, I will conclude this work with stating in what light religion appears to me :

If we suppose a large family of children, who, on any particular day, or particular occasion, make it a custom to present to their parents some token of their affection and gratitude, each of them would make a different offering, and most probably in a different manner.

Some would pay their congratulations in themes of verse and prose, by some little devices, as their genius dictated, or according to what they thought would please ; and, perhaps the least of all, not able to do any of those things, would ramble into the garden, or the field, and gather what it thought the prettiest flower it could find, though, perhaps it might be but a simple weed. The parents would be more gratified by such a variety than if the whole of them had acted on a concerted plan, and each had made exactly the same offering. This would have the cold appearance of contrivance, or the harsh one of control. But of all unwelcome things, nothing would more afflict the parent than to know that the whole of them had afterwards gotten together by the ears, boys and girls, fighting, reviling, and abusing each other about which was the best or the worst present.

Why may we not suppose that the great Father of all is pleased with variety of devotion ; and that the greatest offense we can act is that by which we seek to torment and render each other miserable ? For my own part I am fully satisfied that what I am now doing, with an endeavor to conciliate mankind, to render their condition happy, to unite nations that have hitherto been enemies, and to extirpate the horrid practice of war and break the chains of slavery and oppression, is acceptable in His sight, and being the best service I can perform I act it cheerfully.

I do not believe that any two men, on what are called doctrinal points, think alike who think at all. It is only those who have not thought that appear to agree. . . .

15

Gotthold Ephraim Lessing, *Nathan the Wise Man*

Gotthold Ephraim Lessing (1729–1781), the foremost German playwright before Goethe and Schiller, was also one of the most articulate spokesmen for Enlightenment values in the German-speaking countries. The following speech from *Nathan the Wise Man* offers a parable about religious toleration. Nathan is presenting his case before the Turkish Sultan Saladin.

QUESTIONS TO CONSIDER

1. What do the three rings in Nathan's speech represent?
2. What advice does the judge offer to the squabbling sons? Would that advice have been acceptable to Lord Baltimore (see Reading 13) or Thomas Paine (see Reading 14)?

Nathan : Countless years ago in the East there lived a man who possessed a ring of immeasurable worth, given to him by a loved one. Its stone was an opal which reflected a hundred beautiful colors and had the secret power of making anyone who wore it and believed in it pleasing to God and men. Is it any wonder then that this man in the East never took it from his finger and provided in his will and testament that it should never leave his family? He left the ring to the son he loved the most, providing that he in turn should will the ring to the one of his sons he loved the most and always the best-loved son, not necessarily the eldest, should be lord of the whole family through the sole power of the ring. . . .

The ring thus went from son to son, but finally came to the father of three sons, all of whom obeyed him equally well, so that he could not resist loving them all equally. It happened that this one from time to time, then that one, then the third one — just depending on which one was alone with him without the other two sharing in what came straight from his heart — seemed worthier of the ring to him, and in his softheartedness he would promise it to him. And so that went on as long as it could go on. The time came to die, and the kindly father was embarrassed painfully at having to grieve two of his sons, who were relying on his word. What to do? He sent it to an expert craftsman, placing an order for two others and telling him to spare neither cost nor pains to make them altogether like the original. With cheer and joy he called his sons — each one separately — and gave each one his blessing individually and his ring. Then he died, . . . [but] he was hardly dead before each one came with his ring, and each one wanted to be lord of the family. Investigations, complaints, and fights followed to no avail : no proof could be found for the one true ring. . . .

The sons sued each other, each one swearing before the judge that he took his ring right from his father's hand, which was true, after having already had the promise of lordship through the ring from him for a long time — which was no less true. Each one swore that his father could not have played false with him. Before he would suspect his father of that he would have to accuse his brothers of foul play — however much he had previously been inclined to believe only the best about them — and before long he wanted the satisfaction of seeing the traitors identified and brought to justice. . . .

The Judge said : "If you don't soon produce your father for me, I will dismiss you from my court. Do you think that I am here to solve riddles? Or do you insist on waiting around until the ring opens its mouth? But wait! I have been hearing that the right ring has the miraculous power of making the wearer pleasing to God and men. That fact must be decisive, for the false rings will never be able to do that! Now tell me, whom do two of you love the most? Speak up now! You have

From Gotthold Ephraim Lessing, *Nathan der Weise*, act 3, scene 7. In *Lessings Werke*, vol. 2, ed. Georg Witkowski (Leipzig : Bibliographisches Institut, n.d.), pp. 342–347. Translated by Henry A. Myers.

nothing to say? Are the rings having an effect only on the wearer and no effect outside of him? Each of you loves only himself the most? Oh, then you are all three deceived deceivers! None of your three rings is real. The real ring must be assumed lost: to hide the loss, the father had three replacements made for it. . . .

"And so," the Judge continued, "if you want only my sentence but not my advice, just leave! But my advice to you is this: accept the matter just as it is. If each of you received his ring from his father, let each one sincerely believe his ring to be the real one. It is possible that the father no longer wanted to tolerate the tyranny of the ring in his household, which seems all the more likely since he loved all three of you and loved you equally to the extent that he could not ignore two of you in order to favor one. Go to it! Free of prejudice and corrupting influences, let each one of you pursue what he loves. Let each of you compete to demonstrate the power in his ring — whether this power assists you when you are gentle, when you gladly put up with the faults of others, when you do good works, or when your devotion to God is most sincere. And when the powers of this stone reveal themselves in your children's children, I summon you to appear a thousand times a thousand years from now before this bench. Then a wiser man than I will sit here and give you his verdict. Go!" These were the words of the knowing judge.

Enlightenment, Politics, and Trade

Although French writers and the French language often expressed the spirit and goals of the Enlightenment, no single European nation ever completely dominated this movement. England, France, and Germany provided a number of important writers, often called *philosophes,* who championed the Enlightenment's ideals of reason, progress, liberty, and happiness. The following selections from Locke, Leibniz, Montesquieu, Euler, Rousseau, and Smith not only illustrate the cosmopolitan character of the Enlightenment but also suggest its wide-ranging interests in politics, trade, and the non-European world.

16

John Locke, *The Second Treatise of Civil Government*

John Locke (1632–1704) was an English philosopher of the Glorious Revolution period whose works had a great influence on the people of his own country, on French *philosophes* of the eighteenth-century Enlightenment, and on the colonists who became American revolutionaries. In his political writing, Locke was most concerned with demonstrating that consent of the governed alone bestows legitimacy and that an attempt to rule in defiance of the people's will was tyranny.

Locke's two-volume *Essay Concerning Human Understanding* anticipated scientific psychology with its analysis of how the human mind actually works. As a by-product of his conclusion that both cognition and belief are the results of sensations acting on the mind, he showed that persecuting people for religious beliefs was senseless. Locke believed that people couldn't "help" what went through their minds ; therefore, regulating religious beliefs meant teaching people to lie about what they believed. Although even Locke had some reservations about full political rights for Roman Catholics, Muslims, and atheists, he generally advocated religious toleration.

Even though Locke contributed substantially to the later concept of separation of Church and state, he drew at times on medieval ideas concerning God, humans, and the state. Using the medieval idea that man was God's property, he refuted the notion that kings or other rulers could treat people as their own property. Under the protection of the God to whom they would always belong, the people formed a government to protect their God-given or natural rights of life, liberty, and property.

Locke's reasoning became a mainstay of *constitutionalism,* the theory that the people give authority to governments conditionally as part of a contract. When government officials no longer protect the natural rights of the people, these officials can be removed — by revolution, if no other means are available.

Locke's stress on property as an essential right of the individual makes him an early defender of capitalism in the context of his times. Just as people belong to God because God created them, individuals own what they create with their labor. In Locke's "labor theory of value," raw materials take on higher value as labor turns them into finished commodities. Locke thus gave the efforts of all individuals who aided production credit for creating new value and thus supported capitalistic individualism. Marx and the Marxists later modified this labor theory of value and directed it against the whole capitalist system.

The following excerpts are from Locke's best-known political work, *The Second Treatise of Civil Government.*

QUESTIONS TO CONSIDER

1. What motivation do people have for parting with the liberty that they enjoy in the state of nature?
2. How does a person exchange his or her "natural liberty" for mutual obligations under government?
3. Which rights from the state of nature do people always keep under government?
4. How is government appropriately divided into branches? Are these branches approximately equal in authority or not?
5. When is revolution justified? Who makes this judgment?

The Contract to Preserve Life, Liberty, and Property

To understand political power right and derive it from its origin, we must consider what state all men are naturally in, and that is a state of perfect freedom to order their actions and dispose of their possessions and persons as they think fit, within the bounds of the law of nature, without asking leave or depending upon the will of any other man. [This is a] state also of equality, wherein all the power and jurisdiction is reciprocal, no one having more than another.

Men being . . . by nature all free, equal, and independent, no one can be put out of this estate and subjected to the political power of another without his own consent. The only way whereby any one divests himself of his natural liberty and puts on the bonds of civil society is by agreeing with other men to join and unite into a community for their comfortable, safe, and peaceable living amongst one another, in a secure enjoyment of their properties and a greater security against any that are not of it. This any number of men may do, because it injures not the freedom of the rest ; they are left as they were in the liberty of the state of nature. When any number of men have so consented to make one community or government, they are thereby presently incorporated and make one body politic wherein the majority have a right to act and conclude the rest. . . . And thus that which begins and actually constitutes any political society is nothing but the consent of any number of freemen capable of a majority to unite and incorporate into such a society. And this is that, and that only, which did or could give beginning to any lawful government in the world.

If man in the state of nature be so free . . . , and if he be absolute lord of his own person and possessions, equal to the greatest, and subject to nobody, why will he part with his freedom, why will he give up his empire and subject himself to the dominion and control of any other power ? To which it is obvious to answer that though in the state of nature he has such a right, yet the enjoyment of it is very uncertain and constantly exposed to the invasion of others ; for all being kings as much as he, every man his equal, and the greater part no strict observers of equity and justice, the enjoyment of the property he has in this state is very unsafe, very unsecure. This makes him willing to quit a condition which, however free, is full of fears and continual dangers ; and it is not without reason that he seeks out and is willing to join in society with others who are already united, or have a mind to unite, for the mutual preservation of their lives, liberties, and estates, which I call by the general name "property."

The great and chief end, therefore, of men's uniting into commonwealths and putting themselves under government is the preservation of their property. . . . Though the earth and all inferior creatures be common to all men, yet every man has a property in his own person ; this nobody has any right to but himself. The labor of his body and the work of his hands, we may say, are properly his. Whatsoever then he removes out of the state that nature has provided and left it in, he has mixed his labor with, and joined to it something that is his own, and thereby makes it his property. It being by him removed from the common state nature has placed it in, it has by this labor something annexed to it that excludes

From *Second Treatise*, in *Two Treatises of Civil Government by John Locke* (London : G. Routledge & Sons, 1884), pp. 244–279, passim.

the common right of other men. For this labor being the unquestionable property of the laborer, no man but he can have a right to what that is once joined to, at least where there is enough and as good left in common for others. . . . As much land as a man tills, plants, improves, cultivates, and can use the product of, so much is his property. He by his labor does, as it were, enclose it from the common.

Law-Making and Executive Power

It is reasonable and just that I should have a right to destroy that which threatens me with destruction; for, by the fundamental law of nature . . . when all cannot be preserved, the safety of the innocent is to be preferred; and one may destroy a man who makes war upon him, or has discovered an enmity to his being, for the same reason that he may kill a wolf or a lion, because such men . . . have no other rule but that of force and violence, and so may be treated as beasts of prey. . . .

To avoid this state of war is one great reason of men's putting themselves into society and quitting the state of nature; for where there is an authority, a power on earth from which relief can be had by appeal, there the continuance of the state of war is excluded, and the controversy is decided by that power.

Whenever, therefore, any number of men are so united into one society as to quit every one his executive power of the law of nature and to resign it to the public, there and there only is a political or civil society.

Because it may be too great a temptation to human frailty, apt to grasp at power, for the same persons who have the power of making laws to have also in their hands the power to execute them, whereby they may exempt themselves from obedience to the laws they make, and suit the law, both in its making and execution, to their own private advantage, and thereby come to have a distinct interest from the rest of the community contrary to the end of society and government; therefore, in well ordered commonwealths, where the good of the whole is so considered as it ought, the legislative power is put into the hands of diverse persons who, duly assembled, have by themselves, or jointly with others, a power to make laws; which when they have done, being separated again, they are themselves subject to the laws they have made. . . .

But because the laws that are at once and in a short time made have a constant and lasting force and need a perpetual execution or an attendance thereunto; therefore, it is necessary there should be a power always in being which should see to the execution of the laws that are made and remain in force. And thus the legislative and executive power come often to be separated. There is another power in every commonwealth which . . . contains the power of war and peace, leagues and alliances, and all the transactions with all persons and communities without the commonwealth, and may be called "federative," if anyone pleases. So the thing be understood, I am indifferent as to the name.

Man, being born, as has been proved, with a title to perfect freedom and uncontrolled enjoyment of all the rights and privileges of the law of nature equally with any other man or number of men in the world, has by nature a power not only to preserve his property — that is, his life, liberty, and estate — against the injuries and attempts of other men, but to judge of and punish the breaches of that law in others as he is persuaded the offense deserves, even with death itself in crimes where the heinousness of the fact in his opinion requires it. Every man who has entered into civil society and become a member of any commonwealth has quitted his power to punish offenses against the law of nature in prosecution of his own private judgment. He has given a right to the commonwealth to employ his force for the execution of the judgments of the commonwealth, which, indeed, are his own judgments, they being made by himself or his representative. . . .

[The] end of law is not to abolish or restrain but to preserve and enlarge freedom ; for in all the states of created beings capable of laws, where there is no law, there is no freedom. For liberty is to be free from restraint and violence from others, which cannot be where there is not law ; but freedom is not, as we are told : a liberty for every man to do what he likes — for who could be free, when every other man's humor might domineer over him ? — but a liberty to dispose and order . . . his person, actions, possessions, and his whole property, within the allowance of those laws under which he is, and therein not to be subject to the arbitrary will of another, but freely follow his own.

Right to Remove Tyrannical Government

Since it can never be supposed to be the will of the society that the legislative should have a power to destroy that which every one designs to secure by entering into society, and for which the people submitted themselves to legislators of their own making, whenever the legislators endeavour to take away and destroy the property of the people, or to reduce them to slavery under arbitrary power, they put themselves into a state of war with the people, who are thereupon absolved from any further obedience, and are left to the common refuge which God has provided for all men against force and violence. Whensoever, therefore, the legislative shall transgress this fundamental rule of society, and either by ambition, fear, folly, or corruption, endeavour to grasp themselves or put into the hands of any other an absolute power over the lives, liberties, and estates of the people, by this breach of trust they forfeit the power the people had put into their hands, for quite contrary ends, and it devolves to the people, who have a right to resume their original liberty, and by the establishment of the new legislative (such as they shall think fit) provide for their own safety and security, which is the end for which they are in society. What I have said here concerning the legislative in general, holds true also concerning the supreme executor, who having a double trust put in him, both to have a part in the legislative and the supreme execution of the law, acts against both when he goes about to set up his own arbitrary will as the law of the society. He acts also contrary to his trust when he employs the force, treasure, and offices of the society, to corrupt the representatives, and gain them to his purposes. . . .

The end of government is the good of mankind, and which is best for mankind, that the people should be always exposed to the boundless will of tyranny, or that the rulers should be sometimes liable to be opposed when they grow exorbitant in the use of their power, and employ it for the destruction and not the preservation of the properties of their people ?

If a controversy arise between a prince and some of the people in a matter where the law is silent or doubtful, and the thing be of great consequence, I should think the proper umpire in such a case should be the body of the people. . . . But if the prince or whoever they be in the administration decline that way of determination, the appeal then lies nowhere but to heaven; force between either persons who have no known superior on earth, or which permits no appeal to a judge on earth, being properly a state of war, wherein the appeal lies only to heaven, and in that state the injured party must judge for himself when he will think fit to make use of that appeal and put himself upon it.

17

Gottfried Wilhelm Leibniz, Preface to *Novissima Sinica*

With the Age of Discovery, European intellectual frontiers reached beyond the limits of the Renaissance world, and a new cosmopolitan spirit developed. Europeans gained appreciation for the globe's many races and diverse cultures and recognized that the non-Christian world was not inhabited by savages alone. Indeed, some of these people enjoyed richer, older, and more refined cultures than the Europeans.

Enlightenment intellectuals, disillusioned with the religious intolerance, monarchical despotism, and the institutions and customs of the old order in Europe, found the Chinese moral and political system a refreshing contrast. China was a great ancient civilization that antedated Christian revelation. It was governed by an enlightened literary class, recruited by competitive examinations rather than by accident of birth. According to the Jesuits' accounts, the Chinese separated morality and revealed religion, and Confucianism was a rational philosophy rather than a religious dogma. For all these reasons, such leaders of the Enlightenment as Voltaire and Quesnay looked upon China as a model for a new Europe.

Perhaps the first and greatest Sinophile in Europe during the late seventeenth and early eighteenth centuries was the famous German philosopher-mathematician Gottfried Wilhelm Leibniz (1646–1716). Leibniz's Sinophilism was nurtured primarily by the Jesuit writings on China that he read in the libraries in Vienna, Hanover, Munich, and Berlin. He also maintained a personal correspondence with such erudite Jesuit priests in Peking as Grimaldi, Bouvet, Verbiest, Kircher, Gerbillion, and Lustian. Thoroughly fascinated by Chinese culture, Leibniz admired Confucius, Emperor K'ang-hsi (Leibniz calls him Cam Hi) (see Reading 11), the Chinese language, and the *Book of Changes* (*I-Ching*), as well as many aspects of the Chinese political and social systems. He recognized the importance of Chinese culture in realizing his grand plan for a universal civilization. In the following excerpts from his preface to *Novissima Sinica* (*Latest News of China*), published in 1697, Leibniz argued the need for an intellectual alliance between the two great civilizations — Europe and China. Leibniz believed that Europe excelled in the theoretical and philosophical sciences (mathematics, astronomy, logic, and metaphysics), while China was superior to Europe in practical philosophy and political ethics. Thus he proposed a cultural exchange between the East and the West.

QUESTIONS TO CONSIDER

1. What aspects of Chinese thinking and institutions were appealing to European intellectuals?
2. Why did Sinomania decline in Europe in the nineteenth century? (See Readings 24, 25, 37, and 42.)

I consider it a singular plan of the fates that human cultivation and refinement should today be concentrated, as it were, in the two extremes of our continent, in Europe and in Tschina (as they call it), which adorns the Orient as Europe does the opposite edge of the earth. Perhaps Supreme Providence has ordained such an arrangement, so that, as the most cultivated and distant peoples stretch out their arms to each other, those in between may gradually be brought to a better way of life. . . .

Now the Chinese Empire, which challenges Europe in cultivated area, and certainly surpasses her in population, vies with us in many other ways in almost equal combat, so that now they win, now we. But what should I put down first by way of comparison? To go over everything, even though useful, would be lengthy and is not our proper task in this place. In the useful arts and in practical experience with natural objects we are, all things considered, about equal to them, and each people has knowledge which it could with profit communicate to the other. In profundity of knowledge and in the theoretical disciplines we are their superiors. For besides logic and metaphysics, and the knowledge of things incorporeal, which we justly claim as peculiarly our province, we excel by far in the understanding of concepts which are abstracted by the mind from the material, i.e., in things mathematical, as is in truth demonstrated when Chinese astronomy comes into competition with our own. The Chinese are thus seen to be ignorant of that great light of the mind, the art of demonstration, and they have remained content with a sort of empirical geometry, which our artisans universally possess. They also yield to us in military science, not so much out of ignorance as by deliberation. For they despise everything which creates or nourishes ferocity in men, and almost in emulation of the higher teachings of Christ (and not, as some wrongly suggest, because of anxiety), they are averse to war. They would be wise indeed if they were alone in the world. But as things are, it comes back to this, that even the good must cultivate the arts of war, so that the evil may not gain power over everything. In these matters, then, we are superior.

But who would have believed that there is on earth a people who, though we are in our view so very advanced in every branch of behavior, still surpass us in comprehending the precepts of civil life? Yet now we find this to be so among the

From Donald F. Lach, trans., *The Preface to Leibniz' Novissima Sinica* (Honolulu : University of Hawaii Press, 1957), pp. 68–75. Reprinted by permission of the University of Hawaii Press.

Chinese, as we learn to know them better. And so if we are their equals in the industrial arts, and ahead of them in contemplative sciences, certainly they surpass us (though it is almost shameful to confess this) in practical philosophy, that is, in the precepts of ethics and politics adapted to the present life and use of mortals. Indeed, it is difficult to describe how beautifully all the laws of the Chinese, in contrast to those of other peoples, are directed to the achievement of public tranquility and the establishment of social order, so that men shall be disrupted in their relations as little as possible. Certainly by their own doing men suffer the greatest evils and in turn inflict them upon each other. It is too truly said that "man is a wolf to man." Great indeed is our quite universal folly, in which we, exposed as we are to natural injuries, heap woes on ourselves, as though they were lacking from elsewhere.

What harm, then, if reason has anywhere brought a remedy? Certainly the Chinese above all others have attained a higher standard. In a vast multitude of men they have virtually accomplished more than the founders of religious orders among us have achieved within their own narrow ranks. So great is obedience toward superiors and reverence toward elders, so religious, almost, is the relation of children toward parents, that for children to contrive anything violent against their parents, even by word, is almost unheard of, and the perpetrator seems to atone for his actions even as we make a parricide pay for his deed. Moreover, there is among equals, or those having little obligation to one another, a marvellous respect, and an established order of duties. To us, not enough accustomed to act by reason and rule, these smack of servitude; yet among them, where these duties are made natural by use, they are observed gladly. As our people have noticed in amazement, the Chinese peasants and servants, when they bid farewell to friends, or when they first enjoy the sight of each other after a long separation, behave to each other so lovingly and respectfully that they challenge all the politeness of European magnates. What then would you expect from the mandarins, or from Colai? Thus it happens that scarcely anyone offends another by the smallest word in common conversation. And they rarely show evidences of hatred, wrath, or excitement. With us respect and careful conversation last for hardly more than the first days of a new acquaintance—scarcely even that. Soon familiarity moves in and circumspection is gladly put away for a sort of freedom which is quickly followed by contempt, backbiting, anger, and afterwards enmity. It is just the contrary with the Chinese. Neighbors and even members of a family are so held back by a hedge of custom that they are able to maintain a kind of perpetual courtesy.

To be sure, they are not lacking in avarice, lust, or ambition. . . .

Who indeed does not marvel at the monarch of such an empire? His grandeur almost exceeds human stature, and he is held by some to be a mortal god. His very nod is obeyed. Yet he is educated according to custom in virtue and wisdom and rules his subjects with an extraordinary respect for the laws and with a reverence for the advice of wise men. Endowed with such eminence he seems fit indeed to judge. Nor is it easy to find anything worthier of note than the fact that this greatest of kings, who possesses such complete authority in his own day, anxiously fears posterity and is in greater dread of the judgment of history, than other kings are of representatives of estates and parliaments. Therefore he carefully seeks to avoid actions which might cast a reflection upon his reputation when recorded by the chroniclers of his reign and placed in files and secret archives.

Until the reign of the present emperor, Cam Hi, a prince of almost unparalleled merit, the magistracy opposed any disposition on the part of the ruler to grant the Europeans freedom to practice the Christian religion legally and publicly until its purity should be investigated. This objection rested on no better pretext than that the prince's great and salutary decision to introduce European arts and sciences into China might lead to ruin. In this matter he seems to me to have had individually much more foresight than all his officials. It is further evidence of his personal good judgment that he has brought European and Chinese civilization together. . . .

I remember the Reverend Father Claude Philip Grimaldi, an eminent man of the same Society, telling me in Rome how much he admired the virtue and wisdom of this prince. Indeed (passing by, if I may, the comment on his love of justice, his charity to the populace, his moderate manner of living, and his other merits), Grimaldi asserted that the monarch's marvellous desire for knowledge almost amounted to a faith. For that ruler, whom eminent princes and the greatest men of the empire venerate from afar and revere when near, used to work with Verbiest in an inner suite for three or four hours daily with mathematical instruments and books as a pupil with his teacher. He profited so greatly that he learned the Euclidean theorems, and, having understood trigonometrical calculations, could demonstrate by numbers the phenomena of the stars. And indeed, as the Reverend Father Louis Le Comtes [*sic*], recently returned from there, informs us in a published account of China, the emperor prepared a book on geometry, that he might furnish his sons with the elements of so great a science and the knowledge of so many truths, and bequeath the wisdom which he had brought into his empire as an inheritance to his realm, having in view the happiness of his people even in posterity. For my part I do not see how more admirable resolutions could motivate any man. . . .

And now I learn that by the authority of their king and through the zeal of Hedraeus and Verjus, great men of their order and nation, the Reverend Fathers Gerbillion and Bouvet, French Jesuits, along with four others, who are mathematicians from the Académie des Sciences, have been sent to the Orient to teach the monarch, not only the mathematical arts, but also the essence of our philosophy. But if this process should be continued I fear that we may soon become inferior to the Chinese in all branches of knowledge. I do not say this because I grudge them new light; rather I rejoice. But it is desirable that they in turn teach us those things which are especially in our interest: the greatest use of practical philosophy and a more perfect manner of living, to say nothing now of their other arts. Certainly the condition of our affairs, slipping as we are into ever greater corruption, seems to me such that we need missionaries from the Chinese who might teach us the use and practice of natural religion, just as we have sent them teachers of revealed theology. And so I believe that if someone expert, not in the beauty of goddesses but in the excellence of peoples, were selected as judge, the golden apple would be awarded to the Chinese, unless we should win by virtue of one great but superhuman thing, namely, the divine gift of the Christian religion.

18

Baron de Montesquieu, *The Spirit of the Laws*

Born in the twilight of Louis XIV's reign, Charles de Secondat, Baron de Montesquieu (1689–1755), became one of the Enlightenment's most celebrated leaders. His early writings, particularly his *Persian Letters* (a satirical exposé of intolerance), gave little hint of the durable quality of his profound *The Spirit of the Laws* (1748). In this treatise, Montesquieu broke with earlier French jurists who had justified absolutism by urging uniformity in law and orthodoxy in religion. Instead, Montesquieu urged diversity in politics, tolerance in religion, and respect for the role of history and climate in shaping a nation's legal foundations.

Although revolutionaries such as Thomas Jefferson and Jean Paul Marat invoked his name to justify rebellion, Montesquieu was no revolutionary. He had deep respect for tradition and never sought change through revolution. Like Voltaire, his contemporary, Montesquieu had lived in England and had a keen interest in English politics. In the following selection, describing the English Constitution, he presented an overly idealized view of English politics, but he did affirm for the Enlightenment the valued place of aristocratic leadership in society and the virtues of a constitutional monarchy.

QUESTIONS TO CONSIDER

1. In what ways can the concepts of "balanced constitution" and "separation of powers" be attributed to Montesquieu?
2. Are there any traces of Montesquieu's thought in *The Federalist,* Number 10 (see Reading 27) and the *Declaration of the Rights of Man and of the Citizen* (see Reading 28)?
3. How would you compare Montesquieu's approach to government with that of Jean-Jacques Rousseau (see Reading 20)?

In every government there are three sorts of power; the legislative; the executive, in respect to things dependent on the law of nations; and the executive, in regard to things that depend on the civil law.

By virtue of the first, the prince or magistrate enacts temporary or perpetual laws, and amends or abrogates those that have been already enacted. By the second, he makes peace or war, sends or receives embassies; establishes the public security, and provides against invasions. By the third, he punishes criminals, or determines the disputes that arise between individuals. The latter we shall call the judiciary power, and the other simply the executive power of the state.

From Montesquieu, *The Spirit of the Laws,* vol. 1, trans. Thomas Nugent (London : J. Nourse, 1777), pp. 221–237, passim.

The political liberty of the subject is a tranquillity of mind, arising from the opinion each person has of his safety. In order to have this liberty, it is requisite the government be so constituted as one man need not be afraid of another.

When the legislative and executive powers are united in the same person, or in the same body of magistrates, there can be no liberty; because apprehensions may arise, lest the same monarch or senate should enact tyrannical laws, to execute them in a tyrannical manner.

Again, there is no liberty, if the power of judging be not separated from the legislative and executive powers. Were it joined with the legislative, the life and liberty of the subject would be exposed to arbitrary control; for the judge would then be the legislator. Were it joined to the executive power, the judge might behave with all the violence of an oppressor.

There would be an end of every thing, were the same man, or the same body, whether of the nobles or of the people to exercise those three powers, that of enacting laws, that of executing the public resolutions, and that of judging the crimes or differences of individuals.

Most kingdoms in Europe enjoy a moderate government, because the prince, who is invested with the two first powers, leaves the third to his subjects. In Turkey, where these three powers are united in the sultan's person, the subjects groan under the weight of a most frightful oppression.

In the republics of Italy, where these three powers are united, there is less liberty than in our monarchies. Hence their government is obliged to have recourse to as violent methods for its support, as even that of the Turks; witness the state inquisitors, and the lion's mouth into which every informer may at all hours throw his written accusations.

What a situation must the poor subject be in, under those republics! The same body of magistrates are possessed, as executors of the laws, of the whole power they have given themselves in quality of legislators. They may plunder the state by their general determinations; and as they have likewise the judiciary power in their hands, every private citizen may be ruined by their particular decisions.

The whole power is here united in one body; and though there is no external pomp that indicates a despotic sway, yet the people feel the effects of it every moment.

Hence it is that many of the princes of Europe, whose aim has been levelled at arbitrary power, have constantly set out with uniting in their own persons, all the branches of magistracy, and all the great offices of state.

The executive power ought to be in the hands of a monarch; because this branch of government, which has always need of expedition, is better administered by one than by many: Whereas, whatever depends on the legislative power, is oftentimes better regulated by many than by a single person.

But if there was no monarch, and the executive power was committed to a certain number of persons selected from the legislative body, there would be an end then of liberty; by reason the two powers would be united, as the same persons would actually sometimes have, and would moreover be always able to have, a share in both.

Were the legislative body to be a considerable time without meeting, this would likewise put an end to liberty. For one of these two things would naturally follow ; either that there would be no longer any legislative resolutions, and then the state would fall into anarchy ; or that these resolutions would be taken by the executive power, which would render it absolute.

It would be needless for the legislative body to continue always assembled. This would be troublesome to the representatives, and moreover would cut out too much work for the executive power, so as to take off its attention from executing, and oblige it to think only of defending its own prerogatives, and the right it has to execute.

Again, were the legislative body to be always assembled, it might happen to be kept up only by filling the places of the deceased members with new representatives ; and in that case, if the legislative body was once corrupted, the evil would be past all remedy. When different legislative bodies succeed one another, the people who have a bad opinion of that which is actually sitting, may reasonably entertain some hopes of the next : But were it to be always the same body, the people, upon seeing it once corrupted, would no longer expect any good from its laws ; and of course they would either become desperate, or fall into a state of indolence.

The legislative body should not assemble of itself. For a body is supposed to have no will but when it is assembled ; and besides, were it not to assemble unanimously, it would be impossible to determine which was really the legislative body, the part assembled, or the other. And if it had a right to prorogue itself, it might happen never to be prorogued ; which would be extremely dangerous, in case it should ever attempt to encroach on the executive power. Besides, there are seasons, some of which are more proper than others, for assembling the legislative body : It is fit therefore that the executive power should regulate the time of convening, as well as the duration of those assemblies, according to the circumstances and exigencies of state known to itself.

Were the executive power not to have a right of putting a stop to the encroachments of the legislative body, the latter would become despotic ; for as it might arrogate to itself what authority it pleased, it would soon destroy all the other powers.

But it is not proper, on the other hand, that the legislative power should have a right to stop the executive. For as the execution has its natural limits, it is useless to confine it ; besides, the executive power is generally employed in momentary operations. The power therefore of the Roman tribunes was faulty, as it put a stop not only to the legislation, but likewise to the execution itself ; which was attended with infinite mischiefs.

But if the legislative power in a free government ought to have no right to stop the executive, it has a right, and ought to have the means of examining in what manner its laws have been executed ; an advantage which this government has over that of Crete and Sparta, where the Cosmi and the Ephori gave no account of their administration.

But whatever may be the issue of that examination, the legislative body ought not to have a power of judging the person, nor of course the conduct of him who is intrusted with the executive power. His person should be sacred, because as it is necessary for the good of the state to prevent the legislative body from rendering themselves arbitrary, the moment he is accused or tried, there is an end of liberty.

To prevent the executive power from being able to oppress, it is requisite, that the armies, with which it is intrusted, should consist of the people, and have the same spirit as the people, as was the case at Rome, till the time of Marius. To obtain this end, there are only two ways, either that the persons employed in the army, should have sufficient property to answer for their conduct to their fellow subjects, and be enlisted only for a year, as customary at Rome : Or if there should be a standing army, composed chiefly of the most despicable part of the nation, the legislative power should have a right to disband them as soon as it pleased ; the soldiers should live in common with the rest of the people ; and no separate camp, barracks, or fortress, should be suffered.

When once an army is established, it ought not to depend immediately on the legislative, but on the executive power, and this from the very nature of the thing ; its business consisting more in action than in deliberation.

From a manner of thinking that prevails amongst mankind, they set a higher value upon courage than timorousness, on activity than prudence, on strength than counsel. Hence, the army will ever despise a senate, and respect their own officers. They will naturally slight the orders sent them by a body of men, whom they look upon as cowards, and therefore unworthy to command them. So that as soon as the army depends on the legislative body, the government becomes a military one ; and if the contrary has ever happened, it has been owing to some extraordinary circumstances. It is because the army was always kept divided ; it is because it was composed of several bodies, that depended each on their particular province ; it is because the capital towns were strong places, defended by their natural situation, and not garrisoned with regular troops. Holland, for instance, is still safer than Venice ; she might drown, or starve the revolted troops ; for as they are not quartered in towns capable of furnishing them with necessary subsistence, this subsistence is of course precarious.

Whoever shall read the admirable treatise of Tacitus on the manners of the Germans, will find that it is from them the English have borrowed the idea of their political government. This beautiful system was invented first in the woods.

As all human things have an end, the state we are speaking of will lose its liberty, it will perish. Have not Rome, Sparta, and Carthage perished ? It will perish when the legislative power shall be more corrupted than the executive.

It is not my business to examine whether the English actually enjoy this liberty, or not. It is sufficient for my purpose to observe, that it is established by their laws ; and I inquire no further.

Neither do I pretend by this to undervalue other governments, not to say that this extreme political liberty ought to give uneasiness to those who have only a moderate share of it. How should I have any such design, I who think that even the excess of reason is not always desirable, and that mankind generally find their account better in mediums than in extremes?

19

Léonhard Euler, "Newton's Discovery of the Principle of Gravity"

Because of the wretched condition of eighteenth-century universities, the Enlightenment was not a university-centered movement. Instead, private patrons, many of whom were women, regularly invited *philosophes* to their own salons for discussion of the new learning. Provincial literary societies offered prizes for scientific and philosophical research, and monarchs such as Frederick the Great of Prussia (1740–1786) sponsored scientific research in their royal academies. Never did the Enlightenment become a mass movement, but its international membership kept abreast of scientific developments via a vigorous exchange of letters, which circulated among interested readers much as books from libraries circulate today. To keep people abreast of developments in all fields of learning, the Enlightenment movement expected its more talented members to explain or "popularize" new findings so that anyone eager for new learning could be informed.

One of the Enlightenment's most original and prolific mathematicians was Léonhard Euler (1707–1783), a Swiss scientist who was President of the Mathematical School in Saint Petersburg and a member of the Berlin Academy. In a series of 79 letters to the Princess of Anhalt-Dessau, a niece of King Frederick the Great of Prussia, Euler explained the "new" principles of mathematics, optics, physics, and philosophy. Because of their clarity, precision, and brevity, Euler's *Letters to a German Princess* became one of the most popular and reliable explanations of the Enlightenment's great scientific achievements. The following letter, written on September 3, 1760, explains Sir Isaac Newton's (1641–1727) discovery of gravity.

QUESTIONS TO CONSIDER

1. According to Euler, what is the essence of Newton's achievement?
2. Do you think there would be any religious or secular opposition to Newton's hypotheses? Why? Why not?
3. Are there any political, economic, or social implications of Newton's arguments?
4. Are there any connections between Newton's scientific investigations and the writings of Montesquieu (see Reading 18) and Adam Smith (see Reading 21)?

Weight, or gravity, is a property of all terrestrial bodies, and it extends, likewise, to the moon. Because of gravity the moon presses toward the earth; and gravity regulates her motion just as it directs that of a stone thrown, or of a cannon ball fired off.

To *Newton* we are indebted for this important discovery. This great English philosopher and geometrician, happening one day to be lying under an apple tree, an apple fell upon his head, and suggested to him a multitude of reflections. He readily conceived that gravity was the cause of the apple's falling, by overcoming the force which attached it to the branch. Any person whomever might have made the same reflection ; but the English philosopher pursued it much farther. Would this force have always acted upon the apple, had the tree been a great deal higher ? He could entertain no doubt of it.

But had the height of the tree been equal to that of the moon? Here he found himself at a loss to determine whether the apple would fall or not. In case it should fall, which appeared to him, however, highly probable, since it is impossible to conceive of a limit to the height of the tree, at which it would cease to fall, it must still have a certain degree of gravity forcing it toward the earth ; therefore, if the moon were at the same place, she must be pressed toward the earth by a power similar to that which would act upon the apple. Nevertheless since the moon did not fall on his head, he reasoned that motion might be the cause of this, just as a bomb (i.e., an artillery shell) frequently flies over us, without falling vertically.

This comparison of the motion of the moon to that of a bomb compelled him to examine attentively this question ; and aided by the most sublime geometry, he discovered, that the moon in her motion was subject to the same laws which regulate that of a bomb, and that if it were possible to fire a bomb to the height of the moon, and with the same velocity, the bomb would have the same motion as the moon, with this difference only, that the gravity of the bomb at such a distance from the earth, would be much less than at its surface.

You will see, from this detail, that the first reasonings of the philosopher on this subject were very simple, scarcely differing from those of a peasant ; but Newton soon pushed them far beyond the level of a peasant. It is, then, a very remarkable property of the earth, that not only all bodies near it, but those also which are distant, even as distant as the moon, possess a force pulling them toward the center of the earth, and this force is called gravity, which diminishes in proportion as these bodies are more distant from the earth.

The English philosopher did not stop here. As he knew that the other planets are perfectly similar to the earth, he concluded, that heavenly bodies near planets possess gravity and the gravitational pull is toward the center of each planet. This gravity might be greater or less than on the earth ; in other words, a body of a certain weight on earth, if transported to another planet, might there weigh more or less.

Finally, this power of gravity of each planet also extends to great distances around them ; and as we see that Jupiter has four satellites, and Saturn five, which orbit them just as the moon orbits the earth, one cannot doubt, that the motion of the satellites of Jupiter is regulated by their gravity toward the center of that planet ; and that of the satellites of Saturn by their gravitation toward the center of Saturn. Thus, in the same manner as the moon orbits the earth, and their respective satellites orbit Jupiter and Saturn, all the planets themselves orbit the sun.

From Léonhard Euler, "Sur la découverte de la gravitation universelle faite par le grand Newton," in *Lettres a une Princesse d'Allemagne sur divers sujets de Physique & de Philosophie*, vol. 1 (Saint Petersbourg : Académie Impériale des Sciences, 1768), pp. 116–118. Translated by Philip F. Riley.

Hence *Newton* drew this illustrious and important conclusion: The Sun is endowed with a similar property of attracting all bodies toward its center, by a power which may be called *solar gravity.*

This power of solar gravity extends well beyond the sun, and far beyond all the planets, for it is this power which regulates all their motions. The same great philosopher discovered the means of determining the motion of bodies from the knowledge of the power by which they are attracted to a center; thus he discovered the powers of the planets, and he was able to give an accurate description of their motion. In effect, before Newton we were ignorant of the motion of the heavenly bodies; and to him alone we are indebted for all the progress which we now enjoy in the science of astronomy.

It is astonishing to think how much scientific progress is owed to such a simple but original idea. Had not Newton accidentally been lying in an orchard, and had not the apple by chance fallen on his head, we might, perhaps still have been in the same state of ignorance of the motions of the heavenly bodies, and a multitude of other phenomena depending upon them. . . .

20

Jean-Jacques Rousseau, *The Social Contract*

Like Locke, but in a different way, Jean-Jacques Rousseau (1712–1778) stressed the concept of a *contract* as the basis for a just political system. Although the period in which he wrote falls in the middle of the Enlightenment, his ideas had more in common with those of the Romantic period, which was soon to follow.

Like the Romantics, Rousseau rejected the idea that an increasingly complex civilization was making people better or happier. In his "Discourse on the Origin of Inequality" (1753), he portrays humankind as better off in simpler days before the artificiality and materialism of social institutions corrupted human nature. He consequently contributed to the notion of the "noble savage" (the person of very early society) as honest, faithful, and brave, in contrast with cynical, greedy, and apathetic modern humanity. Later, in *The Social Contract* (1762), he viewed the educated advances of modern times as potentially positive if people would only begin to control their political, social, and educational environments.

While Locke and others of the early Enlightenment believed that individual freedom was the main goal to be pursued by improving political systems, the Romantics attached as much or more importance to demands made by groups (such as nations, classes, and religious denominations) on individuals. Rousseau thought that the sovereign people, united by a "general will," would rightfully dominate individuals, with their own "particular wills," in any issue involving societal interests.

Unlike Locke, who viewed representation as a guarantee that government would be responsive to the people, Rousseau was scornful of a people who delegated authority to representatives rather than constantly participating in legislative decision-making themselves. In his own version of keeping government responsible, Rousseau drew a sharp line between the *state,* as the sovereign union of all citizens, and *government,* as the collective body of institutions and office-holders responsible for implementing the state's laws.

Rousseau was passionately democratic, in the sense of desiring citizens to be constantly involved in political decision-making. He was a bit weak in protecting individuals and minorities from the "general will" because he equated that will — at least when it was well-informed — with public right-mindedness. He was convinced that when people were forced against their own particular wills to obey the general will, they were being led to do what they really would want to do if they understood the matter fully. Thus for Rousseau there was no contradiction in at least occasionally forcing people to be free.

Although little attention was paid to the first edition of *The Social Contract,* by the 1780s Rousseau's work had become a well-known text. Once the French Revolution began in 1789, Rousseau's ideas became instrumental in shaping the politics and ideology of revolutionary France.

QUESTIONS TO CONSIDER

1. What does Rousseau mean when he states that in a good society (a) each member is able to obey only himself or herself; and (b) any member who refuses to obey the general will should be forced to do so?
2. To what extent are private property rights protected in the society that Rousseau describes?
3. Why does Rousseau criticize separation-of-power theories (see Reading 18)?
4. Why does Rousseau think that using representatives is a sign of decadence in society?
5. In his discussion of civil religion, how could Rousseau insist that there is no contradiction between his recommendations that there be no religious intolerance — in fact, that religions with intolerant dogmas be banned — and that banishment and even the death penalty may be justified for offenses to the civil religion?
6. Edmund Burke (see Reading 30) once described Rousseau as "an insane Socrates." Why would Burke say this about Rousseau?
7. How would you compare Rousseau's approach to civil government with that of John Locke (see Reading 16)?

Origin and Terms of the Social Contract

Man was born free, but everywhere he is in chains. This man believes that he is the master of others, and still he is more of a slave than they are. How did that transformation take place? I don't know. How may the restraints on man become legitimate? I do believe I can answer that question. . . .

From Jean-Jacques Rousseau, *Contrat social ou Principes du droit politique* (Paris: Garnier Frères, 1800), pp. 240–332, passim. Translated by Henry A. Myers.

At a point in the state of nature when the obstacles to human preservation have become greater than each individual with his own strength can cope with . . . , an adequate combination of forces must be the result of men coming together. Still, each man's power and freedom are his main means of self-preservation. How is he to put them under the control of others without damaging himself . . . ?

This question might be rephrased : "How is a method of associating to be found which will defend and protect — using the power of all — the person and property of each member and still enable each member of the group to obey only himself and to remain as free as before ?" This is the fundamental problem ; the social contract offers a solution to it.

The very scope of the action dictates the terms of this contract and renders the least modification of them inadmissible, something making them null and void. Thus, although perhaps they have never been stated in so many words, they are the same everywhere and tacitly conceded and recognized everywhere. And so it follows that each individual immediately recovers his primitive rights and natural liberties whenever any violation of the social contract occurs and thereby loses the contractual freedom for which he renounced them.

The social contract's terms, when they are well understood, can be reduced to a single stipulation : the individual member alienates [gives] himself totally to the whole community together with all his rights. This is first because conditions will be the same for everyone when each individual gives himself totally, and secondly, because no one will be tempted to make that condition of shared equality worse for other men. . . .

Once this multitude is united this way into a body, an offense against one of its members is an offense against the body politic. It would be even less possible to injure the body without its members feeling it. Duty and interest thus equally require the two contracting parties to aid each other mutually. The individual people should be motivated from their double roles as individuals and members of the body, to combine all the advantages which mutual aid offers them. . . .

Individual Wills and the General Will

In reality, each individual may have one particular will as a man that is different from — or contrary to — the general will which he has as a citizen. His own particular interest may suggest other things to him than the common interest does. His separate, naturally independent existence may make him imagine that what he owes to the common cause is an incidental contribution — a contribution which will cost him more to give than their failure to receive it would harm the others. He may also regard the moral person of the State as an imaginary being since it is not a man, and wish to enjoy the rights of a citizen without performing the duties of a subject. This unjust attitude could cause the ruin of the body politic if it became widespread enough.

So that the social pact will not become meaningless words, it tacitly includes this commitment, which alone gives power to the others : Whoever refuses to obey the general will shall be forced to obey it by the whole body politic, which means nothing else but that he will be forced to be free. This condition is indeed the one which by dedicating each citizen to the fatherland gives him a guarantee against being personally dependent on other individuals. It is the condition which all political machinery depends on and which alone makes political undertakings legitimate. Without it, political actions become absurd, tyrannical, and subject to the most outrageous abuses.

Whatever benefits he had in the state of nature but lost in the civil state, a man gains more than enough new ones to make up for them. His capabilities are put to good use and developed ; his ideas are enriched, his sentiments made more noble, and his soul elevated to the extent that — if the abuses in this new condition did not often degrade him to a condition lower than the one he left behind — he would have to keep blessing this happy moment which snatched him away from his previous state and which made an intelligent being and a man out of a stupid and very limited animal. . . .

Property Rights

In dealing with its members, the State controls all their goods under the social contract, which serves as the basis for all rights within the State, but it controls them only through the right of first holder which individuals convey to the State. . . .

A strange aspect of this act of alienating [giving away] property rights to the state is that when the community takes on the goods of its members, it does not take these goods away from them. The community does nothing but assure its members of legitimate possession of goods, changing mere claims of possession into real rights and customary use into property. . . . Through an act of transfer having advantages for the public but far more for themselves they have, so to speak, really acquired everything they gave up. . . .

Indivisible, Inalienable Sovereignty

The first and most important conclusion from the principles we have established thus far is that the general will alone may direct the forces of the State to achieve the goal for which it was founded, the common good. . . . Sovereignty is indivisible . . . and is inalienable. . . . A will is general or it is not : it is that of the whole body of the people or only of one faction. In the first instance, putting the will into words and force is an act of sovereignty : the will becomes law. In the second instance, it is only a particular will or an administrative action ; at the very most it is a decree.

Our political theorists, however, unable to divide the source of sovereignty, divide sovereignty into the ways it is applied. They divide it into force and will ; into legislative power and executive power ; into the power to tax, the judicial power, and the power to wage war ; into internal administration and the power to negotiate with foreign countries. Now we see them running these powers together. Now they will proceed to separate them. They make the sovereign a being of fantasy, composed of separate pieces, which would be like putting a man together from several bodies, one having eyes, another arms, another feet — nothing more. Japanese magicians are said to cut up a child before the eyes of spectators, then throw the pieces into the air one after the other, and then cause the child to drop down reassembled and alive again. That is the sort of magic trick our political theorists perform. After having dismembered the social body with a trick worthy of a travelling show, they reassemble the pieces without anybody knowing how. . . .

If we follow up in the same way on the other divisions mentioned, we find that we are deceived every time we believe we see sovereignty divided. We find that the jurisdictions we have thought to be exercised as parts of sovereignty in reality are subordinate to the [one] sovereign power. They presuppose supreme wills, which they merely carry out in their jurisdictions. . . .

Need for Citizen Participation, Not Representation

It follows from the above that the general will is always in the right and inclines toward the public good, but it does not follow that the deliberations of the people always have the same rectitude. People always desire what is good, but they do not always see what is good. You can never corrupt the people, but you can often fool them, and that is the only time that the people appear to will something bad. . . .

If, assuming that the people were sufficiently informed as they made decisions and that the citizens did not communicate with each other, the general will would always be resolved from a great number of small differences, and the deliberation would always be good. But when blocs are formed, associations of parts at the expense of the whole, the will of each of these associations will be general as far as its members are concerned but particular as far as the State is concerned. Then we may say that there are no longer so many voters as there are men present but as many as there are associations. The differences will become less numerous and will yield less general results. Finally, when one of these associations becomes so strong that it dominates the others, you no longer have the sum of minor differences as a result but rather one single [unresolved] difference, with the result that there no longer is a general will, and the view that prevails is nothing but one particular view. . . .

But we must also consider the private persons who make up the public, apart from the public personified, who each have a life and liberty independent of it. It is very necessary for us to distinguish between the respective rights of the citizens and the sovereign and between the duties which men must fulfill in their role as subjects from the natural rights they should enjoy in their role as men.

It is agreed that everything which each individual gives up of his power, his goods, and his liberty under the social contract is only that part of all those things which is of use to the community, but it is also necessary to agree that the sovereign alone is the judge of what that useful part is.

All the obligations which a citizen owes to the State he must fulfill as soon as the sovereign asks for them, but the sovereign in turn cannot impose any obligation on subjects which is not of use to the community. In fact, the sovereign cannot even wish to do so, for nothing can take place without a cause according to the laws of reason, any more than according to the laws of nature [and the sovereign community will have no cause to require anything beyond what is of communal use]. . . .

Government . . . is wrongly confused with the sovereign, whose agent it is. What then is government ? It is an intermediary body established between the subjects and the sovereign to keep them in touch with each other. It is charged with executing the laws and maintaining both civil and political liberty. . . . The only will dominating government . . . should be the general will or the law. The government's power is only the public power vested in it. As soon as [government] attempts to let any act come from itself completely independently, it starts to lose its intermediary role. If the time should ever come when the [government] has a particular will of its own stronger than that of the sovereign and makes use of the public power which is in its hands to carry out its own particular will — when there are thus two sovereigns, one in law and one in fact — at that moment the social union will disappear and the body politic will be dissolved.

Once the public interest has ceased to be the principal concern of citizens, once they prefer to serve State with money rather than with their persons, the State will be approaching ruin. Is it necessary to march into combat ? They will pay some troops and stay at home. Is it necessary to go to meetings ? They will name some deputies and stay at home. Laziness and money finally leave them with soldiers to enslave their fatherland and representatives to sell it. . . .

Sovereignty cannot be represented. . . . Essentially, it consists of the general will, and a will is not represented : either we have it itself, or it is something else ; there is no other possibility. The deputies of the people thus are not and cannot be its representatives. They are only the people's agents and are not able to come to final decisions at all. Any law that the people have not ratified in person is void, it is not a law at all.

Sovereignty and Civil Religion

Now then, it is of importance to the State that each citizen should have a religion requiring his devotion to duty ; however, the dogmas of that religion are of no interest to the State except as they relate to morality and to the duties which each believer is required to perform for others. For the rest of it, each person may have whatever opinions he pleases. . . .

It follows that it is up to the sovereign to establish the articles of a purely civil faith, not exactly as dogmas of religion but as sentiments of social commitment without which it would be impossible to be either a good citizen or a faithful subject. . . . While the State has no power to oblige anyone to believe these articles, it may banish anyone who does not believe them. This banishment is not for impiety but for lack of social commitment, that is, for being incapable of sincerely loving the laws and justice or of sacrificing his life to duty in time of need. As for the person who conducts himself as if he does not believe them after having publicly stated his belief in these same dogmas, he deserves the death penalty. He has lied in the presence of the laws.

The dogmas of civil religion should be simple, few in number, and stated in precise words without interpretations or commentaries. These are the required dogmas : the existence of a powerful, intelligent Divinity, who does good, has foreknowledge of all, and provides for all ; the life to come ; the happy rewards of the just ; the punishment of the wicked ; and the sanctity of the social contract and the laws. As for prohibited articles of faith, I limit myself to one : intolerance. Intolerance characterizes the religious persuasions we have excluded.

21

Adam Smith, *The Wealth of Nations*

In the eighteenth century, "Enlightened Despotism" gave active kingship a new lease on life in Spain and Eastern Europe ; however, in most of Western Europe what remained of popular enthusiasm for extensive monarchical government declined. Particularly in Britain and France, spokesmen for the middle class came to regard much royal regulation as unnecessary.

The political side of this attack on state power was, of course, phrased in terms of keeping governmental functions to the minimum necessary for protecting life, liberty, and property (see Reading 16). Those voicing the economic side of this argument indicted mercantilism for inefficiency and for placing burdens on the people as producers, consumers, and taxpayers for the benefit of special interests favored by government. Mercantilism was the theory that made government responsible for creating a favorable balance of trade, particularly through external tariffs against foreign imports, subsidies and grants of monopolies, and the acquisition of colonies to assure the mother country of steady supplies of cheap raw materials and markets for finished goods.

Leading the economic attack in France were Dr. François Quesnay, a physician who wrote in the 1750s and 1760s, and his followers. Known as "physiocrats" (from *physis,* "nature," and -*crat,* "ruler"), this group advocated letting nature rule in the economic sphere. They compared the free, unregulated, "natural" production and flow of goods with the flow of blood in the human body, with which it would be foolish to interfere. Although the physiocrats, who saw land and agriculture as the source of all proper wealth, were most concerned about productive land use, their phrases *laissez faire* ("let things be made") and *laissez passer* ("let things circulate") furthered the idea that capitalism need only be left alone for nature to take its course and usher in an era of general prosperity.

In England, the comparable aims were summarized simply as "free trade." Free-trade advocates were less concerned about land use than were the physiocrats. Instead, they particularly stressed the notion of enlightened self-interest — people working at what they did best for their own immediate good in a society respecting life, liberty, law, and property — as the means for assuring that goods of the best quality would be produced at the lowest possible prices for consumers throughout the world. Seeing the state as having a very limited role in the national economy, they attempted to show that mercantilistic policies were not only useless but counterproductive : Tariffs and monopolies raised prices for consumers ; subsidies to bail out inefficient producers burdened taxpayers ; and requiring overseas settlers to buy and sell at the mother country's direction was both unfair and indirectly costly to taxpayers, who had to provide the necessary revenue for enforcing trade restrictions overseas.

In 1776, Adam Smith published *An Inquiry into the Nature and Causes of the Wealth of Nations,* an attack on government-regulated economy and a defense of free trade. Today this volume remains the classic work in its field. Although its publication did not have any direct relationship to the American Revolution, by that time many of the American colonists entertained similar notions about British mercantile policy.

QUESTIONS TO CONSIDER

1. Why is Smith convinced that free importing of agricultural products will not harm farmers at home?
2. How does Smith characterize the mentality of merchants and manufacturers, as opposed to that of country gentlemen and farmers?
3. How does Smith rate problems of economic dislocation among the working population if foreign imports are freely allowed?
4. In what exceptional circumstances, according to Smith, may government regulation of foreign trade be necessary?
5. How does Smith describe the effects of raising revenue through taxes on necessary commodities?
6. Is Adam Smith's approach to international trade workable in an international economy in which not all of the trading countries practice laissez-faire economic policies?

The Case for Free Trade and Lower Taxes

By restraining, either by high duties, or by absolute prohibitions, the importation of such goods from foreign countries as can be produced at home, the monopoly of the home-market is more or less secured to the domestic industry employed in producing them. Thus the . . . high duties upon the importation of corn, which in times of moderate plenty amount to a prohibition, give a like advantage to the growers of that commodity. The prohibition of the importation of foreign woollens is equally favourable to the woollen manufacturers. The silk manufacture, though altogether employed upon foreign materials, has lately obtained the same advantage. The linen manufacture has not yet obtained it, but is making great strides towards it. Many other sorts of manufacturers have, in the same manner, obtained in Great Britain, either altogether, or very nearly a monopoly against their countrymen. . . .

That this monopoly of the home-market frequently gives great encouragement to that particular species of industry which enjoys it . . . cannot be doubted. But whether it tends either to increase the general industry of the society, or to give it the most advantageous direction, is not, perhaps, altogether so evident.

From Adam Smith, *An Inquiry into the Nature and Causes of the Wealth of Nations* (1776), ed. Edwin Cannan (London: Methuen, 1904), pp. 418–436, passim; spelling and punctuation slightly modified.

The general industry of the society never can exceed what the capital of the society can employ. As the number of workmen that can be kept in employment by any particular person must bear a certain proportion to his capital, so the number of those that can be continually employed by all the members of a great society, must bear a certain portion to the whole capital of that society, and never can exceed that proportion. No regulation of commerce can increase the quantity of industry in any society beyond what its capital can maintain. It can only divert a part of it into a direction into which it might not otherwise have gone ; and it is by no means certain that this artificial direction is likely to be more advantageous to the society than that into which it would have gone of its own accord.

Every individual is continually exerting himself to find out the most advantageous employment for whatever capital he can command. It is his own advantage, indeed, and not that of the society, which he has in view. But the study of his own advantage naturally, or rather necessarily leads him to prefer that employment which is most advantageous to the society.

First, every individual endeavors to employ his capital as near home as he can, and consequently as much as he can in the support of domestic industry ; provided always that he can thereby obtain . . . ordinary profits. . . .

Thus upon equal or nearly equal profits, every wholesale merchant naturally prefers the home-trade to the foreign trade of consumption. . . . In the home-trade his capital is never so long out of his sight as it frequently is in the foreign trade of consumption. He can know better the character and situation of the persons whom he trusts, and if he should happen to be deceived, he knows better the laws of the country from which he must seek redress. . . . Home is in this manner the center, if I may say so, round which the capitals of the inhabitants of every country are continually circulating, and towards which they are always tending, though by particular causes they may sometimes be driven off and repelled from it towards more distant employments. But a capital employed in the home-trade . . . necessarily puts into motion a greater quantity of domestic industry, and gives revenue and employment to a greater number of the inhabitants of the country, than an equal capital employed in the foreign trade of consumption : and one employed in the foreign trade of consumption has the same advantage over an equal capital employed in the carrying trade. Upon equal, or only nearly equal profits, therefore, every individual naturally inclines to employ his capital in the manner in which it is likely to afford the greatest support to domestic industry, and to give revenue and employment to the greatest number of people of his own country.

Secondly, every individual who employs his capital in the support of domestic industry, necessarily endeavors so to direct that industry, that its produce may be of the greatest possible value.

The produce of industry is what it adds to the subject or materials upon which it is employed. In proportion as the value of this produce is great or small, so will likewise be the profits of the employer. But it is only for the sake of profit that any man employs a capital in the support of industry ; and he will always, therefore, endeavor to employ it in the support of that industry of which the produce is likely to be of the greatest value, or to exchange for the greatest quantity either of money or of other goods. . . .

As every individual, therefore, endeavors as much as he can both to employ his capital in the support of domestic industry, and so to direct that industry that its produce may be of the greatest value; every individual necessarily labors to render the annual revenue of the society as great as he can. He generally, indeed, neither intends to promote the public interest, nor knows how much he is promoting it. By preferring the support of domestic to that of foreign industry, he intends only his own security; and by directing that industry in such a manner as its produce may be of the greatest value, he intends only his own gain, and he is in this, as in many other cases, led by an invisible hand to promote an end which was no part of his intention. Nor is it always the worse for the society that it was no part of it. By pursuing his own interest he frequently promotes that of the society more effectually than when he really intends to promote it. I have never known much good done by those who affected to trade for the public good. It is an affectation, indeed, not very common among merchants, and very few words need be employed in dissuading them from it. . . .

To give the monopoly of the home-market to the produce of domestic industry, in any particular art or manufacture, is in some measure to direct private people in what manner they ought to employ their capitals, and must, in almost all cases, be either a useless or a hurtful regulation. If the produce of domestic can be brought there as cheap as that of foreign industry, the regulation is evidently useless. If it cannot, it must generally be hurtful. It is the maxim of every prudent master of a family, never to attempt to make at home what it will cost him more to make than to buy. The taylor does not attempt to make his own shoes, but buys them of the shoemaker. The shoemaker does not attempt to make his own clothes, but employs a taylor. The farmer attempts to make neither the one nor the other, but employs those different artificers. All of them find it for their interest to employ their whole industry in a way in which they have some advantage over their neighbors, and to purchase with a part of its produce, or what is the same thing, with the price of a part of it, whatever else they have occasion for. . . .

The natural advantages which one country has over another in producing particular commodities are sometimes so great, that it is acknowledged by all the world to be in vain to struggle with them. By means of glasses, hotbeds, and hotwalls, very good grapes can be raised in Scotland, and very good wine too can be made of them at about thirty times the expense for which at least equally good can be brought from foreign countries. Would it be a reasonable law to prohibit the importation of all foreign wines, merely to encourage the making of claret and burgundy in Scotland? But if there would be a manifest absurdity in turning towards any employment, thirty times more of the capital and industry of the country, than would be necessary to purchase from foreign countries an equal quantity of the commodities wanted, there must be an absurdity, though not altogether so glaring, yet exactly of the same kind, in turning towards any such employment a thirtieth, or even a three hundredth part more of either. . . . As long as the one country has those advantages, and the other wants them, it will always be more advantageous for the latter, rather to buy of the former than to make. It is an acquired advantage only, which one artificer has over his neighbor, who exercises another trade; and yet they both find it more advantageous to buy of one another, than to make what does not belong to their particular trades.

Merchants and manufacturers are the people who derive the greatest advantage from this monopoly of the home market. The prohibition of the importation of foreign cattle, and of salt provisions, together with the high duties upon foreign corn, which in times of moderate plenty amount to a prohibition, are not near so advantageous to the graziers and farmers of Great Britain, as other regulations of the same kind are to its merchants and manufacturers. Manufacturers, those of the finer kind especially, are more easily transported from one country to another than corn or cattle. It is in the fetching and carrying manufacturers, accordingly, that foreign trade is chiefly employed. In manufactures, a very small advantage will enable foreigners to undersell our own workmen, even in the home market. It will require a very great one to enable them to do so in the rude produce of the soil. If the free importation of foreign manufacturers were permitted, several of the home manufactures would probably suffer, and some of them, perhaps, go to ruin altogether, and a considerable part of the stock and industry at present employed in them, would be forced to find out some other employment. But the freest importation of the rude produce of the soil could have no such effect upon the agriculture of the country.

If the importation of foreign cattle, for example, were made ever so free, so few could be imported, that the grazing trade of Great Britain could be little affected by it. Live cattle are, perhaps, the only commodity of which the transportation is more expensive by sea than by land. By land they carry themselves to market. By sea, not only the cattle, but their food and their water too must be carried at no small expense and inconveniency. . . .

The Sole Justifications for Restricting Trade

To prohibit by a perpetual law the importation of foreign corn and cattle, is in reality to enact, that the population and industry of the country shall at no time exceed what the rude produce of its own soil can maintain.

There seem, however, to be two cases in which it will generally be advantageous to lay some burden upon foreign, for the encouragement of domestic industry.

The first is when some particular sort of industry is necessary for the defense of the country. The defense of Great Britain, for example, depends very much upon the number of its sailors and shipping. The act of navigation, therefore, very properly endeavors to give the sailors and shipping of Great Britain the monopoly of the trade of their own country, in some cases, by absolute prohibitions, and in others by heavy burdens upon the shipping of foreign countries. . . .

The act of navigation is not favorable to foreign commerce, or to the growth of that opulence which can arise from it. The interest of a nation in its commercial relations to foreign nations is, like that of a merchant with regard to the different people with whom he deals, to buy as cheap and to sell as dear as possible. But it will be most likely to buy cheap, when by the most perfect freedom of trade it encourages all nations to bring to it the goods which it has occasion to purchase; and, for the same reason, it will be most likely to sell dear, when its markets are thus filled with the greatest number of buyers. The act of navigation, it is true, lays no burden upon foreign ships that come to export the produce of British industry. Even the ancient aliens duty, which used to be paid upon all goods exported as well as imported, has, by several subsequent acts, been taken off from the greater part of the articles of exportation. But if foreigners, either by prohibitions or high duties, are hindered from coming to sell, they cannot always afford to come to buy ; because coming without a cargo, they must lose the freight from their own country to Great Britain. By diminishing the number of sellers, therefore, we necessarily diminish that of buyers, and are thus likely not only to buy foreign goods dearer, but to sell our own cheaper, than if there was a more perfect freedom of trade. As defense, however, is of much more importance than opulence, the act of navigation is, perhaps, the wisest of all the commercial regulations of England.

The second case, in which it will generally be advantageous to lay some burden upon foreign for the encouragement of domestic industry, is, when some tax is imposed at home upon the produce of the latter. In this case, it seems reasonable that an equal tax should be imposed upon the like produce of the former. This would not give the monopoly of the home market to domestic industry, nor turn towards a particular employment a greater share of the stock and labor of the country, then what would naturally go to it. It would only hinder any part of what would naturally go to it from being turned away by the tax, into a less natural direction, and would leave the competition between foreign and domestic industry, after the tax, as nearly as possible upon the same footing as before....

The Effects of Taxing Necessities

Taxes imposed with a view to prevent, or even to diminish importation, are evidently as destructive of the revenue of the customs as of the freedom of trade. [Taxes] upon the necessaries of life have nearly the same effect upon the circumstances of the people as a poor soil and a bad climate. Provisions are thereby rendered dearer in the same manner as if it required extraordinary labor and expense to raise them. As in the natural scarcity arising from soil and climate, it would be absurd to direct the people in what manner they ought to employ their capitals and industry, so is it likewise in the artificial scarcity arising from such taxes. To be left to accommodate, as well as they could, their industry to their situation, and to find out those employments in which, notwithstanding their unfavorable circumstances, they might have some advantage either in the home or in the foreign market, is what in both cases would evidently be most for their advantage. To lay a new tax upon them, because they are already overburdened with taxes, and because they already pay too dear for necessaries of life, to make them likewise pay too dear for the greater part of other commodities, is certainly a most absurd way of making amends.

Such taxes, when they have grown up to a certain height, are a curse equal to the barrenness of the earth and the inclemency of the heavens ; and yet it is in the richest and most industrious countries that they have been most generally imposed. No other countries could support so great a disorder. As the strongest bodies only can live and enjoy health, under an unwholesome regimen ; so the nations only, that in every sort of industry have the greatest natural and acquired advantages, can subsist and prosper under such taxes.

The Enlightenment in Russia

Catherine II (r. 1762–1796), Empress of Russia, continued the Westernization begun by Peter the Great (see Reading 12), encouraging the Russian nobility to adopt European customs, ideas, and fashions. Catherine the Great, as she became known, had been deeply interested in Enlightenment thought, corresponded with the most noted philosophers of the time, and wrote plays and essays advocating Enlightenment philosophy. In 1767, she summoned over 500 deputies to Moscow to present to them *The Instruction to the Commissioners for Composing a New Code of Laws.* This document, had it been implemented, would have maintained Russia as an absolute monarchy but would have provided a uniform system of law for all free subjects of the Empire, excluding serfs. The deputies spent four years working on a new legal code. Because of the war with Turkey and the Cossack and peasant revolt of 1773 to 1775, Catherine disbanded the commission before it completed its work. Moreover, the American and French revolutions convinced Catherine of the danger of Enlightenment ideas, which she now attempted to suppress in Russia.

The tragic irony was that Russian nobles who had followed Catherine's directions and immersed themselves in Western enlightened thought were now ordered to cast off those ideas. Many educated noblemen, believing in their natural rights, resented the state's tyranny, as we see illustrated in the second reading. Thus began a process of opposition to the government that culminated in the Russian Revolution of 1917.

22

Catherine the Great, *The Instruction to the Commissioners for Composing a New Code of Laws*

QUESTIONS TO CONSIDER

1. Why would the French *philosophe* Voltaire describe Catherine's *Instructions to the Commissioners* as "the finest monument of the century"?
2. Was Catherine really committed to these reforms? What do these instructions reveal about the approach of "Enlightened Monarchs" to administrative reforms?
3. Are there any connections between Catherine's reforms and those of Mikhail Gorbachev (see Reading 98)?

6. Russia is an European State.

7. This is clearly demonstrated by the following Observations: The Alterations which *Peter the Great* undertook in Russia succeeded with the greater Ease, because the Manners, which prevailed at that Time, and had been introduced amongst us by a Mixture of different Nations, and the Conquest of foreign Territories, were quite unsuitable to the Climate. *Peter the First,* by introducing the Manners and Customs of Europe among the European People in his Dominions, found at that Time such Means as even he himself was not sanguine enough to expect. . . .

9. The Sovereign is absolute; for there is no other Authority but that which centers in his single Person, that can act with a Vigour proportionate to the Extent of such a vast Dominion.

10. The Extent of the Dominion requires an absolute Power to be vested in that Person who rules over it. It is expedient so to be, that the quick Dispatch of Affairs, sent from distant Parts, might make ample Amends for the Delay occasioned by the great Distance of the Places.

11. Every other Form of Government whatsoever would not only have been prejudicial to Russia, but would even have proved its entire Ruin.

12. Another Reason is: That it is better to be subject to the Laws under one Master, than to be subservient to many.

13. What is the true End of Monarchy? Not to deprive People of their natural Liberty; but to correct their Actions, in order to attain the *supreme Good.*

14. The Form of Government, therefore, which best attains this End, and at the same Time sets less Bounds than others to natural Liberty, is that which coincides with the Views and Purposes of rational Creatures, and answers the End, upon which we ought to fix a steadfast Eye in the Regulations of civil Polity.

15. The Intention and the End of Monarchy, is the Glory of the Citizens, of the State, and of the Sovereign.

16. But, from this Glory, a Sense of Liberty arises in a People governed by a Monarch; which may produce in these States as much Energy in transacting the most important Affairs, and may contribute as much to the Happiness of the Subjects, as even Liberty itself. . . .

33. The Laws ought to be so framed, as to secure the Safety of every Citizen as much as possible.

34. The Equality of the Citizens consists in this; that they should all be subject to the same Laws.

35. This Equality requires Institutions so well adapted, as to prevent the Rich from oppressing those who are not so wealthy as themselves, and converting all the Charges and Employments intrusted to them as Magistrates only, to their own private Emolument. . . .

37. In a State or Assemblage of People that live together in a Community, where there are Laws, Liberty can only consist *in doing that which every One ought to do,* and *not to be constrained to do that which One ought not to do.*

From W. F. Reddaway, *Documents of Catherine the Great: The Correspondence with Voltaire and the Instruction of 1767 in the English Text of 1768* (Cambridge: Cambridge University Press, 1931), pp. 216–217, 219, 256. Reprinted by permission of Cambridge University Press.

38. A Man ought to form in his own Mind an exact and clear Idea of what Liberty is. *Liberty is the Right of doing whatsoever the Laws allow* : And if any one Citizen could do what the Laws forbid, there would be no more Liberty ; because others would have an equal Power of doing the same.

39. The political Liberty of a Citizen is the Peace of Mind arising from the Consciousness, that every Individual enjoys his peculiar Safety ; and in order that the People might attain this Liberty, the Laws ought to be so framed, that no one Citizen should stand in Fear of another ; but that all of them should stand in Fear of the same Laws. . . .

250. A Society of Citizens, as well as every Thing else, requires a certain fixed Order : There ought to be *some to govern,* and *others to obey.*

251. And this is the Origin of every Kind of Subjection ; which feels itself more or less alleviated, in Proportion to the Situation of the Subjects.

252. And, consequently, as the Law of Nature commands *Us* to take as much Care, as lies in *Our* Power, of the Prosperity of all the People ; we are obliged to alleviate the Situation of the Subjects, as much as sound Reason will permit.

253. And therefore, to shun all Occasions of reducing People to a State of Slavery, except the *utmost* Necessity should *inevitably* oblige us to do it ; in that Case, it ought not to be done for our own Benefit ; but for the Interest of the State : Yet even that Case is extremely uncommon.

254. Of whatever Kind Subjection may be, the civil Laws ought to guard, on the one Hand, against the *Abuse* of Slavery, and, on the other, against the *Dangers* which may arise from it.

23

A. N. Radishchev, *A Journey from St. Petersburg to Moscow*

Alexander Radishchev (1749–1801) was one of the young noblemen victimized by Catherine's change of mind. At the age of 17, he was sent by her, along with other promising young Russian noblemen, to study at the University of Leipzig. In 1790, he published *A Journey from St. Petersburg to Moscow,* in which he condemned serfdom and pleaded for the establishment of a society based on law, natural rights, and intellectual freedom. Outraged by the work, Catherine had Radishchev arrested, tried, and sentenced to death. She later commuted his sentence to exile in Eastern Siberia.

In the following selection, Radishchev uses a story told by a former judge to express his own condemnation of serfdom. He discusses the "right of first night" : a lord's right to spend the first night with a virgin serf bride. He also expresses his enlightened views of civil and natural law.

QUESTIONS TO CONSIDER

1. What principles expressed in the *Instruction* were flagrantly violated, according to Radishchev?
2. What does Catherine's treatment of Radishchev indicate about her "enlightened" views?

"I have observed from a great many examples that the Russian people are very patient and long-suffering, but when they reach the end of their patience, nothing can restrain them from terrible cruelty. This is just what happened in the case of the assessor. The occasion for it was provided by the brutal and dissolute, or say rather the beastly act of one of his sons.

"In his village there was a good-looking peasant girl who was betrothed to a young peasant of the same village. The assessor's middle son took a liking to her and used every possible means to win her love for himself; but the girl remained true to the promise she had made to her sweetheart, a steadfastness rare but still possible among the peasantry. The wedding was to have taken place on a Sunday. In accordance with the custom current on many landed estates, the bridegroom's father went with his son to the manor house and brought two poods of bridal honey to his master. The young 'nobleman' decided to use this last moment for the gratification of his lust. He took both his brothers with him and, having summoned the bride to the courtyard by a strange boy, gagged her and carried her off to a shed. Unable to utter a sound, she struggled with all her strength against her young master's beastly purpose. At last, overcome by the three of them, she had to yield to force, and the vile monster was just about to carry out his long-cherished purpose when the bridegroom, returning from the manor, entered the yard, saw one of the young masters near the shed, and guessed their evil intention. He called his father to help him and flew faster than lightning to the shed. What a spectacle presented itself to him! Just as he got there they closed the doors of the shed, but the combined strength of the two brothers could not stem the onrush of the maddened bridegroom. Nearby he picked up a stake, ran into the shed, and hit the ravisher of his bride over the back with it. The others wanted to seize the bridegroom, but, seeing his father running with a stake to his assistance, they abandoned their prey, jumped out of the shed, and ran away. But the bridegroom caught up with one of them and broke his head with a blow of the stake. Bent on revenge for this injury, these evildoers went straight to their father and told him that they had met the bride while passing through the village and had jested with her, and that the bridegroom, seeing this, had straightway fallen upon them and beaten them, with the help of his father. As proof they showed him the one brother's wounded head. Infuriated by the wounding of his son, the father burst into a rage. He ordered the three evildoers — as he called the bridegroom, the bride,

From Aleksandr Nikolaevich Radishchev, *A Journey from St. Petersburg to Moscow,* trans. Leo Wiener, ed. Roderick Page Thaler (Cambridge, MA : Harvard University Press, 1958), pp. 96–99, 102–103. © 1958 by the President and Fellows of Harvard College. Reprinted by permission of Harvard University Press.

and the bridegroom's father — to be brought before him without delay. When they appeared before him, the first question he asked them was who had broken his son's head. The bridegroom did not deny that he had done it, and told him everything that had happened. 'How did you dare,' said the old assessor, 'to raise your hand against your master? Even if he had spent the night with your bride on the eve of your wedding, you should have been grateful to him. You shall not marry her. She shall be attached to my house, and you shall all be punished.' After this judgment, he turned the bridegroom over to his sons, and ordered them to flog him mercilessly with the cat-o'-nine-tails. He stood the scourging manfully and watched with indomitable fortitude as they began to subject his father to the same torture. But he could not endure it when he saw his master's children starting to take his bride into the house. The punishment was taking place in the yard. In an instant he snatched her from the hands of her abductors, and the two lovers, now free, ran away from the yard. Seeing this, the master's sons stopped beating the old man and started to pursue them. Seeing that they were catching up with him, the bridegroom snatched a rail out of the fence and prepared to defend himself. Meanwhile the noise attracted other peasants to the manor yard. They sympathized with the young peasant and, infuriated against their masters, they gathered around their fellow to defend him. Seeing all this, the assessor himself ran up, began to curse them, and struck the first man he met so violently with his cane that he fell senseless to the ground. This was the signal for a general attack. They surrounded their four masters and, in short, beat them to death on the spot. They hated them so much that not one wanted to miss the chance to take part in murdering them, as they themselves later confessed. Just at this time the chief of the country police of that district happened to come by with a detachment of soldiers. He was an eyewitness of part of what happened. He had the guilty persons — that is, half the village — put under guard, and instituted an investigation which ultimately reached the criminal court. The case was clearly established, and the guilty persons confessed everything, pleading in their defense only the barbarous acts of their masters, of which the whole province had been cognizant. In the course of my official duty it was incumbent upon me to pass the final sentence of death upon the guilty persons and to commute it to confiscation of property and lifelong penal servitude.

"Upon reviewing the case, I found no sufficient or convincing reason to condemn the offenders. The peasants who had killed their master were guilty of murder. But was it not forced upon them? Was not the murdered assessor himself the cause of it? If in arithmetic a third number follows invariably from two given ones, the consequence was equally inevitable in this case. The innocence of the defendants was, at least for me, a mathematical certainty. If I am going on my way and an evildoer falls upon me and raises a dagger over my head to strike me down, am I to be considered a murderer if I forestall him in his evil deed and strike him down lifeless at my feet? If a Mohock today, having won the universal contempt he deserves, wants to revenge himself for it on me, and, meeting me in a solitary place, attacks me with drawn sword to deprive me of life or at least to wound me, am I guilty if I draw my sword in self-defense and deliver society from a member who disturbs its peace? Can an act be considered prejudicial to the inviolable human rights of a fellow being if I do it to save myself, if it prevents my destruction, if without it my well-being would be forever undone? . . .

"Every man is born into the world equal to all others. All have the same bodily parts, all have reason and will. Consequently, apart from his relation to society, man is a being that depends on no one in his actions. But he puts limits to his own freedom of action, he agrees not to follow only his own will in everything, he subjects himself to the commands of his equals ; in a word, he becomes a citizen. For what reason does he control his passions ? Why does he set up a governing authority over himself ? Why, though free to seek fulfillment of his will, does he confine himself within the bounds of obedience ? For his own advantage, reason will say ; for his own advantage, inner feeling will say ; for his own advantage, wise legislation will say. Consequently, wherever being a citizen is not to his advantage, he is not a citizen. Consequently, whoever seeks to rob him of the advantages of citizenship is his enemy. Against his enemy he seeks protection and satisfaction in the law. If the law is unable or unwilling to protect him, or if its power cannot furnish him immediate aid in the face of clear and present danger, then the citizen has recourse to the natural law of self-defense, self-preservation, and well-being. For the citizen, in becoming a citizen, does not cease to be a man, whose first obligation, arising from his very nature, is his own preservation, defense, and welfare. By his bestial cruelty the assessor who was murdered by the peasants had violated their rights as citizens. At the moment when he abetted the violence of his sons, when he added insult to the heartfelt injury of the bridal pair, when he, seeing their opposition to his devilish tyranny, moved to punish them, then the law that protects a citizen fell into abeyance and its efficacy disappeared ; then the law of nature was reborn, and the power of the wronged citizen, which the positive law cannot take from him when he has been wronged, comes into operation, and the peasants who killed the beastly assessor are not guilty before the law. On rational grounds my heart finds them not guilty, and the death of the assessor, although violent, is just. Let no one presume to seek in reasons of state or in the maintenance of public peace grounds for condemning the murderers of the assessor, who expired in the midst of his wickedness. No matter in what estate heaven may have decreed a citizen's birth, he is and will always remain a man ; and so long as he is a man, the law of nature, as an abundant wellspring of goodness, will never run dry in him, and whosoever dares wound him in his natural and inviolable right is a criminal. Woe to him, if the civil law does not punish him. He will be marked as a pariah by his fellow citizens, and may whosoever has sufficient power exact vengeance against him for his evildoing."

China's Sinocentric World

Imperial China's conduct of foreign relations was somewhat analogous to the way the two superpowers of the post–World War II era, the United States and the Soviet Union, have been dealing with their small allies. China was the Middle Kingdom in the center, and all the countries surrounding it were expected to behave as satellites in the Chinese orbit. By virtue of its imposing territorial expanse, military power, economic affluence, and brilliant old civilization, China developed an ethnocentric notion that it was the center of human civilization, in comparison to which it assumed all other non-Chinese peoples were ipso facto "barbarians," irresistibly attracted and willing to pay homage to the Emperor of China, the "Son of Heaven." Such a Sinocentric world view of Imperial China was reflected in the tribute system which had been institutionalized since the early Ming dynasty (1368–1643) and lasted until the middle of the nineteenth century. Through this system, the reciprocal relationships of compassionate benevolence on the part of the Son of Heaven and humble submission of the junior members of the Sinitic world, such as Korea, Liuqiu (Liu-ch'iu or Ryukyu), Annam (Vietnam), Siam, Burma, Laos, and a host of other peripheral states in Southeast and Central Asia, were regulated and reassured. The Son of Heaven recognized the legitimacy of the rulers of the tributary states by sending imperial envoys to officiate at their investitures and by conferring on them the imperial patent of appointment. The imperial government also sent military and economic aid to the tributary states in times of foreign invasion or natural disasters. The tributary states sent periodic tribute missions to the imperial capital to renew their submission and their acknowledgment of the superiority of the celestial empire. Besides presenting the tribute and local products to the Son of Heaven, they performed the full ceremony of kowtow — three kneelings and nine knockings of the head on the ground — in the audience hall. Kowtow was a symbolic gesture of submission to the Chinese emperor, and this requirement annoyed the European envoys in the nineteenth century as they deemed it to be humiliating.

Trade was another important aspect of the tribute system since a large number of traders accompanied the tributary mission and were allowed to engage in commercial transactions by the imperial government.

24

Ceremonial for Visitors: Court Tribute

The following excerpt shows the rules and protocols governing the tributary missions developed by the Qing (Ch'ing) government in 1764.

QUESTIONS TO CONSIDER

1. How analogous is China's tribute system to the Communist and Western alliance systems of post–World War II? What are the similarities and differences?
2. How do you relate this reading with Emperor Chien-lung's [Qianlong] letter to King George III of England (see Reading 25)?

1. *"As to the countries of the barbarians on all sides that send tribute to Court,* on the east is Korea ; on the southeast, Liu-ch'iu and Sulu ; on the south, Annam and Siam ; on the southwest, Western Ocean, Burma, and Laos. (For the barbarian tribes of the northwest, see under Court of Colonial Affairs.) All send officers as envoys to come to Court and present tributary memorials and pay tribute.

2. *"As to the imperial appointment of kings of (tributary) countries,* whenever the countries which send tribute to Court have a succession to the throne, they first send an envoy to request an imperial mandate at the Court. In the cases of Korea, Annam, and Liu-ch'iu, by imperial command the principal envoy and secondary envoy(s) receive the imperial patent (of appointment) and go (to their country) to confer it. As for the other countries, the patent (of appointment) is bestowed upon the envoy who has come (from his country) to take it back, whereupon an envoy is sent (from that country) to pay tribute and offer thanks for the imperial favor.

3. *"As to the king of Korea,* (the patent) is bestowed upon his wife the same as upon the king. When the son grows up, then he requests that it be bestowed upon him as the heir apparent. In all cases officials of the third rank or higher act as principal and secondary envoys. Their clothing and appearance, and ceremonial and retinue in each case are according to rank. In the cases of Annam and Liu-ch'iu, officials of the Hanlin Academy, the Censorate, or the Board of Ceremonies, of the fifth rank or below, act as principal and secondary envoys ; (the Emperor) specially confers upon them 'unicorn' clothing of the first rank, in order to lend weight to their journey. In ceremonial and retinue they are all regarded as being of the first rank. When the envoys return, they hand back their clothing to the office in charge of it. . . .

6. *"As to tribute objects,* in each case they should send the products of the soil of the country. Things that are not locally produced are not to be presented. Korea, Annam, Liu-ch'iu, Burma, Sulu, and Laos all have as tribute their customary objects. Western Ocean and Siam do not have a customary tribute. . . .

7. *"As to the retainers* (who accompany an envoy), in the case of the Korean tribute envoy there are one attendant secretary, three chief interpreters, 24 tribute guards, 30 minor retainers who receive rewards, and a variable number of minor retainers who do not receive rewards. For Liu-ch'iu, Western Ocean, Siam, and Sulu, the tribute vessels are not to exceed three, with no more than 100 men per vessel ; those going to the capital are not to exceed 20. When Annam, Burma, and Laos send tribute, the men are not to exceed 100, and those going to the capital are not to exceed 20. Those that do not go to the capital are to be retained at the frontier. The frontier officials give them a stipend from the government granary, until the envoy returns to the frontier, when he takes them back to their country.

[8. Presentation of tributary memorials, after arrival at Peking.]

9. *"As to the Court ceremony,* when a tribute envoy arrives at the capital at the time of a Great Audience or of an Ordinary Audience, His Majesty the Emperor

This excerpt is from the 1764 Ch'ien-lung edition of the *Statutes* (Ch'ien-lung hui-tien 56.1-8b), in John K. Fairbank and Ssù-yu Teng, *Ch'ing Administration : Three Studies* (Cambridge : Harvard University Press, 1960), pp. 170–173. Copyright © 1960 by The Harvard-Yenching Institute. These rules and regulations set the standard for the last century and a half of the Qing dynasty (1644–1911).

goes to the T'ai Ho [Taihe] palace and, after the princes, dukes, and officials have audience and present their congratulations, the ushers lead in the tributary envoys and their attendant officers, each of them wearing his country's court dress. They stand in the palace courtyard on the west in the last place. When they hear (the command of) the ceremonial ushers they perform the ceremony of three kneelings and nine knockings of the head [the full kowtow]. They are graciously allowed to sit. Tea is imperially bestowed upon them. All this is according to etiquette (for details see under the Department of Ceremonies). If (a tribute envoy) does not come at the time of an Audience, he presents a memorial through the Board (of Ceremonies) asking for an imperial summons to Court. His Majesty the Emperor goes to a side hall of the palace . . . etc.

[10–13. There follow details concerning further ceremonies, with performances of the kowtow; banquets; and imperial escorts, including those provided for westerners because of their services as imperial astronomers.]

14. "*As to trade,* — when the tribute envoys of the various countries enter the frontier, the goods brought along in their boats or carts may be exchanged in trade with merchants of the interior (China); either they may be sold at the merchants' hongs in the frontier province or they may be brought to the capital and marketed at the lodging house (i.e. the Residence for Tributary Envoys). At the customs stations (lit. passes and fords) which they pass en route, they are all exempted from duty. As to barbarian merchants who themselves bring their goods into the country for trade, — for Korea on the border of Shêng-ching [Shengjing] [Fengtien province], and at Chung-chiang [Zhongjang] [northeast of Chengtu, Szechwan], there are spring and autumn markets, two a year; at Hui-ning [southeast of Lanchow, Kansu], one market a year; at Ch'ing-yüan [Qingyuan] [in Chihli, now Chao-hsien], one market every other year, — (each) with two Interpreters of the Board of Ceremonies, one Ninguta (Kirin) clerk, and one Lieutenant to superintend it. After twenty days the market is closed. For the countries beyond the seas, (the market) is at the provincial capital of Kwangtung [Guangdong]. Every summer they take advantage of the tide and come to the provincial capital (Canton). When winter comes they wait for a wind and return to their countries. All pay duties to the (local) officers in charge, the same as the merchants of the interior (China).

15. "*As to the prohibitions,* — when a foreign country has something to state or to request, it should specially depute an officer to bring a document to the Board (of Ceremonies), or in the provinces it may be memorialized on behalf (of the country) by the Governor-General and Governor concerned. Direct communication to the Court is forbidden. For a tribute envoy's entrance of the frontier and the tribute route which he follows, in each case there are fixed places. Not to follow the regular route, or to go over into other provinces, is forbidden. It is forbidden secretly (i.e. without permission) to buy official costumes which violate the regulations, or books of history, weapons, copper, iron, oil, hemp, or combustible saltpetre; or to take people of the interior or rice and grain out of the frontiers. There are boundaries separating the rivers and seas; to catch fish beyond the boundaries is forbidden. The land frontiers are places of defensive entrenchments where Chinese and foreign soldiers or civilians have established military

colonies or signal-fire mounds, or cultivated rice-fields and set up huts; to abscond and take shelter (on either side) is forbidden. It is forbidden for civil or military officials on the frontier to communicate in writing with foreign countries not on public business. When commissioned to go abroad, to receive too many gifts, or when welcomed in coming and going, privately to demand the products of the locality (i.e. as "squeeze") is forbidden. Offenses against the prohibitions will be considered according to law.

[16. Charity and sympathy to be shown regarding foreign rulers' deaths, calamities, etc.]

17. *"As to the rescue* (of distressed mariners), — when ships of foreign merchants are tossed by the wind into the inner waters (of China), the local authorities should rescue them, report in a memorial the names and number of distressed barbarians, move the public treasury to give them clothing and food, take charge of the boat and oars, and wait for a wind to send them back. If a Chinese merchant vessel is blown by the wind into the outer ocean, the country there can rescue it and give it aid, put a boat in order and send them (the merchants) back, or it may bring them along on a tribute vessel so as to return them. In all such cases an imperial patent is to be issued, praising the king of the country concerned; imperial rewards are to be given to the officers (of the tributary country) in different degrees."

25

Emperor Ch'ien-lung [Qianlong], Letter to King George III

London decided to send an official mission to Beijing on the occasion of the eighty-third birthday of Emperor Qianlong (r. 1735–1795), hoping to alleviate difficulties experienced by British merchants in Canton as a result of China's restrictive and cumbersome rules and regulations for foreign merchants and Chinese official irregularities.

The mission, headed by Lord Macartney, Baron of Lissanoure and a cousin of the Crown, was courteously received by the Chinese government because it was understood to be a tributary mission delivering felicitations from George III (reigned 1760–1820). However, Macartney's mission failed to accomplish its real objectives, even the opening of discussions concerning trade extension and envoy exchange. The Ch'ing court considered Macartney's requests presumptuous and completely out of order. As far as the Ch'ing court was concerned, Macartney's mission had been completed after presenting gifts and offering felicitations to the Emperor on his birthday. In the following letter to King George III, written in 1793, the ostentatious Emperor Ch'ien-lung flatly rejected all the requests presented by Macartney.

QUESTIONS TO CONSIDER

1. What reasons did Emperor Ch'ien-lung cite in his letter for outright rejection of the British demand for a diplomatic and trade relationship?
2. Compare and contrast the Western treaty system with China's tributary system.

You, O King, live beyond the confines of many seas, nevertheless, impelled by your humble desire to partake of the benefits of our civilisation, you have dispatched a mission respectfully bearing your memorial. Your Envoy has crossed the seas and paid his respects at my Court on the anniversary of my birthday. To show your devotion, you have also sent offerings of your country's produce.

I have perused your memorial: the earnest terms in which it is couched reveal a respectful humility on your part, which is highly praiseworthy. In consideration of the fact that your Ambassador and his deputy have come a long way with your memorial and tribute, I have shown them high favour and have allowed them to be introduced into my presence. To manifest my indulgence, I have entertained them at a banquet and made them numerous gifts. I have also caused presents to be forwarded to the Naval Commander and six hundred of his officers and men, although they did not come to Peking, so that they too may share in my all-embracing kindness.

As to your entreaty to send one of your nationals to be accredited to my Celestial Court and to be in control of your country's trade with China, this request is contrary to all usage of my dynasty and cannot possibly be entertained. It is true that Europeans, in the service of the dynasty, have been permitted to live at Peking, but they are compelled to adopt Chinese dress, they are strictly confined to their own precincts and are never permitted to return home. You are presumably familiar with our dynastic regulations. Your proposed Envoy to my Court could not be placed in a position similar to that of European officials in Peking who are forbidden to leave China, nor could he, on the other hand, be allowed liberty of movement and the privilege of corresponding with his own country; so that you would gain nothing by his residence in our midst.

Moreover, our Celestial dynasty possesses vast territories, and tribute missions from the dependencies are provided for by the Department for Tributary States, which ministers to their wants and exercises strict control over their movements. It would be quite impossible to leave them to their own devices. Supposing that your Envoy should come to our Court, his language and national dress differ from that of our people, and there would be no place in which to bestow him. It may be suggested that he might imitate the Europeans permanently resident in Peking and adopt the dress and customs of China, but, it has never been our dynasty's wish to force people to do things unseemly and inconvenient. Besides, supposing I sent an Ambassador to reside in your country, how could you possibly make for him the requisite arrangements? Europe consists of many other nations besides your own: if each and all demanded to be represented at our Court, how

From E. Backhouse and J. O. P. Bland, *Annals and Memoirs of the Court of Peking* (Boston: Houghton Mifflin, 1914), pp. 322–331, passim.

could we possibly consent? The thing is utterly impracticable. How can our dynasty alter its whole procedure and system of etiquette, established for more than a century, in order to meet your individual views? If it be said that your object is to exercise control over your country's trade, your nationals have had full liberty to trade at Canton for many a year, and have received the greatest consideration at our hands. Missions have been sent by Portugal and Italy, preferring similar requests. The Throne appreciated their sincerity and loaded them with favours, besides authorising measures to facilitate their trade with China. You are no doubt aware that, when my Canton merchant, Wu Chao-ping [Wu Zhaoping], was in debt to the foreign ships, I made the Viceroy advance the monies due, out of the provincial treasury, and ordered him to punish the culprit severely. Why then should foreign nations advance this utterly unreasonable request to be represented at my Court? Peking is nearly two thousand miles from Canton, and at such a distance what possible control could any British representative exercise?

If you assert that your reverence for Our Celestial dynasty fills you with a desire to acquire our civilisation, our ceremonies and code of laws differ so completely from your own that, even if your Envoy were able to acquire the rudiments of our civilisation, you could not possibly transplant our manners and customs to your alien soil. Therefore, however adept the Envoy might become, nothing would be gained thereby.

Swaying the wide world, I have but one aim in view, namely, to maintain a perfect governance and to fulfil the duties of the State: strange and costly objects do not interest me. If I have commanded that the tribute offerings sent by you, O King, are to be accepted, this was solely in consideration for the spirit which prompted you to dispatch them from afar. Our dynasty's majestic virtue has penetrated unto every country under Heaven, and Kings of all nations have offered their costly tribute by land and sea. As your Ambassador can see for himself, we possess all things. I set no value on objects strange or ingenious, and have no use for your country's manufactures. This then is my answer to your request to appoint a representative at my Court, a request contrary to our dynastic usage, which would only result in inconvenience to yourself. I have expounded my wishes in detail and have commanded your tribute Envoys to leave in peace on their homeward journey. It behoves you, O King, to respect my sentiments and to display even greater devotion and loyalty in future, so that, by perpetual submission to our Throne, you may secure peace and prosperity for your country hereafter. Besides making gifts (of which I enclose an inventory) to each member of your Mission, I confer upon you, O King, valuable presents in excess of the number usually bestowed on such occasions, including silks and curios — a list of which is likewise enclosed. Do you reverently receive them and take note of my tender goodwill towards you! A special mandate. . . .

In the same letter, a further mandate to King George III dealt in detail with the British ambassador's proposals and the Emperor's reasons for declining them.

You, O King, from afar have yearned after the blessings of our civilisation, and in your eagerness to come into touch with our converting influence have sent an Embassy across the sea bearing a memorial. I have already taken note of your respectful spirit of submission, have treated your mission with extreme favour and loaded it with gifts, besides issuing a mandate to you, O King, and honouring you with the bestowal of valuable presents. Thus has my indulgence been manifested.

Yesterday your Ambassador petitioned my Ministers to memorialise me regarding your trade with China, but his proposal is not consistent with our dynastic usage and cannot be entertained. Hitherto, all European nations, including your own country's barbarian merchants, have carried on their trade with our Celestial Empire at Canton. Such has been the procedure for many years, although our Celestial Empire possesses all things in prolific abundance and lacks no product within its own borders. There was therefore no need to import the manufactures of outside barbarians in exchange for our own produce. But as the tea, silk and porcelain which the Celestial Empire produces, are absolute necessities to European nations and to yourselves, we have permitted, as a signal mark of favour, that foreign *hongs* [merchant firms] should be established at Canton, so that your wants might be supplied and your country thus participate in our beneficence. But your Ambassador has now put forward new requests which completely fail to recognise the Throne's principle to "treat strangers from afar with indulgence," and to exercise a pacifying control over barbarian tribes, the world over. Moreover, our dynasty, swaying the myriad races of the globe, extends the same benevolence towards all. Your England is not the only nation trading at Canton. If other nations, following your bad example, wrongfully importune my ear with further impossible requests, how will it be possible for me to treat them with easy indulgence? Nevertheless, I do not forget the lonely remoteness of your island, cut off from the world by intervening wastes of sea, nor do I overlook your excusable ignorance of the usages of our Celestial Empire. I have consequently commanded my Ministers to enlighten your Ambassador on the subject, and have ordered the departure of the mission. But I have doubts that, after your Envoy's return he may fail to acquaint you with my view in detail or that he may be lacking in lucidity, so that I shall now proceed . . . to issue my mandate on each question separately. In this way you will, I trust, comprehend my meaning. . . .

(3) Your request for a small island near Chusan, where your merchants may reside and goods be warehoused, arises from your desire to develop trade. As there are neither foreign *hongs* nor interpreters in or near Chusan, where none of your ships have ever called, such an island would be utterly useless for your purposes. Every inch of the territory of our Empire is marked on the map and the strictest vigilance is exercised over it all : even tiny islets and far-lying sand-banks are clearly defined as part of the provinces to which they belong. Consider, moreover, that England is not the only barbarian land which wishes to establish . . . trade with our Empire : supposing that other nations were all to imitate your evil example and beseech me to present them each and all with a site for trading purposes, how could I possibly comply? This also is a flagrant infringement of the usage of my Empire and cannot possibly be entertained.

(4) The next request, for a small site in the vicinity of Canton city, where your barbarian merchants may lodge or, alternatively, that there be no longer any restrictions over their movements at Aomen, has arisen from the following causes. Hitherto, the barbarian merchants of Europe have had a definite locality assigned to them at Aomen for residence and trade, and have been forbidden to encroach an inch beyond the limits assigned to that locality. . . . If these restrictions were

withdrawn, friction would inevitably occur between the Chinese and your barbarian subjects, and the results would militate against the benevolent regard that I feel towards you. From every point of view, therefore, it is best that the regulations now in force should continue unchanged. . . .

(7) Regarding your nation's worship of the Lord of Heaven, it is the same religion as that of other European nations. Ever since the beginning of history, sage Emperors and wise rulers have bestowed on China a moral system and inculcated a code, which from time immemorial has been religiously observed by the myriads of my subjects. There has been no hankering after heterodox doctrines. Even the European (missionary) officials in my capital are forbidden to hold intercourse with Chinese subjects; they are restricted within the limits of their appointed residences, and may not go about propagating their religion. The distinction between Chinese and barbarian is most strict, and your Ambassador's request that barbarians shall be given full liberty to disseminate their religion is utterly unreasonable.

It may be, O King, that the above proposals have been wantonly made by your Ambassador on his own responsibility, or peradventure you yourself are ignorant of our dynastic regulations and had no intention of transgressing them when you expressed these wild ideas and hopes. . . . If, after the receipt of this explicit decree, you lightly give ear to the representations of your subordinates and allow your barbarian merchants to proceed to Chêkiang [Zhejiang] and Tientsin [Tianjin], with the object of landing and trading there, the ordinances of my Celestial Empire are strict in the extreme, and the local officials, both civil and military, are bound reverently to obey the law of the land. Should your vessels touch the shore, your merchants will assuredly never be permitted to land or to reside there, but will be subject to instant expulsion. In that event your barbarian merchants will have had a long journey for nothing. Do not say that you were not warned in due time! Tremblingly obey and show no negligence! A special mandate!

Tokugawa "Hostage" System

For almost seven centuries, since General Minamoto Yoritomo assumed the title of shogun[1] in 1192, a dualistic political tradition evolved in Japan. At the apex of the political hierarchy, two authorities shared leadership and maintained a symbiotic relationship. Theoretically, the shogun was recognized as the emperor's delegated military authority, but in practice, the shogun ruled the country as a virtual military dictator while the emperor merely reigned as a semi-divine monarch. Until 1867, three lines of hereditary military families alternated in ruling feudal Japan. The last such rule began in 1603 when General Tokugawa Ieyasu emerged as the unchallenged military master of Japan and became shogun. For the following 264 years, Japan remained under the Tokugawa shogunal rule (1603–1867). Shogun Ieyasu divided up the country among his daimyo,[2] who numbered more than 260. Daimyo

1. Generalissimo or military dictator.
2. Vassals or autonomous territorial lords.

were treated as the personal vassals of the shogun, bound to him by an oath of personal allegiance. In search for stability and to ensure their continuous loyalty and obedience, Ieyasu and his two immediate successors devised very elaborate systems of control, which remained in effect almost without modifications for well over 200 years. The daimyo were subject to a whole series of rules and regulations, which included very elaborate and unique requirements for the Tokugawa vassals known as the Sankin Kotai system or the alternate attendance system. It required all the daimyo to reside in alternate years at the shogunal capital Edo (now Tokyo) in attendance on the shogun. It was a kind of polite hostage system since the daimyo were not permitted to be accompanied by their wives and children to their provinces. Their families were permanently detained in Edo under the watchful eyes of the shogunate. This requirement remained in force except for a brief suspension between 1722 and 1730 for over 200 years until 1862.

26

The Laws for the Military House (Buke Shohatto), 1615

The first laws for the daimyo were promulgated by the second Tokugawa Shogun Hidetada in 1615. They were subsequently reissued a number of times with revisions by his successors.

QUESTIONS TO CONSIDER

1. How would you compare the alternate attendance system of Tokugawa Japan with a similar system of political control in European history?
2. Can Tokugawa Japan be called "a premodern police state"? Why? Why not?

As to the rule that the Daimyos shall come (to the Shogun's Court at Edo) to do service.

In the *Shoku Nihon ki* (*i.e.* The Continuation of the Chronicles of Japan) it is recorded amongst the enactments: —

"Except when entrusted with some official duty no one (dignitary) is allowed at his own pleasure to assemble his whole tribe within the limits of the capital, no one is to go about attended by more than twenty horsemen, etc." Hence it is not permissible to lead about a large force of soldiers. For Daimyos whose revenues range from 1,000,000 koku[1] down to 200,000 koku, the number of twenty horse-

Asiatic Society of Japan, *Transactions*, 38:4 (1911):290, 293–297.
    1. One koku is equivalent to 4.96 bushels (of rice).

men is not to be exceeded. For those whose revenues are 100,000 koku and under the number is to be in the same proportion.

On occasions of official service, however (*i.e.* in time of warfare), the number of followers is to be in proportion to the social standing of each Daimyo.

Laws for the Barons (The Buke Shohatto) of Kwan-ei 22 (5th August, 1635).

[Promulgated by Iyemitsu.]

1. — The taste for the Way of literature, arms, archery and horsemanship is to be the chief object of cultivation.

2. — It is now settled that the Daimyōs and Shōmyōs (*i.e.* the greater and lesser Barons) are to do service by turns at Yedo. They shall proceed hither on service every year in summer during the course of the fourth month. Latterly the numbers of their followers have become excessive. This is at once a cause of wastefulness to the provinces and districts and of hardship to the people. Henceforward suitable reductions in this respect must be made. On the occasions of going up to Kyoto, however, the directions given may be followed. On occasions of government service (*i.e.* military service) the full complement of each Baron must be in attendance.

3. — The erection or repairing of new castles is strictly forbidden. When the moats or ramparts of the present residential castles are to be repaired, whether as regards the stonework, plaster, or earth-work, a report must be made to the *Bugyōsho* (*i.e.* the Magistracy at Yedo) and its direction taken. As regards the (*Yagura, hei* and *mon*) armories, fences and gates, repairs may be made to restore them to their previous conditions.

4. — Whether at Yedo or in any of the provinces whatsoever, if an occurrence of any sort whatsoever should take place, those (Barons and their retainers) who are there at the time are to stay where they are and to await the Shōgun's orders (from Yedo).

5. — Whenever capital punishment is to be inflicted, no matter where, nobody except the functionaries in charge is to be present. But the coroner's directions are to be followed.

6. — The scheming of innovations, the forming of parties and the taking of oaths is strictly forbidden.

7. — There must be no private quarrels whether amongst the (*Kokushu*) greater Barons or (*Ryōshu*) the other Feudatories. Ordinary circumspection and carefulness must be exercised. If matters involving a lengthy arrangement should arise they must be reported to the Magistracy and its pleasure ascertained.

8. — Daimyōs of over 10,000 *koku* income, whether they be lords of provinces (domains) or lords of castles, and the heads of departments (*monogashira*) in personal attendance on them are not to form matrimonial alliances (between members of their families) at their private convenience (*i.e.* they must apply for the Shōgun's permission before doing so).

9. — In social observances of the present day, such as visits of ceremony, sending and return of presents, the formalities of giving and receiving in marriage, the giving of banquets and the construction of residences, the striving after elegance is carried to very great lengths. Henceforth there must be much greater

simplicity in these respects. And in all other matters there must be a greater regard for economy.

10. — There must be no indiscriminate intermingling (of ranks) as regards the materials of dress. Undyed silk with woven patterns *(Shiro-aya)* is only to be worn by Court Nobles *(Kuge)* and others of the highest ranks. Wadded coats of undyed silk may be worn by Daimyōs and others of higher rank. Lined coats of purple silk ; silk coats with the lining of purple ; white gloss silk, coloured silk coats without the badge are not to be worn at random. Coming down to retainers, henchmen, and men-at-arms, the wearing by such persons of ornamental dresses such as silks, damask, brocade or embroideries was quite unknown to the ancient laws, and a stop must be put to it.

11. — Those who may ride in palaquins[2] are all persons of distinction who are connections of the Tokugawa clan ; lords of domains *(Kuni)* and lords of castles having 10,000 *koku* and upwards ; the sons of provincial Daimyō (beneficiaries), lords of castles ; chamberlains and higher functionaries, and the legitimate sons of such (*i.e.* sons by their wives ; but not sons by their concubines) ; persons (of any rank) above fifty years of age ; of the two professions of doctors of medicine and soothsayers (astrologers, *onyōshi*) and invalids and sick persons. Apart from the above named, irregularities must be prohibited ; but those who have applied for and received official permission to ride are not included in the prohibition.

As regard the feudal retainers in the provinces, those who may ride are to be definitely specified in each fief. Court Nobles, Abbots of royal or noble birth, and ecclesiastics of distinction are not to be included in this regulation.

12. — Retainers who have had a disagreement with their original lord are not to be taken into employment by other Daimyōs. If any such are reported as having been guilty of rebellion or homicide they are to be sent back (to their former lord). Any who manifest a refractory disposition must either be sent back or expelled.

13. — When the hostages given by subvassals to their mesne lords have committed an offence requiring punishment by banishment or death, a report in writing of the circumstances must be made to the Magistrates' office and their decision awaited. In case the circumstances were such as to necessitate or justify the instant cutting down of the offender, a personal account of the matter must be given to the Magistrate.

14. — The lesser beneficiaries must honestly discharge the duties of their position and refrain from giving unlawful or arbitrary orders (to the people of their benefices) : they must take care not to impair the resources or well-being of the province or district in which they are.

15. — The roads, relays of post horses, boats, ferries and bridges must be carefully attended to, so as to ensure that there shall be no delays or impediments to quick communication.

16. — No private toll-bars may be erected, nor may any existing ferry be discontinued.

17. — No vessels of over 500 *koku* burden are to be built.

2. A type of vehicle.

18. — The glebelands of shrines and temples scattered throughout the provinces (domains) having been attached to them from ancient times to the present day, are not to be taken from them.

19. — The Christian sect is to be strictly prohibited in all the provinces and in all places.

20. — In case of any unfilial conduct the offender will be dealt with under the penal law.

21. — In all matters the example set by the laws of Yedo is to be followed in all the provinces and places.

All the foregoing provisions, being in conformity with the previous enactments of this (Tokugawa) House, are hereby reimposed and definitely established and must be carefully observed.

The "Buke Shohatto" were again promulgated by the 4th Shōgun Iyetsuna in *1663* (June 28th): only alterations made on this occasion are noted below, the body of the code remaining as before.

In Art. 2—As regards the taking of turns of duty, the Daimyōs and Shōmyōs shall come to Yedo on service every year at the time when the Shōgun fixes the posts which they are to guard. . . .

REVOLUTIONS
AND REBELLIONS

Men and Women in Revolution

The last decades of the eighteenth century ushered in an age of democratic revolution for many of the countries bordering the Atlantic Ocean. Because this age of revolution began first in America, documents such as the Declaration of Independence quickly became models for successive waves of revolution in the old European world and throughout Spanish America. Thomas Jefferson (1743–1826), the primary author of the Declaration of Independence, was feted in Paris, and his writings were read widely throughout France. The writings of other heroes of the American Revolution, such as James Madison (1751–1836), were also studied closely throughout the Atlantic world. This inspirational legacy of the American Revolution was one of its most important contributions to the age of democratic revolution.

Certainly the successful example of America's revolution, its heroes and their writings, inspired the people who steered the early course of the French Revolution, which broke upon France in the summer of 1789. On August 27, 1789, the new National Assembly issued the clearest statement of the goals of the French Revolution, the Declaration of the Rights of Man and of the Citizen, a document heavily influenced by the American Revolution. Despite the importance of this document and the earlier American declaration, neither specifically advanced or even recognized the rights of women. For at least one French woman, Olympe de Gouges (1748–1793), this omission had to be repaired. In 1791, she wrote a Declaration of the Rights of Woman and of the Female Citizen. Unfortunately for de Gouges, France's revolutionary leaders not only rejected her proposal but charged her with treason and ordered her executed.

Edmund Burke (1729–1797), a famous Irish statesman, closely observed both the French and American revolutions. He was sympathetic to the cause of the American colonists, and on the eve of their war for independence, he urged Parliament to consider a policy of conciliation ; but he fervently denounced the French Revolution even before it had reached its radical phase. In 1790, Burke published his *Reflections on the Revolution in France*, in which he stressed the importance of historical institutions and traditions and outlined his views on government and society.

The unfolding drama of revolution in Philadelphia, Boston, and Paris was closely watched in Buenos Aires, Caracas, and Mexico City. By the late eighteenth century, a growing resentment of Spanish political and economic restrictions, coupled with the impact of the American and French revolutions, inspired Spanish American revolutionaries to challenge Spain's colonial control. The immediate cause of the Spanish American revolutions was the French occupation of the Iberian peninsula in 1808. Napoleon's intervention there weakened Spain and provided revolutionary leaders in the New World with the opportunity to declare their independence and begin fighting for it. Many of these leaders looked to the American Constitution in the hope of establishing democratic federal republics in Latin America. Others, such as Simón Bolívar, questioned whether the U.S. model would work in Spanish America.

27

James Madison, *The Federalist*, Number 10

The *Federalist* papers, written by Alexander Hamilton, James Madison, and John Jay in the campaign to gain adoption of the U.S. Constitution by New York State, are considered one of the most important contributions to political thought in America. First published in New York newspapers, the essays defending the new Constitution appeared in book form in 1788. In *The Federalist*, Number 10, Madison discusses how the evil of faction and the danger of majority tyranny can be avoided in a republican union consisting of many diverse interests.

QUESTIONS TO CONSIDER

1. How does James Madison define *faction*? Why did he think the government outlined in the U.S. Constitution could deal with this problem?
2. Would James Madison agree with Rousseau's prescription for government (see Reading 20)?

Complaints are everywhere heard from our most considerate and virtuous citizens, equally the friends of public and private faith and of public and personal liberty, that our governments are too unstable, that the public good is disregarded in the conflicts of rival parties, and that measures are too often decided, not according to the rules of justice and the rights of the minor party, but by the superior force of an interested and overbearing majority. However anxiously we may wish that these complaints had no foundation, the evidence of known facts will not permit us to deny that they are in some degree true. It will be found, indeed, on a candid review of our situation, that some of the distresses under which we labor have been erroneously charged on the operation of our governments; but it will be found, at the same time, that other causes will not alone account for many of our

From *The Federalist* (New York : Colonial Press, 1901), pp. 44–51.

heaviest misfortunes ; and, particularly, for that prevailing and increasing distrust of public engagements and alarm for private rights which are echoed from one end of the continent to the other. These must be chiefly, if not wholly, effects of the unsteadiness and injustice with which a factious spirit has tainted our public administrations.

By a faction I understand a number of citizens, whether amounting to a majority or minority of the whole, who are united and actuated by some common impulse of passion, or of interest, adverse to the rights of other citizens, or to the permanent and aggregate interests of the community.

There are two methods of curing the mischiefs of faction : the one, by removing its causes ; the other, by controlling its effects.

There are again two methods of removing the causes of faction : the one, by destroying the liberty which is essential to its existence ; the other, by giving to every citizen the same opinions, the same passions, and the same interests.

It could never be more truly said than of the first remedy that it was worse than the disease. Liberty is to faction what air is to fire, an aliment without which it instantly expires. But it could not be a less folly to abolish liberty, which is essential to political life, because it nourishes faction than it would be to wish the annihilation of air, which is essential to animal life, because it imparts to fire its destructive agency.

The second expedient is as impracticable as the first would be unwise. As long as the reason of man continues fallible, and he is at liberty to exercise it, different opinions will be formed. As long as the connection subsists between his reason and his self-love, his opinions and his passions will have a reciprocal influence on each other ; and the former will be objects to which the latter will attach themselves. The diversity in the faculties of men, from which the rights of property originate, is not less an insuperable obstacle to a uniformity of interests. The protection of these faculties is the first object of government. From the protection of different and unequal faculties of acquiring property, the possession of different degrees and kinds of property immediately results ; and from the influence of these on the sentiments and views of the respective proprietors ensues a division of the society into different interests and parties.

The latent causes of faction are thus sown in the nature of men ; and we see them everywhere brought into different degrees of activity, according to the different circumstances of civil society. A zeal for different opinions concerning religion, concerning government, and many other points, as well of speculation as of practice ; an attachment to different leaders ambitiously contending for preeminence and power ; or to persons of other descriptions whose fortunes have been interesting to the human passions, have, in turn, divided mankind into parties, inflamed them with mutual animosity, and rendered them much more disposed to vex and oppress each other than to cooperate for their common good. So strong is this propensity of mankind to fall into mutual animosities that where no substantial occasion presents itself the most frivolous and fanciful distinctions have been sufficient to kindle their unfriendly passions and excite their most violent conflicts. But the most common and durable source of factions has been the various and unequal distribution of property. Those who hold and those who are without property have ever formed distinct interests in society. Those who are creditors, and those who are debtors, fall under a like discrimination. A landed interest, a manufacturing interest, a mercantile interest, a moneyed interest, with many lesser interests, grow up of necessity in civilized nations, and divide them into different classes, actuated by different sentiments and views. The regulation of these various and interfering interests forms the principal task of modern legislation and involves the spirit of party and faction in the necessary and ordinary operations of the government.

From this view of the subject it may be concluded that a pure democracy, by which I mean a society consisting of a small number of citizens, who assemble and administer the government in person, can admit of no cure for the mischiefs of faction. A common passion or interest will, in almost every case, be felt by a majority of the whole ; a communication and concert result from the form of government itself ; and there is nothing to check the inducements to sacrifice the weaker party or an obnoxious individual. Hence it is that such democracies have ever been spectacles of turbulence and contention ; have ever been found incompatible with personal security or the rights of property ; and have in general been as short in their lives as they have been violent in their deaths. Theoretic politicians, who have patronized this species of government, have erroneously supposed that by reducing mankind to a perfect equality in their political rights, they would at the same time be perfectly equalized and assimilated in their possessions, their opinions, and their passions.

A republic, by which I mean a government in which the scheme of representation takes place, opens a different prospect and promises the cure for which we are seeking. Let us examine the points on which it varies from pure democracy, and we shall comprehend both the nature of the cure and the efficacy which it must derive from the Union.

The two great points of difference between a democracy and a republic are : first, the delegation of the government, in the latter, to a small number of citizens elected by the rest ; secondly, the greater number of citizens and greater sphere of country over which the latter may be extended.

The effect of the first difference is, on the one hand, to refine and enlarge the public views by passing them through the medium of a chosen body of citizens, whose wisdom may best discern the true interest of their country and whose patriotism and love of justice will be least likely to sacrifice it to temporary or partial considerations. Under such a regulation it may well happen that the public voice, pronounced by the representatives of the people, will be more consonant to the public good than if pronounced by the people themselves, convened for the purpose. On the other hand, the effect may be inverted. Men of factious tempers, of local prejudices, or of sinister designs, may, by intrigue, by corruption, or by other means, first obtain the suffrage, and then betray the interests of the people. The question resulting is, whether small or extensive republics are most favorable to the election of proper guardians of the public weal ; and it is clearly decided in favor of the latter by two obvious considerations.

In the first place it is to be remarked that however small the republic may be the representatives must be raised to a certain number in order to guard against the cabals of a few ; and that however large it may be they must be limited to a certain number in order to guard against the confusion of a multitude. Hence, the number of representatives in the two cases not being in proportion to that of the two constituents, and being proportionally greatest in the small republic, it follows that if the proportion of fit characters be not less in the large than in the small republic, the former will present a greater option, and consequently a greater probability of a fit choice.

In the next place, as each representative will be chosen by a greater number of citizens in the large than in the small republic, it will be more difficult for unworthy candidates to practise with success the vicious arts by which elections are too often carried ; and the suffrages of the people being more free, will be more likely to center on men who possess the most attractive merit and the most diffusive and established characters.

28

Declaration of the Rights of Man and of the Citizen

In the summer of 1789, France exploded into revolution. The French government's inability to find new tax revenues without tampering with the privileged, tax-exempt status of the nobility had forced King Louis XVI (reigned 1774–1792) to call representatives of the clergy, nobility, and Third Estate to assemble at Versailles as the Estates-General. For the first month little happened. Then, on June 17, the leadership of the Third Estate, along with representatives of the clergy and the nobility, openly challenged Louis XVI by overturning the authority of the Estates-General and declaring themselves the National Assembly of France. On July 14, anxious Parisian crowds, driven by rumors of an aristocratic plot to starve the city, attacked the feared prison of the Bastille in search of weapons. At the same time, in widely scattered parts of rural France, peasants assaulted nobles and burned their chateaux. On August 27, the National Assembly issued the document presented below.

QUESTIONS TO CONSIDER

1. Are there any problems reconciling the sentiments of article 2 of *The Declaration of the Rights of Man and of the Citizen* with articles 3, 4, 5, and 6?
2. Are there any traces of the thoughts of Jean-Jacques Rousseau (see Reading 20) in this document?

The representatives of the French people, meeting in National Assembly, considering that ignorance, forgetfulness, or contempt of human rights are the sole causes of public misfortunes and the corruption of governments, have resolved to

From P.-J.-B. Buchez and P. C. Roux, *Histoire parlementaire de la révolution française ; ou Journal des assemblées nationales, depuis 1789 jusqu'en 1815* (Paris : Paulin, 1834–1838), vol. 11, pp. 404–406. Translated by Philip F. Riley.

set forth in solemn declaration the sacred, inalienable and natural rights of man, so that this declaration, constantly before all members of the social body, may unceasingly remind them of their rights and duties; in order that the acts of the legislative power and those of the executive power, may always be compared with the goal of every political institution, and may therefore be more respected; in order that the demands of citizens, founded henceforth on simple and incontestable principles, may be directed to the maintenance of the Constitution and welfare of all.

Consequently, the National Assembly recognizes and proclaims, in the presence of and under the auspices of the Supreme Being, the following rights of man and citizen:

1. Men are born free and remain free and equal in rights. Social distinctions can only be founded on general utility.
2. The end of all political association is the preservation of the natural and inalienable rights of man. These rights are liberty, property, security and resistance to oppression.
3. The source of sovereignty resides essentially in the nation. No body, no individual, may exercise any authority not emanating expressly therefrom.
4. Liberty consists in the power to do whatever does not injure another. Thus the exercise of the natural rights of each man has no other limits than those which assure to every other man the enjoyment of those same rights. These limits may be determined only by law.
5. The law should only prohibit those actions harmful to society. Anything not forbidden expressly by law should not be prevented and no one can be forced to do that which the law does not require.
6. The law is the expression of the general will. All citizens have a right to concur either personally or by their representatives in its formation. The law should be the same for all whether it protects or whether it punishes. All citizens, being equal in its eyes, and equally entitled to all honors, places and public employments according to their abilities without any other distinction than that of their virtues and their talents.
7. No man can be accused, arrested or held in confinement except in those cases determined by law and according to the forms it has prescribed. Any one who promotes, solicits, or executes arbitrary orders must be punished; but all citizens called upon or apprehended by virtue of the law, must immediately obey; he renders himself culpable by resistance.
8. The law should only impose those penalties which are absolutely and clearly necessary, and one may only be punished by a law that has been established and promulgated prior to the offense and legally applied.
9. Every man is presumed innocent until he has been declared guilty, if it is necessary to arrest him, all unnecessary force for securing his person must be severely repressed by law.
10. No one is to be harassed for his opinions, even his religious opinions, provided their expression does not threaten public order as established by law.
11. Freedom of expression of thoughts and opinions is one of the most precious rights of man: every citizen may speak, write, and publish freely, provided he is responsible for the abuse of this liberty in cases determined by law.

12. The guarantee of the rights of man and citizen requires a public force : this force is instituted for the advantage of all and not for the particular benefit of those to whom it is entrusted.

13. To maintain the public force and the expenses of administration, a common tax is indispensable ; it should be assessed equally among all citizens, according to their abilities.

14. All citizens have the right, either by themselves or by their representatives to a free voice in determining the necessity of the public tax, to oversee its use, and to determine its quota, assessment and duration.

15. Society has the right to demand of each public agent an accounting of his administration.

16. Any society in which the guarantee of rights is not assured nor the separation of powers determined, has no constitution at all.

17. The right to property is inviolable and sacred, no one can be deprived of it except in cases of public necessity, verified by law, and on condition of a just and prior indemnity.

29

Olympe de Gouges, *Declaration of the Rights of Woman and of the Female Citizen*

One of the most articulate and outspoken female revolutionaries was Olympe de Gouges, a butcher's daughter, who in 1791 wrote the following declaration. Her proposal called for a national assembly of women, emphasized the importance of education for all women, and suggested that women as well as men should vote. When the French Revolution moved into its most radical phase, called the "Terror" (1793–1794), women such as de Gouges pressed even harder for their rights. Fearful that any such recognition could undermine their own leadership and threaten the revolution, the National Convention charged Olympe de Gouges with treason. She was quickly arrested, tried, and on November 3, 1793, executed by the guillotine.

QUESTIONS TO CONSIDER

1. In light of articles 6, 7, 9, 10, and 12 of *The Declaration of the Rights of Woman and of the Female Citizen*, how would you define the political agenda of Olympe de Gouges?

2. What does article 11, along with Olympe de Gouges's reflections on marriage, suggest about the condition of women in eighteenth-century France?

Mothers, daughters, sisters and representatives of the nation demand to be constituted in a national assembly. Believing that ignorance, omission, or contempt for the rights of women are the only causes of public misfortune and the corruption of governments, we resolve to expose in a solemn declaration the natural, inalienable and sacred rights of woman so that this declaration, constantly exposed to all members of the society, may unceasingly remind them of their rights and duties ; that the actions of women and the actions of men can at any moment harmonize with the goals of all political institutions ; and that the demands of female citizens, founded on simple and incontestable principles, will always support the constitution, good morals, and the happiness of all.

Consequently, the sex superior in beauty and courageous in maternal sufferings recognizes and declares in the presence and under the auspices of the Supreme Being, the following Rights of Woman and of the Female Citizen :

1. Woman is born free and remains equal to man in rights. Social distinctions can be founded only on general utility.
2. The goal of all political association is the preservation of the natural and imprescriptible rights of Woman and Man : These rights are liberty, property, security, and above all resistance to oppression.
3. The source of all sovereignty resides in the nation, which is nothing but the union of Woman and Man : No body, no individual, may exercise any authority not emanating expressly therefrom.
4. Liberty and justice consist of returning all that belongs to another ; thus, the only limits on the exercise of woman's natural rights are the perpetual tyranny wielded by men ; these limits must be reformed by the law of nature and the law of reason.
5. The laws of nature and of reason prohibit all actions harmful to society : Anything not forbidden by these wise and divine laws, cannot be forbidden, and no one can be forced to do that which the law does not require.
6. The law should be the expression of the general will ; all female and male citizens should concur either personally or by their representatives in its formulation ; it should be the same for all : All female and male citizens are equal in its eyes, and equally entitled to all honors, places and public employments according to their abilities without any other distinction than that of their virtues and their talents.
7. No woman is an exception ; she is accused, arrested, and detained in cases determined by law. Women, like men, obey this rigorous law.
8. The law should only impose those penalties which are strictly and absolutely necessary, and one may be punished only by a law that has been established and promulgated prior to the offense and legally applied to women.
9. Once a woman has been declared guilty, the law should be applied rigorously.
10. No one is to be harassed for their fundamental beliefs ; a woman has the right to mount the scaffold ; she also has the right to mount the rostrum, providing that her actions do not threaten lawful public order.

From Olympe de Gouges, *La Nation à La Reine : Les Droits de la Femme* (Paris : Momoro, n.d.[1791]), pp. 6–13, 17–20. Translated by Philip F. Riley.

11. Freedom of expression of thoughts and opinions is one of the most precious rights of woman, since this liberty assures the legitimate paternity of children. Each female citizen must be free to say I am the mother of this child which belongs to you, without being forced by barbarous prejudice to lie ; however, lawful exceptions may be made, if this liberty is abused.

12. The guarantee of the rights of woman and the female citizen ensures a major advantage ; this guarantee must be instituted for the advantage of all, and not for the particular utility of those to whom it is entrusted.

13. To maintain the public force and the expenses of administration, the contributions of woman and man are equal ; she performs all the labor taxes, and all the painful duties ; therefore she should have the same responsibilities, honors, and employment.

14. Female and male citizens have the right, either by themselves or by their representatives, to verify the necessity of the public tax. Women can do this if they are admitted to an equal share of the wealth, public administration, and permitted to determine the amount, basis, collection, and the duration of the tax.

15. The mass of women, joined for tax purposes with men, has the right to demand of each public agent an accounting of his administration.

16. Any society in which the guarantee of rights is not assured nor the separation of powers determined has no constitution at all ; the constitution is invalid if the majority of individuals comprising the nation have not cooperated in its writing.

17. Property belongs to both sexes united or separate ; for each property is an inviolable and sacred right ; no one can be deprived of it, since it is the true patrimony of nature, except in cases of public necessity, verified by law, and on condition of a just and prior indemnity.

Woman, wake-up ; the tocsin of reason is being heard in all the universe ; discover your rights. Nature's powerful empire is no longer surrounded by lies, superstition, prejudice and fanaticism. The flame of truth has dissipated all the clouds of stupidity and usurpation. Enslaved man has multiplied his strength, but he needs your help to break his chains. Having become free, he has become unjust to his companion. Oh Women ! Women, when will you cease being blind ? What are the advantages you have received in this Revolution ? More contempt ? More disdain ? In the centuries of corruption you ruled only over men's foibles. Your old empire is destroyed. How will it be restored ? By convicting men's injustices. The reclamation of your patrimony must be based on the wise decrees of nature. Why should you fear such a fine venture ? The *bon mot* of the Legislator of the wedding feast of Cana ? Do you fear only that our French Legislators, correctors of a morality, long entangled by politics but now out of date, will ask you : women what do you have in common with us ? Everything, you must respond. If they continue in their weakness, by permitting this absurdity to contradict their principles, you must courageously oppose the force of reason to the vain pretensions of superiority ; unite under the banner of philosophy ; deploy all the energy of your character, and you will see these arrogant fellows, not as sycophants groveling at your feet, but proud to share with you the treasures of the Supreme Being. Whatever the barriers before you, it is in your power to break them; you only have to want to break them. . . .

Marriage is a tomb of trust and love. A married woman can with impunity give bastards to her husband and give them also wealth that does not belong to them. An unmarried woman has only one feeble right: Ancient and inhuman laws deny her children the name and the wealth of their father, and no new laws have corrected this. If it is considered a paradox on my part to try to give my sex an honorable and just consistency, I leave to men the glory of doing this; but, while waiting, we can prepare the way by national education, by restoring morality, and by conjugal conventions.

Form for a Social Contract between Man and Woman

We, _____ and _____, moved by our own will, unite ourselves for a lifetime, and for the duration of our mutual inclinations, under the following conditions: We intend and wish to put our wealth in common, while reserving the right to divide in favor of our children and whomever else we might select, recognizing that our property belongs to our children, from whatever bed they proceed, and that all our children have the right to carry the name of their fathers and mothers who have acknowledged them, and we agree to subscribe to the law which punishes those who deny their own blood. We are equally obliged, that in the case of separation, to divide our wealth, and to set aside a lawful portion for our children; and, in the case of perfect union, the spouse who dies first, will ensure that one-half of his property will pass to the children; and if there are no children the survivor will inherit this half-share unless the deceased spouse has made other arrangements.

That is the formula for marriage that I propose to execute. Upon reading this bizarre document, I see rising against me the hypocrites, the prudes, the clergy and all their infernal allies. But I believe this document offers to the wise the moral means of achieving the perfection of a happy government! . . .

I would also wish for a law that would assist widows and young women deceived by the false promises of a man to whom they were attached; I would like this law to force such a deceitful man to keep his promise of engagement, or to pay an indemnity equal to his wealth. I also believe this law should be rigorously applied against women, if it can be proven they have broken their word. I wish at the same time to reiterate a proposal I made in *Le Bonheur primitif de l'homme,* in 1788, that prostitutes be placed in designated quarters. Prostitutes do not contribute to the degradation of morality; it is the women of society. In regenerating the latter, the former will be improved. This chain of fraternal union will, at first, bring disorder, but over time it will be harmonious.

I offer an invincible means to elevate the soul of women; it is to join all the activities of men: If a man finds this impractical, let him share his fortune with a woman, not out of his whim but by the wisdom of the laws. Prejudice falls, morals are purified, and nature recaptures all her rights. Add to this the marriage of priests with the King firmly on his throne, and the French government cannot perish. . . .

30

Edmund Burke, *Reflections on the Revolution in France*

Edmund Burke (1729–1797) was a leading voice of conservatism who denounced the French Revolution even before it had moved into its most radical phase. In 1790, he published *Reflections on the Revolution in France*, in which he condemned the destructiveness of the revolutionary movement and questioned whether the newly elected assembly could produce a better government and society.

QUESTIONS TO CONSIDER

1. What did Edmund Burke find so offensive about the leadership of the French Revolution? What elements of Burke's essay may be cited as the basis for modern political conservatism?
2. In light of Burke's attack on the French Revolution, how could he champion the rights of the American colonists to rebel against King George III?

France, by the perfidy of her leaders, has utterly disgraced the tone of lenient council in the cabinets of princes, and disarmed it of its most potent topics. She has sanctified the dark suspicious maxims of tyrannous distrust ; and taught kings to tremble at (what will hereafter be called) the delusive plausibilities, of moral politicians. Sovereigns will consider those who advise them to place an unlimited confidence in their people, as subverters of their thrones ; as traitors who aim at their destruction, by leading their easy good nature, under specious pretences, to admit combinations of bold and faithless men into a participation of their power. This alone (if there were nothing else) is an irreparable calamity to you and to mankind. . . .

. . . Laws overturned ; tribunals subverted ; industry without vigor ; commerce expiring ; the revenue unpaid, yet the people impoverished ; a church pillaged, and a state not relieved ; civil and military anarchy made the constitution of the kingdom ; every thing human and divine sacrificed to the idol of public credit, and national bankruptcy the consequence ; and to crown all, the paper securities of new, precarious, tottering power, the discredited paper securities of impoverished fraud, and beggared rapine, held out as a currency for the support of an empire, in lieu of the two great recognised species that represent the lasting conventional credit of mankind, which disappeared and hid themselves in the earth from whence they came, when the principle of property, whose creatures and representatives they are, was systematically subverted.

From Edmund Burke, *The Works of Edmund Burke*, vol. 3 (Boston : Chas. C. Little and James Brown, 1839), pp. 57–62, 71–73, 81–83, 97–101, passim.

Were all these dreadful things necessary? Were they the inevitable results of the desperate struggle of determined patriots, compelled to wade through blood and tumult, to the quiet shore of a tranquil and prosperous liberty? No! nothing like it. The fresh ruins of France, which shock our feelings wherever we can turn our eyes, are not the devastation of civil war; they are the sad but instructive monuments of rash and ignorant counsel in time of profound peace. They are the display of inconsiderate and presumptuous, because unresisted and irresistible authority.

This unforced choice, this fond election of evil, would appear perfectly unaccountable, if we did not consider the composition of the national assembly; I do not mean its formal constitution, which, as it now stands, is exceptionable enough, but the materials of which, in a great measure, it is composed, which is of ten thousand times greater consequence than all the formalities in the world. If we were to know nothing of this assembly but by its title and function, no colors could paint to the imagination any thing more venerable. . . .

After I had read over the list of the persons and descriptions elected into the *Tiers Etat,* nothing which they afterwards did could appear astonishing. Among them, indeed, I saw some of known rank; some of shining talents; but of any practical experience in the state, not one man was to be found. The best were only men of theory. But whatever the distinguished few may have been, it is the substance and mass of the body which constitutes its character, and must finally determine its direction. . . .

Judge, sir, of my surprise, when I found that a very great proportion of the assembly (a majority, I believe, of the members who attended,) was composed of practitioners in the law. It was composed, not of distinguished magistrates, who had given pledges to their country of their science, prudence, and integrity; not of leading advocates, the glory of the bar; not of renowned professors in universities; but for the far greater part, as it must in such a number, of the inferior, unlearned, mechanical, merely instrumental members of the profession. There were distinguished exceptions; but the general composition was of obscure provincial advocates, of stewards of petty local jurisdictions, country attorneys, notaries, and the whole train of the ministers of municipal litigation, the fomenters and conductors of the petty war of village vexation. From the moment I read the list, I saw distinctly, and very nearly as it has happened, all that was to follow. . . .

Whenever the supreme authority is vested in a body so composed, it must evidently produce the consequences of supreme authority placed in the hands of men not taught habitually to respect themselves; who had no previous fortune in character at stake; who could not be expected to bear with moderation, or to conduct with discretion, a power, which they themselves, more than any others, must be surprised to find in their hands. . . .

Nothing is a due and adequate representation of a state, that does not represent its ability, as well as its property. But as ability is a vigorous and active principle, and as property is sluggish, inert and timid, it never can be safe from the invasions of ability, unless it be, out of all proportion, predominant in the representation. It must be represented too in great masses of accumulation, or it is not rightly protected. The characteristic essence of property, formed out of the combined principles of its acquisition and conservation, is to be *unequal.* . . .

The power of perpetuating our property in our families is one of the most valuable and interesting circumstances belonging to it, and that which tends the most to the perpetuation of society itself. It makes our weakness subservient to our virtue; it grafts benevolence even upon avarice. The possessors of family wealth, and of the distinction which attends hereditary possession (as most concerned in it) are the natural securities for this transmission. With us, the house of peers is formed upon this principle. It is wholly composed of hereditary property and hereditary distinction; and made therefore the third of the legislature; and in the last event, the sole judge of all property in all its subdivisions. The house of commons too, though not necessarily, yet in fact, is always so composed in the far greater part. Let those large proprietors be what they will, and they have their chance of being among the best, they are at the very worst, the ballast in the vessel of the commonwealth. For though hereditary wealth, and the rank which goes with it, are too much idolized by creeping sycophants, and the blind abject admirers of power, they are too rashly slighted in shallow speculations of the petulant, assuming, short-sighted coxcombs of philosophy. Some decent regulated preëminence, some preference (not exclusive appropriation) given to birth, is neither unnatural, nor unjust, nor impolitic.

It is said, that twenty-four millions ought to prevail over two hundred thousand. True; if the constitution of a kingdom be a problem of arithmetic. This sort of discourse does well enough with the lamp-post for its second: to men who *may* reason calmly, it is ridiculous. The will of the many, and their interest, must very often differ; and great will be the difference when they make an evil choice. A government of five hundred country attorneys and obscure curates is not good for twenty-four millions of men, though it were chosen by eight and forty millions; nor is it the better for being guided by a dozen persons of quality, who have betrayed their trust in order to obtain that power. At present, you seem in every thing to have strayed out of the high-road of nature. The property of France does not govern it. Of course property is destroyed, and rational liberty has no existence. All you have got for the present is a paper circulation, and a stockjobbing constitution: and as to the future, do you seriously think that the territory of France, upon the republican system of eighty-three independent municipalities (to say nothing of the parts that compose them) can ever be governed as one body, or can ever be set in motion by the impulse of one mind? When the national assembly has completed its work, it will have accomplished its ruin. . . .

Government is not made in virtue of natural rights, which may and do exist in total independence of it; and exist in much greater clearness, and in a much greater degree of abstract perfection: but their abstract perfection is their practical defeat. By having a right to every thing, they want every thing. Government is a contrivance of human wisdom to provide for human *wants.* Men have a right that these wants should be provided for by this wisdom. Among these wants is to be reckoned the want, out of civil society, of a sufficient restraint upon their passions. Society requires not only that the passions of individuals should be subjected, but that even in the mass and body as well as in the individuals, the inclinations of men should frequently be thwarted, their will controlled, and their passions brought into subjection. This can only be done *by a power out of themselves*; and not, in the exercise of its function, subject to that will and to those passions which it is its office to bridle and subdue. In this sense the restraints on men, as well as their liberties, are to be reckoned among their rights. But as the liberties and the restrictions vary with times and circumstances, and admit of infinite modifications, they cannot be settled upon any abstract rule ; and nothing is so foolish as to discuss them upon that principle.

The moment you abate any thing from the full rights of men, each to govern himself, and suffer any artificial positive limitation upon those rights, from that moment the whole organization of government becomes a consideration of convenience. This it is which makes the constitution of a state, and the due distribution of its powers, a matter of the most delicate and complicated skill. It requires a deep knowledge of human nature and human necessities, and of the things which facilitate or obstruct the various ends which are to be pursued by the mechanism of civil institutions. The state is to have recruits to its strength, and remedies to its distempers. What is the use of discussing a man's abstract right to food or medicine ? The question is upon the method of procuring and administering them. In that deliberation I shall always advise to call in the aid of the farmer and the physician, rather than the professor of metaphysics.

The science of constructing a commonwealth, or renovating it, or reforming it, is, like every other experimental science, not to be taught *a priori*. Nor is it a short experience that can instruct us in that practical science ; because the real effects of moral causes are not always immediate ; but that which in the first instance is prejudicial may be excellent in its remoter operation ; and its excellence may arise even from the ill effects it produces in the beginning. . . .

The nature of man is intricate ; the objects of society are of the greatest possible complexity : and therefore no simple disposition or direction of power can be suitable either to man's nature, or to the quality of his affairs. When I hear the simplicity of contrivance aimed at and boasted of in any new political constitutions, I am at no loss to decide that the artificers are grossly ignorant of their trade, or totally negligent of their duty. The simple governments are fundamentally defective, to say no worse of them. If you were to contemplate society in but one point of view, all these simple modes of polity are infinitely captivating. In effect each would answer its single end much more perfectly than the more complex is able to attain all its complex purposes. But it is better that the whole should be imperfectly and anomalously answered, than that, while some parts are provided for with great exactness, others might be totally neglected, or perhaps materially injured, by the overcare of a favorite member.

31

Simón Bolívar's Political Ideas

Simón Bolívar (1783–1830), inspired by the ideals and success of the North American and French revolutions, led the struggle for independence in northern South America. After studying and traveling in Europe, he returned to Venezuela in 1807 to participate in the Caracas rebellion to liberate the area. In the subsequent decade, Bolívar led numerous military expeditions to end Spanish control. In 1819, he became president of the new republic of Gran Colombia, but he was unable to prevent the fragmentation of the state into Colombia, Venezuela, and Ecuador by 1830. Bolívar was important both as a military leader and as a political thinker. The following excerpts, reflecting many of his ideas on government, are from his message to the Congress of Angostura (1819), which had met to consider a proposed new constitution for Venezuela.

QUESTIONS TO CONSIDER

1. What advice did Bolívar offer to those forging new governments in Spanish America? Why did Bolívar's ideas appeal to those who advocated dictatorships as the best form of government for Latin America?
2. In light of Dana Munro's analysis of American policy in Latin America (see Reading 49), how accurate is Bolívar's argument that Latin Americans should not "consult the code of Washington"?
3. According to Bolívar, what "civic virtues" were lacking in Latin America, in contrast to the United States, that made the brand of democracy and federalism in North America an inappropriate model for Spanish America?

America, in separating from the Spanish monarchy, found herself in a situation similar to that of the Roman Empire when its enormous framework fell to pieces in the midst of the ancient world. Each Roman division then formed an independent nation in keeping with its location or interests; but this situation differed from America's in that those members proceeded to reestablish their former associations. We, on the contrary, do not even retain the vestiges of our original being. We are not Europeans; we are not Indians; we are but a mixed species of aborigines and Spaniards. Americans by birth and Europeans by law, we find ourselves engaged in a dual conflict: we are disputing with the natives for titles of ownership, and at the same time we are struggling to maintain ourselves in the country that gave us birth against the opposition of the invaders. Thus our position is most extraordinary and complicated. But there is more. As our role has always been strictly passive and our political existence nil, we find that our quest for liberty is now even more difficult of accomplishment; for we, having been placed in a state lower than slavery, had been robbed not only of our freedom but also of the right to exercise an active domestic tyranny. Permit me to explain this paradox.

In absolute systems, the central power is unlimited. The will of the despot is the supreme law, arbitrarily enforced by subordinates who take part in the organized oppression in proportion to the authority that they wield. They are charged with civil, political, military, and religious functions; but, in the final analysis, the satraps of Persia are Persian, the pashas of the Grand Turk are Turks, and the sultans of Tartary are Tartars. China does not seek her mandarins in the homeland of Genghis Khan, her conqueror. America, on the contrary, received everything

From Vicente Lecuna, comp., and Harold A. Bierck, Jr., ed., *Selected Writings of Bolívar*, vol. 1 (Caracas: Banco de Venezuela, 1951), pp. 175–180, passim. Reprinted by permission.

from Spain, who, in effect, deprived her of the experience that she would have gained from the exercise of an active tyranny by not allowing her to take part in her own domestic affairs and administration. This exclusion made it impossible for us to acquaint ourselves with the management of public affairs; nor did we enjoy that personal consideration, of such great value in major revolutions, that the brilliance of power inspires in the eyes of the multitude. In brief, Gentlemen, we were deliberately kept in ignorance and cut off from the world in all matters relating to the science of government.

Subject to the threefold yoke of ignorance, tyranny, and vice, the American people have been unable to acquire knowledge, power, or [civic] virtue. The lessons we received and the models we studied, as pupils of such pernicious teachers, were most destructive. We have been ruled more by deceit than by force, and we have been degraded more by vice than by superstition. Slavery is the daughter of Darkness: an ignorant people is a blind instrument of its own destruction. Ambition and intrigue abuse the credulity and experience of men lacking all political, economic, and civic knowledge; they adopt pure illusion as reality; they take license for liberty, treachery for patriotism, and vengeance for justice. This situation is similar to that of the robust blind man who, beguiled by his strength, strides forward with all the assurance of one who can see, but, upon hitting every variety of obstacle, finds himself unable to retrace his steps.

If a people, perverted by their training, succeed in achieving their liberty, they will soon lose it, for it would be of no avail to endeavor to explain to them that happiness consists in the practice of virtue; that the rule of law is more powerful than the rule of tyrants, because, as the laws are more inflexible, everyone should submit to their beneficent austerity; that proper morals, and not force, are the bases of law; and that to practice justice is to practice liberty. Therefore, Legislators, your work is so much the more arduous, inasmuch as you have to reeducate men who have been corrupted by erroneous illusions and false incentives. Liberty, says Rousseau, is a succulent morsel, but one difficult to digest. Our weak fellow-citizens will have to strengthen their spirit greatly before they can digest the wholesome nutriment of freedom. Their limbs benumbed by chains, their sight dimmed by the darkness of dungeons, and their strength sapped by the pestilence of servitude, are they capable of marching toward the august temple of Liberty without faltering? Can they come near enough to bask in its brilliant rays and to breathe freely the pure air which reigns therein?

Legislators, meditate well before you choose. Forget not that you are to lay the political foundation for a newly born nation which can rise to the heights of greatness that Nature has marked out for it if you but proportion this foundation in keeping with the high plane that it aspires to attain. Unless your choice is based upon the peculiar tutelary experience of the Venezuelan people — a factor that should guide you in determining the nature and form of government you are about to adopt for the well-being of the people — and, I repeat, unless you happen upon the right type of government, the result of our reforms will again be slavery. . . .

The more I admire the excellence of the federal Constitution of Venezuela, the more I am convinced of the impossibility of its application to our state. And, to my way of thinking, it is a marvel that its prototype in North America endures so successfully and has not been overthrown at the first sign of adversity or danger.

Although the people of North America are a singular model of political virtue and moral rectitude ; although the nation was cradled in liberty, reared on freedom, and maintained by liberty alone ; and — I must reveal everything — although those people, so lacking in many respects, are unique in the history of mankind, it is a marvel, I repeat, that so weak and complicated a government as the federal system has managed to govern them in the difficult and trying circumstances of their past. But, regardless of the effectiveness of this form of government with respect to North America, I must say that it has never for a moment entered my mind to compare the position and character of two states as dissimilar as the English–American and the Spanish–American. Would it not be most difficult to apply to Spain the English system of political, civil, and religious liberty ? Hence, it would be even more difficult to adapt to Venezuela the laws of North America. Does not [Montesquieu's] *L'Esprit des lois* state that laws should be suited to the people for whom they are made ; that it would be a major coincidence if those of one nation could be adapted to another ; that laws must take into account the physical conditions of the country, climate, character of the land, location, size, and mode of living of the people ; that they should be in keeping with the degree of liberty that the Constitution can sanction respecting the religion of the inhabitants, their inclinations, resources, numbers, commerce, habits, and customs ? This is the code we must consult, not the code of Washington !

America Asserts Itself

After the defeat of Napoleon, the victorious European powers joined together to preserve the postwar settlement agreed to at the Congress of Vienna in 1815. The suppression of a revolution in Spain and the restoration of the deposed king, Ferdinand VII, caused many to believe that the Europeans also hoped to restore Spanish authority in the western hemisphere, where the Latin American wars for independence had erupted. At the same time, Russia was extending her influence in the western hemisphere. In September 1821, the Tsar issued a decree claiming the west coast of North America down to the fifty-first degree of latitude and ordered foreign ships to stay away from the coastal area. Great Britain strongly objected because Russian claims threatened British interests in the Northwest. In addition, the newly independent Latin American nations had opened their ports to ships of all nations, and the British were involved in a profitable trade that had formerly been a Spanish monopoly. The result was the promulgation of the Monroe Doctrine, which remained an integral part of American foreign policy.

Apart from attempting to maintain the independence of the western hemisphere, America was influencing Europe in other ways. The American experiment with democracy appeared to reform-minded Europeans as worthy of at least selective imitation in the 1830s and 1840s. Alexis de Toqueville, a very observant traveler to America, was a member of the French Chamber of Deputies and eventually joined the opposition to King

Louis Philippe. He was active in French politics after the Revolution of 1848 until the *coup d'état* of Louis Napoleon Bonaparte restored the monarchy in a different form. In 1848, in the preface to the twelfth edition of his best-selling *Democracy in America*, he stressed the usefulness of the American model in some of its aspects for the new French Republic.

The American combination of democracy and capitalism appeared remarkably successful once again after its march had been interrupted by the American Civil War. Andrew Carnegie, as a prominent industrialist, was well qualified to extol the virtues of American progress, both in satisfying many material wants in man's pursuit of happiness and in making philanthropic projects possible on a grand scale through the sheer abundance of the wealth it produced.

32

The Monroe Doctrine

To exclude further British colonization in the western hemisphere, President Monroe included in his annual message to Congress on December 2, 1823, two key ideas — noncolonization and separation of the New World from the Old. These two concepts and the reading that follows have become known as the Monroe Doctrine.

QUESTIONS TO CONSIDER

1. How did President Monroe's statements reflect a new sense of American confidence in foreign affairs?
2. Why did the British and French ignore the presidential statement for much of the nineteenth century?
3. How have subsequent U.S. presidents interpreted the Monroe Doctrine?
4. Are there any parallels between the Monroe Doctrine and the Brezhnev Doctrine? (See Reading 83.)

. . . the American Continents, by the free and independent condition which they have assumed and maintain, are henceforth not to be considered as subjects for future colonization by any European Powers. . . .

It was stated at the commencement of the last session, that a great effort was then making in Spain and Portugal, to improve the condition of the people of those countries, and that it appeared to be conducted with extraordinary modera-

From James D. Richardson, ed., *A Compilation of the Messages and Papers of the Presidents, 1789–1902*, vol. 2 (Washington, DC: Bureau of National Literature and Art, 1903), pp. 209–219, passim.

tion. It need scarcely be remarked that the result has been so far very different from what was then anticipated. Of events in that quarter of the globe, with which we have so much intercourse and from which we derive our origin, we have always been anxious and interested spectators. The citizens of the United States cherish sentiments the most friendly in favor of the liberty and happiness of their fellowmen on that side of the Atlantic. In the wars of the European powers in matters relating to themselves, we have never taken any part, nor does it comport with our policy, so to do. It is only when our rights are invaded or seriously menaced that we resent injuries or make preparation for our defense. With the movements in this Hemisphere we are of necessity more immediately connected, and by causes which must be obvious to all enlightened and impartial observers. The political system of the allied powers is essentially different in this respect from that of America. This difference proceeds from that which exists in their respective Governments; and to the defense of our own, which has been achieved by the loss of so much blood and treasure, and matured by the wisdom of their most enlightened citizens, and under which we have enjoyed unexampled felicity, this whole nation is devoted. We owe it, therefore, to candor and to the amicable relations existing between the United States and those powers to declare that we should consider any attempt on their part to extend their system to any portions of this Hemisphere as dangerous to our peace and safety. With the existing colonies or dependencies of any European power we have not interfered and shall not interfere. But with the Governments who have declared their independence and maintained it, and whose independence we have, on great consideration and on just principles, acknowledged, we could not view any interposition for the purpose of oppressing them, or controlling in any other manner their destiny, by any European power in any other light than as the manifestation of an unfriendly disposition towards the United States. In the war between those new Governments and Spain we declared our neutrality at the time of their recognition, and to this we have adhered, and shall continue to adhere, provided no change shall occur which, in the judgement of the competent authorities of this Government, shall make a corresponding change on the part of the United States indispensable to their security. . . .

Our policy in regard to Europe, which was adopted at an early state of the wars which have so long agitated that quarter of the globe, nevertheless remains the same, which is, not to interfere in the internal concerns of any of its powers; to consider the government *de facto* as the legitimate government for us; to cultivate friendly relations with it, and to preserve those relations by a frank, firm and manly policy, meeting in all instances the just claims of every power, submitting to injuries from none. But in regard to those continents circumstances are eminently and conspicuously different. It is impossible that the allied powers should extend their political system to any portion of either continent without endangering our peace and happiness; nor can anyone believe that our southern brethren, if left to themselves, would adopt it of their own accord. It is equally impossible, therefore, that we should behold such interposition in any form with indifference. If we look to the comparative strength and resources of Spain and those new Governments, and their distance from each other, it must be obvious that she can never subdue them. It is still the true policy of the United States, to leave the parties to themselves, in the hope that other powers will pursue the same course.

33

Alexis de Tocqueville, *Democracy in America*

In 1831, Alexis de Tocqueville (1805–1859) was sent to the United States by
the French government to study American prison and rehabilitation systems
with the thought of applying some new concepts to prison reform in France.
While traveling around the United States, then at the highpoint of Jack-
sonian democracy, de Tocqueville became intrigued by the variety of forces
that made democracy function as it did in America. He was firmly convinced
that democracy in America worked to assure that the will of majorities
among the people prevailed and that it respected the rights of the population in general. His discussion of democracy in America amounts to a defense of it, in spite of his reservations about the role of the masses in
American society and his frequently critical reaction to the behavior of particular Americans he spoke with. He was, after all, representing a constitutional monarchy in his official travels in the United States.

   His classical education introduced de Tocqueville to the idea that humankind has the option of being governed by monarchical, aristocratic, or
democratic principles — or some combination of these — and, in discussing
French society, he writes as if choices among these systems were available
on an ongoing basis; however, he is convinced that Americans will be
prompted by the success of their own system to remain with democracy for
the indefinite future.

QUESTIONS TO CONSIDER

1. What aspects of American democracy does de Tocqueville stress as worthy of
   imitation?
2. What price does de Tocqueville see a nation paying for adhering to democratic
   principles?
3. On what basis does de Tocqueville link American democracy with commer-
   cialism or capitalism?

What Are the Real Advantages which American Society Derives from a Democratic Government?

Democratic laws generally tend to promote the welfare of the greatest possible
number; for they emanate from the majority of the citizens, who are subject to
error, but who cannot have an interest opposed to their own advantage. The laws

of an aristocracy tend, on the contrary, to concentrate wealth and power in the hands of the minority ; because an aristocracy, by its very nature, constitutes a minority. It may therefore be asserted, as a general proposition, that the purpose of a democracy in its legislation is more useful to humanity than that of an aristocracy. . . .

Aristocracies are infinitely more expert in the science of legislation than democracies ever can be. They are possessed of a self-control that protects them from the errors of temporary excitement ; and they form far-reaching designs, which they know how to mature till a favorable opportunity arrives. Aristocratic government proceeds with the dexterity of art ; it understands how to make the collective force of all its laws converge at the same time to a given point. . . .

How does it happen that in the United States, where the inhabitants have only recently immigrated to the land which they now occupy, and brought neither customs nor traditions with them there ; where they met one another for the first time . . . ; where, in short, the instinctive love of country can scarcely exist ; how does it happen that everyone takes as zealous an interest in the affairs of his township, his county, and the whole state as if they were his own? It is because everyone, in his sphere, takes an active part in the government of society.

The lower orders in the United States understand the influence exercised by the general prosperity upon their own welfare. . . . Besides, they are accustomed to regard this prosperity as the fruit of their own exertions. The citizen looks upon the fortune of the public as his own, and he labors for the good of the state, not merely from a sense of pride or duty, but from what I venture to term cupidity. . . . As the American participates in all that is done in his country, he thinks himself obliged to defend whatever may be censured in it ; for it is not only his country that is then attacked, it is himself. . . .

Nothing is more embarrassing in the ordinary intercourse of life than this irritable patriotism of the Americans. A stranger may well be inclined to praise many of the institutions of their country, but he begs permission to blame some things in it, a permission that is inexorably refused. America is therefore a free country in which, lest anybody should be hurt by your remarks, you are not allowed to speak freely of private individuals or of the state . . . , of the authorities, of public or private undertakings, or in short of anything at all except, perhaps the climate and the soil ; and even then Americans will be found ready to defend both as if they had cooperated in producing them. . . .

In America, the lowest classes have conceived a very high notion of political rights, because they exercise those rights ; and they refrain from attacking the rights of others in order that their own may not be violated. While in Europe the same classes sometimes resist even the supreme power, the American submits without a murmur to the authority of the pettiest magistrate. . . .

[T]he political activity that pervades the United States must be seen in order to be understood. No sooner do you set foot upon American ground than you are stunned by a kind of tumult ; a confused clamor is heard on every side, and a thousand simultaneous voices demand the satisfaction of their social wants. Everything is in motion around you ; here the people of one quarter of a town are met to decide upon the building of a church ; there the election of a representative is going on ; a little farther, the delegates of a district are hastening to the town in order to consult upon some local improvements ; in another place, the laborers of a village quit their plows to deliberate upon the project of a road or a public school. Meetings are called for the sole purpose of declaring their disapprobation of the conduct of the government; while in other assemblies citizens salute the authorities of the day as the fathers of their country. Societies are formed which regard drunkenness as the principal cause of the evils of the state, and solemnly bind themselves to give an example of temperance. . . .

To take a hand in the regulation of society and to discuss it is [an American's] biggest concern and, so to speak, the only pleasure [he] knows. This feeling pervades the most trifling habits of life; even the women frequently attend public meetings as a recreation from their household labors. Debating clubs are, to a certain extent, a substitute for theatrical entertainments: an American cannot converse, but he can discuss, and his talk falls into a dissertation. He speaks to you as if he were addressing a meeting; and if he should chance to become warm in the discussion, he will say "Gentlemen" to the person with whom he is conversing. . . . [I]f an American were condemned to confine his activity to his own affairs, he would be robbed of one half of his existence; he would feel an immense void in the life which he is accustomed to lead, and his wretchedness would be unbearable. . . .

[I]t is impossible that the lower orders should take a part in public business without extending the circle of their ideas and quitting the ordinary routine of their thoughts. The humblest individual who cooperates in the government of society acquires a certain degree of self-respect; and as he possesses authority, he can command the services of minds more enlightened than his own. He is canvassed by a multitude of applicants, and in seeking to deceive him in a thousand ways, they really enlighten him. He takes part in political undertakings which he did not originate, but which give him a taste for undertakings of the kind. New improvements are daily pointed out to him in the common property, and this gives him the desire of improving that property which is his own. . . .

Democracy does not give the people the most skillful government, but it produces what the ablest governments are frequently unable to create: namely, an all-pervading and restless activity, a superabundant force, and an energy which is inseparable from it and which may, however unfavorable circumstances may be, produce wonders. These are the true advantages of democracy.

Do you wish to give a certain elevation to the human mind and teach it to regard the things of this world with generous feelings, to inspire men with a scorn of mere temporal advantages, to form and nourish strong convictions and keep alive the spirit of honorable devotedness? Is it your object to refine the habits, embellish the manners, and cultivate the arts, to promote the love of poetry, beauty, and glory? Would you constitute a people fitted to act powerfully upon all other nations, and prepared for those high enterprises which, whatever be their results, will leave a name famous forever in history? If you believe such to be the principal object of society, avoid the government of the democracy, for it would not lead you with certainty to the goal.

But if you hold it expedient to divert the moral and intellectual activity of man to the production of comfort and the promotion of general well-being; if a clear understanding be more profitable to man than genius; if your object is not to stimulate the virtues of heroism, but the habits of peace; if you had rather witness vices than crimes, and are content to meet with fewer noble deeds, provided offenses be diminished in the same proportion; if instead of living in the midst of a brilliant society, you are contented to have prosperity around you ; if, in short, you are of the opinion that the principal object of a government is not to confer the greatest possible power and glory upon the body of the nation, but to ensure the greatest enjoyment and to avoid the most misery to each of the individuals who compose it — if such be your desire, then equalize the conditions of men and establish democratic institutions.

34

Andrew Carnegie, *Triumphant Democracy*

Born in Scotland, Andrew Carnegie (1835–1919) emigrated to the United States at the age of 13. As a young man, he invested heavily in iron and steel and by 1900 had acquired a fortune of more than a half-billion dollars. Carnegie believed that his wealth should serve the public and gave more than $350 million to charitable causes. He also became one of the most articulate champions of American business and politics.

QUESTIONS TO CONSIDER

1. Are technological progress and political democracy the best measures of American achievements?
2. Writing in 1886, Carnegie was convinced that America had achieved equality under the law. Would de Tocqueville agree? (See Reading 33.)
3. Does Carnegie's analysis refute or affirm Marx and Engels's diagnosis of capitalism? Why? (See Reading 36.)

A community of toilers with an undeveloped continent before them, and destitute of the refinements and elegancies of life — such was the picture presented by the Republic sixty years ago. Contrasted with that of to-day, we might almost conclude that we were upon another planet and subject to different primary conditions. The development of an unequaled transportation system brings the products of one section to the doors of another, the tropical fruits of Florida and California to Maine, and the ice of New England to the Gulf States. Altogether life has become vastly better worth living than it was a century ago.

Among the rural communities, the change in the conditions is mainly seen in the presence of labor-saving devices, lessening the work in house and field. Mowing and reaping machines, horse rakes, steam plows and threshers, render man's part easy and increase his productive power. Railroads and highways connect him with the rest of the world, and he is no longer isolated or dependent upon his petty

From Andrew Carnegie, *Triumphant Democracy* (New York : Scribners, 1886), pp. 164–183, passim.

village. Markets for his produce are easy of access, and transportation swift and cheap. If the roads throughout the country are yet poor compared with those of Europe, the need of good roads has been rendered less imperative by the omnipresent railroad. It is the superiority of the iron highway in America which has diverted attention from the country roads. It is a matter of congratulation, however, that this subject is at last attracting attention. Nothing would contribute so much to the happiness of life in the country as such perfect roads as those of Scotland. It is a difficult problem, but its solution will well repay any amount of expenditure necessary. [British historian Thomas] Macaulay's test of the civilization of a people — the condition of their roads — must be interpreted, in this age of steam, to include railroads. Communication between great cities is now cheaper and more comfortable than in any other country. Upon the principal railway lines, the cars — luxurious drawing-rooms by day, and sleeping chambers by night — are ventilated by air, warmed and filtered in winter, and cooled in summer. Passenger steamers upon the lakes and rivers are of gigantic size, and models of elegance.

It is in the cities that the change from colonial conditions is greatest. Most of these — indeed all, excepting those upon the Atlantic coast — have been in great measure the result of design instead of being allowed, like Topsy, to "just grow." In these modern days cities are laid out under definite, far-seeing plans; consequently the modern city presents symmetry of form unknown in mediaeval ages. The difference is seen by contrasting the crooked cowpaths of old Boston with the symmetrical, broad streets of Washington or Denver. These are provided with parks at intervals for breathing spaces; amply supplied with pure water, in some cases at enormous expense; the most modern ideas are embodied in their sanitary arrangements; they are well lighted, well policed, and the fire departments are very efficient. In these modern cities an extensive fire is rare. The lessening danger of this risk is indicated by the steady fall in the rate of fire insurance.

The variety and quality of the food of the people of America excels that found elsewhere, and is a constant surprise to Europeans visiting the States. The Americans are the best-fed people on the globe. Their dress is now of the richest character — far beyond that of any other people, compared class for class. The comforts of the average American home compare favorably with those of other lands, while the residences of the wealthy classes are unequaled. The first-class American residence of to-day in all its appointments excites the envy of the foreigner. One touch of the electric button calls a messenger; two bring a telegraph boy; three summon a policeman; four give the alarm of fire. Telephones are used to an extent undreamt of in Europe, the stables and other out-buildings being connected with the mansion; and the houses of friends are joined by the talking wire almost as often as houses of business. Speaking-tubes connect the drawing-room with the kitchen; and the dinner is brought up "piping hot" by a lift. Hot air and steam pipes are carried all over the house; and by the turning of a tap the temperature of any room is regulated to suit the convenience of the occupant. A passenger lift is common. The electric light is an additional home comfort. Indeed, there is no palace or great mansion in Europe with half the conveniences and scientific appliances which characterize the best American mansions. New York Central Park is no unworthy rival of Hyde Park and the Bois de Boulogne in its display of fine equipages;[1] and in winter the hundreds of graceful sleighs dash-

---

1. Hyde Park and the Bois de Boulogne are parks in London and Paris.

ing along the drives form a picture. The opera-houses, theatres, and public halls of the country excel in magnificence those of other lands, if we except the latter constructions in Paris and Vienna, with which the New York, Philadelphia and Chicago opera-houses rank. The commercial exchanges, and the imposing structures of the life insurance companies, newspaper buildings, hotels, and many edifices built by wealthy firms, not only in New York but in the cities of the West, never fail to excite the Europeans' surprise. The postal system is equal in every respect to that of Europe. Mails are taken up by express trains, sorted on board, and dropped at all important points without stopping. Letters are delivered several times a day in every considerable town, and a ten-cent special delivery stamp insures delivery at once by special messenger in the large cities. The uniform rate of postage for all distances, often exceeding three thousand miles, is only two cents . . . per ounce.

In short, the conditions of life in American cities may be said to have approximated those of Europe during the sixty years of which we are speaking. Year by year, as the population advances, the general standard of comfort in the smaller Western cities rises to that of the East. Herbert Spencer [an English philosopher] was astonished beyond measure at what he saw in American cities. "Such books as I had looked into," said he, "had given me no adequate idea of the immense developments of material civilization which I have found everywhere. The extent, wealth, and magnificence of your cities, and especially the splendors of New York, have altogether astonished me. Though I have not visited the wonder of the West, Chicago, yet some of your minor modern places, such as Cleveland, have sufficiently amazed me by the marvelous results of one generation's activity. Occasionally, when I have been in places of some ten thousand inhabitants, where the telephone is in general use, I have felt somewhat ashamed of our own unenterprising towns, many of which, of fifty thousand inhabitants and more, make no use of it."

Such is the Democracy ; such its conditions of life. In the presence of such a picture can it be maintained that the rule of the people is subversive of government and religion ? Where have monarchical institutions developed a community so delightful in itself, so intelligent, so free from crime or pauperism — a community in which the greatest good of the greatest number is so fully attained, and one so well calculated to foster the growth of self-respecting men — which is the end civilization seeks ?

> "For ere man made us citizens
> God made us men."

The republican is necessarily self-respecting, for the laws of his country begin by making him a man indeed, the equal of other men. The man who most respects himself will always be found the man who most respects the rights and feelings of others.

The rural democracy of America could be as soon induced to sanction the confiscation of the property of its richer neighbors, or to vote for any violent or discreditable measure, as it could be led to surrender the President for a king. Equal laws and privileges develop all the best and noblest characteristics, and these always lead in the direction of the Golden Rule. These honest, pure, contented, industrious, patriotic people really do consider what they would have others do to them. They ask themselves what is fair and right. Nor is there elsewhere in the world so conservative a body of men; but then it is the equality of the citizen — just and equal laws — republicanism, they are resolved to conserve. To conserve these they are at all times ready to fight and, if need be, to die; for, to men who have once tasted the elixir of political equality, life under unequal conditions could possess no charm.

To every man is committed in some degree, as a sacred trust, the manhood of man. This he may not himself infringe or permit to be infringed by others. Hereditary dignities, political inequalities, do infringe the right of man, and hence are not to be tolerated. The true democrat must live the peer of his fellows, or die struggling to become so.

The American citizen has no further need to struggle, being in possession of equality under the laws in every particular. He has not travelled far in the path of genuine Democracy who would not scorn to enjoy a privilege which was not the common birthright of all his fellows.

Global Revolutionary Ferment

The second quarter of the nineteenth century witnessed revolutionary movements committed to the earlier goals of limiting monarchy or replacing it with a republic, as well as new ideas such as nationalism, which was a favorite cause of the Romantics (see Reading 39), and attempts to counteract abuses of the Industrial Revolution. In Britain, the problems of the industrial age were well publicized by reports on outrageous working conditions such as those described in "Women Miners in the English Coal Pits." In Britain, however, the tradition of Parliamentary reform enabled that country to cope with the most obvious and compelling of workers' problems simply by passing new laws.

Marxism, which rejected parliamentary solutions of any sort, was very much a reaction to the abuses of the Industrial Revolution during this same period. Almost ignoring nationalism as an element in revolutionary discontent, Marxist theory established two models for future revolutions, one based on the self-destruction of capitalism, the other on pushing a backward regime over the brink with a coalition of all dissident forces. The models converge in their postrevolutionary stages: (1) dictatorship of the proletariat; (2) creation of a society of abundance; and (3) the withering away of the state.

The goals of the Taiping Rebellion in China, on the other hand, evolved from the religious inspiration of its leader, Hung Hsiu-Ch'uan [Hung Xiuquan] as he met with increasing success. These included a commitment to social equality and to nationalism, specifically the aims of freeing native Chinese from the Manchus and — although this was not evident to Western observers at first — eliminating the dominance of Europeans in parts of China. The most constant element in the Taiping revolutionary message remained moral regeneration through the acceptance of Hung's interpretation of the divine will.

35

"Women Miners in the English Coal Pits"

Political revolution was not the only catalyst changing the global experience. Great Britain was the first country to undergo an industrial revolution, fueled in large part by the abundant coal deposits of Wales, Yorkshire, and Lancashire. Mining, like textile manufacture, was an occupation that exploited women and children. Not only did women and children work for less, their small bodies and nimble limbs permitted them to crawl the narrow tunnels to mine and haul the coal much more easily than men. Despite the clear economic advantages of using women and children in the English mines, by the 1840s there was a growing concern that the social and moral consequences of this exploitation were ruining the miners' family life. Agitation for reform in the mines compelled Parliament to investigate working conditions there and enact reform legislation to correct abuses. The following Parliamentary reports printed in 1842 describe the working conditions for English women miners.

QUESTIONS TO CONSIDER

1. Why would so many women miners prefer to work in the mines without clothing? Why did the women need the heavy belts around their waists and chains between their legs?
2. What was the average work day of these female miners? What was their daily diet? What would be the social and familial cost for these female miners?
3. Karl Marx and Friedrich Engels (see Reading 36) argue that capitalism and industrialism are inherently exploitive of women so that "The bourgeois sees in his wife only an instrument of production." Based upon an analysis of this document, how would you respond to Marx and Engels's argument?

In England, exclusive of Wales, it is only in some of the colliery districts of Yorkshire and Lancashire that female Children of tender age and young and adult women are allowed to descend into the coal mines and regularly to perform the same kinds of underground work, and to work for the same number of hours, as boys and men ; but in the East of Scotland their employment in the pits is general ; and in South Wales it is not uncommon.

    West Riding of Yorkshire : Southern Part. — In many of the collieries in this district, as far as relates to the underground employment, there is no distinction of sex, but the labour is distributed indifferently among both sexes, except that it is comparatively rare for the women to hew or get the coals, although there are nu-

From Great Britain, *Parliamentary Papers*, 1842, vol. XVI, pp. 24, 196.

merous instances in which they regularly perform even this work. In great numbers of the coalpits in this district the men work in a state of perfect nakedness, and are in this state assisted in their labour by females of all ages, from girls of six years old to women of twenty-one, these females being themselves quite naked down to the waist.

'Girls', says the Sub-Commissioner [J. C. Symons], 'regularly perform all the various offices of trapping, hurrying [Yorkshire terms for drawing the loaded coal corves],[1] filling, riddling,[2] tipping, and occasionally getting, just as they are performed by boys. One of the most disgusting sights I have ever seen was that of young females, dressed like boys in trousers, crawling on all fours, with belts round their waists and chains passing between their legs, at day pits at Hunshelf Bank, and in many small pits near Holmfirth and New Mills : it exists also in several other places. I visited the Hunshelf Colliery on the 18th of January : it is a day pit ; that is, there is no shaft or descent ; the gate or entrance is at the side of a bank, and nearly horizontal. The gate was not more than a yard high, and in some places not above 2 feet.

'When I arrived at the board or workings of the pit I found at one of the side-boards down a narrow passage a girl of fourteen years of age in boy's clothes, picking down the coal with the regular pick used by the men. She was half sitting half lying at her work, and said she found it tired her very much, and 'of course she didn't like it'. The place where she was at work was not 2 feet high. Further on were men lying on their sides and getting. No less than six girls out of eighteen men and children are employed in this pit.

'Whilst I was in the pit the Rev Mr Bruce, of Wadsley, and the Rev Mr Nelson, of Rotherham, who accompanied me, and remained outside, saw another girl of ten years of age, also dressed in boy's clothes, who was employed in hurrying, and these gentlemen saw her at work. She was a nice-looking little child, but of course as black as a tinker, and with a little necklace round her throat.

'In two other pits in the Huddersfield Union I have seen the same sight. In one near New Mills, the chain, passing high up between the legs of two of these girls, had worn large holes in their trousers ; and any sight more disgustingly indecent or revolting can scarcely be imagined than these girls at work — no brothel can beat it.

'On descending Messrs Hopwood's pit at Barnsley, I found assembled round a fire a group of men, boys, and girls, some of whom were of the age of puberty ; the girls as well as the boys stark naked down to the waist, their hair bound up with a tight cap, and trousers supported by their hips. (At Silkstone and at Flockton they work in their shifts and trousers.) Their sex was recognizable only by their breasts, and some little difficulty occasionally arose in pointing out to me which were girls and which were boys, and which caused a good deal of laughing and joking. In the Flockton and Thornhill pits the system is even more indecent ; for though the girls are clothed, at least three-fourths of the men for whom they "hurry" work *stark naked,* or with a flannel waistcoat only, and in this state they assist one another to fill the corves 18 or 20 times a day : I have seen this done myself frequently.

1. These were baskets to carry the hewn coal.
2. Sifting and separating of the coal.

'When it is remembered that these girls hurry chiefly for men who are *not* their parents; that they go from 15 to 20 times a day into a dark chamber (the bank face), which is often 50 yards apart from any one, to a man working naked, or next to naked, it is not to be supposed but that where opportunity thus prevails sexual vices are of common occurrence. Add to this the free intercourse, and the rendezvous at the shaft or bullstake, where the corves are brought, and consider the language to which the young ear is habituated, the absence of religious instruction, and the early age at which contamination begins, and you will have before you, in the coal-pits where females are employed, the picture of a nursery for juvenile vice which you will go far and wide above ground to equal.'

Two Women Miners[3]

Betty Harris, age 37 : I was married at 23, and went into a colliery when I was married. I used to weave when about 12 years old; can neither read nor write. I work for Andrew Knowles, of Little Bolton (Lancs), and make sometimes 7s a week, sometimes not so much. I am a drawer, and work from 6 in the morning to 6 at night. Stop about an hour at noon to eat my dinner; have bread and butter for dinner; I get no drink. I have two children, but they are too young to work. I worked at drawing when I was in the family way. I know a woman who has gone home and washed herself, taken to her bed, been delivered of a child, and gone to work again under the week.

I have a belt round my waist, and a chain passing between my legs, and I go on my hands and feet. The road is very steep, and we have to hold by a rope; and when there is no rope, by anything we can catch hold of. There are six women and about six boys and girls in the pit I work in; it is very hard work for a woman. The pit is very wet where I work, and the water comes over our clog-tops always, and I have seen it up to my thighs; it rains in at the roof terribly. My clothes are wet through almost all day long. I never was ill in my life, but when I was lying in.

My cousin looks after my children in the day time. I am very tired when I get home at night; I fall asleep sometimes before I get washed. I am not so strong as I was, and cannot stand my work so well as I used to. I have drawn till I have had the skin off me; the belt and chain is worse when we are in the family way. My feller (husband) has beaten me many a time for not being ready. I were not used to it at first, and he had little patience.

I have known many a man beat his drawer. I have known men take liberties with the drawers, and some of the women have bastards.

Patience Kershaw, age 17, Halifax : I go to pit at 5 o'clock in the morning and come out at 5 in the evening; I get my breakfast, porridge and milk, first; I take my dinner with me, a cake, and eat it as I go; I do not stop or rest at any time for the purpose, I get nothing else until I get home, and then have potatoes and meat, not every day meat.

I hurry in the clothes I have now got on — trousers and a ragged jacket; the bald place upon my head is made by thrusting the corves; I hurry the corves a mile

3. From Great Britain, *Parliamentary Papers*, 1842, vol. XV, p. 84, and ibid., vol. XVII, p. 108.

and more under ground and back ; they weigh 3 cwt. I hurry eleven a day. I wear a belt and chain at the workings to get the corves out. The getters that I work for are naked except their caps ; they pull off all their clothes ; I see them at work when I go up.

Sometimes they beat me if I am not quick enough, with their hands ; they strike me upon my back. The boys take liberties with me sometimes ; they pull me about. I am the only girl in the pit ; there are about 20 boys and 15 men ; all the men are naked. I would rather work in mill than in coal-pit.

Note by Sub-Commissioner Scriven : This girl is an ignorant, filthy, ragged, and deplorable looking object, and such a one as the uncivilized natives of the prairies would be shocked to look upon.

36

Karl Marx and Friedrich Engels, *The Communist Manifesto*

As one of many responses to the suffering brought to European working classes by the Industrial Revolution, Karl Marx (1818–1883), a German radical writer who spent most of his life in France, Belgium, and England, formulated the philosophical and economic theories that still bear his name. In forecasting the downfall of capitalism, Marx proceeded from what he took to be demonstrable facts : (1) All new value comes from living labor. (2) In the material (or real) world, only physical labor (roughly what we would call "blue-collar labor") should be counted as productive living labor. (3) People who do not receive most of the value of what they produce are being cheated. (4) Laborers in a capitalistic system receive none of the new value of what they produce except for a mere subsistence wage. (5) Most of the new value that workers generate is taken from them by capitalists, who do no real work of their own. (6) Increasing unemployment will make the workers' lives unbearable, as competition leads capitalists to replace workers with machines.

Establishing these points as objectively true in his own mind, Marx concluded that capitalism is a system of highway robbery, which deserves not reformation but destruction. According to Marx, capitalism is plagued by a fatal contradiction in its very nature : Its efficient production generates vast quantities of goods, but its ceaseless drive to replace workers with machines renders the proletariat (working population) increasingly unemployed — thus unable to buy and consume these goods. Marx predicted that capitalism would be discredited and destroyed by a crisis of overproduction and underconsumption ; mountains of machine-made goods would remain unbought in stores and warehouses, while unemployed workers would face deprivation without hope. Marx believed that the inevitable revolution would be violent because capitalists in most places would not allow capitalism to be voted out of existence and would use force to defend the remnants of their discredited system.

The Communist Manifesto, from which the following excerpts are taken, was the earliest comprehensive statement of Marx's economic, social, and political views; today this work remains the single most representative and influential document in the history of Marxism. Friedrich Engels (1820–1895), a German textile manufacturer whose family also owned a factory in England, assisted Marx in drafting the document. Despite his very bourgeois background, Engels collaborated for nearly 40 years with Marx in producing works for publication. He also gave Marx financial support.

The *Manifesto* was written in 1847 and published early the following year to promulgate the ideas of a new group, which usually called itself the Communist League. (The term "Communist Party" was used only occasionally.) Previously, Marx and Engels had had some close associations with a group of German exiles called the League of the Just, which advocated a variety of democratic and collectivist principles. In effect, the more radical members of the League of the Just, influenced by Marx, became the nucleus of the Communist League. However, the Communist League was never very strong in members or influence and died of attrition in the early 1850s. In fact, those advocating the revolutionary theory of the *Manifesto* — including Marx and Engels themselves — were later forced by their small numbers to work with the labor reform movements they basically disliked.

It remained for Lenin (see Reading 52) in Russia to renounce the spirit of labor reform and return to advocating violent revolution as first proclaimed in the *Manifesto*.

QUESTIONS TO CONSIDER

1. Marx and Engels say there have always been class antagonisms. Why do they believe that the conflict between the bourgeoisie and the proletariat is different from previous class antagonisms?
2. What does the *Manifesto* mean by the statement that the bourgeoisie has forged the weapons that will be used against it?
3. What, according to Marx and Engels, makes it neither possible nor desirable to reform capitalism?
4. Why do Marx and Engels predict so confidently that Communist society will be free of class antagonisms?
5. Why didn't Western European capitalism self-destruct in the manner predicted by the *Manifesto*?
6. Marx and Engels wrote their *Manifesto* for the industrialized First World rather than for the underdeveloped Third World. Ironically, Marx has had more appeal in nonindustrialized Third World countries of the late twentieth century than in the First World. Why?

Confrontation between Capitalism and Communism

A specter is passing through Europe — the specter of Communism. All the powers of old Europe have joined in a holy crusade against this specter : Pope and Tsar, Metternich and Guizot, French radicals and German police. . . .

Bourgeoisie and Proletarians

The whole (written) history of society up to now has been the history of class struggles. . . .

Modern bourgeois society, rising from the ruins of feudal society, did not do away with class antagonisms. It only substituted new classes, new conditions of oppression and new forms of struggle for the old ones.

Our period, however, the bourgeois period, is distinguished by the fact that it has simplified class antagonisms. All society is splitting more and more into two great hostile camps, into two large classes opposing each other directly : bourgeoisie and proletariat. . . .

Large-scale industry established the world market for which the discovery of America had prepared the way. The world market has given unlimited development to commerce, navigation, and overland communication. This has had a reciprocal effect on the expansion of industry : the bourgeoisie has developed, increased its funds for investment, and forced all the classes left over from the Middle Ages into obscurity to the same extent that commerce, shipping, and railroad construction have expanded.

We can thus see how the modern bourgeoisie is itself the product of a long chain of developments, a series of revolutions in the way production and trade have been carried on.

Each of these stages in the development of the bourgeoisie was accompanied by corresponding political progress (of that class). The bourgeoisie — as an oppressed class under the domination of feudal lords, as an armed and self-governing association in free cities, here in control of an independent urban republic, there serving as a monarchy's tax-paying Third Estate — served to balance the power of the nobility in semi-feudal or absolute monarchies with the growth of hand-tool industry and generally became the mainstay of the large monarchies. Finally, with the establishment of large industry and the world market the bourgeoisie conquered exclusive political domination for itself in modern states with representative governments. Those holding authority in modern states are only a committee looking out for the common class interests of the bourgeoisie.

The bourgeoisie has played a highly revolutionary role in history.

Wherever the bourgeoisie has taken over, it has destroyed all feudal, patriarchal, or idyllic relationships. It has relentlessly broken all those bright, multicolored feudal ties which bound men to their natural leaders, leaving no ties between

From Karl Marx and Friedrich Engels, *Manifest der Kommunistischen Partei* (text of 1848 ; later clarifications by Engels are in parentheses). Berlin : Dietz Verlag, 1955, pp. 5–50, passim. Translated by Henry A. Myers.

man and man except naked interest, the bond of "cash payment" devoid of all feeling. It has drowned the holy ecstasies of religious fervor, of chivalrous enthusiasm, and even of top middle-class sentimentality in the ice-cold water of egotistical calculation. It has reduced personal importance to exchange value and substituted *one* single unscrupulous freedom for countless hard-earned and chartered freedoms. In a word, it has replaced exploitation veiled in religious and political illusions with open, shameless, direct and brutal exploitation.

The bourgeoisie has torn away the halo from every occupation regarded up to now with respect or awe. It has turned the physician, the attorney, the poet and the scientist into its own hired hands.

The bourgeoisie has ripped the ever so sentimental veil from family relationships and reduced them to purely monetary relations. . . .

By rapidly improving all instruments of production and by making communication infinitely easier, the bourgeoisie drags all, even the most barbarian, nations into civilization. The cheap prices of its commodities are the heavy artillery with which it levels all Chinese walls to the ground and with which it forces the most fervent hatred of barbarians for foreigners to give way. It compels all nations to adopt bourgeois methods of production if they want to survive. It forces them to introduce so-called civilization among themselves, that is, to become bourgeois. In short, the bourgeoisie creates a world in its own image.

The bourgeoisie has subjected the countryside to the rule of the city. It has raised enormous cities, greatly increasing the urban population numerically in relation to the rural one, and has thus rescued a significant part of the population from the idiocy of rural life. As it has made the countryside dependent on the city, it has also made barbarian and semi-barbarian peoples dependent on civilized peoples, agricultural populations on bourgeois ones, and the Orient on the Occident. . . .

During its class domination of scarcely one hundred years the bourgeoisie has created more colossal means of production and greater quantities of productive forces than have all past generations together. Subduing forces of nature, introducing machinery, steam navigation, railroads, and telegraphy, applying chemistry to industry and agriculture, clearing whole continents for cultivation, making rivers navigable, conjuring up whole populations to order — as if they were raising them out of the ground — what earlier century could have dreamed that such forces of production were asleep in the womb of associated labor? . . .

The weapons with which the bourgeoisie destroyed feudalism are now turned against the bourgeoisie itself.

The bourgeoisie, however, has not only forged the weapons of its own destruction but has also produced the men who will bear these weapons against them: the modern workers — the *proletarians.*

To the same extent to which the bourgeoisie — that is, capital — develops, the proletariat, the modern working class, also develops. Proletarians live only as long as they can find work, and they find work only as long as their work increases capital. These workers, who must sell themselves piecemeal, are a commodity like any other article of commerce and are therefore exposed to all the uncertainties of competition and to all the fluctuations of the market. . . .

Proletarians and Communists

What is the relationship of the Communists to the proletarians in general?

The Communists are no particular party to be contrasted with other workers' parties.

They have no interests separate from the whole proletariat.

They do not want to shape the proletarian movement in accordance with any special (sectarian) principles. The Communists are distinguished from the rest of the proletarian parties only by the fact that, on one hand, they strongly emphasize the common interests of the world proletariat independent of nationality considerations in the different national struggles of the proletarians and, on the other hand, they always represent the interests of the total movement in the different stages of development which the struggle between the proletariat and the bourgeoisie goes through.

The Communists are thus really the most committed part of workers' parties of all countries, the part which continually drives them further; their understanding of theory gives them insight into the conditions, the course, and the general outcomes of the proletarian movement in advance of the remaining mass of the proletariat.

The most immediate aim of the Communists is the same as that of all other proletarian parties: formation of the proletariat into a class, overthrow of bourgeois domination, and conquest of political power by the proletariat. . . .

On this subject, the Communists can sum up their theory in one phrase: abolition of private property.

We Communists have been accused of wanting to abolish that property which has been personally acquired through the owner's own efforts, property which is supposed to be the basis of all personal freedom, activity, and independence.

Property which has been worked for — acquired through the owner's own efforts! Are you talking about the property of the petty bourgeoisie or that of the small farmers which preceded bourgeois property? We don't need to abolish that: the development of industry has been abolishing it and is abolishing it every day.

Or are you talking about modern bourgeois private property?

Now, does the proletarian's work for wages create any property for him? In no way. It creates capital, i.e., property, which exploits wage labor and which can increase only under the condition that it produces a fresh supply of labor for wages, in order to exploit it in turn. Property in its current form is based on the antagonism of capital and wage labor. Let us observe the nature of this antagonism:

To be a capitalist means to occupy not only a purely personal but also a social position in production. Capital is a community product and can be put into motion only through the common activity of many members, indeed, in the final analysis, only through the common activity of all members of society.

Capital is thus not a personal force, but rather social power.

When capital is thus transformed into property belonging in common to all members of the community, personal property is not being changed into social property. Only the social character of property is changed. It loses its class character. . . .

In bourgeois society, living labor is only a means for increasing stored labor. In Communist society, stored labor is only a means for expanding, enriching, and improving the way workers live.

In bourgeois society, therefore, the past dominates the present; in Communist society, the present dominates the past. In bourgeois society, capital is individual and personal while the active individual person is dependent and depersonalized.

And the bourgeoisie calls the abolition of this relationship the abolition of individuality and freedom! And they are right. It is a question, to be sure, of abolishing bourgeois individuality, independence, and freedom. . . .

Elimination of the family! Even the greatest radicals are horrified over this shameful intention of the Communists.

What is the basis of the present-day family, the bourgeois family? Capital, private gain. In its completely developed form, it exists only for the bourgeoisie; however, it requires two complements to maintain it: deprivation of proletarian family life and public prostitution.

The bourgeois family will naturally disappear with the disappearance of these complements to it, and both complements will disappear when capital disappears. . . .

All bourgeois sayings about family and education, about intimate relations of trust between parents and children, are becoming all the more disgusting as all family ties are torn apart for the proletarians by the development of big industry and their children are transformed into simple articles of trade and labor.

"But you Communists want to introduce the practice of holding women in common!" the whole bourgeoisie shouts back in chorus.

The bourgeois sees in his wife only an instrument of production. He hears that instruments of production are to be utilized for the common good, and naturally he can think of nothing other than that the fate of being common property will also fall to women.

He does not suspect that the real aim is to eliminate the position of women as mere instruments of production.

By the way, nothing is more ridiculous than the highly moral indignation of our bourgeois over the alleged official "community of women" of the Communists. The Communists do not need to introduce the community of women; it has almost always existed.

Our bourgeois men, not satisfied with the fact that the wives and daughters of their proletarians are at their disposal, to say nothing of public prostitution, take great pleasure in alternately seducing each others' wives.

Bourgeois marriage is in reality a community of married women. The most Communists can be accused of is a desire to introduce an official and open community of women, to take the place of a hypocritically concealed one. It goes without saying that with the abolition of the prevailing system of production the community of women arising from it, i.e., legal and illegal prostitution, will disappear.

Communists are further accused of wanting to abolish the fatherland and nationality.

Workers have no fatherland. We cannot take from them what they do not have. When the proletariat first takes over political rule and raises itself to the (leading) class of the nation, the proletariat will be constituting itself as the nation. It will then be "national" itself, although not at all in the bourgeois sense.

More and more national differences and antagonisms are disappearing already among the peoples due to the development of the bourgeoisie, freedom of trade, the world market, the uniformity of industrial production, and the living conditions corresponding with it.

Proletarian dominance will erase them even more. United action, among the civilized countries at least, is one of the basic preconditions for liberating the proletariat.

To the extent that the exploitation of one individual by another is eliminated, the exploitation of one nation by another will be eliminated.

The hostile stance of nations towards each other will disappear as the antagonism of classes inside the nation disappears.

The charges against Communism raised on religious, philosophical and ideological grounds in general do not deserve extensive discussion.

Does it require deep insight to grasp that when human living conditions — and with them social existences and relationships — change, their images, views, and concepts, in a word, their consciousness, will change as well?

What does the history of ideas prove other than that the output of the human mind changes itself to fit changes in material production? The ruling ideas of a period have always been only the ideas of the ruling class. . . .

In short, the Communists support every movement everywhere against existing social and political conditions.

In all these movements, they emphasize the property issue, regardless of how pronounced or faintly developed it is perceived to be, as the fundamental issue of the movement.

Finally, the Communists work everywhere for mutual understanding and support among the democratic parties of all countries.

The Communists scorn any concealment of their views and intentions. They declare openly that their goals can be reached only through the violent overthrow of all social structures which have existed previously. Let the ruling classes tremble at the prospect of a Communist Revolution. The proletarians have nothing to lose from it but their chains. They have a world to win.

Proletarians of all countries, unite!

37

The Taiping Rebellion

In the middle of the nineteenth century, China, under Manchu rule, was confronted with a dynastic crisis. British and French gunboats threatened China from the south, and the Russians encroached upon its territories from the north. Weakness, corruption, and rebellion spread across the land. By far the most serious rebellion was the Taiping Rebellion (1851–1864), started by Hung Hsiu-Ch'uan [Hong Xiuquan] (1814–1864).

The son of a farmer in southern China, Hung aspired to become an Imperial government official. After repeatedly failing the government service examinations, he fell ill in despair; in delirium he saw Jesus Christ, whom he called his Elder Brother. As the Heavenly Younger Brother of Christ, Hung came to believe that he was called to save humankind as the new messiah. His earlier contacts with the Reverend Issachar Roberts, an American Southern Baptist missionary, probably induced Hung's visions. By the late 1840s, his organization, called the God Worshippers Society, had built a large following. Most of his followers were the frustrated and disaffected of southern China who were drawn to Hung's blend of Christian and Chinese ideology.

As his movement grew it spread northward, defeating Imperial troops dispatched to crush the rebellion. In 1851, Hung bestowed upon himself the title of Heavenly King of the "Heavenly Kingdom of Great Peace" ("Taiping Tien-kuo [Taiping Dianquo]"). Within two years, his rebellion had captured Nanking [Nanjing], the second city of the empire, and established a theocratic-military government. The policies of the Taiping leaders in the early period reflected their puritanical spirit. They prohibited opium-smoking, gambling, the use of tobacco and wine, polygamy, the sale of slaves, and prostitution. Their egalitarian ideas, including the equality of the sexes, were reflected in the abolition of footbinding and in the appointment of women as administrators and officers in the Taiping army. They also tried to abolish the private ownership of land and property, and they developed a program for the equal distribution of land. Many of the Taiping programs were thus quite unprecedented and revolutionary in nature. But the initial vigor and idealism were soon lost amid power struggles among the leaders, strategic blunders, poor diplomacy, and corruption. The rebellion faded by the summer of 1864.

The following excerpt is from the basic document of the Taiping Kingdom, called "The Land System of the Heavenly Kingdom." It is a sort of Taiping constitution. This document, first published in 1853, did not confine itself only to the land system but also included programs and policies related to military, civil, religious, financial, judicial, and educational institutions.

QUESTIONS TO CONSIDER

1. What were the egalitarian programs of the Taiping Kingdom?
2. How Christian was the Taiping ideology? How Chinese was it?
3. In what way was the Taiping Rebellion unique in the history of Chinese rebellions?
4. Are there any connections between the Taiping revolutionary programs and those of the French Revolution? (See Reading 28).

All fields are to be divided into nine grades : every *mou*[1] of land, which during the two seasons, both early and late,[2] can produce 1,200 catties [of grain] shall be ranked as a superior field of the first class ; every *mou* that produces 1,100 catties as a superior field of the second class ; and every *mou* that produces 1,000 catties as a superior field of the third class. Every *mou* that produces 900 catties shall be considered as a medium field of the first class ; every *mou* that produces 800 catties as a medium field of the second class ; and every *mou* that produces 700 catties as a medium field of the third class. Every *mou* that produces 600 catties shall be considered as an inferior field of the first class ; every *mou* that produces 500 catties as an inferior field of the second class ; and every *mou* that produces 400 catties as an inferior field of the third class. One *mou* of superior field of the first class shall be considered equal to a *mou* and one-tenth of a superior field of the second class, and to a *mou* and two-tenths of a superior field of the third class ; also to a *mou* and three-and-a-half tenths of a medium field of the first class, to a *mou* and five-tenths of a medium field of the second class, and to a *mou* and seven-and-a-half tenths of a medium field of the third class ; also to two *mou* of an inferior field of the first class, to two *mou* and four-tenths of an inferior field of the second class, and to three *mou* of an inferior field of the third class.

The division of land must be according to the number of individuals, whether male or female ; calculating upon the number of individuals in a household, if they be numerous, then the amount of land will be larger, and if few, smaller ; and it shall be a mixture of the nine classes. If there are six persons in a family, then for three there shall be good land and for three poorer land, and of good and poor each shall have half. All the fields in the empire are to be cultivated by all the people alike. If the land is deficient in one place, then the people must be removed to another, and if the land is deficient in another, then the people must be removed to this place. All the fields throughout the empire, whether of abundant or deficient harvest, shall be taken as a whole : if this place is deficient, then the harvest of that abundant place must be removed to relieve it, and if that place is deficient, then the harvest of this abundant place must be removed in order to relieve the deficient place ; thus, all the people in the empire may together enjoy the abundant happiness of the Heavenly Father, Supreme Lord and Great God. There being fields, let all cultivate them ; there being food, let all eat ; there being clothes, let all be dressed ; there being money, let all use it, so that nowhere does inequality exist, and no man is not well fed and clothed.

All men and women, every individual of sixteen years and upwards, shall receive land, twice as much as those of fifteen years of age and under. Thus, those sixteen of years of age and above shall receive a *mou* of superior land of the first class, and those of fifteen years and under shall receive half that amount, five-tenths of a *mou* of superior land of the first class ; again, if those of sixteen years and above receive three *mou* of inferior land of the third class, then those of fif-

From Franz Michael, *The Taiping Rebellion : History and Documents*, vol. 2, *Documents and Comments* (Seattle : University of Washington Press, 1971), pp. 313–315, 319–320. © 1971 by the University of Washington Press. Reprinted by permission of the University of Washington Press.

    1. One acre equals 6.6 *mou*.
    2. I.e., a two-crop harvest.

teen years and below shall receive half that amount, one and one-half *mou* of inferior land of the third class.

Throughout the empire the mulberry tree is to be planted close to every wall, so that all women may engage in rearing silkworms, spinning the silk, and making garments. Throughout the empire every family should keep five hens and two sows, which must not be allowed to miss their proper season. At the time of harvest, every sergeant shall direct the corporals to see to it that of the twenty-five families under his charge each individual has a sufficient supply of food, and aside from the new grain each may receive, the remainder must be deposited in the public granary. Of wheat, pulse, hemp; flax, cloth, silk, fowls, dogs, etc., and money, the same is true; for the whole empire is the universal family of our Heavenly Father, the Supreme Lord and Great God. . . . For every twenty-five families there must be established one public granary, and one church where the sergeant must reside. Whenever there are marriages, or births, or funerals, all may go to the public granary; but a limit must be observed, and not a cash be used beyond what is necessary. Thus, every family which celebrates a marriage or a birth will be given one thousand cash and a hundred catties of grain. . . .

In every circle of twenty-five families, the work of the potter, the blacksmith, the carpenter, the mason, and other artisans must all be performed by the corporal and privates; when free from husbandry they are to attend to these matters. Every sergeant, in superintending marriages and funeral events in the twenty-five families, should in every case offer a eucharistic sacrifice to our Heavenly Father, the Supreme Lord and Great God; all corrupt ceremonies of former times are abolished.

In every circle of twenty-five families, all young boys must go to church every day, where the sergeant is to teach them to read the Old Testament and the New Testament, as well as the book of proclamations of the true ordained Sovereign. Every Sabbath the corporals must lead the men and women to the church, where the males and females are to sit in separate rows. There they will listen to sermons, sing praises, and offer sacrifices to our Heavenly Father, the Supreme Lord and Great God. . . .

In the creation of an army, for each 13,156 families there must first be a corps general; next there must be five colonels under the command of the corps general; next there must be five captains under the command of each colonel, altogether twenty-five captains; next each of the twenty-five captains must have under his command five lieutenants, altogether 125 lieutenants; next each of the 125 lieutenants must have under his command four sergeants, altogether 500 sergeants; next each of the 500 sergeants must have under his command five corporals, altogether 2,500 corporals; next each of the 2,500 corporals must have under his command four privates, altogether 10,000 privates, the entire army numbering altogether 13,156 men.

After the creation of an army, should the number of families increase, with the increase of five families there shall be an additional corporal; with the increase of twenty-six families there shall be an additional sergeant; with the increase of 105 families there shall be an additional lieutenant; with the increase of 526 families there shall be an additional captain; with the increase of 2,631 families there shall be an additional colonel; with the total increase of 13,156 families there shall be an additional corps general. Before a new corps general is appointed, the colonel and subordinate officers shall remain under the command of the old corps general; with the appointment of a corps general they must be handed over to the command of the new corps general.

Within [the court] and without, all the various officials and people must go every Sabbath to hear the expounding of the Holy Bible, reverently offer their sacrifices, and worship and praise the Heavenly Father, the Supreme Lord and Great God. On every seventh seven, the forty-ninth day, the Sabbath, the colonel, captains, and lieutenants shall go in turn to the churches in which reside the sergeants under their command and expound the Holy books, instruct the people, examine whether they obey the Commandments and orders or disobey the Commandments and orders, and whether they are diligent or slothful. On the first seventh seven, the forty-ninth day, the Sabbath, the colonel shall go to a certain sergeant's church, on the second seventh seven, the forty-ninth day, the Sabbath, the colonel shall then go to another sergeant's church, visiting them all in order, and after having gone the round he must begin again. The captains and lieutenants shall do the same.

Each man throughout the empire who has a wife, sons, and daughters amounting to three or four mouths, or five, six, seven, eight, or nine mouths, must give up one to be a soldier. With regard to the others, the widowers, widows, orphaned, and childless, the disabled and sick, they shall all be exempted from military service and issued provisions from the public granaries for their sustenance.

Throughout the empire all officials must every Sabbath, according to rank and position, reverently present sacrificial animals and offerings, sacrifice and worship, and praise the Heavenly Father, the Supreme Lord and Great God. They must also expound the Holy books; should any dare to neglect this duty, they shall be reduced to husbandmen. Respect this.

Nationalism: Romantics and Realists

Although *Romanticism* stressed a love of nature, the Romantics' view of what was natural and good differed from that held by most eighteenth-century intellectuals during the Enlightenment.

People of the Enlightenment had placed a high value on peace and tranquility. They called the events in England in 1688–1689 the "Glorious Revolution" because it achieved constitutional government with so little apparent bloodshed and praised the American Revolution in the years that immediately followed it for *not* ushering in a period of class-based violence. Many Romantics, on the other hand, saw life itself as an endless struggle in which they were duty bound to participate on the side of justice. We find Romantics entering into the class conflicts of the nineteenth century, usually on the side of the workers, and taking up such causes as the Greek war for liberation from the Turks.

Nationalism was fairly central to the thinking of most Romantics, who rejected the eighteenth-century notion that the universality of man overshadowed ethnic-group differences. They applied the idea that nature delighted in a splendid diversity of peoples and societies. This put them in a radical position after the Treaty of Vienna, which assigned many nationalities to multinational empires and effectively kept some other nationalities, notably the Germans and Italians, from moving toward national union. Even though Romantics generally backed armed conflict for idealistic causes, they did not condone war waged for the old eighteenth-century reasons of dynastic succession or mere balance of power without regard for national identities or higher goals.

Realism challenged Romanticism as an intellectual and cultural force during the last half of the nineteenth century in novels such as Gustave Flaubert's *Madame Bovary,* which focuses on the dullness of middle-class marriage and an intelligent woman's justified despair at its confines, and Émile Zola's *Germinal* with its meticulous attention to detail in portraying the lives of coal-mining families. The Realists in literature and art were committed to portraying life as it really was, but this did not prevent some of them from fervently espousing just causes. Zola, for example, passionately defended Major Alfred Dreyfus, who was falsely accused of treason, as a victim of anti-Jewish prejudice, and Zola faced imprisonment for libel as a result of his journalistic attacks. When realism became a slogan in later nineteenth-century politics, however, it generally referred to using means that work effectively to achieve goals unattainable by "idealists" living in a world of illusions and having moral values too high for the "real" world.

38

Robert Southey, "The Battle of Blenheim"

Robert Southey (1774–1843), English poet, essayist, and historian, illustrates the Romantics' aversion to wars fought for abstract reasons of state or for the acquisition of seemingly random territory. The historical Battle of Blenheim, which took place about 25 miles from Augsburg in Bavaria, had been a major victory for the British, the Austrians, and their allies in the War of the Spanish Succession (1701–1714). In the recounting of the battle in Southey's poem, old Kaspar is not only ignorant of any idea why it was fought but has lost track of the fact that the main "heroes," the Duke of Marlborough and the Austrian Prince Eugene, were on the *other* side, fighting the French and Bavarian forces.

QUESTIONS TO CONSIDER

1. Why might a Romantic poet have condemned the War of the Spanish Succession as not worth the human sacrifices it demanded?
2. What is Southey's view of the sentiments of children in the poem? How do the words of Wilhelmine and Peterkin reflect the Romantics' view of children in general?
3. What, in Kaspar's view, made the victory at Blenheim a great one?

It was a summer evening,
Old Kaspar's work was done,
And he before his cottage door
Was sitting in the sun,
And by him sported on the green
His little grandchild Wilhelmine.

She saw her brother Peterkin
Roll something large and round,
Which he beside the rivulet
In playing there had found;
He came to ask what he found,
That was so large, and smooth, and round.

Old Kaspar took it from the boy,
Who stood expectant by;
And then the old man shook his head,
And, with a natural sigh,
"'Tis some poor fellow's skull," said he,
"Who fell in the great victory."

"I find them in the garden,
For there's many here about;
And often when I go to plough,
The ploughshare turns them out!
For many thousand men," said he,
"Were slain in that great victory."

"Now tell us what 'twas all about,"
Young Peterkin, he cries;
And little Wilhelmine looks up
With wonder-waiting eyes;
"Now tell us all about the war,
And what they fought each other for."

Poems of Robert Southey, edited by Maurice H. Fitzgerald (London : Henry Frowde, 1909), pp. 365–366. (First published 1798)

"It was the English," Kaspar cried,
"Who put the French to rout;
But what they fought each other for,
I could not well make out;
But everybody said," quoth he,
"That 'twas a famous victory.

"My father lived at Blenheim then,
Yon little stream hard by;
They burnt his dwelling to the ground,
And he was forced to fly;
So with his wife and child he fled,
Nor had he where to rest his head.

"With fire and sword the country round
Was wasted far and wide,
And many a childling mother then,
And new-born baby died;
But things like that, you know, must be
At every famous victory.

"They say it was a shocking sight
After the field was won;
For many thousand bodies here
Lay rotting in the sun;
But things like that, you know, must be
After a famous victory.

"Great praise the Duke of Marlbro' won,
And our good Prince Eugene."
"Why 'twas a very wicked thing!"
Said little Wilhelmine.
"Nay .. nay .. my little girl," quoth he,
"It was a famous victory.

"And every body praised the Duke
Who this great fight did win."
"But what good came of it at last?"
Quoth little Peterkin.
"Why that I cannot tell," said he,
"But 'twas a famous victory."

39

Heinrich von Treitschke, Conquest and National Greatness

Heinrich von Treitschke (1834–1896) typifies the nationalistic orientation of the later Romantic period, in which the earlier notion of a harmonious symphony of the talents of all nationalities gave way to strident assertions of the superiority of the writer's own culture. Treitschke was a professor of history and writer of historical works most of his life and used history effectively in support of political ideology. Elected to the new German Reichstag in 1871, he supported the Bismarckian order of things wholeheartedly, including the *Kulturkampf,* designed to give the new Germany an anti-Catholic identity. Treitschke portrayed the subjection of state interests to religious leadership as decadent and typical of the Orient where, in his mind, the other-worldly aspects of religions such as Hinduism and Buddhism kept people from mastering worthwhile knowledge and achieving progress.

Since Treitschke was convinced (1) that theocratic rule was decadent and Oriental and (2) that the papacy had some aim to exert Church power over state decision-makers, it followed that he believed that the papacy was the sort of institution that would have been more at home in Asia than in Europe. In addition, its Roman Catholic supporters could not be really good citizens of any European country, least of all a country committed to Protestantism and progress, which he saw as going together naturally in the new German Empire under Prussian leadership. Like Bismarck, Treitschke was more of a Prussian nationalist than a German one and saw the new united Germany best served by a stress on the Prussian military orientation and doctrine of unswerving loyalty to the state.

QUESTIONS TO CONSIDER

1. How does Treitschke see the relationship between state and society?
2. What makes Treitschke take such a positive view of war?
3. Just why does Treitschke seem to prefer a strong, centrally run state to one characterized by checks and balances?
4. Why are Oriental rulers supposed to have an easy time of it as they hold their subjects down in repressive systems?
5. Why do the Russians get along better with Muslims than with non-Russian Christians?

Society, the State, and War

Society is a confused mess of all possible interests struggling against each other, and if left to itself society would soon become a war of all against all. Law, peace, and order can never emerge from the multiplicity of social interests in their eternal struggle with each other, but only from that power which stands over society, the state furnished with power enough to tame the wild passions of society. Only when we realize this do we begin to have an inkling of what we may call the moral holiness of the state, for it is the state which brings justice and mutual protection into this world of social struggles. . . .

The state is the people [or "nation" (*Volk*)] united by law as an independent power. . . . We know the state as a real entity, not any personified legal fiction. Society, however, has no uniform will: We have no *social* obligations to fulfill. My whole life long it has never occurred to me to think of society in connection with obligations: In that context, I think only of my people or nation, whose honor I attempt to increase as much as I can. . . .

Ideally we should have a balance of political (or state-related) and social activity. The nation tends to bring this about automatically in that it bestirs itself after time periods of irregular duration through war. War is the prime example of politics in action. Over and over again we see the proposition confirmed that the people become a real people or nation only in war. Only great deeds performed in common with the fatherland in mind can forge a bond sufficient to hold a people together. A state with independent constitutional authority, however, can accomplish on a daily basis what war brings about from time to time as a radical bit of medication. Here it is worth noting that the independently functioning organs of the state are more important than what goes on in parliaments for maintaining the balance between political and social activity, for they draw the better citizens into serving the daily needs of the state. . . .

It is a false conclusion people reach when they say that wars are waged for the sake of material things: Modern wars are *not* waged for plundering the material assets of other nations. The key factor is actually the high moral good of national honor, transmitted from generation to generation, which has something absolutely holy in it and requires the individual to sacrifice himself for it. This good remains priceless: It cannot be valued in banknotes and coins. . . . Fichte put all this beautifully[1] when he said that the individual human being sees the realization of his earthly eternity in his fatherland. . . . True, living political consciousness is being conscious of working with the active state, standing upon the achievements of our fathers in order to pass them on to our grandchildren. . . .

The whole theory of three branches of government and their separation has nothing to do with the real world; it is playing games with imaginary concepts. The essence of the state is seen specifically in its unity, and the state is best organized when these powers are unified in the highest hand and an independent one.

From Heinrich von Treitschke, *Politik. Vorlesungen gehalten an der Universität zu Berlin* (Leipzig: Hirzel: 1897–1911), Vol. I, pp. 1–25; Vol. II, pp. 3–339, passim. Translated by Henry A. Myers.

1. Johann Gottlieb Fichte (1762–1814), German philosopher and one of the earliest advocates of German nationalism.

The Theocratic Mindset of the Oriental

The development of theocracies is a given state of affairs for the Oriental with his dream-life, his limited drive to seek out truth, and his need for an authoritarian belief system: This is demonstrated by the incredible longevity [of Oriental states]. If a people can once be mastered by such stifling beliefs and stationary ways of looking at the world as theirs, the state power built on such a mindset will be able to achieve such a subjection of the population and such a duration of rule as few governments of [our part of] the world could ever obtain. . . . In confronting the theocracies of the East, the feeling comes naturally to us that they correspond to the moral development of the people who live under them. . . .

Among all the theocracies of the ancient Orient, we find this [Biblical] one of ancient Israel the most appealing; however, the power to expand, which is characteristic of other theocracies is lacking in it. Foreign policy was never the strength of the Israelites. . . . The Jews conquered now and then, to be sure, but with a very mediocre rate of success. We know very well that a fatherland is the basis of all political greatness and equally well we should know that a people with no fatherland reveals the opposite of real political talent. To be able to apply political talent, it is necessary to possess courage and living love for your people and land. The modern Jew continues to display the opposite of anything which can be called positive, political sense. For this reason it is a truly monstrous state of affairs among us today that the Jews dominate the political press.

Germanic and Russian Monarchies

The kingship of our ancient Germanic past . . . carried the seeds of a great development within it. In general, something noble — even if phantasy-filled and not yet clarified — always characterizes the ancient Germans. Their mythology reveals a splendid imagination where divine things are concerned, one such as not even the ancient Greeks possessed. The thought of a different world to come was already coming to life among them. . . .

Nowadays . . . absolute monarchy is to be found only in one country anywhere in Europe: in Russia. There that governmental form is rooted in the cultural conditions of the people, that is, their social relationships and their lifelong customs. Given rulers of adequate insight there, the system is assured of a long life. It is quite wrong to place — as the radicals among us do — Russian absolutism on the same level with any Prussian equivalent. While the Russian Empire is indeed a half-Asiatic one, our radicals themselves fall into a half-Oriental mindset in misperceiving the German Kaiser's role. The White Tsar is not only the absolute secular ruler, but he heads the Orthodox Church in Russia as well. . . .

Still, external circumstances may induce the [Russian] state not to be so strict in demanding religious conformity. In confronting Muhammedans, this has been particularly true; toward them the Russian Church has always been more tolerant than toward Protestants and Roman Catholics. In dealing with Kirghizes, Kalmuks, and whatever the rest of those appetizing peoples of the Orient may call themselves, pressure for religious conformity serves no valid purpose. The Russians, as half-Orientals, make intuitive use of their natural skills in dealing with Muslims; at the same time, the Muhammedans have the instinctive feeling that Asia halfway owns the Russians. . . .

Whoever judges things objectively is forced to agree that since the Great Elector the political history of Germany has been contained in Prussian history. Every clod of soil which through the sins of the old [Holy Roman / Austrian] emperorship was lost and then won back again owed its recovery to Prussian efforts. . . .

Finally we come to those men of genius who appeared on the stage of history when the spirit of the age recognized them and called upon them to act: Wilhelm I, Bismarck, and Roon, and now we see the decisive struggle of 1866 [the Austro-Prussian War] take place. What did it bring about? Against the will of the rest of Germany, it allowed the Prussian state to create a constitution with its good sword.

40

Otto von Bismarck, Making German Patriotism Effective

Prince Otto von Bismarck (1815–1898) read and admired Romantic literature as a young man. As a main force in the unification of Germany through armed struggle, Bismarck was a hero to many Romantics of his day, such as Treitschke. At the same time, Bismarck was the ultimate *Realpolitiker* or practitioner of pragmatic, ends-justify-the-means measures in serving the Prussian state and later the German Empire. Then as now, Realism and Romanticism stood at opposite ends of an ideological spectrum. Some of the earlier German Romantic revolutionary activists, such as the poet Georg Herwegh, thoroughly rejected Bismarck for practicing a sordid and cynical set of policies to achieve power for his state. What follows is Bismarck's own estimate of what for him was the erratic but probably serviceable nature of German nationalism.

QUESTIONS TO CONSIDER

1. Why might Bismarck indeed be classified among the Romantic thinkers and doers of the nineteenth century?
2. What is distinctly un-Romantic about Bismarck's approach to political activity?
3. How realistic was Bismarck's assessment of German nationalism? Were his remedies for the flaws, as he perceived them, well chosen? Was he correct in emphasizing the need for attachment to a dynasty to make German nationalism durable?

In order that German patriotism should be active and effective, it needs as a rule to hang on the peg of independence upon a dynasty; independent of a dynasty, it rarely comes to the rising point, though in theory it daily does so, in parliament, in the press, in public meeting, in practice the German needs either attachment to a dynasty or the goad of anger, hurrying him into action : the latter phenomenon, however, by its own nature is not permanent. It is as a Prussian, a Hanoverian, a Wurtemberger, a Bavarian or a Hessian, rather than as a German, that he is disposed to give unequivocal proof of patriotism; and in the lower order and the parliamentary groups it will be long before otherwise. We cannot say that the Hanoverian, Hessian, and other dynasties were at any special pains to win the affections of their subjects; but nevertheless the German patriotism of their subjects is essentially conditioned by their attachment to the dynasty after which they call themselves. It is not differences of stock, but dynastic relations upon which in their origin the centrifugal elements repose. It is not attachment to Swabian, Lower Saxon, Thuringian, or other particular stock that counts for most, but the dynastic incorporation with the people of some severed portion of ruling princely family, as in the instances of Brunswick, Brabant, and Wittlesbach dynasties. The cohesion of the kingdom of Bavaria does not rest merely on the Bavarian stock as it is found in South Bavaria and in Austria : the Swabian of Augsburg, the Alleman of the Palatinate, the Frank of the Main, though of widely different blood, call themselves Bavarians with as much satisfaction as does the Old-Bavarian at Munich or Landshut, and for no other reason than that they have been connected with the latter for three generations through the common dynasty. It is to dynastic influences that those stocks which present the most marked characteristics, as the Low-German, the Platt-Deutsch, the Saxon, owe their greater depth and distinctness of differentiation. The German's love of Fatherland has need of a prince on whom it can concentrate its attachment. Suppose that all the German dynasties were suddenly deposed; there would then be no likelihood that German national sentiment would suffice to hold all Germans together from the point of view of international law amid the friction of European politics, even in the form of federated Hanse towns and imperial village communes. The Germans would fall a prey to more closely welded nations if they once lost the tie which resides in the princes' sense of community of rank.

History shows that in Germany the Prussian stock is that of which the individual character is most strongly stamped, and yet no one could decisively answer the question whether, supposing the Hohenzollern dynasty and all its rightful successors to have passed away, the political cohesion of Prussia would survive. Is it quite certain that the eastern and the western divisions, that Pomeranians and Hanoverians, natives of Holstein and Silesia, of Aachen and Konigsberg, would then continue as they now are, bound together in the indisruptable unity of the Prussian state ? Or Bavaria — if the Wittelsbach dynasty were to vanish and leave not a trace behind, would Bavaria continue to hold together in isolated unity ? Some dynasties have many memories which are not exactly of the kind to inspire

From Bismarck's *Memoires,* cited in *Otto von Bismarck, The Man and the Statesman,* selection of works translated by A. J. Butler (London : Smith, Elder & Co., 1898), vol. I, pp. 314–322, passim.

attachment in the heterogeneous fragments out of which their states have, as a matter of history, been formed. . . .

The other nations of Europe have need of no such go-between for their patriotism and national sentiment. Poles, Hungarians, Italians, Spaniards, Frenchmen would under any or without any dynasty preserve their homogeneous national unity. The Teutonic stocks of the north, the Swedes and the Danes, have shown themselves pretty free from dynastic sentiment; and in England, though external respect for the Crown is demanded by good society, and the formal maintenance of monarchy is held expedient by all parties that have hitherto had any share in government, I do not anticipate the disruption of the nation, or that such sentiments as were common in the time of the Jacobites would attain to any practical form if in the course of its historical development the British people should come to deem a change of dynasty or the transition to a republican form of government necessary or expedient. The preponderance of dynastic attachment, and the use of a dynasty as the indispensable cement to hold together a definite portion of the nation calling itself by the name of the dynasty is a specific peculiarity of the German Empire. The particular nationalities, which among us have shaped themselves on the bases of dynastic family and possession, include in most cases heterogeneous elements, whose cohesion rests neither on identity of stock nor on similarity of historical development, but exclusively on the fact of some (in most cases questionable) acquisition by the dynasty whether by the right of the strong, or hereditary succession by affinity or compact of inheritance, or by some reversionary grant obtained from the imperial Court as the price of a vote.

Whatever may be the origin of this factitious union of particularist elements, its result is that the individual German readily obeys the command of a dynasty to harry with fire and sword, and with his own hands to slaughter his German neighbors and kinsfolk as a result of quarrels unintelligible to himself. To examine whether this characteristic be capable of rational justification is not the problem of a German statesman, so long as it is strongly enough pronounced for him to reckon upon it. The difficulty of either abolishing or ignoring it, or making any advance in theory towards unity without regard to this practical limitation, has often proved fatal to the champions of unity.

EMPIRES AND UPHEAVALS

England's Imperial March

The British gained footholds in India, particularly in Bengal in northeast India, through the British East India Company, a privately owned "joint stock company" founded for conducting trade. Supported from time to time by British military strength, the Company took on many of the characteristics of a colonial government in the areas it controlled during the last half of the eighteenth century. The Governor-General of the Company was appointed in large part to carry out the policies of the British Prime Minister and Parliament, which established a Board of Control in 1784 to direct the Company's political activities.

In strengthening the British economic and military position in India, Company officials first attempted to leave Muslim and Hindu religious laws intact, as a sign of British commitment to religious toleration. Eventually, however, high Company officials found some native religious customs intolerable and, with the consent of the Board of Control, began to prohibit them. For example, the practice of getting rid of unwanted newborn infants was tolerated by Hindu custom, but infanticide was a crime by British standards, and consequently the East India Company prohibited it. A highly symbolic case for the Company and its Board was that of *sati* (or *suddhee*), a custom of higher Hindu castes that required widows to burn themselves on their husbands' funeral pyres. By the 1820s, some officials of the Company were not only repulsed by *sati* but had become convinced that — as far as the widows themselves were concerned — it was no longer necessarily a voluntary religious act. Reports had reached officials of men tying widows to their husbands' corpses and standing nearby with long poles to beat the women back into the fire if they tried to escape after the ropes burned through.

The pros and cons of intervening in these cases are weighed in the following selection by Lord William Bentinck, who was appointed Governor-General of the East India Company in 1828.

41

Lord William Bentinck, Comments on Ritual Murder and the Limits of Religious Toleration

QUESTIONS TO CONSIDER

1. Why does Bentinck think it advisable and necessary for the Company to abolish the custom of *sati*?
2. What does *sati* have to do with the British policy of religious toleration?
3. What reaction does Bentinck expect from the Hindus if *sati* is abolished?
4. If *sati* is abolished, what advice does he give for handling possible violations?
5. Would you have approached this situation in the same way as Bentinck or would you have used different reasoning?

Whether the question be to continue or to discontinue the practice of *sati*, the decision is equally surrounded by an awful responsibility. To consent to the consignment year after year of hundreds of innocent victims to a cruel and untimely end, when the power exists of preventing it, is a predicament which no conscience can contemplate without horror. But, on the other hand, if heretofore received opinions are to be considered of any value, to put to hazard by a contrary course the very safety of the British Empire in India, and to extinguish at once all hopes of those great improvements — affecting the condition not of hundreds and thousands but of millions — which can only be expected from the continuance of our supremacy, is an alternative which even in the light of humanity itself may be considered as a still greater evil. It is upon this first and highest consideration alone, the good of mankind, that the tolerance of this inhuman and impious rite can in my opinion be justified on the part of the government of a civilized nation. While the solution of this question is appalling from the unparalleled magnitude of its possible results, the considerations belonging to it are such as to make even the stoutest mind distrust its decision. On the one side, Religion, Humanity, under the most appalling form, as well as vanity and ambition — in short, all the most powerful influences over the human heart — are arrayed to bias and mislead the judgment. On the other side, the sanction of countless ages, the example of all the Mussulman conquerors, the unanimous concurrence in the same policy of our own most able rulers, together with the universal veneration of the people, seem authoritatively to forbid, both to feeling and to reason, any interference in the exercise of their natural prerogative. In venturing to be the first to deviate from this practice it becomes me to show that nothing has been yielded to feeling, but that reason, and reason alone, has governed the decision.

From "Lord William Bentinck on the Suppression of *Sati*, 8 November 1829," in *Speeches and Documents on Indian Policy, 1750–1921*, ed. Arthur B. Keith (Oxford : Oxford University Press, 1922), vol. 1, pp. 208–226.

It must be first observed that of the 463 *satis* occurring in the whole of the Presidency of Fort William, 420 took place in Bengal, Behar, and Orissa, or what is termed the Lower Provinces, and of these latter 287 in the Calcutta Division alone.

It might be very difficult to make a stranger to India understand, much less believe, that in a population of so many millions of people as the Calcutta Division includes, and the same may be said of all the Lower Provinces, so great is the want of courage and of vigour of character, and such the habitual submission of centuries, that insurrection or hostile opposition to the will of the ruling power may be affirmed to be an impossible danger. . . .

If, however, security was wanting against extensive popular tumult or revolution, I should say that the Permanent Settlement, which, though a failure in many other respects and in its most important essentials, has this great advantage at least, of having created a vast body of rich landed proprietors deeply interested in the continuance of the British Dominion and having complete command over the mass of the people. . . .

Were the scene of this sad destruction of human life laid in the Upper instead of the Lower Provinces, in the midst of a bold and manly people, I might speak with less confidence upon the question of safety. In these Provinces the *satis* amount to forty-three only upon a population of nearly twenty millions. It cannot be expected that any general feeling, where combination of any kind is so unusual, could be excited in defense of a rite in which so few participate, a rite also notoriously made too often subservient to views of personal interest on the part of the other members of the family. . . .

But I have taken up too much time in giving my own opinion when those of the greatest experience and highest official authority are upon our records. In the report of the Nizamat Adalat for 1828, four out of five of the Judges recommended to the Governor-General in Council the immediate abolition of the practice, and attest its safety. The fifth Judge, though not opposed to the opinions of the rest of the Bench, did not feel then prepared to give his entire assent. In the report of this year the measure has come up with the unanimous recommendation of the Court. . . . No documents exist to show the opinions of the public functionaires in the interior, but I am informed that nine-tenths are in favour of the abolition. . . .

Having made inquiries, also, how far *satis* are permitted in the European foreign settlements, I find from Dr. Carey that at Chinsurah no such sacrifices had ever been permitted by the Dutch Government. That within the limits of Chandarnagar itself they were also prevented, but allowed to be performed in the British territories. The Danish Government of Serampur has not forbidden the rite, in conformity to the example of the British Government.

It is a very important fact that, though representations have been made by the disappointed party to superior authority, it does not appear that a single instance of direct opposition to the execution of the prohibitory orders of our civil functionaries has ever occurred. How, then, can it be reasonably feared that to the Government itself, from whom all authority is derived, and whose power is now universally considered to be irresistible, anything bearing the semblance of resistance can be manifested? Mr. Wilson also is of opinion that no immediate overt act of insubordination would follow the publication of the edict. The Regulation of

Government may be evaded, the police may be corrupted, but even here the price paid as hush money will operate as a penalty, indirectly forwarding the object of Government.

I venture, then, to think it completely proved that from the native population nothing of extensive combination, or even of partial opposition, may be expected from the abolition. . . .

I have now to submit for the consideration of Council the draft of a regulation enacting the abolition of *satis*. . . . It is only in the previous processes, or during the actual performance of the rite, when the feelings of all may be more or less roused to a high degree of excitement, that I apprehend the possibility of affray or of acts of violence through an indiscreet and injudicious exercise of authority. It seemed to me prudent, therefore, that the police, in the first instance, should warn and advise, but not forcibly prohibit, and if the *sati,* in defiance of this notice, were performed, that a report should be made to the magistrate, who would summon the parties and proceed as in any other case of crime. . . .

The first and primary object of my heart is the benefit of the Hindus. I know nothing so important to the improvement of their future condition as the establishment of a purer morality, whatever their belief, and a more just conception of the will of God. The first step to this better understanding will be dissociation of religious belief and practice from blood and murder. They will then, when no longer under this brutalizing excitement, view with more calmness acknowledged truths. They will see that there can be no inconsistency in the ways of Providence, that to the command received as divine by all races of men, "No innocent blood shall be spilt," there can be no exception ; and when they shall have been convinced of the error of this first and most criminal of their customs, may it not be hoped that others, which stand in the way of their improvement, may likewise pass away, and that, thus emancipated from those chains and shackles upon their minds and actions, they may no longer continue, as they have done, the slaves of every foreign conqueror, but that they may assume their first places among the great families of mankind ? I disown in these remarks, or in this measure, any view whatever to conversion to our own faith. I write and feel as a legislator for the Hindus, and as I believe many enlightened Hindus think and feel.

Descending from these higher considerations, it cannot be a dishonest ambition that the Government of which I form a part should have the credit of an act which is to wash out a foul stain upon British rule, and to stay the sacrifice of humanity and justice to a doubtful expediency ; and finally, as a branch of the general administration of the Empire, I may be permitted to feel deeply anxious that our course shall be in accordance with the noble example set to us by the British Government at home, and that the adaptation, when practicable to the circumstances of this vast Indian population, of the same enlightened principles, may promote here as well as there the general prosperity, and may exalt the character of our nation.

42

Lin Tse-hsü [Lin Zexu], Letter of Moral Admonition to Queen Victoria

Although the English East India Company's trade with China was profitable, the overall balance of trade had remained in China's favor until the early decades of the nineteenth century. European traders bought tea, silk, rhubarb, and other goods from China, but the Chinese found little need for Western goods. A reversal in the trade balance came in the 1830s, and opium importation was one of the most important factors. Opium, forbidden in China, was smuggled into the country from India in ever-increasing quantities, primarily by English East India Company ships through the port of Canton [Guanzhou]. During the years of 1838–1839 alone, more than five million pounds of opium were imported illegally by East India Company ships.

The effects of the illicit trade on Chinese morality and health, as well as on the economy, were so deleterious that Emperor Tao-kuang [Daoguang] (r. 1821–1850) was gravely concerned. He searched for an official who would be able to deal with the opium menace effectively and resolutely. In Lin Tse-hsü [Lin Zexu] he found such a person. A high official in the Imperial government, Lin had enjoyed a wide reputation for his competence and integrity and for his hardline approach toward the proliferation of opium. In December 1838, he was appointed Imperial Commissioner at Canton, with full power to stop the Canton opium traffic.

Lin Tse-hsü arrived in Canton in March 1839 and immediately began to stamp out the opium traffic ; however, it became clear to him that the solution was to stop the supply at its source. The following selection is his letter to Queen Victoria, appealing to the British conscience and demanding an end to the opium trade. The letter was written in the summer of 1839, only a few months before the outbreak of the Opium War in November 1839.

QUESTIONS TO CONSIDER

1. What moral arguments did Commissioner Lin present against the British importation of opium into China ?
2. On the basis of Lin's letter to Queen Victoria and Emperor Qianlong's letter to King George III (see Reading 25), describe China's view of the West, especially of Great Britain. Contrast these views with those expressed by Rudyard Kipling in "The White Man's Burden" (see Reading 43).

A communication : magnificently our great Emperor soothes and pacifies China and the foreign countries, regarding all with the same kindness. If there is profit, then he shares it with the peoples of the world ; if there is harm, then he removes it on behalf of the world. This is because he takes the mind of heaven and earth as his mind.

The kings of your honorable country by a tradition handed down from generation to generation have always been noted for their politeness and submissiveness. We have read your successive tributary memorials saying, "In general our countrymen who go to trade in China have always received His Majesty the Emperor's gracious treatment and equal justice," and so on. Privately we are delighted with the way in which the honorable rulers of your country deeply understand the grand principles and are grateful for the Celestial grace. For this reason the Celestial Court in soothing those from afar has redoubled its polite and kind treatment. The profit from trade has been enjoyed by them continuously for two hundred years. This is the source from which your country has become known for its wealth.

But after a long period of commercial intercourse, there appear among the crowd of barbarians both good persons and bad, unevenly. Consequently there are those who smuggle opium to seduce the Chinese people and so cause the spread of the poison to all provinces. Such persons who only care to profit themselves, and disregard their harm to others, are not tolerated by the laws of heaven and are unanimously hated by human beings. His Majesty the Emperor, upon hearing of this, is in a towering rage. He has especially sent me, his commissioner, to come to Kwangtung, and together with the governor-general and governor jointly to investigate and settle this matter.

All those people in China who sell opium or smoke opium should receive the death penalty. If we trace the crime of those barbarians who through the years have been selling opium, then the deep harm they have wrought and the great profit they have usurped should fundamentally justify their execution according to law. We take into consideration, however, the fact that the various barbarians have still known how to repent their crimes and return to their allegiance to us by taking the 20,183 chests of opium from their storeships and petitioning us, through their consular officer [superintendent of trade], Elliot, to receive it. It has been entirely destroyed and this has been faithfully reported to the Throne in several memorials by this commissioner and his colleagues.

Fortunately we have received a specially extended favor from His Majesty the Emperor, who considers that for those who voluntarily surrender there are still some circumstances to palliate their crime, and so for the time being he has magnanimously excused them from punishment. But as for those who again violate the opium prohibition, it is difficult for the law to pardon them repeatedly. Having established new regulations, we presume that the ruler of your honorable country, who takes delight in our culture and whose disposition is inclined towards us, must be able to instruct the various barbarians to observe the law with care. It is only necessary to explain to them the advantages and disadvantages and then they will know that the legal code of the Celestial Court must be absolutely obeyed with awe.

We find that your country is sixty or seventy thousand *li* [three *li* make one mile] from China. Yet there are barbarian ships that strive to come here for trade for the purpose of making a great profit. The wealth of China is used to profit the barbarians. That is to say, the great profit made by barbarians is all taken from the rightful share of China. By what right do they then in return use the poisonous drug to injure the Chinese people? Even though the barbarians may not necessarily intend to do us harm, yet in coveting profit to an extreme, they have no regard for injuring others. Let us ask, where is your conscience? I have heard that the smoking of opium is very strictly forbidden by your country; that is because the harm caused by opium is clearly understood. Since it is not permitted to do harm to your own country, then even less should you let it be passed on to the harm of other countries — how much less to China! Of all that China exports to foreign countries, there is not a single thing which is not beneficial to people: they are of benefit when eaten, or of benefit when used, or of benefit when resold; all are beneficial. Is there a single article from China which has done any harm to foreign countries? Take tea and rhubarb, for example; the foreign countries cannot get along for a single day without them. If China cuts off these benefits with no sympathy for those who are to suffer, then what can the barbarians rely upon to keep themselves alive? Moreover the woolens, camlets, and longells [i.e., textiles] of foreign countries cannot be woven unless they obtain Chinese silk. If China, again, cuts off this beneficial export, what profit can the barbarians expect to make? As for other food-stuffs, beginning with candy, ginger, cinnamon, and so forth, and articles for use, beginning with silk, satin, chinaware, and so on, all the things that must be had by foreign countries are innumerable. On the other hand, articles coming from the outside to China can only be used as toys. We can take them or get along without them. Since they are not needed by China, what difficulty would there be if we closed the frontier and stopped the trade? Nevertheless our Celestial Court lets tea, silk, and other goods be shipped without limit and circulated everywhere without begrudging it in the slightest. This is for no other reason but to share the benefit with the people of the whole world.

The goods from China carried away by your country not only supply your own consumption and use, but also can be divided up and sold to other countries, producing a triple profit. Even if you do not sell opium, you still have this three-fold profit. How can you bear to go further, selling products injurious to others in order to fulfill your insatiable desire?

Suppose there were people from another country who carried opium for sale to England and seduced your people into buying and smoking it; certainly your honorable ruler would deeply hate it and be bitterly aroused. We have heard heretofore that your honorable ruler is kind and benevolent. Naturally you would not wish to give unto others what you yourself do not want. We have also heard that the ships coming to Canton have all had regulations promulgated and given to them in which it is stated that it is not permitted to carry contraband goods. This indicates that the administrative orders of your honorable rule have been originally strict and clear. Only because the trading ships are numerous, heretofore perhaps they have not been examined with care. Now after this communication has been dispatched and you have clearly understood the strictness of the prohibitory laws of the Celestial Court, certainly you will not let your subjects dare again to violate the law.

We have further learned that in London, the capital of your honorable rule, and in Scotland (Su-ko-lan), Ireland (Ai-lun), and other places, originally no opium has been produced. Only in several places of India under your control such as Bengal, Madras, Bombay, Patna, Benares, and Malwa has opium been planted from hill to hill, and ponds have been opened for its manufacture. For months and years work is continued in order to accumulate the poison. The obnoxious odor ascends, irritating heaven and frightening the spirits. Indeed you, O King, can eradicate the opium plant in these places, hoe over the fields entirely, and sow in its stead the five grains [i.e., millet, barley, wheat, etc.]. Anyone who dares again attempt to plant and manufacture opium should be severely punished. This will really be a great, benevolent government policy that will increase the common weal and get rid of evil. For this, Heaven must support you and the spirits must bring you good fortune, prolonging your old age and extending your descendants. All will depend on this act.

As for the barbarian merchants who come to China, their food and drink and habitation are all received by the gracious favor of our Celestial Court. Their accumulated wealth is all benefit given with pleasure by our Celestial Court. They spend rather few days in their own country but more time in Canton. To digest clearly the legal penalties as an aid to instruction has been a valid principle in all ages. Suppose a man of another country comes to England to trade, he still has to obey the English laws; how much more should he obey in China the laws of the Celestial Dynasty?

Now we have set up regulations governing the Chinese people. He who sells opium shall receive the death penalty and he who smokes it also the death penalty. Now consider this: if the barbarians do not bring opium, then how can the Chinese people resell it, and how can they smoke it? The fact is that the wicked barbarians beguile the Chinese people into a death trap. How then can we grant life only to these barbarians? He who takes the life of even one person still has to atone for it with his own life; yet is the harm done by opium limited to the taking of one life only? Therefore in the new regulations, in regard to those barbarians who bring opium to China, the penalty is fixed at decapitation or strangulation. This is what is called getting rid of a harmful thing on behalf of mankind.

Moreover we have found that in the middle of the second month of this year [April 9] Consul [Superintendent] Elliot of your nation, because the opium prohibition law was very stern and severe, petitioned for an extension of the time limit. He requested a limit of five months for India and its adjacent harbors and related territories, and ten months for England proper, after which they would act in conformity with the new regulations. Now we, the commissioner and others, have memorialized and have received the extraordinary Celestial grace of His Majesty the Emperor, who has redoubled his consideration and compassion. All those who within the period of the coming one year (from England) or six months (from India) bring opium to China by mistake, but who voluntarily confess and completely surrender their opium, shall be exempt from their punishment. After this limit of time, if there are still those who bring opium to China then they will plainly have committed a wilful violation and shall at once be executed according to law, with absolutely no clemency or pardon. This may be called the height of kindness and the perfection of justice.

Our Celestial Dynasty rules over and supervises the myriad states, and surely possesses unfathomable spiritual dignity. Yet the Emperor cannot bear to execute people without having first tried to reform them by instruction. Therefore he especially promulgates these fixed regulations. The barbarian merchants of your country, if they wish to do business for a prolonged period, are required to obey our statutes respectfully and to cut off permanently the source of opium. They must by no means try to test the effectiveness of the law with their lives. May you, O King, check your wicked and sift your vicious people before they come to China, in order to guarantee the peace of your nation, to show further the sincerity of your politeness and submissiveness, and to let the two countries enjoy together the blessings of peace. How fortunate, how fortunate indeed! After receiving this dispatch will you immediately give us a prompt reply regarding the details and circumstances of your cutting off the opium traffic. Be sure not to put this off. The above is what has to be communicated. [Vermilion endorsement :] This is appropriately worded and quite comprehensive.

Imperialism: Three Views

Imperialism — one country's dominating the economic or political affairs of a weaker country — was certainly not new to the nineteenth century ; however, its explosive character and global scale were new. In the eighteenth century, European colonists (with the exception of the United States) had been content to occupy the coastlines of Africa, India, China, and the New World. But by the mid-nineteenth century, a more aggressive imperialism, equipped with new tools of empire, sought a deeper and more permanent penetration of the non-European world. The steam engine, railway, Maxim gun, synthetic quinine, dum-dum bullets, and Colonel Shrapnel's splintering artillery shell were just some of the technical advantages permitting Europeans to build huge empires, particularly in India and Africa. In 1875, for example, Europeans controlled about 10 percent of Africa, but by 1902, they controlled 90 percent of the African continent. Indeed by 1900, one out of ten inhabitants of the entire world was governed by a European nation, and 20 percent of the earth's surface flew a European flag.

A combination of economic, political, religious, and idealistic impulses fueled this nineteenth-century imperialism. Although much has been made of the economic motives, European governments found empire building very expensive ; even though individuals like Cecil Rhodes or companies such as Michelin made fortunes in places like Africa and Vietnam, their governments did not. Winning souls for Christ, advancing national prestige by conquering new lands, "civilizing" non-Europeans by shouldering the "white man's burden" — all these were important factors in imperial policy. Rivalries between European nations and the internal conditions of non-European peoples frequently shaped imperial policy much more than any grand scheme of imperial conquest. In 1883, Sir John Seeley underscored the offhand, haphazard approach of Great Britain's imperial march when he wrote : "We seem, as it were, to have conquered and peopled half the world in a fit of absence of mind."[1]

The first of the following three selections suggests the idealism that was part of this nineteenth-century imperialism ; the other two documents state the Vietnamese and Indian case against European imperialism.

43

Rudyard Kipling, "The White Man's Burden"

No single statement better represents the justification for British imperialism than "The White Man's Burden," written by Rudyard Kipling (1865–1936).

QUESTIONS TO CONSIDER

1. Why would this poem appeal to religious and scientific sentiment in Victorian England ?
2. Compare and contrast Kipling's view of native, nonwhite people with that of Frantz Fanon (see Reading 90).

Take up the White Man's burden —
Send forth the best ye breed —
Go bind your sons to exile
To serve your captives' need ;
To wait in heavy harness,
On fluttered folk and wild —
Your new-caught, sullen peoples,
Half-devil and half-child.

Take up the White Man's burden —
In patience to abide,
To veil the threat of terror
And check the show of pride ;
By open speech and simple,
An hundred times made plain
To seek another's profit,
And work another's gain.

From Rudyard Kipling, *Verse*, Inclusive Edition (New York : Doubleday and Page, 1920), pp. 371–372. Reprinted by permission of Doubleday and Company, Inc.

1. John R. Seeley quoted in L. C. B. Seaman, *Victorian England : Aspects of English and Imperial History, 1837–1901* (London : Methuen, 1973), p. 332.

Take up the White Man's burden —
The savage wars of peace —
Fill full the mouth of Famine
And bid the sickness cease ;
And when your goal is nearest
The end for others sought,
Watch sloth and heathen Folly
Bring all your hopes to nought.

Take up the White Man's burden —
No tawdry rule of kings,
But toil of serf and sweeper —
The tale of common things.
The ports ye shall not enter,
The roads ye shall not tread,
Go mark them with your living,
And mark them with your dead.

Take up the White Man's burden —
And reap his old reward :
The blame of those ye better,
The hate of those ye guard —
The cry of hosts ye humour
(Ah, slowly!) toward the light : —
'Why brought he us from bondage,
Our loved Egyptian night ?'

Take up the White Man's burden —
Ye dare not stoop to less —
Nor call too loud on Freedom
To cloke your weariness ;
By all ye cry or whisper,
By all ye leave or do,
The silent, sullen peoples
Shall weigh your gods and you.

Take up the White Man's burden —
Have done with childish days —
The lightly proferred laurel,
The easy, ungrudged praise.
Comes now, to search your manhood
Through all the thankless years,
Cold, edged with dear-bought wisdom,
The judgment of your peers!

44

Nguyen Dinh Chieu, "Elegy"

Beginning in 1858, France started an aggressive imperial penetration of Vietnam. In 1859, Saigon fell. Reinforced by French troops from China, the French imperial forces began to occupy all of southern Vietnam, known at the time as Cochinchina. Unexpectedly, at a military outpost near Saigon in 1861, the French encountered stiff guerrilla resistance from Vietnamese peasants. In the following selection, the blind Vietnamese writer Nguyen Dinh Chieu explains why his compatriots must honor the memory of those peasants who, though poorly armed and trained, resisted French imperialism.

QUESTIONS TO CONSIDER

1. Does this poet's description of the Vietnamese people verify Rudyard Kipling's description of native "silent, sullen peoples" who would benefit from imperialism? Why? Why not?
2. What does the poem reveal about the character, tactics, and strategy of Vietnamese resistance to French imperialism?

You were not professional soldiers of the provincial militia nor of the capital's guards, experienced in military life and training. You were but inhabitants of villages and hamlets turned partisans to serve the cause of righteousness.

You did not wait until you had been thoroughly trained in the eighteen weapons of the military art. The ninety schemes of military tactics had never been demonstrated for your instruction.

On your back, a shirt of cotton; you did not wait for holsters or cartridge belts.

In your hands, a pointed stick; you did not ask for knives or helmets.

The match for your gunpowder was made of straw; but this did not prevent you from successfully burning the missionary house.[1]

For a sword, you used your kitchen knife; yet you were able to behead the enemies' lieutenant.

Your officers were not compelled to beat the drums in order to urge you forward. You advanced on your own, clambering onto the barricades. You looked upon the enemy as if he did not exist.

From Nguyen Dinh Chieu, "Elegy for Those Who Fought Righteously at Can Quioc (1861)," in Truong Buu Lam, *Patterns of Vietnamese Response to Foreign Intervention: 1858–1900*, Monograph Series no. 11, Southeast Asia Studies, Yale University (Detroit: Cellar Book Shop, 1967), pp. 67–71. Reprinted by permission.

　1. *Missionary house:* the struggle had already assumed a clear anti-Catholic bias.

You were not frightened by the French who shot large and small bullets at you. You forced your way into their camp, risking your life as if you had no material body.

Some of you stabbed, some struck so eagerly that the French soldiers and their mercenaries lost heart.

You screamed in the forefront, you shouted at the rear regardless of the enemies' gunboats, their ships, or their rifles.

You had hoped that your patriotism would serve your country forever. Who could have foreseen that your material body would betray you so soon.

You had thought that your right conduct would earn you victory in the battlefields. Who could have predicted that the horse's skin would so swiftly swathe your corpse.

Now you have returned to the world of the dead for many hundred years; you did not wait for your sword to be suspended on your grave.[2]

On the Can giuoc river, the grass and the trees mark grief along many thousand miles.

At the market of Truong binh,[3] tears fall from young and aged faces.

Had you been bandits or robbers, and therefore condemned to fight, this fate would have been acceptable.[4]

Had you been deserters from your ranks while in charge of the guard of citadels or fortifications, and therefore condemned to redeem your misconduct, you would have deserved this destiny.

But what you felt was that each foot of your land and each shoot of your vegetables, you owed to your king. Your talent must therefore benefit your country.

For a bowl of rice and a cut of cloth — what is the matter with the enemies' ancestors that they come and dispute them with us?

Who causes all the difficulties to our mandarins and our troops that they must taste snow and lie on dew?

Because of whom have our posts and forts been shattered, swaying in the rain and collapsing in the wind?

What was the meaning of life when you were compelled to live with heretics[5] who threw away the incense burner, thrust off the reading stand? The spectacle enhanced your sadness.

What was the meaning of life when you were impressed into the enemy militia and when you had to share their wine and nibble their bread. The situation only accentuated your shame.

---

2. *Your sword to be suspended on your grave:* a brave and righteous soldier in the Warring States period had asked his son to suspend his sword on his tomb to indicate his bravery and righteousness to the passersby. The Vietnamese partisans did not have that privilege.

3. *Truong binh:* the name of a market close to Can giuoc.

4. This sentence alludes to the institution of *don dien* or military colonies in southern Vietnam. In the early years of the Vietnamese occupation of the Mekong Delta, which was then a Cambodian possession, the Vietnamese authorities sent prisoners to clear the land under the supervision of officers of the central government. They established villages and hamlets and were a source of military manpower at the borders.

5. *Heretics:* the text reads *tà dao* or *ta dao,* both meaning heresy. These words came to designate Christianity or the Christians. The struggle was thus undoubtedly anti-Catholic.

You preferred to die fighting the enemy, and return to our ancestors in glory
    rather than survive in submission to the Occidentals and share your
    miserable life with barbarians.
O, now all is finished!
The Lao ngo pagoda, through the five watches of the night, remains quiet
    and cold. You have entrusted the full moon with the care of the
    faithfulness of your heart.
The military posts of the enemies from the Western Seas witnessed for one
    minute how you expressed your resentment. It is to be lamented that
    your unpropitious lot caused you to drift with the outflowing current.
How mournful is an old mother weeping for her young son under the
    midnight lamp, its light flickering around the hut.
How pitiful is a feeble wife in search of her husband; still she falters at the
    doorway though the sun has set.
O, the smoke of your battle has already dissipated, but your right conduct
    shall be recorded for a thousand years.
Let their generals and soldiers establish their camp on the Ben nghe river,[6] we
    shall see who is responsible for the clouds blackening all four horizons.
Our ancestors and parents still live on the land of Dong nai,[7] we shall see who
    will be able to save the next generation.
You are dead, but your debt to your country has been fully honored, and
    your reputation shall be praised by the whole population of the six provinces.
You are dead, but temples and shrines have been erected for your cult, and
    your name shall be cherished by thousands of generations to come.
You fought the enemy during your life. Now, dead, you continue your
    struggle by letting your souls follow and support our garrisons and
    troops. For ten regenerations, you have pledged revenge.
You served your king during your life. Now, dead, you continue to serve him.
    The Imperial edict demonstrates it clearly and a simple word
    "recognition"[8] suffices to compensate you for your noble deeds.
The heroes' tears shall not run dry, and we love you because you acted
    according to the will of Heaven and the people.
The incense sticks burnt in memory of the partisans are the most fragrant,
    and we are grateful to you because you struggled for the king and for the
    land.
O, mourn.

---

6. *Ben nghe river:* the Saigon river; Ben nghe was the ancient name for the Saigon ag-
glomeration.
7. *Dong nai:* the ancient name of southern Vietnam.
8. *"Recognition":* the word refers to the practice of the court whereby it accorded certain privileges to the descendants of men who had performed great deeds.

45

Gandhi: Facing the British in India

Mahatma Gandhi (1869–1948) devoted much of his life to the struggle for Indian rights and independence. In 1903, while living in South Africa, he helped establish *Indian Opinion,* a weekly journal which became an important instrument in the early years of the struggle. The following excerpts are from several articles Gandhi wrote for the journal as India's independence movement was gaining strength.

QUESTIONS TO CONSIDER

1. Why did Gandhi believe that "... the hope of India lies in the British people, rather than in the British government ..."?
2. How did Gandhi characterize Indian nationalism at the turn of the century? Compare this reading with the ideas expressed in Heinrich von Treitschke (see Reading 39) and Rudyard Kipling's poem (see Reading 43) and in Nguyen Dinh Chieu's "Elegy" (see Reading 44). Do these writers express any common elements of nationalism?

More and more, as years go by, a feeling of unrest is growing in India. More and more ... is a spirit of discontent pervading its three hundred millions.... And more and more, as they realize that amid the differences of creed and caste is one basic nationality, does agitation spread and take the form of definite demands for the fulfillment of the solemn assurance of the British Government that they should be given the ordinary rights of British subjects. It is impossible that national aspirations can be forever repressed, and equally impossible for India to remain a "dependency" in an Empire to which it contributes more than half the population. How often have South Africans kicked against the pricks from the Home [colonial government in London] authorities, and felt with indignation that local affairs were not properly understood.... Is it then surprising that the teeming millions of India should be dissatisfied with being ruled by a number of too-often self-sufficient and unsympathetic aliens ignorant of the genius of the people? Not even the "mild" Hindu can bear this forever. Is it possible for the patriotic spirits of a people with the glorious traditions of India to be content with serfdom?...

   ... The root of the trouble seems to be that, although there is a very great sentimental interest taken in India by the people [in Great Britain], there is, unfor-

The first excerpt from *Indian Opinion,* September 2, 1905. In Louis Fischer, ed., *The Essential Gandhi: An Anthology* (New York: Random House, 1962), pp. 115–117, passim; the second, ibid., June 9, 1906. Reproduced by permission of the Navajivan Trust.

tunately, an equally small practical interest taken. Insofar as Indians are "hea-thens" they are interesting, insofar as they are fellow-subjects — well, the Government can look after them. But the members of the Government are too busy seeking their bubble reputation to trouble much with what will not bring place and position. . . .

It seems, then, that the hope of India lies in the British people, rather than in the British Government . . .

[No] people exists that would not think itself happier even under its own bad gov-ernment than it might really be under the good governance of an alien power.

The spirit of political and international liberty is universal and, it may even be said, instinctive. No race appreciates a condition of servitude or subjection to a conquering or an alien race. If we turn our minds to the conditions which anteceded the American War of Independence, it is not difficult to understand how even the suspicion of an assumed superiority will antagonize its prospective victim to the degree of rendering cooperation almost an impossibility.

Yet it is curious how unimaginative so many Britishers are. What they recog-nize as a virtue in themselves is an appalling vice in others, else should we never hear of alleged sedition in Ireland, Egypt, or India. It is normal for a man to desire to be free, even if, actually, he does not merit freedom. But it is the desire itself that, in . . . time, will bring the now impossible aspiration to realization.

It cannot for one moment be alleged that a strange ruler is capable of enter-ing into the intimate thought and feeling, the inmost life, of the ruled in the man-ner that is possible for those of the same or a similar nationality and tradition.

Japan's Emergence as a Modern State

Tokugawa Japan's self-imposed isolation, which had lasted for more than two hundred years, finally came to an end in 1854. In that year, an American, Commodore Matthew C. Perry, brought to Japan from President Fillmore a message expressing his desire to open relations with that country. This re-sulted in the signing of the Treaty of Kanagawa with the Shogunal govern-ment in Edo. This abandonment of the 200-year-old seclusion policy represented a severe blow to the prestige of the Shogunal government in the eyes of the Japanese people. This event ushered in a new era in modern Jap-anese history, marking the beginning of the final collapse of the old order, which was replaced by a modern Japan under the government of Emperor Meiji in 1868.

In 1858, four years after the Kanagawa treaty, Townsend Harris, the first Consul General of the United States, signed a more substantial commercial treaty with the Japanese, the Treaty of Amity and Commerce between the United States and Japan. In accordance with its guidelines, the ratified treaty was to be exchanged in Washington, DC. This provided Japan with the op-portunity to send her envoys to America for the first time ever. The 77-

member entourage of Japan's first Embassy reached Washington, DC and exchanged the ratified treaty on May 22, 1860. President James Buchanan received the Embassy in the White House. This occasion was an important eyeopener for the members of the Japanese Embassy.

In Japan itself, a handful of dedicated leaders of the Meiji Restoration rallied around Emperor Meiji (1867–1912), and launched sweeping political, social, economic, and intellectual reforms. They studied Western institutions carefully, adopting the best features without abandoning Japan's traditional ideals and virtues. This was best exemplified in their effort to enact a constitution. Within the lifetime of Emperor Meiji, Japan experienced the transition from a backward, agrarian, and feudal state into a powerful, modern, industrial, and constitutional monarchy.

Despite the modern transformation of Japan during the Meiji period, many old institutions continued to endure. One of these was the institution of the geisha. The profession of geisha is one of the better-known traditional Japanese entertainment occupations, about which Westerners often have misconceptions.

46

First Japanese Embassy to the United States

The following are excerpts from Vice Ambassador Lord Muragaki's eyewitness account of some of the first official U.S.-Japanese interactions. The first is of the reception given by Secretary of State Lewis Cass in the Embassy's honor. The second is of the White House. Muragaki seems rather unimpressed by American freedom and might.

QUESTIONS TO CONSIDER

1. How do you best describe Lord Muragaki's views of the United States? Was he impressed by what he saw? How? If not, why?
2. Compare and contrast Lord Muragaki's views of the United States with those of Alexis de Tocqueville (see Reading 33).

We arrived at Cass's residence. I wondered about the nature of the ceremony we were going to perform on this occasion, since it was an invitation from the Prime Minister. To our great surprise, however, we found that the hall, passages, and rooms were all packed with hundreds of men and women. Innumerable gas

Masao Miyoshi, *As We Saw Them, The First Japanese Embassy to the United States (1860)* (Berkeley: University of California Press, 1979), pp. 71–72, 131–135. Copyright © 1979 The Regents of the University of California. Reprinted by permission.

lamps were hanging from the ceilings, and the glass chandeliers decorated with gold and silver were reflected in the mirrors. It was as brilliant and dazzling as day. Though we did not know what was happening, we somehow managed to make our way through the crowd to the room where Cass and his family stood, and were greeted by them. Even his grandchildren and daughters came to shake hands with us. Although we sat on chairs, everyone in the room also came to shake our hands. Since there was no interpreter around, I did not understand at all what was being said. The crowd was extremely dense. DuPont took my hand and led me to an adjoining room, where a large table was laid with gold and silver ware. At the center of the table were the Japanese and American flags to express friendship. We had some drinks and food at the table. Soon we were led away to another large room ; its floor was covered with smooth boards. In one corner, there was a band playing something called "music" on instruments that looked like Chinese lutes. Men were in uniform with epaulets and swords, and women with bare shoulders were dressed in thin white clothes. They had those wide skirts around their waists. Men and women moved round the room couple by couple, walking on tiptoe to the tune of the music. It was just like a number of mice running around and around. There was neither taste nor charm. It was quite amusing to watch women's huge skirts spread wider and wider like balloons as they turned. Apparently, high officials and older women, as well as young people, are very fond of this pastime. The men and women went to the table for refreshments, then coming back for another dance. This, we were told, would continue all night. As for myself, I was astonished by the sight, and wondered whether this was a dream or reality. We asked DuPont to say good-night to the host for us, and left for the hotel. Admittedly, this is a nation with no order or ceremony [*rei*], but it is indeed odd that the Prime Minister should invite an ambassador of another country to an event of this sort! My sense of displeasure is boundless : there is no respect for order and ceremony or obligation [*gi*]. The only way to exonerate them is by recognizing that all this absence of ceremony issues from their feeling of friendship.

All is strange,
>   Appearance and language,
>   I must be in a dream-land.

Women are white and beautiful, and they are handsomely dressed with gold and silver decorations. Although I am becoming accustomed to their appearance, I find their reddish hair unattractive, and their eyes look like those of dogs. Now and then, though, I see a black-haired woman who also has black eyes. They must be descendants of some Asian race. Naturally they look very attractive.

Muragaki in the White House :

Intercalary Third Month 28th [May 19, 1860].

Cloudy. As the hour for our presentation to the President of the United States was appointed for twelve o'clock, we made all the necessary preparations with the utmost care. Masaoki (wearing a short sword with silk twined scabbard), I (with a short court sword with gold hilt), and Tadamasa (bearing a sword with scabbard twined in front), were dressed alike in *kariginu* and *eboshi* with light green braided cords, and wore sandals woven of silk threads. Both Morita and Naruse Masanori wore *horoginu,* while the two officers of superintendent's rank put on *su-ō,* and Namura Gorō, our official interpreter, was dressed in *kamishimo,* made of ramie cloth.

　　We drove off in open carriages-and-four, Masaoki with Captain DuPont riding in the first carriage, I with Captain Lee in the second, and Tadamasa with Mr. Ledyard in the third, followed by other members of the Embassy in carriages, and servants on foot. (The First and Second Ambassadors and the Censor each took with them three footmen, one spear-bearer and three retainers, while Morita and Naruse were each accompanied by two retainers, one spear-bearer and one sandal-carrier.) Our procession was headed by a score of men in grey uniform (probably city officials), immediately followed by a band of some thirty musicians, and several mounted cavaliers; then came a group of men, bearing upon their shoulders the despatch box with a red leather cover, and accompanied by the officer in charge, a foreman and an interpreter; these were followed by a long line of carriages in good order, on either side of which marched the guards to the accompaniment of music played by the band. The wide main street was literally packed with vehicles, men and women who were eager to get a glimpse of our procession. We couldn't help smiling, finding ourselves feeling quite elated at representing Japan in such a grand style in the foreign land. I even forgot my limitations as I looked at the wonder registered in the faces of the crowd, as they pressed forward to see our party in strange costumes such as they had never seen nor could have ever imagined.

　　Through the iron gate of the President's official residence, we continued to drive some 140 yards, accompanied by the cavaliers, soldiers and our servants, up to the main entrance of the building. Having left our carriages there, we were conducted up a flight of stone steps and through several rooms, into the anteroom, prepared for the Ambassadors and the Censor. Morita and the rest of the Embassy members were shown into another room. We were ushered into a large oval-shaped room, measuring probably 7 *ken* by 4, with a carpet of beautiful designs in bright blue on the floor; draperies of similar pattern and color hung inside three large glass windows. There were large mirrors on all the walls, and before them, tables of various sizes, on which were placed Japanese lacquered writing boxes and other Japanese articles, which had been presented to Commodore Perry on his visit to Japan. General Lewis Cass came in and greeted us. After he left, Captains DuPont and Lee led us to the Audience Room; Naruse Masanori carried the despatch box, containing the Shogun's letter. (The imperial letter was written on gold-leafed Japanese paper with a picture of flowers and birds, and placed in a plain paulownia casket with a lining of silk brocade, which was tied in the middle with vermilion cords. Its cover was made of purple Chinese satin with tassels of similar color attached to its four corners. The box in which this was contained, was of black lacquer with scarlet silk cords tied in the middle; this box had been handed over to Captain DuPont before the ceremony.) As we approached the Audience Room, the doors to its entrance were swung open on both sides. In the center of the room, which measured approximately 6 *ken* by 13, stood President Buchanan, flanked by high-ranking civil and military officers; at his back were many ladies, young and old, all attired in beautiful dresses. Having entered the room and bowed, Masaoki, I, and Tadamasa advanced to the center of the room. We bowed once again and approached the President. Masaoki delivered a short address, conveying to him the imperial wishes, which was then interpreted by Namura. After his address, Masaoki took the Shogun's letter from the casket, held out by Naruse Masanori, and presented it to the President; the casket was handed over by Naruse to the Secretary of State Cass. We withdrew to the center of the room, whereupon, Morita and the rest of the Embassy were led to the President's seat. We then retired to the anteroom, having expressed our gratification for that occasion.

As we were resting in the anteroom, Captain DuPont came and asked us if the ceremony of presenting the imperial letter according to our customs was completed. We said yes. Thereupon, he conducted us once again to the Audience Room. This time, the President shook hands with each of us, and made a short speech to the effect that the President and the entire American nation rejoiced in establishing friendly relations with Japan for the first time since her declaration of seclusion, and particularly in receiving her first Embassy to the United States, and that they were exceedingly gratified to have received the Shogun's letter of goodwill. He then presented us with a written copy of his address. After that, high-ranking officials came forward and shook hands with us; as the greeting seemed to go on forever, we took the first opportunity to withdraw to the anteroom, after making our final bows. We drove through the same streets back to our hotel.

At four P.M., Captain DuPont and Mr. Ledyard called on us, informing us that it was a Western custom to pay visits to foreign ministers in Washington. We told him that we would visit only ministers of those nations with whom our country had concluded amicable treaties, but not the others; they agreed to our condition. We changed into our travelling costumes, and made a swift round of visits in carriages. When we arrived in front of a minister's residence, we had our visiting cards (bearing our names in both Japanese and English), sent in by our driver, so that we did not even have to get out of our carriage. It was a most convenient custom. We made a round of several residences, but did not even know which minister's house we were visiting. At the British and Dutch ministers', we were shown in and met their wives and children; theirs were beautiful houses. It was already evening when we returned to our hotel.

We gathered together and talked of our experience on this memorable day. The President is a silver-haired man of over seventy years of age, and he has a most genial manner without losing noble dignity. He wore a simple black costume of coat and trousers in the same fashion as any merchant, and had no decoration or sword on him. All the high-ranking officials were dressed in the same way as the President, whereas the army and navy officers wore epaulets (the gold tassels attached to the shoulders, of which the length marked the rank), and gold stripes on the sleeves of their costumes (of which the number represented the rank, three stripes signifying the highest); and they carried a sword at their side. It seemed to us a most curious custom to permit the presence of women on such a ceremonious occasion as today. We remembered how we were received at the Sandwich Islands by the women alone — after the main event at our presentation — with somewhat

greater formalities ; this difference, we attributed, although we were not well acquainted with Western customs and manners, to the fact that the Sandwich Islands constituted a monarchy. The United States is one of the greatest countries
in the world, but the President is only a governor voted in [*nyūsatsu*] every four
years. (There will be a changeover on October 1 this year. We heard them suggest
a certain man ; when we asked how they could tell before the "auction," they answered that this man would be the President, because he was related to the present
one. Judging from such remarks, I don't believe that the fundamental laws of this
country will last much longer.) The President is thus not a king. Nevertheless,
since the Shogun's letter was addressed to him, we adopted such manners of etiquette [*rei*] as were appropriate to a monarch. It was pointless, however, to put on
the formal *kariginu* robe in his honor, since the Americans attach little importance
to hierarchic distinction, and dispense with all ceremony [*reigi*]. We were, however, exceedingly happy and satisfied to have attained the goal of our mission
here, an achievement worthy of any man's ambition, when we learned that the
President was highly appreciative and took pride in receiving the first mission
from Japan in his country before any other. We were told that he was letting the
newspapers show our party dressed in *kariginu*.

47

Ito Hirobumi, "Reminiscences on the Drafting of the New Constitution"

The leading architect of a constitutional government in Japan was Ito
Hirobumi (1841–1909). Entrusted by the emperor with a mission to investigate the workings of European countries, Ito spent 18 months in Europe
from 1882 to 1883. He admired Bismarck's Germany and became convinced that — in form at least — the German imperial constitution of 1871
was best suited for Japan ; but he insisted that the spirit behind the constitution should be Japanese. Among other factors, he was determined to see
the emperor remain the source of political power in the new constitutional order. His liberal critics were fearful of creating an authoritarian government, while conservatives were afraid that the constitution would be too
progressive.

The constitution was promulgated on February 11, 1889, the anniversary of the founding of the nation in 660 B.C., as an imperial gift to the people. It provided for a bicameral parliament or Diet, the first of its kind east of
the Suez. The following memoir was written by Ito Hirobumi, the four-time
premier, just before his death in 1909. The document reflects the author's
views on the importance of adopting the Western concept of popular participation in government without sacrificing Japanese political traditions.

QUESTIONS TO CONSIDER

1. What aspects of Western political institutions, particularly those of Germany, were attractive to Ito Hirobumi?
2. What were the native political institutions that the author valued most in framing the constitution?
3. Was the Meiji constitution a democratic document?

Draft of the New Constitution

It was in the month of March, 1882, that His Majesty ordered me to work out a draft of a constitution to be submitted to his approval. No time was to be lost, so I started on the 15th of the same month for an extended journey to different constitutional countries to make as thorough a study as possible of the actual workings of different systems of constitutional government, of their various provisions, as well as of theories and opinions actually entertained by influential persons on the actual stage itself of constitutional life. I took young men with me, who all belonged to the élite of the rising generation, to assist and to cooperate with me in my studies. I sojourned about a year and a half in Europe, and having gathered the necessary materials, in so far as it was possible in so short a space of time, I returned home in September, 1883. Immediately after my return I set to work to draw up the Constitution. I was assisted in my work by my secretaries, prominent among whom were the late Viscount K. Inouyé, and the Barons M. Itō and K. Kanéko, and by foreign advisers, such as Professor Roesler, Mr. Piggott, and others.

Peculiar Features of the National Life

It was evident from the outset that mere imitation of foreign models would not suffice, for there were historical peculiarities of our country which had to be taken into consideration. For example, the Crown was, with us, an institution far more deeply rooted in the national sentiment and in our history than in other countries. It was indeed the very essence of a once theocratic State, so that in formulating the restrictions on its prerogatives in the new Constitution, we had to take care to safeguard the future realness or vitality of these prerogatives, and not to let the institution degenerate into an ornamental crowning piece of the edifice. At the same time, it was also evident that any form of constitutional régime was impossible without full and extended protection of honor, liberty, property, and personal security of citizens, entailing necessarily many important restrictions on the powers of the Crown.

From Rusaku Tsunoda et al., eds., *Sources of Japanese Tradition* (New York : Columbia University Press, 1958), pp. 673–676. © 1958, Columbia University Press. Reprinted by permission of Columbia University Press.

Emotional Elements in Social Life of People

On the other hand, there was one peculiarity of our social conditions that is without parallel in any other civilized country. Homogeneous in race, language, religion, and sentiments, so long secluded from the outside world, with the centuries-long traditions and inertia of the feudal system, in which the family and quasi-family ties permeated and formed the essence of every social organization, and moreover with such moral and religious tenets as laid undue stress on duties of fraternal aid and mutual succor, we had during the course of our seclusion unconsciously become a vast village community where cold intellect and calculation of public events were always restrained and even often hindered by warm emotions between man and man. . . .

. . . It must, of course, be admitted that this social peculiarity is not without beneficial influences. It mitigates the conflict, serves as the lubricator of social organisms, and tends generally to act as a powerful lever for the practical application of the moral principle of mutual assistance between fellow citizens. But unless curbed and held in restraint, it too may exercise baneful influences on society, for in a village community, where feelings and emotions hold a higher place than intellect, free discussion is apt to be smothered, attainment and transference of power liable to become a family question of a powerful oligarchy, and the realization of such a régime as constitutional monarchy to become an impossibility, simply because in any representative régime free discussion is a matter of prime necessity, because emotions and passions have to be stopped for the sake of the cool calculation of national welfare, and even the best of friends have often to be sacrificed if the best abilities and highest intellects are to guide the helm. Besides, the dissensions between brothers and relatives, deprived as they usually are of safety-valves for giving free and hearty vent to their own opinions or discontents, are apt to degenerate into passionate quarrels and overstep the bounds of simple differences of opinion. The good side of this social peculiarity had to be retained as much as possible, while its baneful influences had to be safeguarded. These and many other peculiarities had to be taken into account in order to have a constitution adapted to the actual condition of the country.

Conflict Between the Old and New Thoughts

Another difficulty equally grave had to be taken into consideration. We were just then in an age of transition. The opinions prevailing in the country were extremely heterogeneous, and often diametrically opposed to each other. We had survivors of former generations who were still full of theocratic ideas, and who believed that any attempt to restrict an imperial prerogative amounted to something like high treason. On the other hand there was a large and powerful body of the younger generation educated at the time when the Manchester theory was in vogue, and who in consequence were ultra-radical in their ideas of freedom. Members of the bureaucracy were prone to lend willing ears to the German doctrinaires of the reactionary period, while, on the other hand, the educated politicians among the people having not yet tasted the bitter significance of administrative responsibility, were liable to be more influenced by the dazzling words and lucid theories of Montesquieu, Rousseau, and other similar French writers. A work entitled *History of Civilization,* by Buckle, which denounced every form of government as an unnecessary evil, became the great favorite of students of all the higher schools, including the Imperial University. On the other hand, these same students would not have dared to expound the theories of Buckle before their own conservative fathers. At that time we had not yet arrived at the stage of distinguishing clearly between political opposition on the one hand, and treason to the established order of things on the other. The virtues necessary for the smooth working of any constitution, such as love of freedom of speech, love of publicity of proceedings, the spirit of tolerance for opinions opposed to one's own, etc., had yet to be learned by long experience.

Draft of the Constitution Completed

It was under these circumstances that the first draft of the Constitution was made and submitted to His Majesty, after which it was handed over to the mature deliberation of the Privy Council. The Sovereign himself presided over these deliberations, and he had full opportunities of hearing and giving due consideration to all the conflicting opinions above hinted at. I believe nothing evidences more vividly the intelligence of our august Master than the fact that in spite of the existence of strong undercurrents of an ultra-conservative nature in the council, and also in the country at large, His Majesty's decisions inclined almost invariably towards liberal and progressive ideas, so that we have been ultimately able to obtain the Constitution as it exists at present.

48

Geisha: *Glimpse of Unfamiliar Japan*

The term *geisha* was first used in the middle of the eighteenth century during the Tokugawa period (1600–1868), and the first geisha were male entertainers. But in time, women came to dominate the profession. Aspiring geisha had to have good looks and more importantly good training in various traditional arts such as classical dancing, playing a stringed instrument called the shamisen, singing, games, and flirtatious conversation. Some of the ambitious geisha were even trained in the tea ceremony, flower arranging, calligraphy, and painting. Training began early for girls, often as young as eight or nine, from poor families who were adopted into geisha houses and worked as maid servants for a few years as part of their early apprenticeship. When they reached the age of about 13, they were admitted to full apprenticeship, which lasted about five years. Upon successful completion of the apprenticeship, these girls had to pass an examination of their artistic skills at their local geisha registry before the senior members of the geisha union. Successful geisha candidates then registered at the local registry and were ready to receive assignments. They were hired to entertain customers at dinner parties or at certain restaurants. In recent decades, the profession of geisha has suffered a decline as a result of the inroad of the Western-style bar hostesses. But the geisha house today still enjoys the special favor of the Japanese politicians who prefer to conduct political negotiations at a geisha house rather than at Western-style restaurants.

The following excerpt is an account of the Japanese geisha and a geisha party described by Lafcadio Hearn (1850–1904), an Anglo-Irish-Greek who went to Japan in 1890 and became a Japanese citizen, taking the Japanese name Koizumi Yagumo. He became one of the most popular Western writers on Japan at the turn of the century.

QUESTIONS TO CONSIDER

1. How do you compare geisha with the women in a comparable entertainment profession in the West?
2. Why do you think the Japanese politicians generally prefer geisha houses to Western-style restaurants for conducting political negotiations?
3. Why would a woman become a geisha?

The robed guests take their places, quite noiselessly and without speech, upon the kneeling-cushions. The lacquered services are laid upon the matting before them by maidens whose bare feet make no sound. For a while there is only smiling and flitting, as in dreams. You are not likely to hear any voices from without, as a banqueting-house is usually secluded from the street by spacious gardens. At last the master of ceremonies, host or provider, breaks the hush with the consecrated formula: "*O-somatsu degozarimasu ga! — dōzo o-hashi!*" whereat all present bow silently, take up their hashi (chopsticks), and fall to. But hashi, deftly used, cannot be heard at all. The maidens pour warm saké into the cup of each guest without making the least sound; and it is not until several dishes have been emptied, and several cups of saké absorbed, that tongues are loosened.

Then, all at once, with a little burst of laughter, a number of young girls enter, make the customary prostration of greeting, glide into the open space between the ranks of the guests, and begin to serve the wine with a grace and dexterity of which no common maid is capable. They are pretty; they are clad in very costly robes of silk; they are girdled like queens; and the beautifully dressed hair of each is decked with mock flowers, with wonderful combs and pins, and with curious ornaments of gold. They greet the stranger as if they had always known him; they jest, laugh, and utter funny little cries. These are the geisha,[1] or dancing-girls, hired for the banquet.

Samisen[2] tinkle. The dancers withdraw to a clear space at the farther end of the banqueting-hall, always vast enough to admit of many more guests than ever

Lafcadio Hearn, *Glimpse of Unfamiliar Japan*, vol. II (Boston: Houghton Mifflin and Co., 1894), pp. 525–533.
    1. The Kyōto word is *maiko*.
    2. Guitars of three strings.

assemble upon common occasions. Some form the orchestra, under the direction of a woman of uncertain age ; there are several samisen, and a tiny drum played by a child. Others, singly or in pairs, perform the dance. It may be swift and merry, consisting wholly of graceful posturing, — two girls dancing together with such coincidence of step and gesture as only years of training could render possible. But more frequently it is rather like acting than like what we Occidentals call dancing, — acting accompanied with extraordinary waving of sleeves and fans, and with a play of eyes and features, sweet, subtle, subdued, wholly Oriental. There are more voluptuous dances known to geisha, but upon ordinary occasions and before refined audiences they portray beautiful old Japanese traditions, like the legend of the fisher Urashima, beloved by the Sea God's daughter ; and at intervals they sing ancient Chinese poems, expressing a natural emotion with delicious vividness by a few exquisite words. And always they pour the wine, — that warm, pale yellow, drowsy wine which fills the veins with soft contentment, making a faint sense of ecstasy, through which, as through some poppied sleep, the commonplace becomes wondrous and blissful, and the geisha Maids of Paradise, and the world much sweeter than, in the natural order of things, it could ever possibly be.

The banquet, at first so silent, slowly changes to a merry tumult. . . .

Notwithstanding all this apparent comradeship, a certain rigid decorum between guest and geisha is invariably preserved at a Japanese banquet. However flushed with wine a guest may have become, you will never see him attempt to caress a girl ; he never forgets that she appears at the festivities only as a human flower, to be looked at, not to be touched. The familiarity which foreign tourists in Japan frequently permit themselves with geisha or with waiter-girls, though endured with smiling patience, is really much disliked, and considered by native observers an evidence of extreme vulgarity.

For a time the merriment grows ; but as midnight draws near, the guests begin to slip away, one by one, unnoticed. Then the din gradually dies down, the music stops ; and at last the geisha, having escorted the latest of the feasters to the door, with laughing cries of *Sayōnara*, can sit down alone to break their long fast in the deserted hall.

Such is the geisha's rôle. But what is the mystery of her ? What are her thoughts, her emotions, her secret self ? What is her veritable existence beyond the night circle of the banquet lights, far from the illusion formed around her by the mist of wine ? . . .

The girl begins her career as a slave, a pretty child bought from miserably poor parents under a contract, according to which her services may be claimed by the purchasers for eighteen, twenty, or even twenty-five years. She is fed, clothed, and trained in a house occupied only by geisha ; and she passes the rest of her childhood under severe discipline. She is taught etiquette, grace, polite speech ; she has daily lessons in dancing ; and she is obliged to learn by heart a multitude of songs with their airs. Also she must learn games, the service of banquets and weddings, the art of dressing and looking beautiful. Whatever physical gifts she may have are carefully cultivated. Afterwards she is taught to handle musical instruments : first, the little drum (*tsudzumi*), which cannot be sounded at all without considerable practice ; then she learns to play the samisen a little, with a plectrum of tortoise-shell or ivory. At eight or nine years of age she attends banquets, chiefly as a drum-player. She is then the most charming little creature imaginable, and already knows how to fill your wine-cup exactly full, with a single toss of the bottle and without spilling a drop, between two taps of her drum.

Thereafter her discipline becomes more cruel. Her voice may be flexible enough, but lacks the requisite strength. In the iciest hours of winter nights, she must ascend to the roof of her dwelling-house, and there sing and play till the blood oozes from her fingers and the voice dies in her throat. The desired result is an atrocious cold. After a period of hoarse whispering, her voice changes its tone and strengthens. She is ready to become a public singer and dancer.

In this capacity she usually makes her first appearance at the age of twelve or thirteen. If pretty and skillful, her services will be much in demand, and her time paid for at the rate of twenty to twenty-five sen (Japanese cent) per hour. Then only do her purchasers begin to reimburse themselves for the time, expense, and trouble of her training ; and they are not apt to be generous. For many years more all that she earns must pass into their hands. She can own nothing, not even her clothes.

At seventeen or eighteen she has made her artistic reputation. She has been at many hundreds of entertainments, and knows by sight all the important personages of her city, the character of each, the history of all. Her life has been chiefly a night life ; rarely has she seen the sun rise since she became a dancer. She has learned to drink wine without ever losing her head, and to fast for seven or eight hours without ever feeling the worse. She has had many lovers. To a certain extent she is free to smile upon whom she pleases ; but she has been well taught, above all else, to use her power of charm for her own advantage. She hopes to find Somebody able and willing to buy her freedom, — which Somebody would almost certainly thereafter discover many new and excellent meanings in those Buddhist texts that tell about the foolishness of love and the impermanency of all human relationships.

United States Expansion: Two Views

U.S. involvement in Latin America sharply increased after the Spanish-American War of 1898 when the United States helped Cuba achieve its independence from Spain. A few years later, during Theodore Roosevelt's administration, the United States aided the Panamanian revolutionaries in their effort to secede from Colombia. Cuba and Panama included in their new constitutions the right of American intervention to guarantee their independence and enhance stability. When the United States began to build a canal through the Isthmus of Panama, both that nation and Cuba became virtual American protectorates, and U.S. influence spread extensively throughout Central America and the Caribbean.

Meanwhile, in the Latin American nations, powerful landholding interests and local militias collaborated to suppress rebellions and reforms ; civil wars rather than legitimate elections became institutionalized as a mechanism for transferring power. Because of this chronic instability, Roosevelt announced, as a "corollary" to the Monroe Doctrine, that the United States had the right to intervene to prevent "chronic wrongdoing" and European interference. Although the United States hoped to encourage political stability in the area by supervising elections and enacting financial reforms, the most controversial "remedy" for instability was U.S. military intervention, which frequently occurred at the request of an incumbent regime. For nearly three decades, these interventions helped stabilize governments in Nicaragua, Cuba, the Dominican Republic, Haiti, and Mexico. In most cases, however, one of the most important legacies of U.S. involvement was a U.S.-trained local militia or National Guard, which remained aligned with conservative interests to block reforms and suppress revolutionary movements.

Dana Munro, the author of the first reading in this section, examines the motives behind U.S. policy in Latin America during these years. He served as a foreign service officer in the State Department and represented the United States in Panama, Nicaragua, and Haiti during the period 1921–1932 ; thus he was involved in implementing the policies he describes. The selection by Francisco García Calderón reflects the reaction of Latin American intellectuals toward U.S. expansionism at the turn of the century. He was a prominent Peruvian diplomat who represented his nation at the Paris Peace Conference in 1918 and in the League of Nations.

49

Dana Munro, "The Objectives of U.S. Policy in Latin America"

In the following selection, Dana Munro, a U.S. diplomat and historian, staunchly defends the goals of U.S. policy in Latin America during the early decades of the twentieth century. He declares that they were "neither sinister nor sordid."

QUESTIONS TO CONSIDER

1. According to Munro, what conditions in Latin America threatened the independence of various states?
2. Why did that instability pose a threat to U.S. national security?
3. What were the consequences of discouraging revolutions in Central America and the Caribbean? Consider this policy with reference to conditions in Mexico (see Reading 54).
4. How did the United States attempt to encourage economic improvements in Latin America? What were the obstacles to economic development there?

It would be impossible to deny that many of the American government's actions were ill-judged and unfortunate in their results. As we look back on the story, however, it seems clear that the motives that inspired its policy were basically political rather than economic. What the United States was trying to do, throughout the period with which this study has dealt [1900–1921], was to put an end to conditions that threaten the independence of some of the Caribbean states and were consequently a potential danger to the security of the United States. Revolutions must be discouraged ; the bad financial practices that weakened the governments and involved them in trouble with foreigners must be reformed ; and general economic and social conditions, which were a basic cause of instability, must be improved. The Platt Amendment was an effort to achieve these purposes in Cuba and the Roosevelt Corollary to the Monroe Doctrine meant that the United States would seek to achieve them in other Caribbean states.

The same purpose inspired the policy of successive administrations from Theodore Roosevelt to Woodrow Wilson. The methods used in attempting to achieve them varied from one administration to another, but more because of accumulating experience and increasing involvement than because of any difference in the ultimate goals. Each successive Secretary of State took up Caribbean problems where his predecessor had left them, in most cases making no abrupt change in the way in which they were being handled. . . .

Throughout the period between 1901 and 1921, the first objective of American policy in the Caribbean was to discourage revolutions. Revolutions, and the interstate wars that often rose out of them, were the chief cause of controversies with European powers because they endangered foreign lives and property and disrupted the government's finances so that it could not meet foreign claims. Frequent civil wars were also an obstacle to any sort of material or social progress. A government that had to devote all of its resources simply to maintaining itself in power could do little road building and little for public education, and an atmosphere of insecurity discouraged private enterprises in agriculture or industry.

The improvement of economic conditions was a second objective. There could be little basic improvement in the political situation while the masses of the people were poverty stricken and illiterate. A part of the Dominican bond issue of 1908 was used for public works, though little was accomplished, and the proposed loan for Nicaragua was to have provided funds to build a railroad. In Haiti and the Dominican Republic the occupation authorities had ambitious programs of road-building, port improvement, and sanitation. All economic development, however, had to be carried on with the limited funds available from the countries' own revenues or from loans, because it would hardly have been possible before 1921 to ask the United States Congress to make grants to aid another country.

In discussing their policy, officials in the State Department sometimes held out the hope of increased trade and new fields for American investment as a third objective. It is doubtful, however, whether these considerations really had any great influence in the formulation of policy. There is little evidence that the American government made any important effort to promote trade, and with the exception of Cuba the countries which the United States tried particularly to help were too small and too poor in natural resources to offer attractive opportunities for foreign enterprises.

These objectives, whatever we may think of the way in which the American government tried to attain them, were neither sinister nor sordid. Many critics of the United States' policy, however, maintained that there was a fourth purpose to forward the selfish interests of American businessmen and bankers. To what extent this charge is justified is one of the questions that must be considered in any study of dollar diplomacy and intervention.

50

Francisco García Calderón, "Imperialism of Decadence"

In this selection, Francisco García Calderón, a Peruvian diplomat and writer, sharply criticizes U.S. policy and private commercial interests for exploiting Latin Americans. He also warns of the dangers of cultural imperialism.

QUESTIONS TO CONSIDER

1. Was García Calderón justified in thinking that ". . . loans concluded with the monarchs of North American finance have reduced the people to a new slavery"?
2. According to the author, what were some of the differences which divided the two Americas? Were his judgments valid or were they based on false assumptions? How did these differences exacerbate U.S. relations with Latin America?
3. Why did García Calderón regard the United States as a threat to Latin America's cultural identity? Were his concerns justified?
4. Compare Calderón's views of the American character with those expressed by Alexis de Toqueville (see Reading 33). Are there similarities? If so, what are they, and why do they exist?

Interventions have become more frequent with the expansion of frontiers. The United States have recently intervened in the territory of Acre, there to found a republic of rubber gatherers; at Panama, there to develop a province and construct a canal; in Cuba, under cover of the Platt Amendment, to maintain order

From Francisco García Calderón, *Latin America : Its Rise and Progress* (London : T. F. Unwin, 1913), pp. 392–393.

in the interior ; in Santo Domingo, to support the civilising revolution and over-throw the tyrants ; in Venezuela, and in Central America, to enforce upon these nations, torn by intestine disorders, the political and financial tutelage of the im-perial democracy. In Guatemala and Honduras the loans concluded with the mon-archs of North American finance have reduced the people to a new slavery. Supervision of the customs and the dispatch of pacificatory squadrons to defend the interests of the Anglo-Saxon have enforced peace and tranquility : such are the means employed. The New York American announces that Mr. Pierpont Morgan proposes to encompass the finances of Latin America by a vast network of Yankee banks. Chicago merchants and Wall Street financiers created the Meat Trust in the Argentine. The United States offer millions for the purpose of con-verting into Yankee loans the moneys raised in London during the last century by the Latin American States ; they wish to obtain a monopoly of credit. It has even been announced, although the news hardly appears probable, that a North Amer-ican syndicate wished to buy enormous belts of land in Guatemala, where the En-glish tongue is the obligatory language. The fortification of the Panama Canal, and the possible acquisition of the Galapagos Island in the Pacific, are fresh mani-festations of imperialistic progress. . . .

Warnings, advice, distrust, invasion of capital, plans of financial hegemony all these justify the anxiety of the southern peoples. . . . Neither irony nor grace nor scepticism, gifts of the old civilizations, can make way against the plebeian bru-tality, the excessive optimism, the violent individualism of the [North American] people.

All these things contribute to the triumph of mediocrity ; the multitude of primary schools, the vices of utilitarianism, the cult of the average citizen, the transatlantic M. Homais,[1] and the tyranny of opinion noted by Tocqueville ; and in this vulgarity, which is devoid of traditions and has no leading aristocracy, a re-turn to the primitive type of the redskin, which has already been noted by close observers, is threatening the proud democracy. From the excessive tension of wills, from the elementary state of culture, from the perpetual unrest of life, from the harshness of the industrial struggle, anarchy and violence will be born in the future. In a hundred years men will seek in vain for the "American soul," the "gen-ius of America," elsewhere than in the undisciplined force or the violence which ignores moral laws. . . .

Essential points of difference separate the two Americas. Differences of lan-guage and therefore of spirit ; the difference between Spanish Catholicism and multiform Protestantism of the Anglo-Saxons ; between the Yankee individualism and the omnipotence of the State natural to the nations of the South. In their ori-gin, as in their race, we find fundamental antagonism ; the evolution of the North is slow and obedient to the lessons of time, to the influences of custom ; the history of the southern peoples is full of revolutions, rich with dreams of an unattainable perfection.

---

1. M. Homais is a character in Gustave Flaubert's *Madame Bovary* (1857). He is the prime ex-ample of the bland nineteenth-century bourgeoisie.

AN ERA OF GLOBAL VIOLENCE

China, Russia, and Mexico in Upheaval

During the first decade of the twentieth century, when many people around the world found their lives disrupted by imperialism, industrialization, and modernization, they began to organize and press for reforms. This effort was especially evident in the powerful demands for change erupting in China, Russia, and Mexico. In the case of China, some wanted to terminate the alien Manchu rule by taking direct action. Of these, the most prominent was Sun Yat-sen (1866–1925), who, although trained as a physician, decided to devote his full attention to organizing a revolution to overthrow the Manchus, restore Chinese rule, and establish a federal republic. Following an abortive attempt to stage an uprising in 1895, he fled the country and traveled extensively to organize a revolution and gain support from Chinese living overseas. While he was in Europe, from 1897 to 1898, his famous Three Principles of the People [Sanmin Zhuyi] — nationalism, democracy, and the people's livelihood — were germinated.

In Russia, Tsar Nicholas II (reigned 1894–1917), the last of the Romanovs, was unwilling to concede to any of the Russian people's demands for reforms until the outbreak of revolution on January 9, 1905. At that time, Russia had been at war with Japan for almost a year, and the populace was becoming increasingly disenchanted by the nation's military losses abroad. On January 9, known as "Bloody Sunday," a group of workers led by Father George Gapon marched to the Winter Palace in St. Petersburg to present the tsar with a list of their grievances and political and economic demands. The unarmed workers were met at the bridge by soldiers. After firing two warning shots into the air, the soldiers, ordered not to allow the procession to cross the river, fired point-blank into the crowd. With that shooting, the revolution of 1905 began. After almost a year of strikes and violence, the tsar issued the October Manifesto, which promised civil liberties, a limited suffrage, and a Duma (a limited two-house assembly).

The quest for reforms in Mexico began with a revolt against the continuing dictatorship of Porfirio Díaz (1830–1915), who had dominated the nation since his first election to the presidency in 1876. Díaz had created a highly centralized police state and suppressed individual freedom. He had also attracted many foreign investors who, lured by generous concessions, helped Mexico industrialize and modernize. Although the material benefits of the "Age of Díaz" created a powerful and prosperous elite, they also prompted a reexamination of the character of Mexican society. This process stirred strong nationalistic sentiments that led to the Mexican Revolution, the first major social and political upheaval in modern Latin American history. When the revolution began, it was led by Francisco Madero, the son of a wealthy land-owning family, who opposed Díaz in the nation's presidential elections of 1910.

51

Manifesto of the Chinese United League

In 1905, under Sun Yat-sen's leadership, a number of Chinese revolutionary groups joined together in Tokyo to form the Chinese United League [Tongmenghui], the forerunner of the Kuomintang [Guomindang], or Chinese Nationalist Party. On October 10, 1911, a military mutiny engineered by the United League broke out in Wuchang, in central China. The revolution spread to other cities and provinces, becoming a national movement that ended centuries of Imperial rule and marked the birth of the Chinese Republic.

The central ideas of China's first modern political revolution, formulated by Sun Yat-sen, are contained in the 1905 Manifesto issued at the founding of the Chinese United League in Tokyo. In the following excerpt from that document, note the plans for equalization of land ownership and for a three-stage revolution, which Sun saw as a necessary period of adjustment before the Chinese people could enjoy democracy.

QUESTIONS TO CONSIDER

1. How revolutionary were the programs proclaimed in Sun Yat-sen's document?
2. According to Sun Yat-sen, what were the three stages of revolution?
3. In retrospect, how did China's politics evolve after the fall of the Manchu dynasty?

By order of the Military Government, on the _____ day, _____ month, _____ year of Tien-yun [Dianyun], the Commander-in-Chief of the Chinese National Army proclaims the purposes and platform of the Military Government to the people of the nation:

From Ssu-yu Teng and John K. Fairbank, *China's Response to the West: A Documentary Survey, 1839–1923* (Cambridge, Mass.: Harvard University Press, 1954), pp. 227–229 © 1954, 1979 by the President and Fellows of Harvard College; © 1982 by Ssu-yu Teng and John K. Fairbank. Reprinted by permission of Harvard University Press.

Now the National Army has established the Military Government, which aims to cleanse away two hundred and sixty years of barbarous filth, restore our four-thousand-year-old fatherland, and plan for the welfare of the four hundred million people. Not only is this an unavoidable obligation of the Military Government, but all our fellow-nationals should also take it as their own responsibility. We recall that, since the beginning of our nation the Chinese have always ruled China ; although at times alien peoples have usurped the rule, yet our ancestors were able to drive them out and restore Chinese sovereignty so that they could hand down the nation to posterity. Now the men of Han [i.e., the Chinese] have raised a righteous [or patriotic] army to exterminate the northern barbarians. This is a continuation of heroic deeds bequeathed to us by our predecessors, and a great righteous cause lies behind it ; there is none among us Chinese who does not understand this. But the revolutions in former generations, such as the Ming Dynasty and the Taiping Heavenly Kingdom, were concerned only with the driving out of barbarians and the restoration of Chinese rule. Aside from these they sought no other change. We today are different from people of former times. Besides the driving out of the barbarian dynasty and the restoration of China, it is necessary also to change the national polity and the people's livelihood. And though there are a myriad ways and means to achieve this goal, the essential spirit that runs through them all is freedom, equality, and fraternity. Therefore in former days there were heroes' revolutions, but today we have a national revolution [*Kuo-min ko-ming* [Guomin Geming], lit., revolution of the people of the country]. "National revolution" means that all people in the nation will have the spirit of freedom, equality, and fraternity ; that is, they will all bear the responsibility of revolution. The Military Government is but their agent. From now on the people's responsibility will be the responsibility of the Military Government, and the achievements of the Military Government will be those of the people. With a cooperative mind and concerted effort, the Military Government and the people will thus perform their duty. Therefore we proclaim to the world in utmost sincerity the outline of the present revolution and the fundamental plan for the future administration of the nation.

1. *Drive Out the Tartars:* The Manchus of today were originally the eastern barbarians beyond the Great Wall. They frequently caused border troubles during the Ming dynasty ; then when China was in a disturbed state they came inside Shanhaikuan [Shanhaiguan], conquered China, and enslaved our Chinese people. Those who opposed them were killed by the hundreds of thousands, and our Chinese have been a people without a nation for two hundred and sixty years. The extreme cruelties and tyrannies of the Manchu government have now reached their limit. With the righteous army poised against them, we will overthrow that government, and restore our sovereign rights. Those Manchu and Chinese military men who have a change of heart and come over to us will be granted amnesty, while those who dare to resist will be slaughtered without mercy. Chinese who act as Chinese traitors in the cause of the Manchus will be treated in the same way.

2. *Restore China:* China is the China of the Chinese. The government of China should be in the hands of the Chinese. After driving out the Tartars we must restore our national state. Those who dare to act like Shih Ching-t'ang [Shi Jingtang] or Wu San-kuei [Wu Sangui] [both were traitors] will be attacked by the whole country.

3. *Establish the Republic:* Now our revolution is based on equality, in order to establish a republican government. All our people are equal and all enjoy political rights. The president will be publicly chosen by the people of the country. The parliament will be made up of members publicly chosen by the people of the country. A constitution of the Chinese Republic will be enacted, and every person must abide by it. Whoever dares to make himself a monarch shall be attacked by the whole country.

4. *Equalize Land Ownership:* The good fortune of civilization is to be shared equally by all the people of the nation. We should improve our social and economic organization, and assess the value of all the land in the country. Its present price shall be received by the owner, but all increases in value resulting from reform and social improvements after the revolution shall belong to the state, to be shared by all the people, in order to create a socialist state, where each family within the empire can be well supported, each person satisfied, and no one fail to secure employment. Those who dare to control the livelihood of the people through monopoly shall be ostracized.

The above four points will be carried out in three steps in due order. The first period is government by military law. When the righteous army has arisen, various places will join the cause. The common people of each locality will escape from the Manchu fetters. Those who come upon the enemy must unite in hatred of him, must join harmoniously with the compatriots within their ranks and suppress the enemy bandits. Both the armies and the people will be under the rule of military law. The armies will do their best in defeating the enemy on behalf of the people, and the people will supply the needs of the armies, and not do harm to their security. The local administration, in areas where the enemy has been either already defeated or not yet defeated, will be controlled in general by the Military Government, so that step by step the accumulated evils can be swept away. Evils like the oppression of the government, the greed and graft of officials, the squeeze of government clerks and runners, the cruelty of tortures and penalties, the tyranny of tax collections, the humiliation of the queue — shall all be exterminated together with the Manchu rule. Evils in social customs, such as the keeping of slaves, the cruelty of foot-binding, the spread of the poison of opium, the obstructions of geomancy (*feng-shui*), should also all be prohibited. The time limit for each district (*hsien*) is three years. In those *hsien* where real results are achieved before the end of three years, the military law shall be lifted and a provisional constitution shall be enacted.

The second period is that of government by a provisional constitution. When military law is lifted in each *hsien,* the Military Government shall return the right of self-government to the local people. The members of local councils and local officials shall all be elected by the people. All rights and duties of the Military Government toward the people and those of the people toward the government shall be regulated by the provisional constitution, which shall be observed by the Military Government, the local councils, and the people. Those who violate the law shall be held responsible. Six years after the securing of peace in the nation the provisional constitution shall be annulled and the constitution shall be promulgated.

The third period will be government under the constitution. Six years after the provisional constitution has been enforced a constitution shall be made. The military and administrative powers of the Military Government shall be annulled ; the people shall elect the president, and elect the members of parliament to organize the parliament. The administrative matters of the nation shall proceed according to the provisions of the constitution.

Of these three periods the first is the period in which the Military Government leads the people in eradicating all traditional evils and abuses ; the second is the period in which the Military Government gives the power of local self-government to the people while retaining general control over national affairs ; the third is the period in which the Military Government is divested of its powers, and the government will by itself manage the national affairs under the constitution. It is hoped that our people will proceed in due order and cultivate their free and equal status ; the foundation of the Chinese Republic will be entirely based on this.

[The last paragraph of the manifesto consists of an exhortation to the Chinese people to rise to the occasion, support the ever-faithful Military Government, and shoulder the responsibility of protecting the country and preserving their own ancient and superior race.]

52

V. I. Lenin, *What Is to Be Done?*

By the 1890s, events in Western Europe had largely discredited the basic ideas of the *Communist Manifesto* that capitalist leaders would never tolerate meaningful reform and that workers would never attain a higher standard of living or political rights by peaceful means. Most adult male workers could vote by then ; labor unions were not only tolerated but successful in gaining higher real wages for workers ; political parties favoring the working masses were electing more representatives to legislative bodies. Such previously committed Marxists as Germany's Eduard Bernstein wanted to maintain Marxist goals of aiding the economic, political, and social advance of the workers but — in view of changed political conditions — to do so through political parties, platforms, and elections.

In Russia, however, a militant orthodox movement was headed by Vladimir Illyich Ulyanov (1870–1924), who used the alias of "Nikolai Lenin." He is usually referred to by his real initials and his assumed last name : V. I. Lenin. Lenin's first claim to historical significance was moving the center of Marxist orthodoxy to Russia, since Western Europe was adopting a (for him) watered-down version of Marxism, which he derisively called "Bernstein-ism." Looking at conditions in his own Russia, Lenin insisted that the working class was more miserable than ever, that no political rights were in sight for workers, and that the tsarist regime really did not intend to allow either political or economic reforms. In other words, what was true for Marx and Engels in the 1840s in Western Europe was no longer true for Western European Marxists in the twentieth century but was still true for Russian Bolsheviks.

Equally important was Lenin's success in clarifying the primary role of the Party as the "vanguard" of the proletariat in the revolutionary struggle. Marx and Engels had never determined how much authority the Party should have; they viewed the Communist Revolution as the result of capitalism's self-destruction and heightened class-consciousness of the proletariat. In his early work *What Is To Be Done?* (1902), Lenin made it plain that the Party would lead, the workers would follow, and the Party itself would be led by a relatively small group of professionals. In the excerpts below, we find Lenin berating those within the movement who want the freedom to criticize those positions that he believes harmonize with true Marxism. He is equally impatient with those who place too much value on spontaneity within the movement, rather than accepting the guidance of those who stick with (for him) true Marxist theory.

Before the 1860s, Marxists made a distinction between themselves as Communists and others as Socialists, but between the 1860s and the period immediately following the Russian Revolution of 1917, most Marxists used the terms "Socialist" and "Social-Democrat" for themselves. Roughly a year after Lenin wrote *What Is To Be Done?,* his wing of the Russian Social-Democratic Party took the name "Bolshevik" (from the Russian word for majority) for itself. Following the Bolshevik victory over the Provisional Government after World War I, Lenin decided to change the Party's name from "Social-Democratic" to "Communist."

QUESTIONS TO CONSIDER

1. What is the point of Lenin's parable of the "marshy road"?
2. What can Lenin mean when he insists: "We are too 'free' to go where we please ..."?
3. Why is trade-union consciousness inadequate as a basis for revolutionary change?
4. Do you find Lenin sharing Rousseau's notion of the "General Will"? Why or why not?

"Freedom" is a grand word, but under the banner of Free Trade the most predatory wars were conducted: under the banner of "free labour," the toilers were robbed. The term "freedom of criticism" contains the same inherent falsehood. Those who are really convinced that they have advanced science, would demand, not freedom for the new views to continue side by side with the old, but the substitution of the old views by the new views.

We are marching in a compact group along a precipitous and difficult path, firmly holding each other by the hand. We are surrounded on all sides by enemies, and are under their almost constant fire. We have combined voluntarily, especially for the purpose of fighting the enemy and not to retreat into the adjacent marsh,

From V. I. Lenin, *What Is To Be Done?* (Peking: Foreign Language Press, 1975), pp. 14–35, passim and p. 112.

the inhabitants of which, right from the very outset, have reproached us with having separated ourselves into an exclusive group, and with having chosen the path of struggle instead of the path of conciliation. And now several in our crowd begin to cry out : Let us go into this marsh! And when we begin to shame them, they retort : How conservative you are! Are you not ashamed to deny us the right to invite you to take a better road!

Oh yes, gentlemen! You are free, not only to invite us, but to go yourselves wherever you will, even into the marsh. In fact, we think that the marsh is your proper place, and we are prepared to render *you* every assistance to get there. Only, let go of our hands, don't clutch at us, and don't besmirch the grand word "freedom"; for we too are "free" to go where we please, free, not only to fight against the marsh, but also those who are turning towards the marsh....

We said that *there could not yet be* Social-Democratic consciousness among the workers. This consciousness could only be brought to them from without. The history of all countries shows that the working class, exclusively by its own effort, is able to develop only trade-union consciousness, *i.e.,* it may itself realise the necessity for combining in unions, to fight against the employers and to strive to compel the government to pass necessary labour legislation, etc.

The theory of Socialism, however, grew out of the philosophic, historical and economic theories that were elaborated by the educated representatives of the propertied classes, the intellectuals. The founders of modern scientific Socialism, Marx and Engels, themselves belonged to the bourgeois intelligentsia.

Similarly, in Russia, the theoretical doctrine of Social-Democracy arose quite independently of the spontaneous growth of the labour movement; it arose as a natural and inevitable outcome of the development of ideas among the revolutionary Socialist intelligentsia....

The lack of training of the majority of the revolutionists, being quite a natural phenomenon, could not have aroused any particular fears. Since the tasks were properly defined, since the energy existed for repeated attempts to fulfil these tasks, the temporary failures were not such a great misfortune. Revolutionary experience and organisational skill are things that can be acquired provided the desire is there to acquire these qualities, provided the shortcomings are recognised — which in revolutionary activity is more than half-way towards removing them!

It was a great misfortune, however, when this consciousness began to grow dim (it was very lively among the workers of the group mentioned), when people appeared — and even Social-Democratic organs — who were prepared to regard shortcomings as virtues, who tried even to put a *theoretical* basis to *slavish cringing before spontaneity*....

Since there can be no talk of an independent ideology being developed by the masses of the workers in the process of their movement, then *the only choice is :* Either bourgeois, or Socialist ideology. There is no middle course (for humanity has not created a "third" ideology, and, moreover, in a society torn by class antagonisms there can never be a non-class or above-class ideology). Hence, to belittle Socialist ideology *in any way,* to *deviate from it in the slightest degree* means strengthening bourgeois ideology. There is a lot of talk about spontaneity, but the *spontaneous* development of the labour movement leads to its becoming subordinated to bourgeois ideology....

I could go on analysing the rules, but I think that what has been said will suffice. A small, compact core, consisting of reliable, experienced and hardened workers, with responsible agents in the principal districts and connected by all the rules of strict secrecy with the organisations of revolutionists, can, with the wide support of the masses and without an elaborate set of rules, perform *all* the functions of a trade-union organisation, and perform them, moreover, in the manner Social-Democrats desire. Only in this way can we secure the *consolidation* and development of a *Social-Democratic* trade-union movement, in spite of the gendarmes.

It may be objected that an organisation which is so loose that it is not even formulated, and which even has no enrolled and registered members, cannot be called an organisation at all. That may very well be. I am not out for names. But this "organisation without members" can do everything that is required, and will, from the very outset, guarantee the closest contact between our future trade unionists and Socialism. Only an incorrigible utopian would want a *wide* organisation of workers, with elections, reports, universal suffrage, etc., under autocracy.

The moral to be drawn from this is a simple one. If we begin with the solid foundation of a strong organisation of revolutionists, we can guarantee the stability of the movement as a whole, and carry out the aims of both Social-Democracy and of trade unionism. If, however, we begin with a wide workers' organisation, supposed to be more "accessible" to the masses, when as a matter of fact it will be most accessible to the gendarmes, and will make the revolutionists most accessible to the police, we shall neither achieve the aims of Social-Democracy nor of trade unionism; we shall not escape from our primitiveness. . . .

53

Maxim Gorky, "January 9"

The following selection is from "January 9," a story by Maxim Gorky (1868–1936), written in 1906. Gorky was a participant in the march to the Winter Palace on Bloody Sunday. He indicates that the violence perpetrated against the workers destroyed their faith in the tsar as well as their belief that change could be initiated by him alone. It was a harsh lesson, and one that had far-ranging consequences.

QUESTIONS TO CONSIDER

1. Why did the Petersburg workers believe the Russian tsar would not allow them to be turned away or hurt?
2. Why did Bloody Sunday initiate a revolution in Russia?
3. Besides the events on Bloody Sunday, what were some of the other underlying social and economic causes of the Russian Revolution?

The crowd resembled a dark ocean wave; barely awakened by the first gust of the storm, it moved forward slowly; the grey faces of people were like the turbid foamy crest of a wave.

Their eyes glistened excitedly, but people looked at one another as though not believing their own decision, having surprised themselves. Words circled over the crowd like small grey birds.

They spoke softly, seriously, as if justifying themselves before one another.

"It's impossible to endure any longer, that's why we have come . . . "

"Without a reason, they won't touch the people . . ."

"Is it possible 'he' doesn't understand this ? . . ."

More than anything they talked about "him," convincing each other that "he" was kind, loving, and understood everything . . . But the words which created his image were colorless. It seemed as though for a long time — and perhaps never — they had not thought seriously about "him," had not imagined him as a real living person, did not know what he was like, and even poorly understood why "he" existed and what he could do. But today "he" was needed, all hastened to understand him, and not knowing the real person, they unwittingly created in their imagination something formidable. Their hopes were great; they needed greatness for their own support. . . .

When the crowd poured out onto the street along the river's edge, it saw before it a long broken line of soldiers, blocking the path to the bridge, but this thin grey fence did not stop the people. There was nothing threatening in the figures of the soldiers; they hopped up and down, warming their cold feet, waving their hands, bumping against one another. Before them, beyond the river, the people saw the dark house — there "he" awaited them — the tsar, the ruler of the house. Great and strong, kind and loving, he could not, of course, order his soldiers to forbid the people to go to him, the people who love him and wish to speak with him about their need.

But nevertheless many faces were shadowed with doubt and the people in the front of the crowd slowed their step. Some glanced backwards, others went off to the side, and all tried to show one another that they knew about the soldiers, that this did not surprise them. Several looked peacefully at the golden angel, glistening high in the sky on the dismal fortress; others smiled. . . .

And suddenly something spewed forth into the air dryly and irregularly, quaked, and thrashed the crowd with tens of invisible whips. For a second all voices suddenly seemed to freeze. The mass slowly continued to march forward.

"Blank cartridges . . . " someone said; another asked in a colorless voice.

But here and there groans could be heard; at the feet of the crowd lay several bodies. A woman, moaning loudly, gripping her chest with her hand, lunged forward with quick steps toward the bayonets poised to meet her.

And again the crack of a gun volley, still louder, still more uneven. Those standing at the fence heard the planks quivering — just as though some kind of invisible teeth were chewing them. And one projectile shot along the wooden fence and breaking off small slivers threw them into people's faces. People fell in twos, in threes, dropped to the ground, ran limping off into nowhere, crawled along the

M. Gorky, "January 9" (9-e ianvaria), *Polnoe sobranie sochinenii: khudozhestvennye proizvedeniia v dvadtsati piati tomakh* (Nauka: Moscow, 1968–), VIII (1970), pp. 349, 352, 354, 355. Translated by Mary Louise Loe.

snow, and everywhere, all over the snow, bright red stains blazed forth. Oozing and steaming, they drew all eyes to them. . . . The crowd fell back, stopped for a moment, froze, and suddenly, a wild tremendous howl of a hundred voices rang out. It burst forth and began to flow through the air in a continuous tremulous cacophony of shrieks, sharp pain, horror, protest, sad bewilderment, and cries for help.

With their heads bowed, people ran forward in groups to gather up the dead and wounded. The wounded also shouted, shook their fists; all faces suddenly became transformed, all eyes glazed with madness. . . . There was a singeing horror, which like freezing iron froze the heart, stiffened the body, and forced people to look around with open eyes at the blood being devoured by the snow, at the bloodied faces, hands, clothes, at the corpses strangely peaceful in contrast to the frantic movements of the living. . . .

. . . Everything permanent and familiar was overthrown, smashed, and had vanished. Everyone, more or less clearly, felt depressed and strangely alone, defenseless before the cynical and harsh force which recognized neither rights nor the law. All lives were in its hands; and it was able to sow death unaccountably among the mass of people; it was able to destroy the living in the way it chose and as many as it chose. Nobody could hold it back. Nobody could communicate with it. It was all-powerful and calmly displayed the limitlessness of its strength, thoughtlessly filling the streets with corpses, filling them with blood. Its bloody, mad caprice was seen clearly. It inspired unanimous anxiety, caustic fear, a devastated soul. And it insistently set one thinking of the need to create plans for a new defense of the individual, for new preparations for the protection of life.

54

Francisco Madero, Plan of San Luis Potosí

During the 1910 presidential election campaign in Mexico, the aging dictator, Porfirio Díaz, had his opponent Madero arrested and imprisoned and easily "won" the controlled election. After his release from prison, Madero fled to San Antonio, Texas, where he issued his famous Plan of San Luis Potosí. This plan called for the nullification of the recent elections and urged Mexicans to take up arms against the government on November 20, 1910, a date that signified the beginning of the Mexican Revolution.

QUESTIONS TO CONSIDER

1. What were the conditions in Mexico that Madero believed required the use of force in order to change?
2. Why did Madero emphasize political reform? Was he wrong to believe that a political transformation must precede economic and social change?

3. Consider Madero's ideas with reference to those expressed by John Locke (see Reading 16), Jean-Jacques Rousseau (see Reading 20), and Sun Yat-Sen (see Reading 51).

Peoples, in their constant efforts for the triumph of the ideal of liberty and justice, are forced, at precise historical moments, to make their greatest sacrifices.

Our beloved country has reached one of those moments. A force of tyranny which we Mexicans were not accustomed to suffer after we won our independence oppresses us in such a manner that it has become intolerable. In exchange for that tyranny we are offered peace, but peace full of shame for the Mexican nation, because its basis is not law, but force ; because its object is not the aggrandizement and prosperity of the country, but to enrich a small group who, abusing their influence, have converted the public charges into fountains of exclusively personal benefit, unscrupulously exploiting the manner of lucrative concessions and contracts.

The legislative and judicial powers are completely subordinated to the executive ; the division of powers, the sovereignty of the States, the liberty of the common councils, and the rights of the citizens exist only in writing in our great charter ; but, as a fact, it may almost be said that martial law constantly exists in Mexico ; the administration of justice, instead of imparting protection to the weak, merely serves to legalize the plunderings committed by the strong ; the judges instead of being the representatives of justice, are the agents of the executive, whose interests they faithfully serve ; the chambers of the union have no other will than that of the dictator ; the governors of the States are designated by him and they in their turn designate and impose in like manner the municipal authorities.

From this it results that the whole administrative, judicial, and legislative machinery obeys a single will, the caprice of General Porfirio Díaz, who during his long administration has shown that the principal motive that guides him is to maintain himself in power and at any cost.

For many years profound discontent has been felt throughout the Republic, due to such a system of government, but General Díaz with great cunning and perseverance, has succeeded in annihilating all independent elements, so that it was not possible to organize any sort of movement to take from him the power of which he made such bad use. The evil constantly became worse, and the decided eagerness of General Díaz to impose a successor upon the nations in the person of Mr. Ramon Corral carried that evil to its limit and caused many of us Mexicans, although lacking recognized political standing, since it had been impossible to acquire it during the 36 years of dictatorship, to throw ourselves into the struggle to recover the sovereignty of the people and their rights on purely democratic grounds. . . .

In Mexico, as a democratic Republic, the public power can have no other origin nor other basis than the will of the people, and the latter can not be subordinated to formulas to be executed in a fraudulent manner. . . .

From United States Congress, Senate Subcommittee on Foreign Relations, *Revolutions in Mexico*, 62nd Congress, 2nd Session (Washington, DC : Government Printing Office, 1913), pp. 730–736, passim.

For this reason the Mexican people have protested against the illegality of the last election and, desiring to use successively all the recourses offered by the laws of the Republic, in due form asked for the nullification of the election by the Chamber of Deputies, notwithstanding they recognized no legal origin in said body and knew beforehand that, as its members were not the representatives of the people, they would carry out the will of General Díaz, to whom exclusively they owe their investiture.

In such a state of affairs the people, who are the only sovereign, also protested energetically against the election in imposing manifestations in different parts of the Republic; and if the latter were not general throughout the national territory, it was due to the terrible pressure exercised by the Government, which always quenches in blood any democratic manifestation, as happened in Puebla, Vera Cruz, Tlaxcala, and in other places.

But this violent and illegal system can no longer subsist.

I have very well realized that if the people have designated me as their candidate for the Presidency it is not because they have had an opportunity to discover in me the qualities of a statesman or of a ruler, but the virility of the patriot determined to sacrifice himself, if need be, to obtain liberty and to help the people free themselves from the odious tyranny that oppresses them.

From the moment I threw myself into the democratic struggle I very well knew that General Díaz would not bow to the will of the nation, and the noble Mexican people, in following me to the polls, also knew perfectly the outrage that awaited them; but in spite of it, the people gave the cause of liberty a numerous contingent of martyrs when they were necessary and with wonderful stoicism went to the polls and received every sort of molestation.

But such conduct was indispensable to show to the whole world that the Mexican people are fit for democracy, that they are thirsty for liberty, and that their present rulers do not measure up to their aspirations.

Besides, the attitude of the people before and during the election, as well as afterwards, shows clearly that they reject with energy the Government of General Díaz and that, if those electoral rights had been respected, I would have been elected for President of the Republic.

Therefore, and in echo of the national will, I declare the late election illegal and, the Republic being accordingly without rulers, provisionally assume the Presidency of the Republic until the people designate their rulers pursuant to the law. In order to attain this end, it is necessary to eject from power the audacious usurpers whose only title of legality involves a scandalous and immoral fraud.

With all honesty I declare that it would be a weakness on my part and treason to the people, who have placed their confidence in me, not to put myself at the front of my fellow citizens, who anxiously call me from all parts of the country, to compel General Díaz by force of arms, to respect the national will.

World War I: Battle

World War I (1914–1918) was the second most destructive war in modern history, and the Battle of the Somme (July 1 to November 18, 1916), fought on the chalky scrublands of northwestern France, was the bloodiest battle ever fought by the British Army. On the first day of the battle, the British Army suffered 57,470 casualties: 19,240 dead, 35,493 wounded, 2152 missing, and 585 captured. In the first ten minutes of the attack, one German observer estimated that 14,000 British soldiers fell to the deadly German machine-gun and artillery fire; and in the first 24 hours of the battle, the British Army counted more dead than the combined British deaths of the Crimean, Boer, and Korean wars.

Nothing in the first two years of fighting had prepared the soldiers for these huge losses. In the summer of 1916, British and German soldiers — separated by a desolate, shell-ravaged "no man's land" — peered at each other from zigzagged lines of trenches. Both armies had adjusted to the troglodyte horrors of trench warfare, where the best weapons often were "clubs, ax handles, daggers, medieval man traps, and crossbows, primitive catapults."[1] But even then death came slowly and painfully. Philip Gibbs of the *Daily Telegraph* reported that "the horrors of the first aid post were standard — men hold their intestines in both hands, broken bones tearing the flesh, arteries spurting blood, maimed hands, empty eye sockets, pierced chests, skin hanging down in tatters from the burned face, missing lower jaws . . . men with chunks of steel in their lungs and bowels vomiting great gobs of blood, men with legs and arms torn from their trunks, men without noses and their brains throbbing through open scalps. . . ."[2]

Survivors of battle sought safety and refuge in their trenches. But here the horror of combat only continued: "the incredible mud, into which horses and men sometimes sank clear out of sight, the stench of excrement and rotted flesh and explosives and mustard gas, the maggots that writhed underfoot and oozed up from the cracks in the dried mud, the rats, gorged on human meat (they preferred eyes and livers), some of them as big as terriers and as bold as cats, the churned-up battlefields lost and won and lost again, a dozen times since 1914, in which the earth itself seemed to be composed of dead bodies, where arms and legs and heads protruded through trench walls and had to be covered with empty sandbags or chopped off with shovels and buried."[3]

To break the deadlock of two years of immobility, the British High Command ordered the Somme offensive to crack open the Western Front and break the German Army's hold on northern France. However, slaughter rather than victory awaited the 120,000 British soldiers who attacked the German lines on July 1, 1916, the first day of the Somme offensive.

---

1. From Michael Kernan, "Day of Slaughter on the Somme." *The Washington Post,* June 27, 1976, p. C1.
2. Cited in ibid.
3. Ibid.

55

Slaughter on the Somme

The following are excerpts from the diaries of three British soldiers who participated in the Battle of the Somme.

QUESTIONS TO CONSIDER

1. What do the diary entries reveal about the soldiers' views of authority, the enemy, and the press?
2. What do the diary entries reveal about the soldiers' sense of duty?

Diary of Private Tom Easton

A beautiful summer morning, though we'd had a bit of rain earlier. The skylarks were just singing away. Then the grand mine went up, it shook the earth for nearly a minute, and we had to wait for the fallout. The whistles blew and we stepped off one yard apart going straight forward. We were under orders not to stop or look or help the wounded. Carry on if you're fit, it was. . . .

Men began to fall one by one. . . . One officer said we were OK, all the machine-guns were firing over our heads. This was so until we passed our own front line and started to cross No Man's Land. Then trench machine-guns began the slaughter from the La Boiselle salient [German positions]. Men fell on every side screaming. Those who were unwounded dare not attend to them, we must press on regardless. Hundreds lay on the German barbed wire which was not all destroyed and their bodies formed a bridge for others to pass over and into the German front line.

There were few Germans, mainly in machine-gun posts. These were bombed out, and there were fewer still of us, but we consolidated the lines we had taken by preparing firing positions on the rear of the trenches gained, and fighting went on all morning and gradually died down as men and munitions on both sides became exhausted.

When we got to the German trenches we'd lost all our officers. They were all dead, there was no question of wounded. About 25 of us made it there. . . .

. . . Yes, as we made our way over the latter stages of the charge, men dropped all around like ninepins. Apart from machine-guns, the German artillery was also very active, great sheets of earth rose up before one. Every man had to fend for himself as we still had to face the Germans in their trenches when we got there.

From Michael Kernan, "Day of Slaughter on the Somme," *The Washington Post,* June 27, 1976, pp. C1, C5, passim. © 1976, The Washington Post. Reprinted by permission.

I kept shouting for my MOTHER to guide me, strange as it may seem. Mother help me. Not the Virgin Mother but my own maternal Mother, for I was then only 20 years of age.

Diary of Captain Reginald Leetham

I got to my position and looked over the top. The first thing I saw in the space of a tennis court in front of me was the bodies of 100 dead or severely wounded men lying there in our own wire. . . . I sent my runner 200 yards on my right to get into touch with our right company, who should have been close beside me. He came back and reported he could find nothing of them. It subsequently transpired that they never reached the front line as their communication trenches had caught it so much worse than mine, and the communication trench was so full of dead and dying, that they could not get over them. . . . Those three battalions [2500 men] who went over were practically annihilated. Every man went to his death or got wounded without flinching. Yet in this war, nothing will be heard about it, the papers have glowing accounts of great British success. . . . 60 officers went out lots of whom I knew. I believe 2 got back without being wounded. . . .

The dead were stretched out on one side [of the trench] one on top of the other six high. . . . To do one's duty was continually climbing over corpses in every position. . . . Of the hundreds of corpses I saw I only saw one pretty one — a handsome boy called Schnyder of the Berkshires who lay on our firestep shot through the heart. There he lay with a sandbag over his face : I uncovered it as I knew he was an officer. I wish his Mother could have seen him — one of the few whose faces had not been mutilated.

The 2nd Middlesex came back with 22 men out of 600. . . .

Diary of Subaltern Edward G. D. Liveing

There was the freshness and splendor of a summer morning over everything. . . .

Just in front the ground was pitted by innumerable shellholes. . . . More holes opened suddenly every now and then. Here and there a few bodies lay about. Farther away, before our front line and in No Man's Land, lay more. In the smoke one could distinguish the second line advancing. One man after another fell down in a seemingly natural manner, and the wave melted away. In the background, where ran the remains of the German lines and wire, there was a mask of smoke, the red of the shrapnel bursting amid it. As I advanced I felt as if I was in a dream, but I had all my wits about me. We had been told to walk. Our boys, however, rushed forward with splendid impetuosity. . . .

A hare jumped up and rushed towards me through the dry yellowish grass, its eyes bulging with fear. . . . At one time we seemed to be advancing in little groups. I was at the head of one for a moment or two only to realize shortly afterwards that I was alone. I came up to the German wire. Here one could hear men shouting to one another and the wounded groaning above the explosions of shells and bombs and the rattle of machine-guns. . . .

Suddenly I cursed. I had been scalded in the left hip. A shell, I thought, had blown up in a waterlogged crump hole and sprayed me with boiling water. Letting go of my rifle, I dropped forward full length on the ground. My hip began to smart unpleasantly, and I felt a curious warmth stealing down my left leg. I thought it was the boiling water that had scalded me. Certainly my breeches looked as if they were saturated with water. I did not know they were saturated with blood.

56

"World War I: A Frenchman's Recollections"

Not all the casualties were on the battlefield. Certainly one of the most devastating aspects of World War I was its effect upon the civilian populations, particularly in the small towns and villages. This particular account is from the recollections of François Carlotti (1907 —), who draws upon his boyhood memories to describe the effects of the Great War upon the French town of Auneau, located 15 kilometers west of the cathedral city of Chartres.

QUESTIONS TO CONSIDER

1. Does this set of recollections suggest anything about the quality of civilian morale in France during the Great War?
2. Do these recollections coupled with the diary entries (see Reading 55) help to explain the appeal of fascism (see Reading 66) to some of the men and women who survived the battles and devastation of World War I?

The first leaves fell at the end of October. After the defeat at the frontiers, the retreat, the miracle of the Marne, the stabilization of the line in the trenches was necessary to give France time to recover her balance.

And then the High Command and government, appalled by the losses that surpassed imagining, probably found themselves little disposed to reveal the truth.

Up to this point we had only bad news of those wounded who, evacuated to the interior, had succeeded in getting a letter or a message through, and they were not many. One had lost a leg and another had been hit in the stomach. We had showed them much sympathy, them and their families. We should soon envy them.

François Carlotti, "World War I: A Frenchman's Recollections," *The American Scholar* 57:2(Spring 1988):286–288. Copyright © 1988 by the author. By permission of the publishers.

When the two gendarmes who had stayed at headquarters started to go on their rounds with the official notices, "Died on the field of Honor," a terrified silence fell on the town, the villages, and the hamlets.

Gustave was killed, the little clerk who had once worked for my father and who had looked so handsome in his cavalryman's uniform.

Arsène, Alcide, Jules, Léon, Kléber, Maurice, Rémi, Raoul — all killed. Georges, the son of the fat ironmonger in the marketplace, who had studied in Paris and come back with advanced ideas — talking English, putting up little hurdles in the field to jump over as he ran, teaching the boys to play with a queer sort of ball that wasn't even round — killed.

Alphonse, Clothaire, Emile, Etienne, Firmin, Marceau, Raymond, Victor — killed, killed. . . .

The grief was often the more terrible because in most cases it was an only son.

And then there were the three Cochon brothers.

The Cochons were one of those families of small market-gardeners who grew their crops by the banks of the river. Every morning, the wife threaded on her shoulder straps, took up the shafts of the enormous wheelbarrow, and set out through the town to sell her mountain of fresh vegetables while her husband stayed home working in the garden.

Tall, spare, bony, mother Cochon was always the first to set out and the last to return. She had four men in the house.

The eldest daughter, married to an employee of the railway from far away, had made her home with him there in the Capdenac region where he had a good job.

The father remained at home with his three sons, who had been born one after the other within the space of five years. The three boys had all done very well at school, while also giving a helping hand at home when required. They had passed their leaving certificates before rejoining their father to toil with him from dawn to dusk.

Yet, despite all their work, their plot of land did not suffice to provide a livelihood for the whole family, and, in turn, one or two of the boys went to work for wages. They were not living as lodgers, like Belgians or Bretons who, at St. Jean, poured from the trains in serried ranks with their round hats and their clogs, their working boots slung round their necks — no, they worked as neighbors who were well favored, eating at their master's table. These Cochons were good boys who would never have worked less than their father.

Happy lads, not bothered by jokes on their name, always the first to sound the trumpet and bang the drum of the town band, first over the parallel bars or the vaulting horse, or leaders at the dance in the *mairie* on holidays.[1]

The father died while the eldest boy was away doing his training. The other two boys slaved away in the garden, working all the harder because the first born did not return home when the youngest son left. And after his three years' service, this youngest son faced mobilization and war.

---

1. In French *cochon* means pig. The *mairie* was the town hall.

When the gendarmes arrived that morning, Mme. Cochon received them standing, with the one word: "Which?" "Auguste," replied one of them and laid the little notice on the table.

"Ah, Auguste, my first born, my strongest and my bravest." A slow shudder passed across her face, but she didn't flinch.

And then, as the gendarmes stood their ground, shifting from one foot to the other, she looked them full in the face, till one of them, gathering all his courage, managed to say, "And Désiré," putting the official notification on the table as he left. "Désiré, my most handsome, my most gentle, the golden-haired one." Now she trembled from head to foot, murmuring. "Auguste . . . Désiré . . . Auguste . . . Désiré . . .," ever more softly, as though she was clasping them.

When the gendarmes returned, a month later, she turned towards them from her seat in the corner of the fireplace without looking at them and asked: "Is it Marcel?" They bowed their heads, unable to speak.

"Ah, Marcel, my baby, my last, my dearest, O Marcel." And then suddenly a terrible cry rent the air and carried down to the river. "Marcel, Marcel. Now there are no more Cochons."

Without hearing, the gendarme forced himself to read the paper. "Cochon, Marcel, sergeant, infantry . . . heroic conduct . . . citation . . . *croix de guerre.*"[2] She repeated her crazy, despairing threnody, "No more Cochons, no more Cochons."

From that day she hardly ever went out except to walk to her husband's grave. Those who met her would often hear her muttering. "No more Cochons . . . there are no more." But no one ever saw her cry.

She died at the onset of winter.

And there were still four years of war to come. The long hopeless agonies in the military hospitals, the boys of *classe 16,*[3] called up at eighteen, who would never see their twentieth year, men who were wounded three times, bandaged up, nursed and healed, who returned yet again to the line never to return, the atrocious deaths in the gas attacks. There was the terrible winter of 1916–17 when even wild animals were frozen to death; and the insane spring offensives of 1917 when for a moment one thought oneself back in the bloodiest days of the summer of 1914, when training regiments were rushed into the line to plug the yawning gaps that held fast, never bending under the shells and the hail of the machine guns. The Americans arrived, the diabolical long-range guns shelled Paris, the last great German offensive began, which again reached the Marne, and the final victorious counter-offensive was launched.

There was the great Roger who fell on November 8.

When it was all ended and there was no family left to ask for the return of their corpses, they remained on their battlefields — the three brothers, with the vast army of shadows in the great military cemeteries, neat and orderly where they rest, hidden forever, the bravery, the gaiety, the youth of this people of France, who were — like the men of Athens before them — the adornment of the world.

2. French military decoration for valor in battle.
3. This was the draft levy of 1916.

World War I: Diplomacy

Diplomatic efforts to end the First World War began in earnest in 1915 and continued through the Treaty of Brest-Litovsk of March 3, 1918, between Russia and Germany; the Armistice of November 11, 1918, between the Allies and Germany; and the comprehensive peace treaties of 1919. But European diplomats, concerned with ending the war on terms favorable to their own nations, often gave scant regard to the national aspirations of other peoples. For example, Arab leaders who sought to establish independent states had to accept vague promises from Great Britain and France. The Chinese were shocked to learn, after the Treaty of Versailles in 1919, that the Western powers had assigned German colonial rights in China to Japan.

By the time the Western diplomats assembled in Versailles, the enthusiasm that had greeted President Wilson's Fourteen Points peace proposal had melted away. The Allied powers did not permit Germany to participate in the Versailles deliberations; however, they did assign to Germany and her allies full responsibility for causing the war and insisted that Germany pay for damages incurred during the fighting. The United States refused to join the new League of Nations, and Wilson's plea for dismantling the Western colonial empires went unheeded.

The following selections suggest some of the global effects of the diplomacy of World War I.

57

Sir Henry McMahon, Letter to Ali Ibn Husain

Sir Henry McMahon, British High Commissioner in Egypt, and Ali Ibn Husain, the Sherif of Mecca, exchanged ten letters from 1915 to 1916. The following excerpt from a letter written October 24, 1915, shows Britain's aim — to enlist Arab support against Britain's enemy Turkey in return for hints of British support of an independent Arab state.

QUESTIONS TO CONSIDER

1. Do the suggestions made in the McMahon letter provide a perspective on the contemporary political problems in the Middle East (see Readings 91 and 92)?
2. Did the British government have the legal and moral authority to promise the birth of an Arab state?

As for those regions lying within those frontiers wherein Great Britain is free to act without detriment to the interests of her ally, France, I am empowered in the name of the Government of Great Britain to give the following assurances and make the following reply to your letter:

(1) Subject to the above modifications, Great Britain is prepared to recognise and support the independence of the Arabs in all the regions within the limits demanded by the Sherif of Mecca.

(2) Great Britain will guarantee the Holy Places against all external aggression and will recognise their inviolability.

(3) When the situation admits, Great Britain will give to the Arabs her advice and will assist them to establish what may appear to be the most suitable forms of government in those various territories.

(4) On the other hand, it is understood that the Arabs have decided to seek the advice and guidance of Great Britain only, and that such European advisers and officials as may be required for the formation of a sound form of administration will be British.

(5) With regard to the vilayets [provinces] of Bagdad and Basra, the Arabs will recognise that the established position and interests of Great Britain necessitate special administrative arrangements in order to secure these territories from foreign aggression, to promote the welfare of the local populations and to safeguard our mutual economic interests.

I am convinced that this declaration will assure you beyond all possible doubt of the sympathy of Great Britain towards the aspirations of her friends the Arabs and will result in a firm and lasting alliance, the immediate results of which will be the expulsion of the Turks from the Arab countries and the freeing of the Arab peoples from the Turkish yoke, which for so many years has pressed heavily upon them.

58

The Balfour Declaration

To enlist Jewish support for the war, Arthur James Balfour, British Foreign Secretary, wrote the following letter to Lord Rothschild, a prominent Jewish leader, and had it printed in *The Times*. The letter contains the official statement that soon became known as the Balfour Declaration.

From Great Britain, *Parliamentary Papers*, 1939, Misc. No. 3, Cmd. 5957.

QUESTIONS TO CONSIDER

1. Why did the British government wait until 1917 to publicly support the desire of the Jewish people for a state?
2. What are the contemporary implications of Lord Balfour's statement: ". . . it being clearly understood that nothing shall be done which may prejudice the civil and religious rights of existing non-Jewish communities in Palestine" (see Reading 92)?

Foreign Office
November 2nd, 1917

Dear Lord Rothschild:

I have much pleasure in conveying to you, on behalf of His Majesty's Government, the following declaration of sympathy with Jewish Zionist aspirations which has been submitted to, and approved by, the Cabinet:

His Majesty's Government view with favor the establishment in Palestine of a national home for the Jewish people, and will use their best endeavors to facilitate the achievement of this object, it being clearly understood that nothing shall be done which may prejudice the civil and religious rights of existing non-Jewish communities in Palestine, or the rights and political status enjoyed by Jews in any other country.

I should be grateful if you would bring this declaration to the knowledge of the Zionist Federation.

Yours,

Arthur James Balfour

59

Woodrow Wilson, "Speech on the Fourteen Points"

On January 8, 1918, President Woodrow Wilson, speaking before a joint session of Congress, put forth his Fourteen Points proposal for ending the war. In this speech, he established the basis of a peace treaty and the foundation of a League of Nations.

From *The Times* (London), November 9, 1917.

QUESTIONS TO CONSIDER

1. Can one reconcile points V and XIII of Wilson's Fourteen Points with articles 22 and 156 of the Treaty of Versailles (see Reading 60)?
2. An underlying assumption of the Fourteen Points is that America should use its power to ensure that the world "be made fit and safe to live in . . ." Is this the proper policy of the United States? Why? Why not?

We entered this war because violations of right had occurred which touched us to the quick and made the life of our own people impossible unless they were corrected and the world secured once for all against their recurrence. What we demand in this war, therefore, is nothing peculiar to ourselves. It is that the world be made fit and safe to live in; and particularly that it be made safe for every peace-loving nation which, like our own, wishes to live its own life, determine its own institutions, be assured of justice and fair dealing by the other peoples of the world as against force and selfish aggression. All the peoples of the world are in effect partners in this interest, and for our own part we see very clearly that unless justice be done to others it will not be done to us. The programme of the world's peace, therefore, is our programme; and that programme, the only possible programme, as we see it, is this:

    I. Open covenants of peace, openly arrived at, after which there shall be no private international understanding of any kind but diplomacy shall proceed always frankly and in the public view.

    II. Absolute freedom of navigation upon the seas, outside territorial waters, alike in peace and in war, except as the seas may be closed in whole or in part by international action for the enforcement of international covenants.

    III. The removal, so far as possible, of all economic barriers and the establishment of an equality of trade conditions among all the nations consenting to the peace and associating themselves for its maintenance.

    IV. Adequate guarantees given and taken that national armaments will be reduced to the lowest point consistent with domestic safety.

    V. A free, open-minded, and absolutely impartial adjustment of all colonial claims, based upon a strict observance of the principle that in determining all such questions of sovereignty the interests of the populations concerned must have equal weight with the equitable claims of the government whose title is to be determined.

    VI. The evacuation of all Russian territory and such a settlement of all questions affecting Russia as will secure the best and freest cooperation of the other nations of the world in obtaining for her an unhampered and

From Woodrow Wilson, "Speech on the Fourteen Points," *Congressional Record,* 65th Congress, 2nd Session, 1918, pp. 680–681.

unembarrassed opportunity for the independent determination of her own political development and national policy and assure her a sincere welcome into the society of free nations under institutions of her own choosing ; and, more than a welcome, assistance also of every kind that she may need and may herself desire. The treatment accorded Russia by her sister nations in the months to come will be the acid test of their good will, of their comprehension of her needs as distinguished from their own interests, and of their intelligent and unselfish sympathy.

VII. Belgium, the whole world will agree, must be evacuated and restored, without any attempt to limit the sovereignty which she enjoys in common with all other free nations. No other single act will serve as this will serve to restore confidence among the nations in the laws which they have themselves set and determined for the government of their relations with one another. Without this healing act the whole structure and validity of international law is forever impaired.

VIII. All French territory should be freed and the invaded portions restored, and the wrong done to France by Prussia in 1871 in the matter of Alsace-Lorraine, which has unsettled the peace of the world for nearly fifty years, should be righted, in order that peace may once more be made secure in the interest of all.

IX. A readjustment of the frontiers of Italy should be effected along clearly recognizable lines of nationality.

X. The peoples of Austria-Hungary, whose place among the nations we wish to see safeguarded and assured, should be accorded the freest opportunity of autonomous development.

XI. Rumania, Serbia, and Montenegro should be evacuated ; occupied territories restored ; Serbia accorded free and secure access to the sea ; and the relations of the several Balkan states to one another determined by friendly counsel along historically established lines of allegiance and nationality ; and international guarantees of the political and economic independence and territorial integrity of the several Balkan states should be entered into.

XII. The Turkish portions of the present Ottoman Empire should be assured a secure sovereignty, but the other nationalities which are now under Turkish rule should be assured an undoubted security of life and an absolutely unmolested opportunity of autonomous development, and the Dardanelles should be permanently opened as a free passage to the ships and commerce of all nations under international guarantees.

XIII. An independent Polish state should be erected which should include the territories inhabited by indisputably Polish populations, which should be assured a free and secure access to the sea, and whose political and economic independence and territorial integrity should be guaranteed by international covenant.

XIV. A general association of nations must be formed under specific covenants for the purpose of affording mutual guarantees of political independence and territorial integrity to great and small states alike. . . .

60

The Treaty of Versailles

On June 28, 1919, the Allied powers presented the Treaty of Versailles to Germany for signature. The following excerpts are from key territorial and political clauses.

QUESTIONS TO CONSIDER

1. Can British policy, as suggested in the McMahon letter and the Balfour Declaration (see Readings 57 and 58), be reconciled with the mandate system of article 22 of the Treaty of Versailles?
2. In what ways did articles 231 and 232 of the Treaty of Versailles assist Adolf Hitler in gaining power (see Reading 67)?

Article 22. Certain communities formerly belonging to the Turkish Empire have reached a stage of development where their existence as independent nations can be provisionally recognised subject to the rendering of administrative advice and assistance by a Mandatory [i.e., a Western power] until such time as they are able to stand alone. The wishes of these communities must be a principal consideration in the selection of the Mandatory....

Article 42. Germany is forbidden to maintain or construct any fortifications either on the left bank of the Rhine or on the right bank to the west of a line drawn 50 kilometres to the East of the Rhine.

Article 45. As compensation for the destruction of the coal mines in the north of France and as part payment towards the total reparation due from Germany for the damage resulting from the war, Germany cedes to France in full and absolute possession, with exclusive right of exploitation, unencumbered and free from all debts and charges of any kind, the coal mines situated in the Saar Basin....

Article 49. Germany renounces in favor of the League of Nations, in the capacity of trustee, the government of the territory defined above.

At the end of fifteen years from the coming into force of the present Treaty the inhabitants of the said territory shall be called upon to indicate the sovereignty under which they desire to be placed.

Alsace-Lorraine. The High Contracting Parties, recognizing the moral obligation to redress the wrong done by Germany in 1871 both to the rights of France and to the wishes of the population of Alsace and Lorraine, which were separated from their country in spite of the solemn protest of their representatives at the Assembly of Bordeaux, agree upon the following....

From *The Treaty of Versailles and After : Annotations of the Text of the Treaty* (Washington, DC : Government Printing Office, 1944), passim.

Article 51. The territories which were ceded to Germany in accordance with the Preliminaries of Peace signed at Versailles on February 26, 1871, and the Treaty of Frankfort of May 10, 1871, are restored to French sovereignty as from the date of the Armistice of November 11, 1918.

The provisions of the Treaties establishing the delimitation of the frontiers before 1871 shall be restored. . . .

Article 119. Germany renounces in favor of the Principal Allied and Associated Powers all her rights and titles over her overseas possessions. . . .

Article 156. Germany renounces, in favour of Japan, all her rights, title and privileges . . . which she acquired in virtue of the Treaty concluded by her with China on March 6, 1898, and of all other arrangements relative to the Province of Shantung. . . .

Article 159. The German military forces shall be demobilised and reduced as prescribed hereinafter.

Article 160. By a date which must not be later than March 31, 1920, the German Army must not comprise more than seven divisions of infantry and three divisions of cavalry.

After that date the total number of effectives in the Army of the States constituting Germany must not exceed 100,000 men, including officers and establishments of depots. The Army shall be devoted exclusively to the maintenance of order within the territory and to the control of the frontiers.

The total effective strength of officers, including the personnel of staffs, whatever their composition, must not exceed four thousand. . . .

Article 231. The Allied and Associated Governments affirm and Germany accepts the responsibility of Germany and her allies for causing all the loss and damage to which the Allied and Associated Governments and their nationals have been subjected as a consequence of the war imposed upon them by the aggression of Germany and her allies.

Article 232. The Allied and Associated Governments recognize that the resources of Germany are not adequate, after taking into account permanent diminutions of such resources which will result from other provisions of the present Treaty, to make complete reparation for all such loss and damage.

The Allied and Associated Governments, however, require, and Germany undertakes, that she will make compensation for all damage done to the civilian population of the Allied and Associated Powers and to their property during the period of the belligerency of each as an Allied or Associated Power against Germany.

61

Memorandum of the General Syrian Congress

When Arab leaders learned of article 22 in the Treaty of Versailles, which established Western rule ("mandates") in parts of the former Ottoman Empire (comprising present-day Syria, Lebanon, Jordan, and Israel), they denounced the mandate system and reminded the Allies of President Wilson's promise. The following memorandum was addressed to the King-Crane Commission on July 2, 1919. The King-Crane Commission was an Allied commission sent by the Supreme Allied Council in Paris to oversee the substitution of Western mandates for Ottoman rule.

QUESTIONS TO CONSIDER

1. Why would the General Syrian Congress seek technical and economic assistance from the United States and not from a closer, European power?
2. Are there any connections between this document's position on the question of a Jewish homeland in Palestine and the sentiments expressed in the Palestinian National Charter (see Reading 92)?

We the undersigned members of the General Syrian Congress, meeting in Damascus on Wednesday, July 2nd, 1919, made up of representatives from the three Zones, viz., The Southern, Eastern, and Western, provided with credentials and authorizations by the inhabitants of our various districts, Moslems, Christians, and Jews, have agreed upon the following statement of the desires of the people of the country who have elected us. . . .

  1. We ask absolutely complete political independence for Syria. . . .

  2. We ask that the Government of this Syrian country should be a democratic civil constitutional Monarchy on broad decentralization principles, safeguarding the rights of minorities, and that the King be the Emir Feisal, who carried on a glorious struggle in the cause of our liberation and merited our full confidence and entire reliance.

  3. Considering the fact that the Arabs inhabiting the Syrian area are not naturally less gifted than other more advanced races and that they are by no means less developed than the Bulgarians, Serbians, Greeks, and Roumanians at the beginning of their independence, we protest against Article 22 of the Covenant of the League of Nations, placing us among the nations in their middle stage of development which stand in need of a mandatory power.

  4. In the event of the rejection of the Peace Conference of this just protest for certain considerations that we may not understand, we, relying on the declara-

From *Foreign Relations of the United States : Paris Peace Conference,* vol. 12 (Washington, DC : Government Printing Office, 1919), pp. 780–781.

tions of President Wilson that his object in waging war was to put an end to the ambition of conquest and colonization, can only regard the mandate mentioned in the Covenant of the League of Nations as equivalent to the rendering of economical and technical assistance that does not prejudice our complete independence. And desiring that our country should not fall a prey to colonization and believing that the American Nation is farthest from any thought of colonization and has no political ambition in our country, we will seek the technical and economic assistance from the United States of America, provided that such assistance does not exceed 20 years.

5. In the event of America not finding herself in a position to accept our desire for assistance, we will seek this assistance from Great Britain, also provided that such does not prejudice our complete independence and unity of our country and that the duration of such assistance does not exceed that mentioned in the previous article.

6. We do not acknowledge any right claimed by the French Government in any part whatever of our Syrian country and refuse that she should assist us or have a hand in our country under any circumstances and in any place.

7. We oppose the pretensions of the Zionists to create a Jewish commonwealth in the southern part of Syria, known as Palestine, and oppose Zionist migration to any part of our country; for we do not acknowledge their title but consider them a grave peril to our people from the national, economical, and political points of view. Our Jewish compatriots shall enjoy our common rights and assume the common responsibilities.

Stalin's Revolution

Joseph Vissarionovich Dzhugashvili (1879–1953), much better known as "Stalin" (man of steel), the cover name he assumed as a Bolshevik revolutionary, was a native of Russian Georgia who arose from modest peasant origins to become probably the twentieth century's most successful dictator.

Stalin gained Lenin's trust in Bolshevik affairs through his unwavering support of Lenin in all controversies against all critics. With Lenin's backing, Stalin became the first editor of *Pravda,* the Bolshevik (and later Communist Party) newspaper, in 1912. Although Stalin logged an adventurous revolutionary career as a young man, leading robberies on wagon trains to get funds for the Bolsheviks, for example, he had considerable literary talent, particularly when it came to marshalling unwieldy facts and fictions in the service of politically useful conclusions. After the revolution, Stalin took on the gray, routine sort of desk work which the higher-profile Bolsheviks found dull and distasteful. He soon headed the ministry that checked the new Soviet bureaucracy for inefficiency, and in 1922 he became General Secretary of the Communist Party, a post that enabled him to put his friends and supporters in higher offices.

Stalin's crudeness and inclination to brutality offended Lenin not long before the latter died in 1924, but within a few years after Lenin's death,

Stalin was firmly in control of both the Communist Party and the Soviet government. Holding firm to the reins of police-state power, Stalin eliminated personal opponents by the hundreds, real or imagined ideological opponents by the thousands, and "class enemies" by the millions. His program of industrializing Russia at the expense of agriculture and consumer-goods production was successful enough to provide the Russians with armaments to resist the German invasion during World War II, but his insistence on thoroughly collectivizing agriculture left Soviet farmers without much motivation to produce and led to decades of regular and severe food shortages in the same country which, under the tsars, had exported agricultural surpluses.

Unlike Hitler, Stalin was very patient. He took his time in killing off opposition, and he waited for international opportunities to ripen before seizing them with great speed and skill. Stalin's ability to get Hitler's approval for the Soviet annexation of Latvia, Lithuania, Estonia, and some of eastern Poland is a remarkable example of his diplomatic skill but perhaps less so than his incorporation of these territories into the Soviet Union as "republics" after Hitler's defeat with very little opposition from the Western allies.

On his way to becoming dictator of the USSR, Stalin was able to discredit several of the leading veterans of the Bolshevik Revolution, particularly Leon Trotsky (1879–1940) and Grigori Zinoviev (1883–1936). He attributed to them a utopian desire to lead postrevolutionary Russia into headlong conflicts with capitalist countries to spread the Communist Revolution internationally before a workable form of collectivism had been established at home in the USSR. This is the theme of the following selection.

Notice Stalin's use of the terms "socialism" and "Social Democrat." After the Bolshevik Revolution, Lenin began referring to "socialism" as the collectivist, intermediary stage through which Russia was to pass on the way to "communism," the final stage of Marxist revolutionary development. While the *Party,* as the guiding force toward this end, was the *Communist* Party, Soviet government and society were to be *socialist* until a society of abundance would prevail and the state would wither away, leaving a *communist* society with no need for government in any usual sense. Meanwhile, Soviet vocabulary usage shifted to turn "Social Democrats" into those moderate and compromising advocates of collectivism who failed to accept Bolshevik leadership.

62

Stalin, "Socialism in One Country"

QUESTIONS TO CONSIDER

1. Why does Stalin insist that building socialism in the USSR must be the Party's first priority?

2. What does Stalin find false about the international orientation of his opponents?
3. What does Stalin believe to be the proper international role of the Communist Party of the Soviet Union?

Formerly, the victory of the revolution in one country was considered impossible, on the assumption that it would require the combined action of the proletarians of all or at least of a majority of the advanced countries to achieve victory over the bourgeoisie. Now this point of view no longer fits in with the facts. Now we must proceed from the possibility of such a victory; for the uneven and spasmodic character of the development of the various capitalist countries under the conditions of imperialism, the development within imperialism of catastrophic contradictions leading to inevitable wars, the growth of the revolutionary movement in all countries of the world — all this leads, not only to the possibility, but also to the necessity of the victory of the proletariat in individual countries. The history of the revolution in Russia is direct proof of this. At the same time, however, it must be borne in mind that the overthrow of the bourgeoisie can be successfully accomplished only when certain absolutely necessary conditions exist, in the absence of which there can be even no question of the proletariat taking power. . . .

But the overthrow of the power of the bourgeoisie and establishment of the power of the proletariat in one country does not yet mean that the complete victory of socialism has been ensured. After consolidating its power and leading the peasantry in its wake the proletariat of the victorious country can and must build a socialist society. But does this mean that it will thereby achieve the complete and final victory of socialism, i.e., does it mean that with the forces of only one country it can finally consolidate socialism and fully guarantee that country against intervention and consequently, also against restoration? No, it does not. For this the victory of the revolution in at least several countries is needed. Therefore, the development and support of revolution in other countries is an essential task of the victorious revolution. Therefore the revolution which has been victorious in one country must regard itself not as a self-sufficient entity, but as an aid, as a means for hastening the victory of the proletariat in other countries. . . .

What is meant by the *possibility* of the victory of socialism in one country?

It means the possibility of solving the contradictions between the proletariat and peasantry by means of the internal forces of our country, the possibility of the proletariat seizing power and using that power to build a complete socialist society in our country, with the sympathy and support of the proletarians of other countries, but without the preliminary victory of the proletarian revolution in other countries.

Without such a possibility, building socialism is building without prospects, building without being sure that socialism will be completely built. It is no use engaging in building socialism without being sure that we can build it completely, without being sure that the technical backwardness of our country is not an *insuperable* obstacle to the building of a complete socialist society. To deny such a pos-

From "The Foundations of Leninism," and "Concerning Questions of Leninism," in J. V. Stalin, *Problems of Leninism* (Peking : Foreign Languages Press, 1976), pp. 36–37, 212–222, passim.

sibility means disbelief in the cause of building socialism, departure from Leninism.

What is meant by the *impossibility* of the complete, final victory of socialism in one country without the victory of the revolution in other countries?

It means the impossibility of having a full guarantee against intervention, and consequently against the restoration of the bourgeois order, without the victory of the revolution in at least a number of countries. To deny this indisputable thesis means departure from internationalism, departure from Leninism. . . .

Let us turn to Lenin. Here is what he said about the victory of socialism in one country even before the October Revolution, in August 1915:

> Uneven economic and political development is an absolute law of capitalism. Hence, the victory of socialism is possible first in several or even in one capitalist country taken separately. The victorious proletariat of that country, having expropriated the capitalists and *organized its own socialist production,*[1] would stand up *against* the rest of the world, the capitalist world, attracting to its cause the oppressed classes of other countries, raising revolts in those countries against the capitalists, and in the event of necessity coming out even with armed force against the exploiting classes and their states. (See Vol. XVIII, pp. 232–33.)[2]

What is meant by Lenin's phrase "having . . . organized its own socialist production" which I have stressed? It means that the proletariat of the victorious country, having seized power, *can* and *must* organize its own socialist production. And what does "organize socialist production" mean? It means completely building a socialist society. It scarcely needs proof that this clear and definite statement of Lenin's requires no further comment. Otherwise Lenin's call for the seizure of power by the proletariat in October 1917 would be incomprehensible. . . .

In other words, we can and must build a complete socialist society; for we have at our disposal all that is necessary and sufficient for this building.

I think it would be difficult to express oneself more clearly. . . .

One can only wonder why we took power in October 1917 if we did not count on completely building socialism.

We should not have taken power in October 1917 — this is the conclusion to which the inherent logic of Zinoviev's line of argument leads us.

I assert further that in the highly important question of the victory of socialism Zinoviev has gone *counter* to the definite decisions of our Party, as registered in the well-known resolution of the Fourteenth Party Conference.

Let us turn to this resolution. Here is what it says about the victory of socialism in one country:

> "The existence of two directly opposite social systems gives rise to the constant menace of capitalist blockade, of other forms of economic pressure, of armed intervention, or restoration. Consequently, the only guarantee of the *final victory of socialism,* i.e., *the guarantee against restoration,*[3] is a victorious socialist revolution in a

---

1. My italics — Joseph Stalin.
2. "On the Slogan for a United States of Europe."
3. My italics — Joseph Stalin.

number of countries. . . ." "Leninism teaches that the *final* victory of socialism, *in the sense of a full guarantee against the restoration*[4] of bourgeois relationships, is possible only on an international scale. . . ." "But it *does not follow*[5] from this that it is impossible to build a *complete socialist society*[6] in a backward country like Russia, without the 'state aid' (Trotsky) of countries more developed technically and economically."

[W]hat is our country, the country "that is building socialism," if not the base of the world revolution? But can it be a real base of the world revolution if it is incapable of completely building a socialist society? Can it remain the mighty centre of attraction for the workers of all countries that it undoubtedly is now, if it is incapable of achieving victory at home over the capitalist elements in our economy, the victory of socialist construction? I think not. But does it not follow from this that disbelief in the victory of socialist construction, the dissemination of such disbelief, will lead to our country being discredited as the base of the world revolution? And if our country is discredited the world revolutionary movement will be weakened. How did Messrs. the Social-Democrats try to scare the workers away from us? By preaching that "the Russians will not get anywhere." What are we beating the Social-Democrats with now, when we are attracting a whole series of workers' delegations to our country and thereby strengthening the position of communism all over the world? By our successes in building socialism. Is it not obvious, then, that whoever disseminates disbelief in our successes in building socialism thereby indirectly helps the Social-Democrats, reduces the sweep of the international revolutionary movement, and inevitably departs from internationalism? . . .

I think that disbelief in the victory of socialist construction is the principal error of the "New Opposition." In my opinion, it is the principal error because from it spring all the other errors of the "New Opposition." The errors of the "New Opposition" on the questions of NEP, state capitalism, the nature of our socialist industry, the role of the co-operatives under the dictatorship of the proletariat, the methods of fighting the kulaks, the role and importance of the middle peasantry — all these errors are to be traced to the principal error of the opposition, to disbelief in the possibility of completely building a socialist society by the efforts of our country.

What is disbelief in the victory of socialist construction in our country?

It is, first of all, lack of confidence that, owing to certain conditions of development in our country, the main mass of the peasantry *can be drawn* into the work of socialist construction.

It is, secondly, lack of confidence that the proletariat of our country, which holds the key positions in our national economy, *is capable* of drawing the main mass of the peasantry into the work of socialist construction.

It is from these theses that the opposition tacitly proceeds in its arguments about the paths of our development — no matter whether it does so consciously or unconsciously.

4. Id.
5. Id.
6. Id.

63

Stalin, *On the Draft Constitution of the USSR*

By 1936, Stalin had suppressed all significant opposition to his dictatorship and saw no harm in granting the people of the USSR a more democratic constitution than Lenin had given them. The ruthless practice of Stalin's police state made the democratic guarantees of the new constitution worthless until many decades later; nonetheless, the fact that they existed on paper and were confirmed in the Brezhnev era eventually helped dissidents and reformers to demand more freedom for individuals and the Soviet republics as the fulfillment of what the Soviet Constitution promised.

Stalin's defense of the draft of his new constitution, which follows in a much abridged form, shows him perfectly at home in extolling some of the monumental fictions that characterized his regime: the people's support for his programs, the success of collectivized agriculture, and the freedom of the republics of the USSR to secede if they should want to do so.

QUESTIONS TO CONSIDER

1. According to Stalin, why has the time come for a new constitution for the USSR?
2. What sort of evidence does he introduce to show the success of his regime?
3. Why is it proper — but also "safe" — to allow Soviet republics to secede?

Comrade Stalin's appearance on the rostrum is greeted by all present with loud and prolonged cheers. All rise. Shouts from all parts of the hall: "Hurrah for Comrade Stalin!" "Long live Comrade Stalin!" "Long live the Great Stalin!" "Hurrah for the great genius, Comrade Stalin!" "Vivat!" [Long may he live!], "Rot' Front!" [Red Front] "Glory to Comrade Stalin!"

Commission and Its Tasks

Comrades, the . . . complete victory of the socialist system in all spheres of the national economy is now a fact.

And what does this mean?

It means that the exploitation of man by man has been abolished, eliminated, while the socialist ownership of the instruments and means of production has been established as the unshakable foundation of our Soviet society. (Prolonged applause.)

Report delivered at the Extraordinary Eighth Congress of Soviets of the USSR, November 25, 1936. Text in J. V. Stalin, *Problems of Leninism* (Peking: Foreign Languages Press, 1976), pp. 795–834, passim.

As a result of all these changes in the sphere of the national economy of the U.S.S.R., we now have a new, socialist economy, which knows neither crises nor unemployment, which knows neither poverty nor ruin, and which provides our citizens with every opportunity to lead a prosperous and cultured life.

Such, in the main, are the changes which have taken place in the sphere of our *economy* during the period from 1924 to 1936.

In conformity with these changes in the economy of the U.S.S.R., the *class structure* of our society has also changed.

The landlord class, as you know, had already been eliminated as a result of the victorious conclusion of the Civil War. As for the other exploiting classes, they have shared the fate of the landlord class. The capitalist class in the sphere of industry has ceased to exist. The kulak class in the sphere of agriculture has ceased to exist. And the merchants and profiteers in the sphere of trade have ceased to exist. Thus all the exploiting classes have now been eliminated.

There remains the working class.

There remains the peasant class.

There remains the intelligentsia.

But it would be a mistake to think that these social groups have undergone no change during this period, that they have remained the same as they were, say, in the period of capitalism.

Take, for example, the working class of the U.S.S.R. By force of habit, it is often called the proletariat. But what is the proletariat? The proletariat is a class bereft of the instruments and means of production, under an economic system in which the instruments and means of production belong to the capitalists and in which the capitalist class exploits the proletariat.

The proletariat is a class exploited by the capitalists. But in our country, as you know, the capitalist class has already been eliminated, and the instruments and means of production have been taken from the capitalists and transferred to the state, the leading force of which is the working class. Consequently, there is no longer a capitalist class which could exploit the working class. Consequently, our working class, far from being bereft of the instruments and means of production, on the contrary, possesses them jointly with the whole people. And since it possesses them, and the capitalist class has been eliminated, all possibility of the working class being exploited is precluded. This being the case, can our working class be called a proletariat? Clearly, it cannot. Marx said that if the proletariat is to emancipate itself, it must crush the capitalist class, take the instruments and means of production from the capitalists, and abolish the conditions of production which give rise to the proletariat. Can it be said that the working class of the U.S.S.R. has already brought about these conditions for its emancipation? Unquestionably, it can and must be said. And what does this mean? This means that the proletariat of the U.S.S.R. has been transformed into an entirely new class, into the working class of the U.S.S.R., which has abolished the capitalist economic system, which has established the socialist ownership of the instruments and means of production and is directing Soviet society along the road to communism.

As you see, the working class of the U.S.S.R. is an entirely new working class, a working class emancipated from exploitation, the like of which the history of mankind has never known before.

Let us pass on to the question of the peasantry. It is customary to say that the peasantry is a class of small producers, with its members atomized, scattered over the face of the land, delving away in isolation on their small farms with their backward technical equipment; that they are slaves to private property and are exploited with impunity by landlords, kulaks, merchants, profiteers, usurers, and the like. And, indeed, in capitalist countries the peasantry, if we take it in the mass, is precisely such a class. Can it be said that our present-day peasantry, the Soviet peasantry, taken in the mass, resembles that kind of peasantry? No, that cannot be said. There is no longer such a peasantry in our country. Our Soviet peasantry is an entirely new peasantry. In our country there are no longer any landlords and kulaks, merchants and usurers who could exploit the peasants. Consequently, our peasantry is a peasantry emancipated from exploitation. Further. Our Soviet peasantry, its overwhelming majority, is a collective-farm peasantry, i.e., it bases its work and wealth not on individual labour and on backward technical equipment, but on collective labour and up-to-date technical equipment. . . . The economy of our peasantry is based, not on private property, but on collective property, which has grown up on the basis of collective labour. . . .

Finally, the very nature of the activities of the intelligentsia has changed. Formerly it had to serve the wealthy classes, for it had no alternative. Today it must serve the people, for there are no longer any exploiting classes. And that is precisely why it is now an equal member of Soviet society, in which, side by side with the workers and peasants, pulling together with them, it is engaged in building the new, classless, socialist society.

As you see, it is an entirely new, working intelligentsia, the like of which you will not find in any other country on earth. . . .

The picture of the changes in the social life of the U.S.S.R. would be incomplete without a few words about the changes in yet another sphere. I have in mind the sphere of *national* relationships in the U.S.S.R. As you know, within the Soviet Union there are about 60 nations, national groups and nationalities. The Soviet state is a multi-national state. Clearly, the question of the relations among the peoples of the U.S.S.R. cannot but be of prime importance for us.

The Union of Soviet Socialist Republics, as you know, was formed in 1922, at the First Congress of Soviets of the U.S.S.R. It was formed on the principles of equality and voluntary affiliation of the peoples of the U.S.S.R. The Constitution now in force, adopted in 1924, was the first Constitution of the U.S.S.R. That was the period when relations among the peoples had not yet been properly adjusted, when survivals of distrust toward the Great-Russians had not yet disappeared, and when centrifugal forces still continued to operate. Under those conditions it was necessary to establish fraternal co-operation among the peoples on the basis of economic, political, and military mutual aid by uniting them in a single, federal, multi-national state. The Soviet power had a very clear conception of the difficulties attending this task. . . .

Since then 14 years have elapsed. A period long enough to test the experiment. And what do we find? This period has shown beyond a doubt that the experiment of forming a multi-national state based on socialism has been completely successful. This is an unquestionable victory of the Leninist national policy. (Prolonged applause.)

How is this victory to be explained?

The absence of exploiting classes, which are the principal organizers of strife between nations; the absence of exploitation, which cultivates mutual distrust and kindles nationalist passions; the fact the power is in the hands of the working class, which is the foe of all enslavement and the true vehicle of the ideas of internationalism; the actual practice of mutual aid among the peoples in all spheres of economic and social life; and, finally, the flourishing of the national culture of the peoples of the U.S.S.R., culture which is national in form and socialist in content — all these and similar factors have brought about a radical change in the aspect of the peoples of the U.S.S.R.; their feeling of mutual distrust has disappeared, a feeling of mutual friendship has developed among them, and thus real fraternal co-operation among the peoples has been established within the system of a single federal state.

As a result, we now have a fully formed multi-national socialist state, which has stood all tests, and whose stability might well be envied by any national state in any part of the world. (Loud applause.)

Such are the changes which have taken place during this period in the sphere of *national relationships* in the U.S.S.R. . . .

Specific Features of the Draft Constitution

How are all these changes in the life of the U.S.S.R. reflected in the Draft of the new Constitution? . . .

[H]aving organized industry and agriculture on new, socialist lines, with a new technical base, the Soviet power has today attained a position where agriculture in the U.S.S.R. is producing one and a half times as much as was produced in pre-war times, where industry is producing seven times more than was produced in pre-war times, and where the national income has increased fourfold compared with pre-war times. All these are facts, not promises. (Prolonged applause.)

Further, the Soviet power has abolished unemployment, has introduced the right to work, the right to rest and leisure, the right to education, has provided better material and cultural conditions for the workers, peasants and intelligentsia, and has ensured the introduction of universal, direct and equal suffrage with secret ballot for its citizens. All these are facts, not promises. (Prolonged applause.) . . .

[There is a] group of critics [who] maintains that the absence of freedom for parties in the U.S.S.R. is a symptom of the violation of the principles of democratism.

I must admit that the Draft of the new Constitution does preserve the regime of the dictatorship of the working class, just as it also preserves unchanged the present leading position of the Communist Party of the U.S.S.R. (Loud applause.) If the esteemed critics regard this as a flaw in the Draft Constitution, that is only to be regretted. We Bolsheviks regard it as a merit of the Draft Constitution. (Loud applause.) As to freedom for various political parties, we adhere to somewhat different views. A party is a part of a class, its most advanced part. Several parties, and consequently, freedom for parties, can exist only in a society in which there are antagonistic classes whose interests are mutually hostile and irreconcilable —

in which there are, say, capitalists and workers, landlords and peasants, kulaks and poor peasants, etc. But in the U.S.S.R. there are no longer such classes as the capitalists, the landlords, the kulaks, etc. In the U.S.S.R. there are only two classes, workers and peasants, whose interests — far from being mutually hostile — are, on the contrary, friendly. Hence, there is no ground in the U.S.S.R. for the existence of several parties, and, consequently, for freedom for these parties. In the U.S.S.R. there is ground only for one party, the Communist Party. In the U.S.S.R. only one party can exist, the Communist Party, which courageously defends the interests of the workers and peasants to the very end. And that it defends the interests of these classes not at all badly, of that there can hardly be any doubt. (Loud applause.)

They talk of democracy. But what is democracy? Democracy in capitalist countries, where there are antagonistic classes, is, in the last analysis, democracy for the strong, democracy for the propertied minority. . . .

[An amendment has been proposed] that we completely delete from the Constitution Article 17, which reserves to the Union Republics the right of free secession from the U.S.S.R. I think that this proposal is a wrong one and therefore should not be adopted by the congress. The U.S.S.R. is a voluntary union of Union Republics with equal rights. To delete from the Constitution the article providing for the right of free secession from the U.S.S.R. would be to violate the voluntary character of this union. Can we agree to this step? I think that we cannot and should not agree to it. It is said that there is not a single Republic in the U.S.S.R. that would want to secede from the U.S.S.R., and that therefore Article 17 is of no practical importance. It is, of course, true that there is not a single Republic that would want to secede from the U.S.S.R. But this does not in the least mean that we should not fix in the Constitution the right of Union Republics freely to secede from the U.S.S.R. In the U.S.S.R. there is not a single Union Republic that would want to subjugate another Union Republic. But that does not in the least mean that we ought to delete from the Constitution of the U.S.S.R. the article dealing with the equality of rights of the Union Republics. . . .

Soviet Industrialization

In 1932, John Scott (1912–1976), a 20-year-old American college student, left the United States to work as a welder in the Soviet Union. Disturbed by the conditions of the American depression, Scott hoped that the Russian Revolution of 1917 had destroyed social inequality and injustice, and that a better society was being created. Soviet reality turned out to be quite different from his expectations, but Scott remained in the Soviet Union for five years and eventually returned to the United States with a Russian wife. In *Behind the Urals,* he offers a vivid description of life in Magnitogorsk, Russia's new city of steel, located on the eastern slopes of the Ural Mountains. These were the years of the first Five-Year Plan, whose two major goals were industrialization and collectivization of the countryside. Scott lived and worked in the harsh, freezing conditions along with Soviet workers — some of whom had been sent there as punishment for being rich peasants (*kulaks*). He vividly describes the chronic shortages of everything from bread to welding rods; the frequent, often fatal, accidents of inexperienced, underfed workers; and the ever-present bureaucratic red tape. Yet Scott also was a witness to the hope, optimism, and commitment of many of these people who believed that their personal sacrifices would benefit all humankind. This work offers a detached and penetrating documentation of the tensions, problems, and heroic tasks confronting the men and women engaged in erecting the first Communist society.

64

John Scott, *Behind the Urals*

QUESTIONS TO CONSIDER

1. According to John Scott's observations, what were some of the social problems encountered in trying to meet the goals for industrialization set by the first Five-Year Plan?
2. In the process of collectivization, how did the peasants and the Communist Party decide who were the rich peasants? What was their fate?

The big whistle on the power house sounded a long, deep, hollow six o'clock. All over the scattered city-camp of Magnitogorsk, workers rolled out of their beds or bunks and dressed in preparation for their day's work.

I climbed out of bed and turned on the light. I could see my breath across the room as I woke my roommate, Kolya. Kolya never heard the whistle. Every morning I had to pound his shoulder for several seconds to arouse him.

We pushed our coarse brown army blankets over the beds and dressed as quickly as we could — I had good American long woolen underwear, fortunately; Kolya wore only cotton shorts and a jersey. We both donned army shirts, padded and quilted cotton pants, similar jackets, heavy scarves, and then ragged sheepskin coats. We thrust our feet into good Russian 'valinkis' — felt boots coming up to the knee. We did not eat anything. We had nothing on hand except tea and a few potatoes, and there was no time to light a fire in our little home-made iron stove. We locked up and set out for the mill.

It was January, 1933. The temperature was in the neighborhood of thirty-five below. A light powdery snow covered the low spots on the ground. The high spots were bare and hard as iron. A few stars cracked in the sky and some electric

From John Scott, *Behind the Urals: An American Worker in Russia's City of Steel* (Bloomington, IN: Indiana University Press, 1973), pp. 9–10, 15–21, passim.

lights twinkled on the blast furnaces. Otherwise the world was bleak and cold and almost pitch-dark.

It was two miles to the blast furnaces, over rough ground. There was no wind, so our noses did not freeze. I was always glad when there was no wind in the morning. It was my first winter in Russia and I was not used to the cold. . . .

By the time the seven o'clock whistle blew, the shanty was jammed full of riggers, welders, cutters, and their helpers. It was a varied gang, Russians, Ukrainians, Tartars, Mongols, Jews, mostly young and almost all peasants of yesterday, though a few, like Ivanov, had long industrial experience. There was Popov, for instance. He had been a welder for ten years and had worked in half a dozen cities. On the other hand, Khaibulin, the Tartar, had never seen a staircase, a locomotive, or an electric light until he had come to Magnitogorsk a year before. His ancestors for centuries had raised stock on the flat plains of Kazakhstan. They had been dimly conscious of the Czarist government; they had had to pay taxes. Reports of the Kirghiz insurrection in 1916 had reached them. They had heard stories of the October Revolution; they even saw the Red Army come and drive out a few rich landlords. They had attended meetings of the Soviet, without understanding very clearly what it was all about, but through all this their lives had gone on more or less as before. Now Shaimat Khaibulin was building a blast furnace bigger than any in Europe. He had learned to read and was attending an evening school, learning the trade of electrician. He had learned to speak Russian, he read newspapers. His life had changed more in a year than that of his antecedents since the time of Tamerlane. . . .

I took my mask and electrodes and started out for No. 3. On the way I met Shabkov, the ex-kulak; a great husky youth with a red face, a jovial voice, and two fingers missing from his left hand.

'Well, Jack, how goes it?' he said, slapping me on the back. My Russian was still pretty bad, but I could carry on a simple conversation and understood almost everything that was said.

'Badly,' I said. 'All our equipment freezes. The boys spend half their time warming their hands.'

'Nichevo, that doesn't matter,' said the disfranchised rigger's brigadier. 'If you lived where I do, in a tent, you wouldn't think it so cold here.'

'I know you guys have it tough,' said Popov, who had joined us. 'That's what you get for being kulaks.'

Shabkov smiled broadly. 'Listen, I don't want to go into a political discussion, but a lot of the people living down in the "special" section of town are no more kulaks than you.'

Popov laughed. 'I wouldn't be surprised. Tell me, though, how did they decide who was to be dekulakized?'

'Ah,' said Shabkov, 'that's a hell of a question to ask a guy that's trying to expiate his crimes in honest labor. Just between the three of us, though, the poor peasants of the village get together in a meeting and decide: 'So-and-so has six horses; we couldn't very well get along without those in the collective farm; besides he hired a man last year to help on the harvest.' They notify the GPU, and there you are. So-and-so gets five years. They confiscate his property and give it to the new collective farm. Sometimes they ship the whole family out. When they came to ship us out, my brother got a rifle and fired several shots at the GPU officers. They fired back. My brother was killed. All of which, naturally, didn't make it any better for us. We all got five years, and in different places. I heard my father died in December, but I'm not sure.' . . .

Popov and I set about welding up a section of the bleeder pipe on the blast furnace. He gave me a break and took the outside for the first hour. Then we changed around. From the high scaffolding, nearly a hundred feet above the ground, I could see Kolya making the rounds of his thirty-odd welders, helping them when they were in trouble, swearing at them when they spent too much time warming their hands. People swore at Kolya a good deal too, because the scaffolds were unsafe or the wages bad.

It was just about nine-fifteen when I finished one side of the pipe and went around to start the other. The scaffold was coated with about an inch of ice, like everything else around the furnaces. The vapor rising from the large hot-water cooling basin condensed on everything and formed a layer of ice. But besides being slippery, it was very insecure, swung down on wires, without any guys to steady it. It swayed and shook as I walked on it. I always made a point of hanging on to something when I could. I was just going to start welding when I heard someone sing out, and something swished down past me. It was a rigger who had been working up on the very top.

He bounced off the bleeder pipe, which probably saved his life. Instead of falling all the way to the ground, he landed on the main platform about fifteen feet below me. By the time I got down to him, blood was coming out of his mouth in gushes. He tried to yell, but could not. There were no foremen around, and the half-dozen riggers that had run up did not know what to do. By virtue of being a foreigner I had a certain amount of authority, so I stepped in and said he might bleed to death if we waited for a stretcher, and three of us took him and carried him down to the first-aid station. About halfway there the bleeding let up and he began to yell every step we took.

I was badly shaken when we got there, but the two young riggers were trembling like leaves. We took him into the little wooden building, and a nurse with a heavy shawl over her white gown showed us where to put him. 'I expect the doctor any minute,' she said ; 'good thing, too, I wouldn't know what the hell to do with him.'

The rigger was gurgling and groaning. His eyes were wide open and he seemed conscious, but he did not say anything. 'We should undress him, but it is so cold in here that I am afraid to,' said the nurse. Just then the doctor came in. I knew him. He had dressed my foot once when a piece of pig iron fell on it. He took his immense sheepskin off and washed his hands. 'Fall ?' he asked, nodding at the rigger.

'Yes,' I said.

'How long ago ?'

'About ten minutes.'

'What's that ?' asked the doctor, looking at the nurse and indicating the corner of the room with his foot. I looked and for the first time noticed a pair of ragged valinkis sticking out from under a very dirty blanket on the floor.

'Girder fell on his head,' said the nurse.

'Well,' said the doctor, rolling up his sleeves, 'let's see what we can do for this fellow.' He moved over toward the rigger, who was lying quietly now and looking at the old bearded doctor with watery blue eyes. I turned to go, but the doctor stopped me.

'On your way out, please telephone the factory board of health and tell them I simply must have more heat in this place,' he said.

I did the best I could over the telephone in my bad Russian, but all I could get was, 'Comrade, we are sorry, but there is no coal.'

I was making my way unsteadily back to the bleeder pipe on No. 3 when Kolya hailed me. 'Don't bother to go up for a while, the brushes burnt out on the machine you were working on. They won't be fixed for half an hour or so.' I went toward the office with Kolya and told him about the rigger. I was incensed and talked about some thorough checkup on scaffoldings. Kolya could not get interested. He pointed out there was not enough planking for good scaffolds, that the riggers were mostly plowboys who had no idea of being careful, and that at thirty-five below without any breakfast in you, you did not pay as much attention as you should.

'Sure, people will fall. But we're building blast furnaces all the same, aren't we?' and he waved his hand toward No. 2 from which the red glow of flowing pig iron was emanating. He saw I was not satisfied. 'This somewhat sissified foreigner will have to be eased along a little,' he probably said to himself. He slapped me on the back. 'Come on in the office. We are going to have a technical conference. You'll be interested.'

Fascism: Three Faces

Fascism, the only new comprehensive political philosophy of the twentieth century, appeared in every industrialized country in the 1920s or 1930s.

In Japan, Kita Ikki (1885–1937) was the foremost proponent of national socialist reform, and his book *Outline for the Reconstruction of Japan* (1919) became the bible of Japanese fascists. Kita advocated a complete reorganization of Japanese polity: a military takeover of the government to free the emperor from his selfish and weak advisors; nationalization of land and capital; and an aggressive, expansionist foreign policy, especially on the Asian mainland, to help solve Japan's shortage of natural resources, relieve the population pressure, and free Asia from Western influence.

European fascists, on the other hand, generally tended to avoid rigorous, positive definitions of their programs, concentrating instead on the political and economic failures of democracy and communism. Of all the fascist leaders, Benito Mussolini (1883–1945) has made, perhaps, the clearest and most complete theoretical statement of the fascist ideology. Mussolini denounced the class war and celebrated the fascist cult of violence and death. Adolf Hitler (1889–1945), though heavily influenced by Mussolini, emphasized propaganda and the special role of race in the development of his National Socialist (Nazi) form of German fascism.

65

Kita Ikki, *Outline for the Reconstruction of Japan*

Following World War I, Japan experimented with parliamentary democracy at home and pursued internationalism abroad. But Japanese radicals, both right- and left-wing, had little confidence in parliamentary solutions for social problems. Radical nationalists, particularly ultranationalistic young army officers, found inspiration for the future in the thought and writings of Kita Ikki (1885–1937). This advocate of national socialism was implicated in the abortive military coup d'état of February 26, 1936, and was executed in 1937.

QUESTIONS TO CONSIDER

1. Why would Kita Ikki urge that the study of English be abolished?
2. Are there any parallels between Kita Ikki's and Mussolini's views of war and violence (see Reading 66)?

The Emperor of the People

Suspension of the Constitution : In order to establish a firm base for national reorganization, the Emperor, with the aid of the entire Japanese nation and by invoking his imperial prerogatives, shall suspend the Constitution for a period of three years, dissolve the two houses of the Diet, and place the entire country under martial law.

   The true significance of the Emperor : We must make clear the fundamental principle that the Emperor is the sole representative of the people and the pillar of the state. . . .

   Abolition of the peerage system : By abolishing the peerage system, we shall be able to remove the feudal aristocracy which constitutes a barrier between the Emperor and the people. In this way the spirit of the Meiji Restoration shall be proclaimed.

   The House of Peers shall be replaced by the Deliberative Council which shall review decisions made by the House of Representatives. The Deliberative Council may reject for a single time only any decisions of the House of Representatives.

   The members of the Deliberative Council shall consist of men distinguished in various fields of activities, elected by each other or appointed by the Emperor.

   Popular election : All men twenty-five years of age and above shall have the right to elect and be elected to the House of Representatives, exercising their rights with full equality as citizens of Great Japan. Similar provisions shall apply to

From David John Lu, *Sources of Japanese History*, vol. 2 (New York : McGraw-Hill, 1974), pp. 131–136. Reprinted by permission.

all local self-governing bodies. No women shall be permitted to participate in politics.

Restoration of people's freedom : Existing laws which restrict people's freedom and circumvent the spirit of the constitution shall be abolished. These laws include the civil service appointment ordinance, peace preservation law, press act, and publication law.

National reorganization Cabinet : A national reorganization Cabinet shall be formed during the time martial law is in effect. In addition to the existing ministries, the Cabinet shall establish such ministries of industries as described below and add a number of ministers without portfolio. Members of the reorganization Cabinet shall be selected from outstanding individuals throughout the country, avoiding those who are presently connected with military, bureaucratic, financial, or party cliques. . . .

Granting of imperial estate : The Emperor shall set a personal example by granting to the state, the lands, forests, shares and similar properties held by the Imperial Household. The expenses of the Imperial Household shall be limited to thirty million yen per annum appropriated from the national treasury. However, the Diet may authorize additional expenditure if the need arises.

Limitation on Private Property

Limitation on private property. No Japanese family shall possess property in excess of one million yen. A similar limitation shall apply to Japanese citizens holding property overseas. No one shall be permitted to make a gift of property to those related by blood or to others, or to transfer his property by other means with the intent of circumventing this limitation.

Nationalization of excess amount over limitation on private property : Any amount which exceeds the limitation on private property shall revert to the state without compensation. No one shall be permitted to resort to the protection of present laws in order to avoid remitting such excess amount. Anyone who violates these provisions shall be deemed a person thinking lightly of the example set by the Emperor and endangering the basis of national reorganization. As such, during the time martial law is in effect, he shall be charged with the crimes of endangering the person of the Emperor and engaging in internal revolt and shall be punished by death.

Three Principles for Disposition of Lands

Limitation on private landholding : No Japanese family shall hold land in excess of 100,000 yen in current market value. . . .

. . . Lands held in excess of the limitation on private landholding shall revert to the state. . . .

Popular ownership of lands reverted to state : The state shall divide the lands granted by the Imperial Household and the lands reverted to it from those whose holdings exceed the limitation and distribute such lands to farmers who do not possess their own lands. These farmers shall gain title to their respective lands by making annual installment payments to the state. . . .

Lands to be owned by the state: Large forests, virgin lands which require large capital investment, and lands which can best be cultivated in large lots shall be owned and operated by the state.

Control of Large Capital

Limitation on private property: No private industry shall exceed the limit of 10,000,000 yen in assets. A similar limitation shall apply to private industries owned by Japanese citizens overseas.

Nationalization of industries exceeding the limitation: Any industry whose assets exceed the limitation imposed on private industry shall be collectivized and operated under state control. . . .

Industrial Organization of the State

No. 1. Ministry of Banking: The assets of this ministry shall come from the money expropriated from large banks whose assets exceed the limitation on private industry and from individuals whose net worth exceeds the limitation on private property. . . .

No. 2. Ministry of Navigation: Ships and other assets expropriated from private lines in excess of the limitation on private property shall be utilized mainly for transoceanic voyages in order to attain supremacy of the seas. [The ministry shall also] engage in shipbuilding (naval and commercial) and other activities. . . .

No. 3. Ministry of Mines: Large mines whose assets or market values exceed the limitation on private industry shall be expropriated and operated by this ministry. . . .

No. 4. Ministry of Agriculture: Management of nationally owned lands; management of Taiwan sugar industry and forestry; development of Taiwan, Hokkaido, Karafuto (Southern Sakhalin), and Chōsen (Korea); development of South and North Manchuria and colonies to be acquired in the future; and management of large farms when acquired by the state.

No. 5. Ministry of Industries: Various large industries expropriated by the state shall be reorganized, unified, and expanded to form a truly large industrial combine through which all types of industries may acquire competitive advantages now possessed by comparable foreign industries. The ministry shall also operate industries urgently needed by the nation but not undertaken by private parties. Naval Steel Works and Military Ordinance Factories shall be placed under this ministry's jurisdiction and be operated by it. . . .

Railways whose assets do not exceed the limitation on private industry shall be open to private operation.

Vast income of the national treasury: The vast income realized by the industrial ministries shall be sufficient for the expenditures of various service ministries and guarantee adequate living conditions for the people as described below. Therefore, with the exception of basic income taxes, all other inequitable taxes shall be abolished. Without exception, all industrial ministries shall be taxed in a manner similar to all private industries. . . .

Rights of Workers

Functions of the Ministry of Labor: A Ministry of Labor shall be established within the Cabinet to protect the rights of all workers employed by state-owned and privately owned industries. Industrial disputes shall be submitted to the Ministry of Labor for arbitration in accordance with a law to be enacted independently. . . .

Working hours: Working hours shall be uniformly set at eight hours a day. Wages shall be paid for Sundays and holidays when no work is performed. Farm workers shall receive additional wages for the overtime work performed during the busy farming seasons.

Distribution of profits to workers: One half of the net profits of private industries shall be distributed to workers employed in such industries. All workers, mental and physical, shall participate in the profit distribution proportionate to their salaries or wages. Workers shall elect their own representatives to participate in the industry's management planning and bookkeeping. Similar provisions shall apply to farm workers and landlords.

Workers employed in state-owned industries shall receive semi-annual bonuses in lieu of the profit distribution. . . .

Establishment of employee-shareholder system: Every private corporation shall set up a provision under which physical and mental workers in their employment shall have the right to become stockholders of the corporation.

Protection of tenant farmers: The state shall enact a separate law, based on the basic human rights, to protect tenant farmers tilling the lands owned by small landlords whose holdings do not exceed the limitation on private lands.

Women's labor: Women's labor shall be free and equal to that of men. However, after the reorganization, the state shall make it a matter of national policy that the burden of labor shall not rest on the shoulders of women. In order to prepare women to replace men in providing needed labor in a national emergency, women shall receive education equal to that of men.

People's Right to Live

Children's right to live: Children under fifteen years of age without both parents or father, having rights as children of the state, shall be uniformly supported and educated by the state. . . .

Support of the aged and disabled: The state shall assume the responsibility of supporting those men and women sixty years of age or over who are poor and not having their natural born or adopted sons. Similar support shall be given to those disabled and crippled persons who are poor, unable to work, and without fathers and sons.

Rights to education: National (compulsory) education shall last for a period of ten years from ages six to sixteen. Similar education shall be given to both male and female. There shall be instituted a fundamental reform in the educational system. . . .

English shall be abolished and Esperanto shall become the second language. . . .

Rights of the State

Continuation of the conscript system : The state, having rights to existence and development among the nations of the world, shall maintain the present conscript system in perpetuity. . . .

Positive right to start war : In addition to the right to self-defense, the state shall have the right to start a war on behalf of other nations and races unjustly oppressed by a third power. (As a matter of real concern today, the state shall have the right to start a war to aid the independence of India and preservation of China's integrity.)

As a result of its own development, the state shall also have the right to start a war against those nations who occupy large colonies illegally and ignore the heavenly way of the co-existence of all humanity. (As a matter of real concern today, the state shall have the right to start a war against those nations which occupy Australia and Far Eastern Siberia for the purpose of acquiring them.)

66

Benito Mussolini, "The Political and Social Doctrine of Fascism"

Capitalizing on the economic and political unrest of Italy following World War I, Benito Mussolini (1883–1945) came to power after his black-shirted fascists marched on Rome in 1922. In 1932, Mussolini, with the help of Giovanni Gentile, wrote the following definition of Italian fascism.

QUESTIONS TO CONSIDER

1. How did Mussolini view democracy, socialism, and pacifism?
2. Why would Mussolini's passionate embrace of heroism and violence appeal to so many Italians (and others) in the 1920s?

The years which preceded the March to Rome were years of great difficulty, during which the necessity for action did not permit of research or any complete elaboration of doctrine. The battle had to be fought in the towns and villages. There was much discussion, but — what was more important and more sacred — men died. They knew how to die. Doctrine, beautifully defined and carefully elucidated, with headlines and paragraphs, might be lacking ; but there was to take its

From Benito Mussolini, "The Political and Social Doctrine of Fascism," *International Conciliation*, 306 (January 1935), pp. 5–17, passim. Reprinted by permission of the Carnegie Endowment for International Peace.

place something more decisive — Faith. Even so, anyone who can recall the events of the time through the aid of books, articles, votes of congresses, and speeches of great and minor importance — anyone who knows how to research and weigh evidence — will find that the fundamentals of doctrine were cast during the years of conflict. It was precisely in those years that Fascist thought armed itself, was refined, and began the great task of organization. The problem of the relation between the individual citizen and the State; the allied problems of authority and liberty; political and social problems as well as those specifically national — a solution was being sought for all these while at the same time the struggle against Liberalism, Democracy, Socialism, and the Masonic bodies was being carried on, contemporaneously with the "punitive expedition." But, since there was inevitably some lack of system, the adversaries of Fascism have disingenuously denied that it had any capacity to produce a doctrine of its own, though that doctrine was growing and taking shape under their very eyes, even though tumultuously; first, as happens to all ideas in their beginnings, in the aspect of a violent and dogmatic negation, and then in the aspect of positive construction which has found its realization in the laws and institutions of the regime as enacted successively in the years 1926, 1927 and 1928.

Fascism is now a completely individual thing, not only as a regime, but as a doctrine. And this means that today Fascism, exercising its critical sense upon itself and upon others, has formed its own distinct and peculiar point of view, to which it can refer and upon which, therefore, it can act in the face of all problems, practical or intellectual, which confront the world.

And above all, Fascism, the more it considers and observes the future and the development of humanity quite apart from political considerations of the moment, believes neither in the possibility nor the utility of perpetual peace. It thus repudiates the doctrine of Pacifism — born of a renunciation of the struggle and an act of cowardice in the face of sacrifice. War alone brings up to its highest tension all human energy and puts the stamp of nobility upon the peoples who have the courage to meet it. All other trials are substitutes, which never really put men into the position where they have to make the great decision — the alternative of life or death. Thus a doctrine which is founded upon this harmful postulate of peace is hostile to Fascism. And thus hostile to the spirit of Fascism, though accepted for what use they can be in dealing with particular political situations, are all the international leagues and societies which, as history will show, can be scattered to the winds when once strong national feeling is aroused by any motive — sentimental, ideal, or practical. This anti-pacifist spirit is carried by Fascism even into the life of the individual; the proud motto of the Squadrista, *"Me ne frego"* (I do not fear), written on the bandage of the wound, is an act of philosophy not only stoic, the summary of a doctrine not only political — it is the education to combat, the acceptance of the risks which combat implies, and a new way of life for Italy. Thus the Fascist accepts life and loves it, knowing nothing of and despising suicide: he rather conceives of life as duty and struggle and conquest, life which should be high and full, lived for oneself, but above all for others — those who are at hand and those who are far distant, contemporaries, and those who will come after.

This "demographic" policy of the regime is the result of the above premise. Thus the Fascist loves in actual fact his neighbor, but this "neighbor" is not merely a vague and undefined concept, this love for one's neighbor puts no obstacle in the way of necessary educational severity, and still less to differentiation of status and to physical distance. Fascism repudiates any universal embrace, and in order to live worthily in the community of civilized peoples watches its contemporaries with vigilant eyes, takes good note of their state of mind and, in the changing trend of their interests, does not allow itself to be deceived by temporary and fallacious appearances.

Such a conception of life makes Fascism the complete opposite of that doctrine, the base of the so-called scientific and Marxian Socialism, the materialist conception of history ; according to which the history of human civilization can be explained simply through the conflict of interests among the various social groups and by the change and development in the means and instruments of production. That the changes in the economic field — new discoveries of raw materials, new methods of working them, and the inventions of science — have their importance no one can deny ; but that these factors are sufficient to explain the history of humanity excluding all others is an absurd delusion. Fascism, now and always, believes in holiness and in heroism ; that is to say, in actions influenced by no economic motive, direct or indirect. And if the economic conception of history be denied, according to which theory men are no more than puppets, carried to and fro by the waves of chance, while the real directing forces are quite out of their control, it follows that the existence of an unchangeable and unchanging class war is also denied — the natural progeny of the economic conception of history. And above all Fascism denies that class war can be the preponderant force in the transformation of society. These two fundamental concepts of Socialism being thus refuted, nothing is left of it but the sentimental aspiration — as old as humanity itself — towards a social convention in which the sorrows and sufferings of the humblest shall be alleviated. But here again Fascism repudiates the conception of "economic" happiness, to be realized by Socialism and, as it were, at a given moment in economic evolution to assure to everyone the maximum of well-being. Fascism denies the materialist conception of happiness as a possibility, and abandons it to its inventors, the economists of the first half of the nineteenth century : that is to say, Fascism denies the validity of the equation, well-being = happiness, which would reduce men to the level of animals, caring for one thing only — to be fat and well-fed — and would thus degrade humanity to a purely physical existence.

After Socialism, Fascism combats the whole complex system of democratic ideology, and repudiates it, whether in its theoretical premises or in its practical application. Fascism denies that the majority, by the simple fact that it is a majority, can direct human society ; it denies that numbers alone can govern by means of a periodical consultation, and it affirms the immutable, beneficial, and fruitful inequality of mankind, which can never be permanently leveled through the mere operation of a mechanical process such as universal suffrage. The democratic regime may be defined as from time to time giving the people the illusion of sovereignty, while the real effective sovereignty lies in the hands of other concealed and irresponsible forces. Democracy is a regime nominally without a king, but it is ruled by many kings — more absolute, tyrannical, and ruinous than one sole king, even though a tyrant. This explains why Fascism, having first in 1922 (for reasons of expediency) assumed an attitude tending towards republicanism, renounced this point of view before the March to Rome ; being convinced that the question of political form is not today of prime importance, and after having studied the examples of monarchies and republics past and present reached the conclusion that monarchy or republicanism are not to be judged, as it were, by an absolute standard ; but that they represent forms in which the evolution — political, historical, traditional, or psychological — of a particular country has expressed itself.

67

Adolf Hitler, *Mein Kampf*

Adolf Hitler (1889–1945) became Chancellor of Germany in 1933 and ruled Germany until 1945. In 1943, in the midst of World War II, the U.S. State Department translated and published the following extract of Hitler's National Socialist (Nazi) program, which was originally published in the first volume of Hitler's book *Mein Kampf (My Struggle).*

QUESTIONS TO CONSIDER

1. What were Hitler's views on the racial characteristics of Germans ?
2. According to Hitler, what was the function of propaganda ?

The basic racial elements are differently situated, not only territorially but also in individual cases within the same territory. Nordic men exist side by side with Eastern types ; Easterners, with Dinarics ; both of these types, with Westerners ; and everywhere among them are mixed types. On the one hand this is a great disadvantage : The German folk lacks that sure instinct of the herd which has its roots in the unity of blood and, especially in moments when great danger threatens, preserves the nation from collapse, in as much as with such a folk all small internal distinctions will then immediately disappear and the common enemy will be faced with the closed front of the uniform herd. In the existence side by side of our most varied component racial elements, which have remained unmixed, lies the foundation of that which we designate with the word superindividualism. In peaceful times it may sometimes perform good services for us, but, considered all in all, it has deprived us of world supremacy. If the German folk, in its historical development, had possessed that herdlike unity which other peoples have enjoyed, the German Reich would today be mistress of the globe. World history would have taken another course, and no one can tell whether in this way

From Raymond Murphy, *National Socialism : Basic Principles, Their Application by the Nazi Party's Foreign Organization, and the Use of Germans Abroad for Nazi Aims* (Washington, DC : Government Printing Office, 1943), pp. 845–849, passim.

that might not have been attained which so many deluded pacifists are hoping today to wheedle by moaning and whining : A peace supported not by the palm branches of tearful pacifistic female mourners but founded by the victorious sword of a master race (Herrenvolk) which places the world in the service of a higher culture. . . .

Propaganda

In this regard one proceeded from the very correct principle that the size of the lie always involves a certain factor of credibility, since the great mass of a people will be more spoiled in the innermost depths of its heart, rather than consciously and deliberately bad. Consequently, in view of the primitive simplicity of its mind it is more readily captivated by a big lie than by a small one, since it itself often uses small lies but would be, nevertheless, too ashamed to make use of big lies. Such an untruth will not even occur to it, and it will not even believe that others are capable of the enormous insolence of the most vile distortions. Why, even when enlightened, it will still vacillate and be in doubt about the matter and will nevertheless accept as true at least some cause or other. Consequently, even from the most impudent lie something will always stick.

To whom must propaganda appeal ? To the scientific mind or to the less educated masses ?

The task of propaganda does not lie in a scientific education of the individual but in pointing out to the masses definite facts, processes, necessities, etc., the significance of which in this way is first to be brought within the masses' range of vision.

The art lies exclusively therein, to do this in such an excellent way that a universal conviction arises of the reality of a fact, of the necessity of a process, of the correctness of something necessary, etc. Since it is not and cannot be necessary in itself, since its task, just as in the case of a placard, consists of bringing something before the attention of the crowd and not in the instruction of those who are scientifically trained or are seeking education and insight, its efficacy must always be oriented more to the emotions and only in a very restricted way to the so-called "intellect."

All propaganda has to appeal to the people and its intellectual level has to be set in accordance with the receptive capacities of the most-limited persons among those to whom it intends to address itself. The larger the mass of men to be reached, the lower its purely intellectual level will have to be set. . . .

The art of propaganda lies precisely therein, that, comprehending the great masses' world of emotions and imagination, it finds the way, in a psychologically correct form, to the attention and, further, to the hearts of the great masses.

The receptive capacity of the great masses is very restricted, its understanding small. On the other hand, however, its forgetfulness is great. On account of these facts all effective propaganda must restrict itself to very few points and impress these by slogans, until even the last person is able to bring to mind what is meant by such a word.

. . . In general the art of all truly great popular leaders at all times consists primarily in not scattering the attention of a people but rather in concentrating it always on one single opponent. The more unified this use of the fighting will of a people, the greater will be the magnetic attractive force of a movement and the more powerful the force of its push. It is a part of the genius of a great leader to make even quite different opponents appear as if they belonged only to one category, because the recognition of different enemies leads weak and unsure persons only too readily to begin doubting their own cause.

When the vacillating masses see themselves fighting against too many enemies, objectivity at once sets in and raises the question whether really all the others are wrong and only one's own people or one's own movement is right.

Therewith, however, appears already the first weakening of one's own force. Consequently, a number of intrinsically different opponents must always be comprehended together, so that in the view of the masses of one's own adherents the fight is only being carried on against one enemy alone. This strengthens the faith in one's own cause and increases the bitterness toward the aggressor against this cause.

In all cases in which there is a question of the fulfillment of apparently impossible demands or tasks, the entire attention of a people must be concentrated only on this one question, in such a way as if being or non-being actually depends on its solution. Only in this way will one make a people willing and capable of really great accomplishments and exertions.

Patterns of Genocide

Genocide, the systematic, mass killing of men, women, and children because they seemingly pose political, racial, or religious threats to the state, has become increasingly commonplace in the twentieth century. The following selections illustrate just how common genocide has become.

In the Soviet Union, genocide occurred between 1928 and 1939, when at least ten million Russians were killed or died in prison camps. The purpose of this slaughter, carried out by Stalin and his executioners, was to annihilate anyone defined as an enemy of the state — a label arbitrarily applied to instill terror. This genocide succeeded in giving Stalin and his men complete control of the Soviet Union.

The motives for Nazi genocide are equally clear. Adolf Hitler and his Nazi followers were determined to exterminate "racially inferior" Europeans — especially Jews — from Nazi-occupied Europe. Between 1939 and 1945, three million Poles ; uncounted thousands of Slavs, Gypsies, and Russians ; and at least seven million Jews were killed.

Pol Pot, the leader of the Cambodian Khmer Rouge Communist Party, created another genocidal terror when he implemented one of the most theoretical and brutal Communist revolutions of the twentieth century. Convinced that the Khmer Rouge Communists could achieve a Cambodian worker's paradise immediately, one of its officers told the Cambodian head of state, Prince Norodom Sihanouk: "We want to have our name in history as the ones who can reach total communism with one leap forward. . . . We want to be known as the only communist party to communize a country without a step-by-step policy, without going through socialism."[1] To achieve this goal, between 1975 and 1979 the Khmer Rouge liquidated more than a million Cambodians.

68

Nadezhda Mandelstam, *Hope Against Hope*

In the 1930s, Nadezhda Mandelstam (1899–1980) experienced the Soviet terror. Her husband, Osip Mandelstam (1891–1938), recognized today as the greatest Russian poet of the twentieth century, was persecuted because he portrayed Stalin as a tyrant in one of his poems. He was sentenced in 1938 to five years of hard labor in a camp in Vladivostok, but he died within the first year. Nadezhda first learned that her husband had died when a package she had sent him was returned, and she was told that the addressee was dead.

QUESTIONS TO CONSIDER

1. What was the justification given in Stalin's Russia for the arrest, imprisonment, and execution of "enemies of the state"?
2. How did those who had not been arrested behave during Stalin's terror?
3. What are the long-term consequences for the Soviet Union of Stalin's genocide (see Readings 82 and 98)?

When I used to read about the French Revolution as a child, I often wondered whether it was possible to survive during a reign of terror. I now know beyond doubt that it is impossible. Anybody who breathes the air of terror is doomed, even if nominally he manages to save his life. Everybody is a victim — not only those who die, but also all the killers, ideologists, accomplices and sycophants who close their eyes or wash their hands — even if they are secretly consumed with re-

Excerpted from *Hope Against Hope: A Memoir* by Nadezhda Mandelstam, pp. 297–298, 304–305, 316–317, 369–371. Translated from the Russian by Max Hayward with introduction by Clarence Brown. Copyright © 1970 Atheneum Publishers. English translation copyright © 1970 Atheneum Publishers. Introduction copyright © 1970 Atheneum Publishers. Reprinted with the permission of Atheneum Publishers, an imprint of Macmillan Publishing Company.

1. Marlowe Hood, "The Lesser Evil: An Interview with Norodom Sihanouk," *The New York Review of Books,* March 14, 1985, p. 24.

morse at night. Every section of the population has been through the terrible sickness caused by terror, and none has so far recovered, or become fit again for normal civic life. It is an illness that is passed on to the next generation, so that the sons pay for the sins of the fathers and perhaps only the grandchildren begin to get over it — or at least it takes on a different form with them.

Who was it who dared say that we have no "lost generation" here? The fact that he could utter such a monstrous untruth is also a consequence of terror. One generation after another was "lost" here, but it was a completely different process from what may have happened in the West. Here people just tried to go on working, struggling to maintain themselves, hoping for salvation, and thinking only about their immediate concerns. In such times your daily round is like a drug. The more you have to do, the better. If you can immerse yourself in your work, the years fly by more quickly, leaving only a gray blur in the memory. Among the people of my generation, only a very few have kept clear minds and memories. In M.'s generation, everybody was stricken by a kind of sclerosis at an early stage.

True as this is, however, I never cease to marvel at our hardiness. After Stalin's death my brother Evgeni said to me: "We still do not realize what we have been through." Not long ago, as I was traveling in an overcrowded bus, an old woman pushed up against me and I found my arm was bearing the whole weight of her body. "That must be killing you," she said suddenly. "No," I replied, "we're as tough as the devil." "As tough as the devil?" she said, and laughed. Somebody nearby also laughingly repeated the phrase, and soon the whole bus was saying it after us. But then the bus stopped and everybody started to push toward the exit, jostling each other in the usual way. The little moment of good humor was over. . . .

When life becomes absolutely intolerable, you begin to think the horror will never end. In Kiev during the bombardment I understood that even the unbearable can come to an end, but I was not yet fully aware that it often does so only at death. As regards the Stalinist terror, we always knew that it might wax or wane, but that it might end — this we could never imagine. What reason was there for it to end? Everybody seemed intent on his daily round and went smilingly about the business of carrying out his instructions. It was essential to smile — if you didn't, it meant you were afraid or discontented. This nobody could afford to admit — if you were afraid, then you must have a bad conscience. Everybody who worked for the State — and in this country even the humblest stall-keeper is a bureaucrat — had to strut around wearing a cheerful expression, as though to say: "What's going on is no concern of mine, I have very important work to do, and I'm terribly busy. I am trying to do my best for the State, so do not get in my way. My conscience is clear — if what's-his-name has been arrested, there must be good reason." The mask was taken off only at home, and then not always — even from your children you had to conceal how horror-struck you were; otherwise, God save you, they might let something slip in school. . . . Some people had adapted to the terror so well that they knew how to profit from it — there was nothing out of the ordinary about denouncing a neighbor to get his apartment or his job. But while wearing your smiling mask, it was important not to laugh — this could look suspicious to the neighbors and make them think you were indulging in sacrilegious mockery. We have lost the capacity to be spontaneously cheerful, and it will never come back to us. . . .

I think he exaggerated the extent to which our secret police went in for ordinary detective work. They were not in the least bit interested in *real* facts — all they wanted were lists of people to arrest, and these they got from their network of informers and the volunteers who brought them denunciations. To meet their quotas, all they needed were names of people, not details about their comings and goings. During interrogations they always, as a matter of routine, collected "evidence" against people whom they had no intention of arresting — just in case it was ever needed. I have heard of a woman who heroically went through torture rather than give "evidence" against Molotov! was asked for evidence against Liuba Ehrenburg, whom he had never even met. He managed to send word about this from the forced-labor camp, and Liuba was warned — apparently Akhmatova passed on the message to her. Liuba could not believe it: "What Spasski? I don't know him." She was still naïve in those days, but later she understood everything.

In the torture chambers of the Lubianka they were constantly adding to the dossiers of Ehrenburg, Sholokhov, Alexei Tolstoi, and others whom they had no intention of touching. Dozens, if not hundreds of people were sent to camps on a charge of being involved in a "conspiracy" headed by Tikhonov and Fadeyev! Among them was Spasski. Wild inventions and monstrous accusations had become an end in themselves, and officials of the secret police applied all their ingenuity to them, as though reveling in the total arbitrariness of their power. Their basic principle was just what Furmanov had told us at the end of the twenties: "Give us a man, and we'll make a case." On the day we had spent at Stenich's apartment, his name was almost certainly already on a list of persons due to be arrested — his telephone number would have been found in Diki's address book, and no further information about him was needed.

The principles and aims of mass terror have nothing in common with ordinary police work or with security. The only purpose of terror is intimidation. To plunge the whole country into a state of chronic fear, the number of victims must be raised to astronomical levels, and on every floor of every building there must always be several apartments from which the tenants have suddenly been taken away. The remaining inhabitants will be model citizens for the rest of their lives — this will be true for every street and every city through which the broom has swept. The only essential thing for those who rule by terror is not to overlook the new generations growing up without faith in their elders, and to keep on repeating the process in systematic fashion. Stalin ruled for a long time and saw to it that the waves of terror recurred from time to time, always on an even greater scale than before. But the champions of terror invariably leave one thing out of account — namely, that they can't kill everyone, and among their cowed, half-demented subjects there are always witnesses who survive to tell the tale....

The only link with a person in prison was the window through which one handed parcels and money to be forwarded to him by the authorities. Once a month, after waiting three or four hours in line (the number of arrests was by now falling off, so this was not very long), I went up to the window and gave my name. The clerk behind the window thumbed through his list — I went on days when he dealt with the letter "M" — and asked me for my first name and initial. As soon as I replied, a hand stretched out of the window and I put my identity papers and some money into it. The hand then returned my papers with a receipt and I went away. Everybody envied me because I at least knew that my husband was alive and where he was. It happened only too often that the man behind the window barked : "No record. . . . Next!" All questions were useless — the official would simply shut his window in your face and one of the uniformed guards would come up to you. Order was immediately restored and the next in line moved up to the window. If anybody ever tried to linger, the guard found ready allies among the other people waiting.

There was generally no conversation in the line. This was the chief prison in the Soviet Union, and the people who came here were a select, respectable and well-disciplined crowd. There were never any untoward events, unless it was a minor case of someone asking a question — but persons guilty of such misconduct would speedily retreat in embarrassment. The only incident I saw was when two little girls in neatly starched dresses once came in. Their mother had been arrested the previous night. They were let through out of turn and nobody asked what letter their name began with. All the women waiting there were no doubt moved by pity at the thought that their own children might soon be coming here in the same way. Somebody lifted up the elder of the two, because she was too small to reach the window, and she shouted through it : "Where's my mummy?" and "We won't go to the orphanage. We won't go home." They just managed to say that their father was in the army before the window was slammed shut. This could have been the actual case, or it could have meant that he had been in the secret police. The children of Chekists were always taught to say that their father was "in the army" — this was to protect them from the curiosity of their schoolmates, who, the parents explained, might be less friendly otherwise. Before going abroad on duty, Chekists also made their children learn the new name under which they would be living there. . . . The little girls in the starched dresses probably lived in a government building — they told the people waiting in line that other children had been taken away to orphanages, but that they wanted to go to their grandmother in the Ukraine. Before they could say any more, a soldier came out of a side door and led them away. The window opened again and everything returned to normal. As they were being led away, one woman called them "silly little girls," and another said : "We must send ours away before it's too late."

These little girls were exceptional. Children who came and stood in line were usually as restrained and silent as grown-ups. It was generally their fathers who were arrested first — particularly if they were military people — and they would then be carefully instructed by their mothers on how to behave when they were left completely alone. Many of them managed to keep out of the orphanages, but that depended mainly on their parents' status — the higher it had been, the less chance the children had of being looked after by relatives. It was astonishing that life continued at all, and that people still brought children into the world and had families. How could they do this, knowing what went on in front of the window in the building on Sophia Embankment?

69

Rudolf Hoess, Eyewitness to Hitler's Genocide

Although the Nazis did experiment with mass shootings to kill *unter-menschen* (subhumans), they eventually adopted a form of killing that used Cyclon-B gas in their extermination camps. The following account, given at the Nuremberg War Crimes Tribunal (1945–1946), is the testimony of Rudolf Hoess, a member of the Nazi Party (NSDAP), who commanded the extermination camp at Auschwitz.

QUESTIONS TO CONSIDER

1. What parts of Rudolf Hoess's testimony suggest the mechanistic, industrialized approach of the Nazis' genocide?
2. What are the moral and political implications of Hoess's admission that not only the security police (Gestapo) but also the German Army (Wehrmacht) and physicians cooperated in Hitler's genocide?

I, Rudolf Franz Ferdinand Hoess, being first duly sworn, depose and say as follows:

1. I am forty-six years old, and have been a member of the NSDAP since 1922; a member of the SS since 1934; a member of the Waffen-SS since 1939. I was a member from 1 December 1934 of the SS Guard Unit, the so-called Deathshead Formation *[Totenkopf Verband]*.

2. I have been constantly associated with the administration of concentration camps since 1934, serving at Dachau until 1938; then as Adjutant in Sachenhausen from 1938 to May 1, 1940, when I was appointed Commandant of Auschwitz. I commanded Auschwitz until 1 December 1943, and estimate that at least 2,500,000 victims were executed and exterminated there by gassing and burning, and at least another half million succumbed to starvation and disease making a total dead of about 3,000,000. This figure represents about 70% to 80% of all persons sent to Auschwitz as prisoners, the remainder having been selected and used for slave labor in the concentration camp industries. Included among the executed and burnt were approximately 20,000 Russian prisoners of war (previously screened out of Prisoner of War cages by the Gestapo) who were delivered at Auschwitz in Wehrmacht transports operated by regular Wehrmacht officers, 100,000 German Jews, and great numbers of citizens, mostly Jewish from Holland, France, Belgium, Poland, Hungary, Czechoslovakia, Greece, or other coun-

Office of the U.S., Chief of Counsel for the Prosecution of Axis Criminality, *Nazi Conspiracy and Aggression* (Washington, DC: Government Printing Office, 1947), vol. 6, pp. 787–790 (PS-3868).

tries. We executed about 400,000 Hungarian Jews alone at Auschwitz in the summer of 1944. . . .

4. Mass executions by gassing commenced during the summer 1941 and continued until fall 1944. I personally supervised executions at Auschwitz until the first of December 1943 and know by reason of my continued duties . . . that these mass executions continued as stated above. All mass executions by gassing took place under the direct orders, supervisions, and responsibility of RSHA [Reich Security Main Office]. I received all orders for carrying out these mass executions directly from RSHA. . . .

6. The "final solution" of the Jewish question meant the complete extermination of all Jews in Europe. I was ordered to establish extermination facilities at Auschwitz in June 1941. At that time, there were already in the general government three other extermination camps; Belzek, Treblinka, and Wolzek. These camps were under the *Einsatzkommando* of the Security Police and SD. I visited Treblinka to find out how they carried out their extermination. The Camp Commandant at Treblinka told me that he had liquidated 80,000 in the course of one-half year. He was principally concerned with liquidating all the Jews from the Warsaw ghetto. He used monoxide gas and I did not think that his methods were very efficient. So when I set up the extermination building at Auschwitz, I used Cyclon B, which was a crystallized prussic acid which we dropped into the death chamber from a small opening. It took from 3 to 15 minutes to kill the people in the death chamber depending upon climatic conditions. We knew when the people were dead because their screaming stopped. We usually waited about one-half hour before we opened the doors and removed the bodies. After the bodies were removed our special commandos took off the rings and extracted the gold from the teeth of the corpses.

7. Another improvement we made over Treblinka was that we built our gas chambers to accommodate 2,000 people at one time, whereas at Treblinka their 10 gas chambers only accommodated 200 people each. The way we selected our victims was as follows: we had two SS doctors on duty at Auschwitz to examine the incoming transports of prisoners. The prisoners would be marched by one of the doctors who would make spot decisions as they walked by. Those who were fit for work were sent into the Camp. Others were sent immediately to the extermination plants. Children of tender years were invariably exterminated since by reason of their youth they were unable to work. Still another improvement we made over Treblinka was that at Treblinka the victims almost always knew that they were to be exterminated and at Auschwitz we endeavored to fool the victims into thinking that they were to go through a delousing process. Of course, frequently they realized our true intentions and we sometimes had riots and difficulties due to that fact. Very frequently women would hide their children under their clothes but of course when we found them we would send the children in to be exterminated. We were required to carry out these exterminations in secrecy but of course the foul and nauseating stench from the continuous burning of bodies permeated the entire area and all of the people living in the surrounding communities knew that exterminations were going on at Auschwitz.

8. We received from time to time special prisoners from the local Gestapo office. The SS doctors killed such prisoners by injections of benzine. Doctors had orders to write ordinary death certificates and could put down any reason at all for the cause of death.

9. From time to time we conducted medical experiments on women inmates, including sterilization and experiments relating to cancer. Most of the people who died under these experiments had been already condemned to death by the Gestapo. . . .

I understand English as it is written above. The above statements are true; this declaration is made by me voluntarily and without compulsion; after reading over the statements, I have signed and executed the same at Nuremberg, Germany, on the fifth day of April 1946.

Rudolf Franz Ferdinand Hoess

Subscribed and sworn to before me this 5th day of April 1946, at Nuremberg, Germany
Smith W. Brookhart Jr., Lt. Colonel, IGD

70

François Ponchaud, *Cambodia: Year Zero*

Once the Khmer Rouge took the Cambodian capital city of Phnom Penh in April 1975, they started to move people out of the cities into the countryside for a massive re-education program. At the same time, the Angkar (the "Higher Committee") began the systematic killing of those Cambodians associated with the governments of Lon Nol and Norodom Sihanouk. But, in addition to these political killings, the Khmer Rouge started to annihilate any Cambodian man, woman, or child who threatened the revolution or refused to obey orders. Between 1975 and 1979 over a million Cambodians, out of a population of seven million, fell in the Khmer Rouge killing fields. François Ponchaud, a French Roman Catholic priest, lived and worked in Cambodia for many years but was forced to leave Phnom Penh with the last convoy of foreigners on May 8, 1975. Although living in Paris, he continued to work with Cambodian refugees, interviewing them and recording their stories while the Khmer Rouge's genocide was underway. The following excerpts describe the experiences of a schoolteacher, court clerk, and physician during this period.

QUESTIONS TO CONSIDER

1. How did the Angkar decide which Cambodians would die?
2. How would you compare and contrast the methods and motives for genocide in the Nazi (see Reading 69) and Cambodian examples? Are there parallels? Why? Why not?

A Schoolteacher's Story

At the beginning of January 1976, . . . twenty of us were sentenced to death for traveling without permission. We were taken away in a truck with our hands tied behind our backs. One Khmer Rouge sat behind with a gun and two more sat in front with the driver. One of us managed to free himself and secretly untied eleven others. Then one of us tried to kill the Khmer Rouge sitting in the back of the truck, but the guards in front saw him and turned around and started shooting. The twelve who had their hands free jumped down from the truck and dived into the Mongkol Borei River by the side of the road, then disappeared into the forest. The other eight were killed on the spot.

A Court Clerk's Account of an Execution

In October 1975, the Angkar chose us to cut bamboo at O Ta Tam, near Phnom Rodaong, for eighteen days. One afternoon we were in a group of thirty wagons carting bamboo to the national highway. We had loaded and were about to turn around when we saw a military truck enter the forest carrying about ten young men and girls. A moment later we heard shots, then the truck came back empty. We were very frightened, and harnessed up to go home. Then we heard moaning and somebody calling for help. One of our group, named Sambath, went over and saw a young man with bullet wounds in both arms and one thigh, and his arms still tied behind his back. Sambath untied him, gave him a little rice, and told him how to get to the road to the west. On the way home Sambath told us, "That young man told me that the people who had been shot hadn't done anything wrong, they had simply gone to look for food in the forest, so they weren't working with their group. That's why they were killed."

A Physician's Description of His Prison Camp

When we got out of the train at the station in Sisophon a reception committee was waiting for us. Loudspeakers welcomed us and asked all "specialists" to step forward: doctors, architects, schoolteachers, students, technicians, and skilled workers of all kinds. The Angkar was going to need them. I didn't move, but a man who had been a nurse under me and was now a Khmer Rouge cadre recognized me and strongly advised me to tell them my true identity or risk punishment. Then all the "specialists" were taken to Preah Neth Preah, where we had to work the land as before. One day we were taken to Chup, a village on the road between Siem Reap and Sisophon. There the Khmer Rouge received us with open arms and gave us three meals a day! That was a real treat! At one big meeting, attended by 397 "specialists," a Khmer Rouge asked us to write our biographies and set down our desiderata. He even invited us to come up to the platform and offer our suggestions as to how the country could be better run. Teachers and students went up and began criticizing the Angkar for not giving people anything to eat, and for treating the sick with medicine that was more like rabbit dung than real pills; they asked for the bonzes to be reinstated and the pagodas reopened, and the high schools and universities, and for everyone to be allowed to visit his family, et cetera.

The Khmer Rouge said nothing, but we could see plainly enough that they didn't like it. After we had written our autobiographies they called out the names of twenty young people who had been most outspoken in their criticism, tied their hands behind their backs the way you tie a parrot's wings, and took them to Sisophon, where they were put in prison.

The rest of us went back to the village of Preah Neth Preah. A month later, on January 6, the Khmer Rouge came to get some of us and took us to the Battambang prison. There were forty-five of us, and we were the first "guests" of the prison since the new regime began. We had to write out our autobiographies several more times. Each time the cadres became more insistent: "You've made good progress since the last time but we know that some of you are still not telling the whole truth! We know what that truth is, why hide it? The Angkar doesn't want to kill you, don't be afraid! By acting the way you are, you show that you have not been converted." After three sessions, one of my friends revealed that he had been an army doctor. A week later he disappeared.

We had been there two weeks when the group of twenty young people interned at Sisophon were brought in; their arms were still tied at all times, even during meals, and the ropes had cut deep furrows. We also saw a former lieutenant colonel of the government army brought in, and about twenty [republican] MPs. After a few days they were taken away one at a time and we didn't see them again.

Now and then one of us was summoned for a "meeting," and sometimes the person did not come back. At the end of two and one-half months in prison fifteen of us were taken to the Van Kandal pagoda, which had also been made into a prison. There were three buildings in the pagoda: The doors and windows of one were kept permanently shut — that was where the prisoners were beaten, and some people had been in it for seven months. The windows of the second building were opened from time to time. The third building, where I was put, was for prisoners who stayed only a short time, usually two or three weeks. Its doors and windows were always open until 6:00 P.M. We had reeducation sessions, study meetings, we were subjected to constant interrogations. Those of us who were European-trained doctors and engineers were questioned even more than the others, because we were suspected of having worked with the imperialists or been engaged in secret activities.

In the evening, when we were taking our bath in the Stung Sangker, we saw other prisoners bathing, for although the houses on the other bank were always shut up, there were prisoners in them too. After ten days we were given a black garment and a gray and red *krama* [scarf] and put in a truck. Half the group was let out at Poy Saman and the other half at Kauk Khmwn, to go on working in the fields. That was April 6, 1976.

World War II: Asia and Europe

As a solution to post–World War I Japanese economic and security problems, the Japanese military in Manchuria, known as the Kwangtung Army,[1] without prior approval of the Tokyo government seized control of Mukden, a key administrative center in Manchuria in September 1931. Within a few months, the Kwangtung Army had placed all of Manchuria under its military control by driving out the Chinese military and creating the "puppet state" of Manchukuo in 1932. The Japanese invasion of Manchuria marked the beginning of a decade and a half of military domination by the Japanese government, and it put Japan on a collision course with the United States. To protect Manchuria, the Japanese military continued to nibble away at Chinese territory adjacent to Manchukuo. Continued Japanese encroachment of Chinese sovereignty finally led to an all-out war with China, on July 7, 1937. Quite unexpectedly, the war with China dragged on and the Nationalist Chinese government in Nanjing refused to surrender even after Japan sealed the entire coastal provinces of China. Isolated internationally, Japan desperately sought an end to a further expansion of the seemingly endless war in China, trying to resort to a war of attrition, but was unable to do so on its own terms. Increasingly Japan blamed the Soviet Union, the United States, and Great Britain for China's continuing resistance. The United States showed its displeasure with Japan's aggression toward China by adopting a series of economic sanctions. In the summer of 1938, Washington placed an embargo on shipments of aircraft, arms, and other war material to Japan; in July 1939, it abrogated a commercial treaty with Japan; and in the fall of 1940, the embargo was expanded to include scrap iron and steel. In July 1941, the export of American oil to Japan was banned. Great Britain, the British Commonwealth, and the Dutch East Indies joined the oil embargo. This cut Japan's oil imports by 90 percent and compelled Japan to make a crucial decision between giving up China, including Manchuria, or invading the oil-rich Dutch East Indies and risking war with the United States, Britain, China, and the Dutch. With Nazi Germany and Fascist Italy on its side, the Japanese government chose the road to war.[2] This led to the Pearl Harbor attack on December 7, 1941.

The war in Europe began when Adolf Hitler (1889–1945) pushed Germany into it by declaring war on Poland on September 1, 1939. Hitler's new "lightning war" (*blitzkrieg*) in Poland was followed by German victories in Denmark, Norway, Holland, and Belgium; the climax was the stunning de-

1. Three northeastern provinces of China are often known as Manchuria. As part of the peace settlement following Japan's defeat of Russia in 1905, Japan took over the Russian leasehold in the Liaotung Peninsula in southern Manchuria and tsarist railway and economic rights in Manchuria. A Japanese governor-general administered the leased territory, including the railway zone. The Japanese army stationed in Liaotung Peninsula to guard the Japanese interest in Manchuria was known as the Kwangtung Army.
2. Impressed by the German military successes in Europe, the Japanese government signed a Tripartite Pact with Germany and Italy and became a member of the Axis alliance in September 1941.

feat of France on June 17, 1940. Hitler's quick victories whetted the appetites for war of his Axis allies — Italy and Japan. On June 10, 1940, Italy pounced on France ; after the defeat of France, Japan accelerated its timetable for Pacific expansion by occupying northern French Indochina on September 22, 1940.

Surprisingly, despite the Axis Alliance between Berlin, Rome, and Tokyo (1940), there was very little effort devoted to coordinating war plans. In part, this lack of effort was due to the personality of Adolf Hitler. Hitler, like all politicians, changed his mind and altered plans, but by 1937 he had become convinced that Germany could achieve greatness only through war. Hitler wanted a short war : First Germany would win key battles in the west, then turn east and defeat the Soviet Union, establishing a European continental empire. Despite the size and reputation of the French army, Hitler held France in contempt. Although he respected England, he did not believe that England would fight once France was defeated. An isolated Soviet Union, Hitler believed, would be an easy prey for his *blitzkrieg* style of war.

Hitler miscalculated. His diagnosis of France was correct, but he misread Winston Churchill (1874–1965), England's wartime prime minister, and he severely underestimated the resiliency and military power of the Soviet Union. Though suffering huge losses throughout the war, the Soviet Union destroyed more than 600 German divisions ; the Battle of Stalingrad (1942) marked the end of *blitzkrieg* and turned the tide against Germany. Hitler also underestimated the economic and military capacity of the United States. Inexplicably but fatefully, he declared war on the United States on December 11, 1941.

The following documents outline Hitler's plans for war in 1937, detail America's peacetime commitment to help Great Britain resist Hitler, and present Tojo's defense of Japan's aggression.

71

The Hossbach Memorandum

At a secret meeting with his key advisors on November 5, 1937, Adolf Hitler (the Fuehrer) expressed his views on how the next European war would come. Colonel Friedrich Hossbach, Hitler's adjutant, recorded Hitler's comments. The following memorandum summarizes Hitler's views on war and suggests how Hitler linked military and political strategy.

QUESTIONS TO CONSIDER

1. According to the Hossbach Memorandum, what were the best conditions for Germany to declare war?
2. Why was Hitler inclined to go to war in 1938 rather than 1943?

The aim of German policy was to make secure and to preserve the racial community and to enlarge it. It was therefore a question of space.

The German racial community comprised over 85 million people and, because of their number and the narrow limits of habitable space in Europe, constituted a tightly packed racial core such as was not to be met in any other country and such as implied the right to a greater living space than in the case of other peoples. . . .

Germany's future was therefore wholly conditional upon the solving of the need for space, and such a solution could be sought, of course, only for a foreseeable period of about one to three generations. . . .

The question for Germany ran : where could she achieve the greatest gain at the lowest cost.

German policy had to reckon with two hate-inspired antagonists, Britain and France, to whom a German colossus in the center of Europe was a thorn in the flesh, and both countries were opposed to any further strengthening of Germany's position either in Europe or over seas ; in support of this opposition they were able to count on the agreement of all their political parties. Both countries saw in the establishment of German military bases overseas a threat to their own communications, a safeguarding of German commerce, and, as a consequence, a strengthening of Germany's position in Europe. . . .

Germany's problem could only be solved by means of force and this was never without attendant risk. The campaigns of Frederick the Great for Silesia and Bismarck's wars against Austria and France had involved unheard-of risk, and the swiftness of the Prussian action in 1870 had kept Austria from entering the war. If one accepts as the basis of the following exposition the resort to force with its attendant risks, then there remain still to be answered the questions "when" and "how." In this matter there were three cases to be dealt with :

Case 1 : Period 1943–1945

After this date only a change for the worse, from our point of view, could be expected.

The equipment of the army, navy, and Luftwaffe, as well as the formation of the officer corps, was nearly completed. Equipment and armament were modern ; in further delay there lay the danger of their obsolescence. In particular, the secrecy of "special weapons" could not be preserved forever. The recruiting of reserves was limited to current age groups ; further drafts from older untrained age groups were no longer available.

Our relative strength would decrease in relation to the rearmament which would by then have been carried out by the rest of the world. If we did not act by 1943–45, any year could, in consequence of a lack of reserves, produce the food crisis, to cope with which the necessary foreign exchange was not available, and this must be regarded as a "waning point of the regime." Besides, the world was expecting our attack and was increasing its counter-measures from year to year. It

From *Auswartiges Amt : Documents on German Foreign Policy,* Series D (Washington, DC : Government Printing Office, 1949), vol. 1, pp. 29–49, passim.

was while the rest of the world was still preparing its defenses that we were obliged to take the offensive.

Nobody knew today what the situation would be in years 1943–45. One thing only was certain, that we could not wait longer.

On the one hand there was the great *Wehrmacht,* and the necessity of maintaining it at its present level, the aging of the movement and of its leaders; and on the other, the prospect of a lowering of the standard of living and of a limitation of the birth rate, which left no choice but to act. If the Fuehrer was still living, it was his unaltered resolve to solve Germany's problem of space at the latest by 1943–45. The necessity for action before 1943–45 would arise in cases 2 and 3.

Case 2

If internal strife in France should develop into such a domestic crisis as to absorb the French Army completely and render it incapable of use for war against Germany, then the time for action against the Czechs had come.

Case 3

If France is so embroiled by a war with another state that she cannot "proceed" against Germany.

For the improvement of our politico-military position our first objective, in the event of our being embroiled in war, must be to overthrow Czechoslovakia and Austria simultaneously in order to remove the threat to our flank in any possible operation against the West. In a conflict with France it was hardly to be regarded as likely that the Czechs would declare war on us on the very same day as France. The desire to join in the war would, however, increase among the Czechs in proportion to any weakening on our part and then her participation could clearly take the form of an attack toward Silesia, toward the north or toward the west.

If the Czechs were overthrown and a common German-Hungarian frontier achieved, a neutral attitude on the part of Poland could be the more certainly counted on in the event of a Franco-German conflict. Our agreements with Poland only retained their force as long as Germany's strength remained unshaken. In the event of German setbacks Polish action against East Prussia, and possibly against Pomerania and Silesia as well, had to be reckoned with. . . .

The degree of surprise and the swiftness of our action were decisive factors for Poland's attitude. Poland — with Russia at her rear — will have little inclination to engage in war against a victorious Germany.

Military intervention by Russia must be countered by the swiftness of our operations; however, whether such an intervention was a practical contingency at all was, in view of Japan's attitude, more than doubtful.

Should case 2 arise — the crippling of France by civil war — the situation thus created by the elimination of the most dangerous opponent must be seized upon *whenever it occurs* for the blow against the Czechs.

The Fuehrer saw case 3 coming definitely nearer; it might emerge from the present tensions in the Mediterranean, and he was resolved to take advantage of it whenever it happened, even as early as 1938.

72

The Atlantic Charter

President Franklin D. Roosevelt's concern over the war in Europe sharply increased in 1940 with the collapse of France and the potential expansion of Hitler's empire to the New World if Britain fell. In September, Roosevelt tried to strengthen Britain's ability to resist by exchanging American destroyers for the right to lease naval and air bases in British Commonwealth territories. The following spring, although the United States was technically neutral, Roosevelt urged the passage of the Lend-Lease Act to provide war materials to those nations fighting the Axis powers. While taking these important steps on the road to war, President Roosevelt outlined his objectives and the national interest in his 1941 State of the Union Address, which became known as his "Four Freedoms" speech.

Later that summer, Roosevelt and Churchill met for a shipboard conference off Argentia, Newfoundland, and forged a closer alignment with their joint statement of war aims known as the Atlantic Charter.

QUESTIONS TO CONSIDER

1. Why would the influential Japanese newspaper *Asahi* regard the Atlantic Charter, particularly its fourth article, as a de facto declaration of war by the United States and Great Britain (see Reading 65)?
2. Would Woodrow Wilson approve of this charter? Why? Why not? (See Reading 59.)

Joint declaration of the President of the United States of America and the Prime Minister, Mr. Churchill, representing His Majesty's Government in the United Kingdom, being met together, deem it right to make known certain common principles in the national policies of their respective countries on which they base their hopes for a better future for the world.

First, their countries seek no aggrandizement, territorial or other;

Second, they desire to see no territorial changes that do not accord with the freely expressed wishes of the peoples concerned;

Third, they respect the right of all peoples to choose the form of government under which they will live; and they wish to see sovereign rights and self-government restored to those who have been forcibly deprived of them;

Fourth, they will endeavor, with due respect for their existing obligations, to further the enjoyment by all states, great or small, victor or vanquished, of access, on equal terms, to the trade and to the raw materials of the world which are needed for their economic prosperity;

From U.S. Department of State, *Peace and War: United States Foreign Policy, 1931–1941,* Publication 1983 (Washington, DC: Government Printing Office, 1943), pp. 718–719.

Fifth, they desire to bring about the fullest collaboration between all nations in the economic field with the object of securing, for all, improved labor standards, economic advancement, and social security;

Sixth, after the final destruction of the Nazi tyranny, they hope to see established a peace which will afford to all nations the means of dwelling in safety within their own boundaries, and which will afford assurance that all the men in all the lands may live out their lives in freedom from fear and want;

Seventh, such a peace should enable all men to traverse the high seas and oceans without hindrance;

Eighth, they believe that all the nations of the world, for realistic as well as spiritual reasons, must come to the abandonment of the use of force. Since no future peace can be maintained if land, sea, or air armaments continue to be employed by nations which threaten, or may threaten, aggression outside of their frontiers, they believe, pending the establishment of a wider and permanent system of general security, that the disarmament of such nations is essential. They will likewise aid and encourage all other practicable measures which will lighten for peace-loving peoples the crushing burden of armaments.

Franklin D. Roosevelt
Winston S. Churchill

73

"Tojo Makes Plea of Self Defense"

Soon after Japan's defeat in World War II, 28 Japanese leaders[1] who had held high posts in the Japanese government and military between 1928 and 1945 were apprehended by the U.S. occupation authorities and charged with 55 counts of war crimes, which were grouped in three categories: (1) crimes against peace (first 36 counts), namely, the planning, preparation, initiation or waging of a declared or undeclared war of aggression, or a war in violation of international law, treaties, agreements, or assurances, or participation in a common plan, or conspiring for the accomplishment of any of the foregoing; (2) murder (counts 37 through 52), and (3) conventional war crimes, namely, violations of the laws or customs of war, and crimes against humanity, namely, murder, extermination, enslavement, deportation, and other inhumane acts committed before or during the war (counts 53, 54, and 55).[2] They were tried by the International Military Tribunal for the Far East (I.M.T.F.E.) which was created on January 19, 1946, by the Supreme Com-

---

1. Among them were four former prime ministers, four former foreign ministers, five former war ministers, two former navy ministers, four former ambassadors, and four field commanders.
2. Charter of the International Military Tribunal for the Far East, Section II, Article 5 in Richard H. Minear, *Victor's Justice, The Tokyo War Crimes Trial* (Princeton, NJ: Princeton University Press, 1971), pp. 186–187.

mander of the Allied Powers in Japan in accordance with the directive of the U.S. Joint Chiefs of Staff. The Supreme Commander of the Allied Powers, General Douglas MacArthur appointed 11 justices to the bench, one from each of the 11 victorious nations.[3] After nearly two and a half years of trial, despite a vigorous defense by the defense counsels, the defendants themselves, and the jurists including one of the justices, on the grounds that they had acted in self-defense of their nation, all 25 defendants were found guilty.[4] Seven of them — former Prime Minister, General Hideki Tojo, former Foreign Minister Koki Hirota, and five generals — received death sentences by hanging, and the remaining 18 received various prison terms, ranging from seven years to life. Eight of the 11 justices supported the judgment of the tribunal. Justice Radhabinod Pal of India, the leading dissenter, questioned, among other things, the justness of the victors' deciding whether or not the vanquished resorted to war in self-defense. Justice Pal was apprehensive that the notion that "might makes right" would become an accepted rule in the international system. On December 23, 1948, the seven defendants were hanged at Sugamo Prison in Tokyo.

During the trial, General Hideki Tojo, leader of the hawkish ultranationalistic faction of the Imperial Army of Japan, who became Prime Minister in October 1941, less than two months before the Pearl Harbor attack and remained in that post until July 1944, justified what he and Japan did in the name of national survival and anti-communism. In a 60,000-word written testimony, he accused the United States and Britain of forcing Japan into war and accepted full responsibility for his and Japan's actions. He also strongly defended Emperor Hirohito's innocence in starting the war. The following excerpts are an edited version of a *New York Times* report of the trial.

QUESTIONS TO CONSIDER

1. Was the judgment at the Tokyo trial an exercise in victors' justice, as alleged by some jurists? Why? Why not?
2. How valid was the argument put up by Tojo and other defendants at the trial that Japan was forced by the United States and Britain into war?
3. Should a sovereign nation retain complete freedom of action concerning questions vital to its existence?

Defiantly the 63 year old career soldier who attempted suicide two years ago on the heels of the Japanese surrender, told the eleven-nation court that the Western Allies maneuvered so as to force Japan to fire the first shot "in self-defense" to preserve her "national existence."

3. The eleven nations were : the United States, the Republic of China, the United Kingdom, the Soviet Union, Australia, Canada, France, the Netherlands, New Zealand, India, and the Philippines.

4. Of the original 28 defendants, two had died during the trial and one had been determined mentally unfit and dismissed.

Japan's leaders, including Emperor Hirohito, Tojo testified, went to war reluctantly and only after peaceful means of settlement had been exhausted. Economic pressure had brought the nation in 1941 "to the point of annihilation," he asserted. But Japan attempted to fight the war honorably, Tojo implied.

His government had no intention of making the Pearl Harbor attack a sneak affair, Tojo said. . . .

The treatment of prisoners, he indicated, could in part be explained by Japanese psychology.

As for the Doolittle fliers[1] who were caught after the attack on Tokyo in April 1942, their execution, he asserted, followed "the atrocities they committed in violation of international law and regulations" in the bombing of civilian population.

Tojo, the last but one of the remaining twenty-five top war leaders of Japan to open his defense, gave his testimony in a 60,000-word affidavit. A defense attorney began reading the document to the court while Tojo sat erect in the witness box, earphones clamped to his head. . . .

In effect a long bill of indictment against the Allied nations, restating in much detail Japan's pre-war charges of blockade, encirclement, bad faith and aid to a "hostile" China. Tojo's affidavit roundly attacked the prosecution's main contention that the Japanese leaders formed a conspiracy for war.

"I fail utterly to understand the reasoning of the prosecution in this fantastic accusation," Tojo wrote.

Under the Japanese imperial system with its "fundamental and unchangeable administrative processes," he asserted, such a conspiracy, continuing over a long period and involving many changes of administration was "unthinkable to persons of reason and intelligence."

For Japan's defeat in the war Tojo said he as Premier accepted full responsibility, but he challenged the "legal or criminal" responsibility that the Allied prosecutors attach to him.

"Never at any time did I ever conceive that the waging of this war would or could be challenged by the victors as an international crime," his affidavit concluded "or that regularly constituted officials of the vanquished nation would be charged individually as criminals under any recognized international law or under alleged violations of treaties between nations."

In one long passage of the affidavit Tojo made vigorous effort to exculpate Emperor Hirohito from all blame for the war as a sovereign who constantly pressed his Ministers to seek other means of settlement but who eventually was powerless to alter the course of events.

"Even though some explanation of this point has previously been given by me, further exposition should be made so that, with regard to the Emperor's position, there be no possibility of misconstruction," Tojo wrote. "That to me is quite important."

"The Emperor had no free choice in the governmental structure setting up the Cabinet and Supreme Command. He was not in a position to reject the recommendations and advice of the Cabinet and the High Command."

1. James H. Doolittle, an American general, then Lt. Col., led the first daring air raid on Tokyo with 16 B-25 bombers which took off from the U.S.S. Hornet on April 18, 1942, at the height of World War II.

Although Hirohito might have advanced personal "hopes and wishes" through Marquis Koichi Kido, Lord Keeper of the Privy Seal, Tojo said, even such imperial expressions were subject to Cabinet and military examination.

"The recommendations and suggestions after this careful examination had to be approved by the Emperor and never to be rejected," the statement said. "That was the position of the Emperor beforehand during this most perplexing period in the history of the Japanese Empire."

"These facts being what they are," this part of the argument concluded, "it was solely upon the Cabinet and the Supreme Command that responsibility lay for the political, diplomatic and military affairs of the nation. Accordingly, full responsibility for the decision of Dec. 1, 1941 for war is that of the Cabinet Ministers and members of the High Command and absolutely not the responsibility of the Emperor."

Tojo asserted two main factors forced Japan into war, first "pressure" by Britain and the United States and second national fear of communism.

While the United States and Britain, he wrote, would have been content with nothing less than Japan's evacuation of China and abandonment by the Japanese of all advantages they had gained there in almost ten years of warfare, Japan feared the "bolshevization of Asia" would be the result. To this thesis Tojo reverted several times.

In the Konoye Cabinet of 1939 in which he served as War Minister, Tojo said he expressed this viewpoint regarding the "unconditional withdrawal" from China as sought by the United States.

"Chinese contempt for Japan will expand if we retire from China unconditionally because of United States duress. Relations between Japan and China will grow worse coupled with the thorough-going resistance against Japan maintained by the Communists in China. Certainly China Incident No. 2 and China Incident No. 3 would result, and the repercussions at our loss of prestige would be keenly felt in Manchuria and Korea."

During his own Premiership (Oct. 18, 1941 to July 22, 1944) and up to the end of the war, Tojo asserted, Japan's policy was to preserve peace with Russia despite urgings from Germany, although the Soviet Union after Yalta[2] "actually had pledged itself to enter the war against Japan on the promise of territorial gains even while the (nonaggression) treaty was still valid and that nation actually attacked Japan while the agreement still was in force."

Japan has always been deeply concerned over communism in Asia, Tojo said.

"She realized that the activities of the Chinese Communist party were among the important causes preventing the establishment of peace between Japan and China in the China Incident," he went on. "Thus she made the joint prevention of communism one of the conditions for settlement of the Incident and also made prevention of communism an essential policy among the independent states of East Asia.

"This was all done with a view to saving East Asia from the danger of bolshevization and at the same time to making herself a barrier against world

---

2. In February 1945, three Allied leaders, Franklin D. Roosevelt, Winston Churchill, and Joseph Stalin, met at Yalta to confer on the execution of the war and the postwar settlement.

bolshevization. The present condition of the world two years after the end of World War II eloquently tells how important these barriers were for the peace of the world."

Tojo used a large part of his affidavit to set out what he argued was a "cold war" waged by Britain and the United States against Japan in the Nineteen Thirties and which he argued, forced upon Japan nearly every step she took outside her borders, including her understanding with the Berlin-Rome Axis.

On more than one occasion, after Japan was cut off from food, rubber and petroleum by Allied economic measures after her credits had been frozen and after the United States began on a tremendously expanding arms program, Tojo said Japanese leaders feared armed attack in the Pacific.

"We did not anticipate at the time (1940–41) that America was so directing the war as to force Japan to make the first overt act," he wrote.

Such measures as the construction of air bases in French Indo-China, to which the Allies objected as presaging aggression, Tojo said were "protection against attacks from the south." From this direction, Japan's leaders thought, he said, might come an "onslaught by the 'have' nations against the Japanese Empire."[3]

Hiroshima: The Atomic Bomb

At 8:15 A.M. on August 6, 1945, the *Enola Gay,* an American B-29, dropped an atomic bomb on Hiroshima, Japan. Within minutes, Hiroshima was obliterated and a holocaust was created. Hiroshima was the seventh-largest city in Japan, with a population of about a quarter of a million, reduced from a pre-war population of 400,000 as a result of the wartime evacuation programs. It had been the principal administrative, commercial, and military center of southwestern Japan. The headquarters of the Second Army and of a regional army were located there, and it was one of the largest military logistical centers.

The decision to drop the bomb on Hiroshima was made by President Truman within a few days after the first successful test explosion of an atomic bomb on July 16, 1945. Truman, afraid that a half million more American lives would be lost if the war against Japan continued, decided to bring Japan to her knees with the bomb. When Japan rejected the Potsdam Declaration, issued on July 25, calling for unconditional surrender, the president gave the final order to drop the bomb on Hiroshima.

The strength of the Hiroshima bomb was approximately equivalent to that of 20,000 tons of TNT. This was a small bomb when compared with today's megaton-class hydrogen bomb, but it completely leveled the city and killed a great many people. The exact number of dead and injured will never be known, but according to a U.S. estimate, between 70,000 and 80,000 were killed, with an equal number injured. A survey conducted by the

---

3. "Have" nations refer, in this case, particularly to the United States and Britain.

Hiroshima city survey section in 1946 showed that the number dead and missing reached well over 120,000. The heat emanating from the blast was so intense that the shadows of two men, one sitting and the other standing 200 yards from ground zero, are still to be seen, imprinted in the granite. These two men were obviously vaporized by the flash. More than half of the deaths were caused by burns; additional deaths resulted either from falling debris or from other injuries caused by the "fire-wind." Many who lived through the blast succumbed later to the effects of radiation. One of the tragic results of the bomb was the instant creation of thousands of orphans.

74

President Truman's Decision

The following selection shows how President Truman made his decision to use the atomic bomb.

QUESTIONS TO CONSIDER

1. Was it necessary to use the atomic bomb to end the war against Japan?
2. How has the atomic bomb changed the nature of major power relations since World War II? Is a world war more likely or unlikely to occur because of the nuclear bomb?

It was their [an advisory committee on the use of the new weapon] recommendation that the bomb be used against the enemy as soon as it could be done. They recommended further that it should be used without specific warning and against a target that would clearly show its devastating strength. I had realized, of course, that an atomic bomb explosion would inflict damage and casualties beyond imagination. On the other hand, the scientific advisers of the committee reported, "We can propose no technical demonstration likely to bring an end to the war; we see no acceptable alternative to direct military use." It was their conclusion that no technical demonstration they might propose, such as over a deserted island, would be likely to bring the war to an end. It had to be used against an enemy target.

The final decision of where and when to use the atomic bomb was up to me. Let there be no mistake about it. I regarded the bomb as a military weapon and never had any doubt that it should be used. The top military advisers to the President recommended its use, and when I talked to Churchill he unhesitatingly told me that he favored the use of the atomic bomb if it might aid to end the war.

From Harry S. Truman, *Memoirs by Harry S. Truman*, Vol. 1, *Year of Decisions* (New York : Doubleday, 1955), pp. 419–421. Reprinted by permission of Margaret Truman Daniel.

In deciding to use this bomb I wanted to make sure that it would be used as a weapon of war in the manner prescribed by the laws of war. That meant that I wanted it dropped on a military target. I had told Stimson that the bomb should be dropped as nearly as possible upon a war production center of prime military importance.

Stimson's staff had prepared a list of cities in Japan that might serve as targets. Kyoto, though favored by General Arnold as a center of military activity, was eliminated when Secretary Stimson pointed out that it was a cultural and religious shrine of the Japanese.

Four cities were finally recommended as targets: Hiroshima, Kokura, Niigata, and Nagasaki. They were listed in that order as targets for the first attack. The order of selection was in accordance with the military importance of these cities, but allowance would be given for weather conditions at the time of the bombing. Before the selected targets were approved as proper for military purposes, I personally went over them in detail with Stimson, Marshall, and Arnold, and we discussed the matter of timing and the final choice of the first target. . . .

On July 28 Radio Tokyo announced that the Japanese government would continue to fight. There was no formal reply to the joint ultimatum of the United States, the United Kingdom, and China. There was no alternative now. The bomb was scheduled to be dropped after August 3 unless Japan surrendered before that day.

On August 6, the fourth day of the journey home from Potsdam, came the historic news that shook the world. I was eating lunch with members of the *Augusta's* crew when Captain Frank Graham, White House Map Room watch officer, handed me the following message:

TO THE PRESIDENT
FROM THE SECRETARY OF WAR
Big bomb dropped on Hiroshima August 5 at 7 :15 P.M. Washington time. First reports indicate complete success which was even more conspicuous than earlier test.

I was greatly moved. I telephoned Byrnes aboard ship to give him the news and then said to the group of sailors around me, "This is the greatest thing in history. It's time for us to get home."

75

A Child's View of the Bomb

Eyewitness accounts of young school children were compiled by Professor Arata Osada, former rector of Hiroshima University. The following selection describes what a third-grade boy experienced on the morning of the atomic explosion.

QUESTIONS TO CONSIDER

1. What have we learned from the Hiroshima experience?
2. Some argue that the decision to drop the atomic bomb on Japan — and not on Germany — was racially motivated. How true is this charge?

We heard a voice saying, "Air raid alarm."

I hurried home and was playing. This is because I was already used to this sort of thing. Then the alert ended and I went back to school. The teacher doesn't come so we start talking again. Pretty soon we heard a hum and saw a little aeroplane in the sky to the south-east. And this gradually grew larger and came over our heads. I was watching the aeroplane the whole time. I can't tell whether it is a foreign plane or a Japanese plane. Then suddenly a thing like a white parachute came falling. Five or six seconds later everything turned yellow in one instant. It felt the way it does when you get the sunlight straight in your eye. A second or two later, CRASH! there was a tremendous noise. Everything became dark and stones and roof tiles came pouring down on our heads. For a while I was unconscious. A whole lot of lumber came piling around my hips and I wanted to protest, Stop, that hurts! I came to again with the pain. I quickly crawled outside. There were lots of people lying around there; the faces of most of them were charred. I got out to the street and just as I heaved a sigh of relief my right hand suddenly began to hurt. When I looked closely at it I found that the skin of my right arm was peeled off from my elbow to my fingers and it was all red. I wanted to go home right away and I figured out the direction and started to walk toward the house when I heard a voice call, "Sumi-chan!" and I turned and looked and it was my sister. Her clothes were torn to rags and her face was so changed that I was amazed.

The two of us started off toward the house together, but the house was flattened and there was no one there. We searched around the neighborhood and then came back and looked and there was Father. Father was pulling off the roof and trying to get something out. But then he seemed to give that up and he came toward us.

When I asked, "Mother?" he said tiredly, "She's dead."

I felt as though someone had knocked me on the head. Everything went blank and I couldn't think of anything.

After a little while Father said, "What happened to your head?"

When I touched it, it was all gritty. When I put my hand on the back of my head, my hand was all stained red with blood. Mother got a five inch nail stuck in her head and died instantly.

Pretty soon a muddy rain began to fall so we went under the railroad bridge. The railroad bridge was making a sputtering noise as it smouldered. When the rain stopped it suddenly got cold. We went close to a house that was burning and

From Arata Osada, comp., *Children of the A-Bomb: The Testament of the Boys and Girls of Hiroshima* (New York: G. P. Putnam's Sons, 1959), pp. 129–131. Reprinted by permission of G. P. Putnam's Sons. Copyright © 1959 by Dr. Arata Osada.

warmed ourselves at the fire. A lot of people were warming themselves. There was hardly a single unhurt person among them. Faces were swollen up, lips were black.

There was one who was waving the Japanese flag as though he had gone insane, and shouting, "Banzai!"

There was another one walking around proclaiming, "I am a General of the Army."

I got terribly thirsty so I went to the river to drink. From upstream a great many black and burned corpses came floating down the river. I pushed them away and drank the water. At the margin of the river there were corpses lying all over the place. Among them were some who weren't dead yet and there were some children who were screaming, "Mother! Mother!" When I saw the corpses I was already so used to it I didn't think anything of it. There were also some people who came tottering to the edge of the river and fell in and died just like that. Pretty soon my sister too — was it because of her burns? — fell down on the road.

Nuclear War: Contrasting Perceptions

Since a few years after World War II, the non-Communist world has generally followed a policy of "containment." At the same time, the advent of nuclear weaponry has made the nuclear issue a main factor in determining how to implement containment and in raising questions concerning its risks.

Since the late 1950s, the two terms "deterrence" and "détente" (the latter meaning roughly "relaxation of tensions") have characterized contrasting perceptions of foreign policy throughout the Western world. Most government leaders in the West have favored a combination of the two, seeking to deter Communist expansion through threats of retaliation while relaxing tensions with the Soviet bloc at the same time. There is no agreement, however, on the proportions of détente and deterrence.

Although science in theory is not ideological, the nuclear issue leads to different perceptions of what is supposed to be scientific fact, and these perceptions often divide along ideological lines. In the past quarter century, those favoring a greater degree of détente in dealing with the Soviet Union have generally stressed the threat of nuclear destruction as a real possibility. Firm advocates of deterrence, on the other hand, usually accept the idea of nuclear war as the ultimate tragedy for humankind but come to a different conclusion: The main priority should be preparedness, to assure that no aggressor will risk retaliation in kind by unleashing nuclear warfare. Some proponents of deterrence go so far as to challenge the idea that nuclear war would be the end of meaningful civilization — although no one denies that it would be a disaster of the first magnitude.

The selections below illustrate some of the main stances in this ongoing debate. Edward Teller, who did the pioneering work on the hydrogen bomb, insists that the nuclear issue need not change the West's basic reliance on deterrence. Even though the nuclear issue has generated little public debate in the Soviet Union, Andrei Sakharov, the Soviet physicist who worked on the Soviet hydrogen bomb in its early stages, was active in urging both sides to pursue meaningful détente through his statements published in the West. His efforts won him the Nobel Peace Prize in 1975 but also led to his "internal exile" by Soviet authorities who restricted him to the city of Gorki. In the final selection in this section, Professor Hans Bethe, a Cornell University physicist and a member of the Manhattan Project, and Robert McNamara, Secretary of Defense under Presidents Kennedy and Johnson, propose as an ultimate goal for the twenty-first century "a state of mutual deterrence at the lowest force levels consistent with stability."

76

Edward Teller, "Dangerous Myths about Nuclear Arms"

Edward Teller (1908—) is a native of Hungary who emigrated to the United States in 1935 and taught physics at George Washington University. He subsequently worked on the development of the hydrogen bomb and is sometimes referred to as its "father."

QUESTIONS TO CONSIDER

1. Why would Edward Teller consider civil defense to be such an important part of nuclear strategy?
2. How would you evaluate his arguments in light of the arguments of Robert McNamara and Hans Bethe (see Reading 78)?

Educating people about the nature and actual perils of nuclear weapons would not be easy under any circumstances. It is almost impossible when elementary facts are guarded by strict regulations of secrecy. Given such conditions, dangerous myths develop and proliferate.

The reality of nuclear weapons is grim enough. Exaggerations about them are apt only to paralyze us. Some of the current myths have grown from misinterpreted scientific studies; others seem to be based on simple wishful thinking. They all have one accurate assessment of our problems and will prevent the development of workable plans to preserve peace.

Myth 1 : The Soviet and American nuclear stockpiles are close to identical. A nuclear freeze would stop the arms race and offer improved mutual protection.

From Edward Teller, "Dangerous Myths about Nuclear Arms," *Reader's Digest*, November 1982. Reprinted by permission.

Neither the United States nor the Soviet Union publishes information on its current arsenals, and secrecy laws prevent me from discussing even the available estimates. There is, however, an officially released fact : between 1966 and 1981 the total megatonnage of the American nuclear arsenal was reduced to less than one-half its former size. The Soviet arsenal has rapidly increased in yield, accuracy and diversity during the same period and currently includes a total nuclear explosive power in excess of what the United States ever had. . . .

Myth 2 : Each nation has the power to destroy the other totally. Mutual destruction can most surely be avoided by disarming.

Our nuclear defense strategy, Mutually Assured Destruction, has the most appropriate acronym of MAD. The theory : if the Soviet Union and the United States have their urban populations at risk, then neither will attempt a first strike.

The Soviets have never agreed to the ideas on which MAD is based. The landmass of the U.S.S.R. is more than twice that of the United States ; its urban concentration proportionately much lower. The Soviets' civil-defense planning may well enable them to lose fewer people in a nuclear conflict than the 20 million or more casualties they suffered in World War II. . . .

Disarmament (as opposed to simple surrender) must be based on openness or trust. The extreme reticence of the Soviets to allow on-site inspections has been a continuing problem since 1958. Our basis for trust has not grown since. . . .

Myth 3 : Stopping U.S. weapons research and development will help make the world safer from the destructive effects of nuclear weapons.

For more than 25 years the primary purpose of U.S. weapons laboratories has been to make nuclear weapons less indiscriminately destructive. Cleaner bombs (with less fallout), smaller, more militarily effective weapons, and neutron bombs useful for battlefield defense (with less civilian damage than that created by a conventional artillery barrage) are among the results.

Furthermore, extremely important research is being conducted on systems to defend against incoming nuclear missiles. For example, exploding a very small nuclear bomb near an attack missile as it enters the upper-to-middle atmosphere over our nation would have no effects on the ground and negligible effects on the atmosphere, but could totally disarm the incoming missile without detonating it. Such a system, used to protect our vulnerable missile silos, could be an important first step in improving both our current retaliatory position and directing our policy toward defense. The nuclear-freeze movement would end further work on what could be the best defense systems.

The Soviets have already deployed an antiballistic-missile system around Moscow. We have the right to deploy a similar system but have not done so. The Soviet-American antiballistic-missile treaty is now being reviewed. We should change our policy and emphasize defense rather than retaliation.

Myth 4 : If a large number of nuclear weapons were exploded, fallout would pollute food and water supplies, making combatant countries uninhabitable. The spread of radioactive fallout throughout the world would end life on earth.

Fallout is part of many myths, and one of the common misunderstandings has to do with the durability and extent of its effects.

The radioactivity of fallout declines rapidly. For example, if 1000 rems per hour (a lethal dose) were released by a bomb, seven hours later the dose would be 100 rems per hour (far below lethal). In 49 hours radiation from this fallout would be reduced to 10 rems per hour. In 100 days the radiation would be 0.1 rems, comparable to the amount received from a chest X-ray. . . .

Myth 5: The explosion of nuclear weapons in the atmosphere will bring an end to life on this planet by damaging the ozone layer.

This new doomsday myth is gaining popularity. What we know today about the ozone layer suggests that if weapons larger than half-megaton bombs — such as only the Soviets possess — were exploded in the atmosphere, they would generate considerable amounts of nitrogen oxides at high altitudes. These oxides continue to destroy ozone over a protracted period. If the ozone were depleted, more ultraviolet radiation would reach the earth.

Assuming a worst-case scenario — a nuclear attack in which 5000 weapons, all of 1-to-20-megaton size, were exploded in the atmosphere — there would probably be a 50-percent decrease in the ozone layer over the Northern Hemisphere during the following year. (In the next few years, the ozone layer would return to about 80 percent of normal.) If this occurred, people would suffer rapid sunburn and a significant increase in skin cancer. Some ultraviolet-sensitive species could be extinguished, and some serious ecological changes might follow. However, our survival can be considered certain.

More detailed scientific information about the ozone layer is needed and should be gathered on an international basis. In the meantime, limiting the explosive power of all individual nuclear weapons to 400 kilotons would effectively eliminate the possibility of any significant damage to the ozone layer. Such a limitation should become an important part of disarmament talks.

Myth 6: Civil defense is without value in saving lives and may actually increase the risk of war.

This is perhaps the most dangerous myth of all.

Today some Soviet nuclear missiles may carry an explosive force a thousand times greater than the 15-kiloton Hiroshima bomb. However, while the vertical force of the explosion increases a thousand times, the horizontal distance over which such bombs produce equal damage increases much more slowly. For example, a one-megaton bomb, while almost 70 times more powerful than the Hiroshima bomb, produces equal damage over only about four times the distance. . . .

Under Soviet civil-defense plans, nonessential city workers would be evacuated if the immediate danger of war (or intent for a Soviet first strike) arose. The evacuees would build crude but effective shelters in the countryside according to well-prepared instructions. (Tests of the Soviet shelter plans at Oak Ridge National Laboratory show them to be excellent.) With optimum conditions, these plans would allow the Soviet Union to protect all but about 5 to 10 percent of its people from a full retaliatory strike. Well over 50 percent of the unprepared U.S. population would die in a nuclear attack. This need not be so. Comparable civil-defense planning in the United States could save 100 million more lives. . . .

Our first step toward stability, toward improving the prospects for peace and for the security of all people, must be the replacement of myths with knowledge. Only then can we approach the best possible solutions. They will not be perfect. But they will offer the chance for improvement — of changing mutually assured destruction into a decent chance of survival, of maintaining sufficient military strength to coax Soviet leaders toward real detente. If our salvation is to be real, it must be based on fact, not fantasy.

77

Andrei Sakharov, "An Open Letter to Dr. Sidney Drell"

Andrei D. Sakharov (1921–1989) was one of the Soviet Union's foremost nuclear physicists. In 1975, he was awarded the Nobel Peace Prize for his advocacy of nuclear disarmament. In 1980, Soviet authorities arrested him and ordered him to leave Moscow and remain in internal exile in the city of Gorki. He remained there until his release which occurred soon after President Mikhail Gorbachev's inauguration in 1985.

QUESTIONS TO CONSIDER

1. What cautionary advice does Sakharov offer with regard to the strong pacifist sentiments in the West? What evidence is there to support his statement that pro-Soviet elements have penetrated key positions in Western societies — especially in the mass media?
2. What are some of Sakharov's suggestions for long-term reduction of East-West tensions?
3. What recent conflicts have occurred to raise the danger that "A nuclear war could result from a conventional war" as Sakharov warned?

Precisely because an all-out nuclear war means collective suicide, we can imagine that a potential aggressor might count on a lack of resolve on the part of the country under attack to take the step leading to that suicide, i.e., it could count on its victim capitulating for the sake of saving what could be saved. Given that, if the aggressor has a military advantage in some of the variants of conventional warfare or — which is also possible *in principle* — in some of the variants of partial (limited) nuclear war, he would attempt to use the fear of further escalation to force the enemy to fight the war on his (the aggressor's) own terms. There would be little cause for joy if, ultimately, the aggressor's hopes proved false and the aggressor country perished along with the rest of mankind.

You consider it necessary to achieve a restoration of strategic parity in the field of conventional arms. Now take the next logical step — while nuclear weapons exist it is also necessary to have strategic parity in relation to those variants of limited or regional nuclear warfare which a potential enemy could impose, i.e., it is really *necessary* to examine in detail the various scenarios for both conventional and nuclear war and to analyze the various contingencies. It is of course not possible to analyze fully all these possibilities or to ensure security entirely. But I am at-

From Andrei Sakharov, "An Open Letter to Dr. Sidney Drell," February 2, 1983 (in response to a speech by Dr. Drell at Grace Cathedral in San Francisco, October 23, 1982). In *Foreign Affairs*, Summer 1983, pp. 1010–1016, passim. Reprinted by permission of Mr. Efrem Yankelevich, authorized by Mr. Andrei Sakharov.

tempting to warn of the opposite extreme — "closing one's eyes" and relying on one's potential enemy to be perfectly sensible. As always in life's complex problems, some sort of compromise is needed. . . .

I know that pacifist sentiments are very strong in the West. I deeply sympathize with people's yearning for peace, for a solution to world problems by peaceful means; I share those aspirations fully. But, at the same time, I am certain that it is absolutely necessary to be mindful of the specific political, military, and strategic realities of the present day and to do so objectively without making any sort of allowances for either side; this also means that one should not proceed from an a priori assumption of any special peace-loving nature in the socialist countries due to their supposed progressiveness or the horrors and losses they have experienced in war. Objective reality is much more complicated and far from anything so simple. People both in the socialist and the Western countries have a passionate inward aspiration for peace. This is an extremely important factor, but, I repeat, itself alone does not exclude the possibility of a tragic outcome.

What is necessary now, I believe, is the enormous practical task of education so that specific, exact, and historically and politically meaningful objective information can be made available to all people, information that will enjoy their trust and not be veiled with dogma and propaganda. Here one must take into account that, in the countries of the West, pro-Soviet propaganda has been conducted for quite a long time and is very goal-oriented and clever, and that pro-Soviet elements have penetrated many key positions, particularly in the mass media.

The history of the pacifist campaigns against the deployment of missiles in Europe is telling in many respects. After all, many of those participating in those campaigns entirely ignore the initial cause of NATO's "dual decision" — the change in strategic parity in the 1970s in favor of the U.S.S.R. — and, when protesting NATO's plans, they have not advanced any demands on the U.S.S.R. Another example: President Carter's attempt to take a minimal step toward achieving balance in the area of conventional arms, i.e., to introduce draft registration, met with stiff resistance. Meanwhile, balance in the area of conventional arms is a necessary prerequisite for reducing nuclear arsenals. For public opinion in the West to assess global problems correctly, in particular the problems of strategic parity both in conventional and in nuclear weapons, a more objective approach, one which takes the real world strategic situation into account, is vitally needed.

A second group of problems in the field of nuclear weapons about which I should make a few supplementary remarks here concerns the talks on nuclear disarmament. For these talks to be successful the West should have something that it can give up! The case of the "Euromissiles" once again demonstrates how difficult it is to negotiate from a position of weakness. Only very recently has the U.S.S.R. apparently ceased to insist on its unsubstantiated thesis that a rough nuclear parity now exists and therefore everything should be left as it is.

Now, the next welcome step would be the reduction of the number of missiles — which must include a fair assessment of the *quality* of missiles and other means of delivery (i.e., the number of charges deliverable by each carrier, its range and accuracy, and its degree of vulnerability — the last being greater for aircraft and less for missiles; most likely, it would be expedient to use your criterion, or analogous ones). And what is absolutely at issue here is not moving the missiles beyond the Urals but *destroying* them. After all, rebasing is too "revers-ible." Of course, one also must not consider powerful Soviet missiles, with mobile launchers and several warheads, as being equal to the now-existing Pershing I, the British and French missiles, or the bombs on short-range bombers — as the Soviet side sometimes attempts to do for purposes of propaganda.

No less important a problem is that of the powerful silo-based missiles. At present the U.S.S.R. has a great advantage in this area. Perhaps talks about the limitation and reduction of these most destructive missiles could become easier if the United States were to have MX missiles, albeit only potentially (indeed, that would be best of all). . . .

A specific danger associated with silo-based missiles is that they can be de-stroyed relatively easily as a result of enemy attack. . . . At the same time, they can be used to destroy enemy launch sites in an amount four to five times larger than the number of missiles used for the attack. A country with large numbers of silo-based missiles (at the present time this is primarily the U.S.S.R., but if the United States carries out a major MX program, then it too) could be "tempted" to use such missiles first before the enemy destroys them. In such circumstances the presence of silo-based missiles constitutes a destabilizing factor.

In view of the above, it seems very important to me to strive for the abolition of powerful silo-based missiles at the talks on nuclear disarmament. While the U.S.S.R. is the leader in this field there is very little chance of its easily relinquish-ing that lead. If it is necessary to spend a few billion dollars on MX missiles to alter this situation, then perhaps this is what the West must do. But, at the same time, if the Soviets, in deed and not just in word, take significant verifiable measures for reducing the number of land-based missiles (more precisely, for destroying them), then the West should not only abolish MX missiles (or not build them!) but carry out other significant disarmament programs as well.

On the whole I am convinced that nuclear disarmament talks are of enor-mous importance and of the highest priority. They must be conducted con-tinuously — in the brighter periods of international relations but also in the periods when relations are strained — and conducted with persistence, foresight, firmness and, at the same time, with flexibility and initiative. In so doing, political figures should not think of exploiting those talks, and the nuclear problem in gen-eral, for their own immediate political gains but only for the long-term interests of their country and the world. And the planning of the talks should be included in one's general nuclear strategy as its most important part — on this point as well I am in agreement with you!

The third group of problems which should be discussed here is political and social in nature. A nuclear war could result from a conventional war, while a con-ventional war is, as is well known, a result of politics. We all know that the world is not at peace. There are a variety of reasons for this — national, economic, and so-cial reasons, as well as the tyranny of dictators. . . .

The hot spots of local conflicts are not dying but are rather threatening to grow into global wars. All this is greatly alarming.

The most acutely negative manifestation of Soviet policies was the invasion of Afghanistan which began in December 1979 with the murder of the head of state. Three years of appallingly cruel anti-guerrilla war have brought incalculable suffering to the Afghan people, as attested by the more than four million refugees in Pakistan and Iran.

It was precisely the general upsetting of world equilibrium caused by the invasion of Afghanistan and by other concurrent events which was the fundamental reason that the SALT II agreement was not ratified. I am with you in regretting this but I cannot disregard the reasons I have just described. . . .

In conclusion I again stress how important it is that the world realize the absolute inadmissibility of nuclear war, the collective suicide of mankind. It is impossible to win a nuclear war. What is necessary is to strive, systematically though carefully, for complete nuclear disarmament based on strategic parity in conventional weapons. As long as there are nuclear weapons in the world, there must be a strategic parity of nuclear forces so that neither side will venture to embark on a limited or regional nuclear war. Genuine security is possible only when based on a stabilization of international relations, a repudiation of expansionist policies, the strengthening of international trust, openness and pluralization in the socialist societies, the observance of human rights throughout the world, the rapprochement — convergence — of the socialist and capitalist systems, and worldwide coordinated efforts to solve global problems.

78

Robert S. McNamara and Hans A. Bethe, "Reducing the Risk of Nuclear War"

Robert S. McNamara (1916 —), former President of Ford Motor Company, served as Secretary of Defense under Presidents Kennedy and Johnson. Later he served as the President of the World Bank. Hans A. Bethe (1906 —) was one of the leading physicists in the Manhattan Project that developed the first atomic bomb. In 1958–1959, he was a member of the United States Delegation to Discussions on Discontinuance of Nuclear Weapons Tests at Geneva. He was awarded a Nobel Prize in Physics in 1967 for his work on nuclear energy production in stars.

QUESTIONS TO CONSIDER

1. What are the views of Hans Bethe and Robert McNamara concerning President Reagan's approach to enhanced security, the Strategic Defense Initiative (SDI)?
2. What sort of a balance between deterrence and détente do Hans Bethe and Robert McNamara attempt to strike, in order to promote peace and stability?

The superpowers' arsenals hold some 50,000 nuclear warheads. Each, on the average, is far more destructive than the bomb that obliterated Hiroshima. Just one of our thirty-six strategic submarines has more firepower than man has shot against man throughout history. Thousands of nuclear weapons are ready for immediate use against targets close to hand or half a globe away, but just a few hundred warheads could utterly demolish the largest nation.

To deter war, each side seeks to persuade the other, and itself, that it is prepared to wage a nuclear war that would have the military objectives of a bygone age. What is known of Soviet nuclear war plans is open to interpretation, but these plans appear to rely on tactics derived from Russia's pre-nuclear military experience. Current US defense policy calls for nuclear forces that are sufficient to support a "controlled and protracted" nuclear war, that could eliminate the Soviet leadership, and that would even permit the United States to "prevail."

Nuclear warfighting notions lead to enormous target lists and huge forces. Our 11,000 strategic warheads are directed against some 5000 targets. And NATO's war plans are based on early first use of some 6000 tactical nuclear weapons in response to a Soviet conventional attack. Both NATO and the Warsaw Pact countries routinely train their forces for nuclear operations. War-fighting doctrines create a desire for increasingly sophisticated nuclear weapons which technology always promises to satisfy but never does. Today both sides are committed to programs that will threaten a growing portion of the adversary's most vital military assets with increasingly swift destruction. . . .

These armories and war plans are more than macabre symbols for bolstering self-confidence. Both Moscow and Washington presume that nuclear weapons are likely to be used should hostilities break out. But neither knows how to control the escalation that would almost certainly follow. No one can tell in advance what response any nuclear attack might bring. No one knows who will still be able to communicate with whom, or what will be left to say, or whether any message could possibly be believed.

When our secretary of defense, Caspar Weinberger, was asked whether it really would be possible to control forces and make calculated decisions amid the destruction and confusion of nuclear battle, he replied, "I just don't have any idea. I don't know that anybody has any idea." Surely it is reckless to stake a nation's survival on detailed plans for something about which no one has any idea.

It would be vastly more reckless to attempt a disarming first strike. Nevertheless, the arms race is driven by deep-seated fears held by each side that the other has, or is seeking, the ability to execute just such a strike. . . .

That a first strike is not a rational Soviet option has also been stated by President Reagan's own Scowcroft Commission, which found that no combination of attacks from Soviet submarines and land-based ICBMs could catch our bombers on the ground as well as our Minutemen in their silos. In addition, our submarines at sea, which carry a substantial percentage of our strategic warheads, are invulnerable : in the race between techniques to hide submarines and those to find them, the fugitives have always been ahead and are widening their lead. . . .

Excerpt from *Toward a New Security : Lessons of the Forty Years Since Trinity*, a report of the Union of Concerned Scientists (Boston, 1985), pp. 42–49 ; adapted from an article by Robert S. McNamara and Hans A. Bethe, with assistance from Kurt Gottfried, in the July 1985 issue of *The Atlantic Monthly*. Reprinted by permission.

Despite all such facts, the warfighting mania and the fear of a first strike are eroding confidence in deterrence. Though both sides are aware that a nuclear war that engaged even a small fraction of their arsenals would be an unparalleled disaster, each is vigorously developing and deploying new weapons systems that it will view as highly threatening when the opponent also acquires them. Thus our newest submarines will soon carry missiles accurate enough to destroy Soviet silos. When the Soviets follow suit, as they always do, their offshore submarines will for the first time pose a simultaneous threat to our command centers, bomber bases and Minuteman ICBMs.

The absurd struggle to improve the ability to wage "the war that cannot be fought" has shaken confidence in the ability to avert that war. The conviction that we must change course is shared by groups and individuals as diverse as the freeze movement, the president, the Catholic bishops, the bulk of the nation's scientists, the president's chief arms control negotiator, and ourselves. All are saying, directly or by implication, that nuclear warheads serve no military purpose whatsoever. They are not weapons. They are totally useless except to deter one's opponent from using his warheads. Beyond this point the consensus dissolves, because the changes of direction being advocated follow from very different diagnoses of our predicament.

The president's approach has been to launch the Strategic Defense Initiative (SDI), a vast program for creating an impenetrable shield that would protect the entire nation against a missile attack and would therefore permit the destruction of all offensive nuclear weapons. The president and the secretary of defense remain convinced that this strategic revolution is at hand. . . .

Virtually all others associated with the SDI now recognize that such a leakproof defense is so far in the future, if indeed it ever proves feasible, that it offers no solution to our present dilemma. They therefore advocate other forms of ballistic missile defense. These alternative systems range from defense of hardened targets (for example, missile silos and command centers) to partial protection of our population.

For the sake of clarity we will call these alternative programs Star Wars II, to distinguish them from the president's original proposal, which we will label Star Wars I. It is essential to understand that these two versions of Star Wars have diametrically opposed objectives. The president's program, if achieved, would substitute defensive for offensive forces. In contrast, Star Wars II systems have one characteristic in common: they would all require that we continue with offensive forces but add the defensive systems to them.

And that is what causes the problem. President Reagan, in a little-remembered sentence in the speech announcing his Strategic Defense Initiative on March 23, 1983, said, "If paired with offensive systems, [defensive systems] can be viewed as fostering an aggressive policy, and no one wants that." The president was concerned that the Soviets would regard a decision to supplement our offensive forces with defenses as an attempt to achieve a first-strike capability. That is exactly how they are interpreting our program; that is why they say there will be no agreement on offensive weapons until we give up Star Wars.

Before any further discussion of why Star Wars II will accelerate the arms race, it would be useful to examine why the president's original proposal, Star Wars I, will prove an unattainable dream in our lifetime.

The reason is clear. There is no evidence that any combination of the "defensive technologies" now on the most visionary of horizons can undo the revolution wrought by the invention of nuclear explosives. "War" is only one of the concepts whose meanings were changed forever at Hiroshima. "Defense" is another. Before Hiroshima, defense relied on attrition — exhausting an enemy's human, material, and moral resources. The Royal Air Force won the Battle of Britain by attaining a 10 percent attrition rate against the Nazi air force, because repeated attacks could not be sustained against such odds. The converse, a 90 percent effective defense, could not preserve us against even one modest nuclear attack.

. . . The term "defensive technologies" may conjure up images of mighty fortifications, but it refers to delicate instruments: huge mirrors of exquisite precision, ultrasensitive detectors of heat and radiation, optical systems that must find and aim at a one-foot target thousands of miles away and moving at four miles per second, and so forth. All these marvels must work near the theoretical limit of perfection; even small losses in precision would lead to unacceptably poor performance. . . .

. . . If the Soviets were about to demolish us with a nuclear attack, they would surely not shrink from destroying our unmanned space platforms. And they have had nuclear-armed ABM interceptors ideally suited to that task for two decades. Such weapons could punch a large hole in our shield of space platforms, through which the Soviet first strike could immediately be launched. Hence any defense based on orbiting platforms is fatally vulnerable, or, as Edward Teller has put it, "lasers in space won't fill the bill — they must be deployed in great numbers at terrible cost and could be destroyed in advance of an attack." The wide variety of countermeasures that have been developed during decades of ABM research show that every other proposed space defense scheme has its own Achilles' heel.

The prospect of achieving the goal of Star Wars I has been succinctly put by Robert S. Cooper, the Pentagon's director of advanced research: "There is no combination of gold or platinum bullets that we see in our technology arsenal . . . that would make it possible to do away with our strategic offensive ICBM forces." Until there are inventions that have not even been imagined, a defense robust and cheap enough to replace deterrence will remain a pipe dream. Emotional appeals that defense is morally superior to deterrence are therefore "pernicious," as former Secretary of Defense James Schlesinger has said, because "in our lifetime, and that of our children, cities will be protected by the forbearance of those on the other side, or through effective deterrence." . . .

The authors have personally observed and participated in the nuclear competition for decades. The US invention of the atomic bomb was the most remarkable technical breakthrough in military history. And yet the Soviet Union, though devastated by war and operating from a technological base far weaker than ours, was able to create nuclear forces that gave it a plausible deterrent in an astonishingly short time. Virtually every technical initiative in the nuclear arms race has come from the United States, but the net result has been a steady erosion of American security. There is no evidence that space weapons will be an exception, for a nuclear blunderbuss can foil sophistication.

Then why are the Soviets so worried by Star Wars? Because strategic defense probably could succeed if the Russians played dead. For that reason they must respond. This will require vast expenditures they can ill afford, and will ultimately diminish their security. But that is equally true for us, whether we recognize it or not.

To summarize, these rationales for Star Wars II propose to achieve a superior strategic posture by combining unattainable technical goals with a policy rooted in concepts whose validity died at Hiroshima.

The public's intuitive awareness of the unacceptable risk posed by our present nuclear strategy is well founded. Our security demands that we replace that defense policy with one that is in firm touch with nuclear reality. If neither Star Wars I nor Star Wars II is the answer, what is?

The risk of catastrophic escalation of nuclear operations, and the futility of defense, lead us to base our proposal on the axiom that any initiation of nuclear warfare against a similarly armed opponent would be an irrational act. Hence, as we have said, nuclear weapons must have only one purpose — that of preventing their use. They must not do less; they cannot do more. Thus, a restricting of nuclear forces designed to reduce the risk of nuclear war must be our goal. All policies, every existing program, and each new initiative must be judged in that light.

Post-Hiroshima history has taught us three lessons that shape the present proposal. First, all our technological genius and economic prowess cannot make us secure if they leave the Soviet Union insecure; we can have either mutual security or mutual insecurity. Second, while profound differences and severe competition will surely continue to mark US-Soviet relations, the nuclear arms race is a burden to both sides, and it is in our mutual interest to rid ourselves of its menace. And third, no realistic scheme that would rid us of all nuclear weapons has ever been formulated.

The ultimate goal, therefore, should be a state of mutual deterrence at the lowest force levels consistent with stability. That requires invulnerable forces that could, unquestionably, respond to any attack and inflict unacceptable damage. If those forces are to remain limited, it is equally essential that they not threaten the opponent's deterrent. These factors would combine to produce a stable equilibrium in which the risk of nuclear war would be very remote.

This kind of deterrence posture should not be confused with the one currently prevailing among US and Soviet nuclear forces. The 25,000 warheads that each nation possesses did not come about through any plan but simply descended on the world as a consequence of continuing technical innovations and the persistent failure to recognize that nuclear explosives are not weapons in any traditional sense.

The forces we propose could include a mix of submarines, bombers, and ICBMs. The land-based components should be made invulnerable in themselves by some combination of mobile ICBMs and reductions in the number of warheads per missile. Two considerations would determine the ultimate size of the force: that it deter attack with confidence, and that any undetected or sudden violation of arms control treaties would not imperil this deterrence. We believe that, ultimately, strategic forces having as few as 10 percent of the currently deployed warheads would meet these criteria, and tactical forces could be eliminated entirely. In short, the present inventory of 50,000 warheads could be cut to perhaps 2000.

Before this goal is reached, other nuclear powers (China, France, Great Britain, and possibly others) will have to be involved in the process of reducing nuclear arsenals, lest their weapons disturb the strategic equilibrium. And, it would be wise to resume negotiations towards a comprehensive test ban forbidding all underground nuclear explosions. Such a ban has always been viewed as an important impediment to the development of nuclear weapons by nations now possessing them.

The proposed changes in US and Soviet strategic and tactical forces would require, as would the president's SDI, complementary changes in NATO and Warsaw Pact conventional forces, or appropriate increases in NATO's conventional power. If the latter was necessary, it could be achieved at a fraction of the costs we will incur if we continue on our present course.

Having identified our goal, how can we move toward it? Some of our new policies would depend solely on us; others would require Soviet cooperation. The former should be governed by the dictum attributed to President Eisenhower, that "we need what we need." Were we to drop futile warfighting notions, we would see that many things we already have or are busily acquiring are either superfluous or downright dangerous to us, no matter what the Soviets do. Tactical nuclear weapons in Europe are a prime example, and the administration's policy of reducing their numbers should be accelerated. Other examples are programs that will haunt us when the Soviets copy them: sophisticated antisatellite weapons, sea-based cruise missiles, and highly accurate submarine-launched ballistic missiles. We are more dependent on satellites than the Soviets, and more vulnerable to attack from the sea. Many of these weapons are valid bargaining chips because they threaten the Soviets, just as so much of their arsenal gratuitously threatens us.

THE COLD WAR

As World War II drew to a close, the United States and the Soviet Union rapidly emerged as the arbiters of the world; their mutual suspicions about each other's designs deepened, and their relationship became increasingly confrontational. The post-war world, which was envisioned and shaped by the Allied leaders during wartime at such conferences as Cairo, Yalta, and Potsdam, did not turn out as these leaders had hoped — at least as far as the United States, China, and Great Britain were concerned. In the first two years of the post-war period, the world became increasingly polarized. Despite the pledges made at the Yalta Conference in February 1945 that "free and unfettered elections" would be held in liberated Poland, Stalin imposed a Communist regime. Soon, all of Central and Eastern Europe was swept into the Russian orbit.

But nowhere else were the tensions between the United States and the Soviet Union more clearly present than in the two bisected nations, Korea and Germany — particularly the former. During the war, at the Cairo Conference, the Allied leaders issued a declaration that Korea, which had been a colony of Japan since 1910, would become free and independent. Two days after the first atomic bomb was dropped on Hiroshima and six days before Japan's surrender, the Soviet Union finally declared war on Japan, as agreed at Yalta, and the Red Army crossed into Korea three weeks before the Americans. By then, President Harry S. Truman had had second thoughts about the need for Soviet participation in the war against Japan. To prevent the rapidly advancing Red Army from overrunning the Korean peninsula, the United States proposed to the Soviets a line at the thirty-eighth parallel, dividing the United States troops in the south from those of the Soviet Union in the north. This line, which was casually drawn in the last days of the war, has continued to be a source of international conflict and enormous suffering for the Korean people.

Meanwhile, the Soviet Union's expansionistic designs in northern Iran and Turkey and its support of the insurgency in Greece were being countered by the United States containment policy. In 1947, President Truman declared that the United States would provide military and economic support to any country threatened by Communist aggression. In accordance with this "Truman Doctrine," money and supplies poured into Greece, and the insurgency was crushed by 1949. This move by the United States is usually regarded as the start of the cold war. The Truman Doctrine led to the Marshall Plan, aimed at rebuilding Europe, as well as to the policy of military defense and collective security provided by the North Atlantic Treaty Organization (NATO), which went into operation in August 1949. After the French defeat in Indochina in 1954, John Foster Dulles, Secretary of State under President Eisenhower, took the initiative to extend the collective security system to Southeast Asia.

After the death of Joseph Stalin (1879–1953), the new Soviet leadership asserted that a less rigid foreign and domestic policy was needed. Coexistence — rather than confrontation — would be the new theme in foreign policy, while domestic policy was aimed at relaxing controls and improving the standard of living in the Soviet Union and throughout Eastern Europe.

In 1956, Nikita Khrushchev, the new Communist Party Chairman (1953–1964), shocked the Twentieth Party Congress by denouncing the "cult of the individual" and the crimes of Joseph Stalin. Unintentionally his speech, designed to tighten his control over the party apparatus, contributed to further unrest in Eastern Europe. By saluting the special case of Yugoslavian communism, Khrushchev hinted that differing styles of communism within Eastern Europe were acceptable. But in 1956, when rioting and political unrest erupted in Poland and Hungary, Khrushchev sent in the Red Army to restore control. Despite the blatant crushing of these revolts, Soviet leadership under Leonid I. Brezhnev (1964–1982) permitted a relaxation of political controls within Eastern Europe. Even in Hungary there was a thaw ; but it was in 1968 in Czechoslovakia that the most daring attempts to democratize government were made. The Soviets responded to the Czech rebellion with strong military force and justified their actions with the policy known as the Brezhnev Doctrine.

Khrushchev had made it plain that peaceful coexistence was not exactly peace. While he, and Brezhnev after him, ruled out warfare between the USSR and the industrial countries of the West, he defended Soviet aid to groups waging civil wars or "wars of national liberation." Soviet policy remained one of giving aid to movements hostile to Western influence, and countries of the West generally advocated a policy of containing Communism.

As a result, the cold war was characterized by adversarial relations between the USSR and Western countries, but the actual wars waged between forces fighting in the name of Marxist revolution and their opponents were regional ones in the Third World. Twice, in Korea and Vietnam, the United States fought with its own troops in regional Asian wars, while in 1979 the USSR intervened in Afghanistan with the Soviet Army, but Soviet forces were never in direct combat against those of the United States or any other NATO country, and the geographical sphere of the fighting remained almost completely confined to the countries where the wars had begun.

In the late 1980s, the failure of Marxist economic systems in Eastern Europe to provide a good standard of living and the failure of political systems there to win even the grudging approval of the bulk of the populations led to the collapse of one Communist regime after another. Even the USSR, under Gorbachev, abandoned many basic Marxist principles. Although the forces of democracy and capitalism did not reverse their earlier defeats in China, Cuba, and much of Indo-China, the cold war appeared to be ending for the two major contending groups. Soviet agreement to German unification in a fashion that spelled the end of a Marxist East Germany, the granting of massive food aid by the NATO countries to combat severe food shortages in the USSR, and some coordination of Soviet and American policies to counteract the Iraqi occupation of Kuwait were only some of the many striking events that indicated that in Eastern Europe, Western Europe, and North America at the very least, the last decade of the twentieth century would see the end of the cold war.

79

The Truman Doctrine

By 1947, Greece was in the midst of a civil war that appeared to Washington to be a Communist-led revolution, which, if successful, would threaten Turkey, the Middle East, Africa, and all of Europe. When the British notified Washington that they could no longer guarantee stability in the eastern Mediterranean, President Truman asked the U.S. Congress for military and economic aid for both Greece and Turkey. With strong bipartisan support, Congress approved the funds and implemented the Truman Doctrine, which declared the U.S. determination to pursue a policy of containment by aiding nations attempting to resist Communist pressure. In the following address, given to Congress on March 12, 1947, President Truman outlined the nature of the crisis in Greece and Turkey as well as U.S. responsibilities in the postwar era.

QUESTIONS TO CONSIDER

1. Why did President Truman believe that the governments of Greece and Turkey were unable to resolve their internal problems and needed assistance? Why did he recommend that the United States, rather than the United Nations, provide economic and military aid to Greece and Turkey? What were the "broad implications" of extending that aid?
2. Why did President Truman believe that the national security of the United States was at stake in Greece and Turkey?
3. Are there similarities between President Truman's ideals and goals and those expressed by Woodrow Wilson in his "Fourteen Points" address to Congress (see Reading 59) and the Atlantic Charter (see Reading 72)?

The gravity of the situation which confronts the world today necessitates my appearance before a joint session of the Congress.

The foreign policy and the national security of this country are involved.

One aspect of the present situation, which I wish to present to you at this time for your consideration and decision, concerns Greece and Turkey. . . .

From U.S. Congress, *Congressional Record*, 80th Congress, 1st Session, 1947, XCIII, pp. 1980–1981.

The very existence of the Greek state is today threatened by the terrorist activities of several thousand armed men, led by Communists, who defy the Government's authority at a number of points, particularly along the northern boundaries. A commission appointed by the United Nations Security Council is at present investigating disturbed conditions in northern Greece and alleged border violations along the frontier between Greece on the one hand and Albania, Bulgaria, and Yugoslavia on the other.

Meanwhile, the Greek Government is unable to cope with the situation. The Greek Army is small and poorly equipped. It needs supplies and equipment if it is to restore the authority of the Government throughout Greek territory.

Greece must have assistance if it is to become a self-supporting and self-respecting democracy.

The United States must supply this assistance. We have already extended to Greece certain types of relief and economic aid but these are inadequate.

There is no other country to which democratic Greece can turn.

No other nation is willing and able to provide the necessary support for a democratic Greek Government.

The British Government, which has been helping Greece, can give no further financial or economic aid after March 31. Great Britain finds itself under the necessity of reducing or liquidating its commitments in several parts of the world, including Greece.

We have considered how the United Nations might assist in this crisis. But the situation is an urgent one requiring immediate action, and the United Nations and its related organizations are not in a position to extend help of the kind that is required.

It is important to note that the Greek Government has asked for our aid in utilizing effectively the financial and other assistance we may give to Greece, and in improving its public administration. It is of the utmost importance that we supervise the use of any funds made available to Greece, in such a manner that each dollar spent will count toward making Greece self-supporting, and will help to build an economy in which a healthy democracy can flourish.

No government is perfect. One of the chief virtues of a democracy, however, is that its defects are always visible and under democratic processes can be pointed out and corrected. The Government of Greece is not perfect. Nevertheless it represents 85 percent of the members of the Greek Parliament who were chosen in an election last year. Foreign observers, including 692 Americans, considered this election to be a fair expression of the views of the Greek people.

The Greek Government has been operating in an atmosphere of chaos and extremism. It has made mistakes. The extension of aid by this country does not mean that the United States condones everything that the Greek Government has done or will do. We have condemned in the past, and we condemn now, extremist measures of the right or the left. We have in the past advised tolerance, and we advise tolerance now.

Greece's neighbor, Turkey, also deserves our attention.

The future of Turkey as an independent and economically sound state is clearly no less important to the freedom-loving peoples of the world than the future of Greece. The circumstances in which Turkey finds itself today are considerably different from those of Greece. Turkey has been spared the disasters that have beset Greece. And during the war, the United States and Great Britain furnished Turkey with material aid.

Nevertheless, Turkey now needs our support.

Since the war, Turkey has sought financial assistance from Great Britain and the United States for the purpose of effecting that modernization necessary for the maintenance of its national integrity.

That integrity is essential to the preservation of order in the Middle East.

The British Government has informed us that, owing to its own difficulties, it can no longer extend financial or economic aid to Turkey.

As in the case of Greece, if Turkey is to have the assistance it needs, the United States must supply it. We are the only country able to provide that help.

I am fully aware of the broad implications involved if the United States extends assistance to Greece and Turkey, and I shall discuss these implications with you at this time.

One of the primary objectives of the foreign policy of the United States is the creation of conditions in which we and other nations will be able to work out a way of life free from coercion. This was a fundamental issue in the war with Germany and Japan. Our victory was won over countries which sought to impose their will, and their way of life, upon other nations.

To insure the peaceful development of nations, free from coercion, the United States has taken a leading part in establishing the United Nations. The United Nations is designed to make possible lasting freedom and independence for all its members. We shall not realize our objectives, however, unless we are willing to help free peoples to maintain their free institutions and their national integrity against aggressive movements that seek to impose upon them totalitarian regimes. This is no more than a frank recognition that totalitarian regimes imposed on free peoples, by direct or indirect aggression, undermine the foundations of international peace and hence the security of the United States.

The peoples of a number of countries of the world have recently had totalitarian regimes forced upon them against their will. The Government of the United States has made frequent protests against coercion and intimidation, in violation of the Yalta agreement, in Poland, Rumania, and Bulgaria. I must also state that in a number of other countries there have been similar developments.

At the present moment in world history nearly every nation must choose between alternative ways of life. The choice is too often not a free one.

One way of life is based upon the will of the majority, and is distinguished by free institutions, representative government, free elections, guaranties of individual liberty, freedom of speech and religion, and freedom from political oppression.

The second way of life is based upon the will of a minority forcibly imposed upon the majority. It relies upon terror and oppression, a controlled press and radio, fixed elections, and the suppression of personal freedoms.

I believe that it must be the policy of the United States to support free peoples who are resisting attempted subjugation by armed minorities or by outside pressures.

I believe that we must assist free peoples to work out their own destinies in their own way.

I believe that our help should be primarily through economic and financial aid, which is essential to economic stability and orderly political processes.

The world is not static and the status quo is not sacred. But we cannot allow changes in the status quo in violation of the Charter of the United Nations by such methods as coercion, or by such subterfuges as political infiltration. In helping free and independent nations to maintain their freedom, the United States will be giving effect to the principles of the Charter of the United Nations.

It is necessary only to glance at a map to realize that the survival and integrity of the Greek nation are of grave importance in a much wider situation. If Greece should fall under the control of an armed minority, the effect upon its neighbor, Turkey, would be immediate and serious. Confusion and disorder might well spread throughout the entire Middle East.

Moreover, the disappearance of Greece as an independent state would have a profound effect upon those countries in Europe whose peoples are struggling against great difficulties to maintain their freedoms and their independence. . . .

It would be an unspeakable tragedy if these countries, which have struggled so long against overwhelming odds, should lose that victory for which they sacrificed so much. Collapse of free institutions and loss of independence would be disastrous not only for them but for the world. Discouragement and possibiy failure would quickly be the lot of neighboring peoples striving to maintain their freedom and independence.

Should we fail to aid Greece and Turkey in this fateful hour, the effect will be far reaching to the West as well as to the East.

We must take immediate and resolute action.

I therefore ask the Congress to provide authority for assistance to Greece and Turkey in the amount of $400,000,000 for the period ending June 30, 1948. In requesting these funds, I have taken into consideration the maximum amount of relief assistance which would be furnished to Greece out of the $350,000,000 which I recently requested that the Congress authorize for the prevention of starvation and suffering in countries devastated by the war.

In addition to funds, I ask the Congress to authorize the detail of American civilian and military personnel to Greece and Turkey, at the request of those countries, to assist in the tasks of reconstruction, and for the purpose of supervising the use of such financial and material assistance as may be furnished. I recommend that authority also be provided for the instruction and training of selected Greek and Turkish personnel.

Finally, I ask that the Congress provide authority which will permit the speediest and most effective use, in terms of needed commodities, supplies, and equipment, of such funds as may be authorized.

If further funds, or further authority, should be needed for purposes indicated in this message, I shall not hesitate to bring the situation before the Congress. On this subject the executive and legislative branches of the Government must work together.

This is a serious course upon which we embark.

I would not recommend it except that the alternative is much more serious.

The United States contributed $341,000,000,000 toward winning World War II. This is an investment in world freedom and world peace.

The assistance that I am recommending for Greece and Turkey amounts to little more than one-tenth of 1 percent of this investment. It is only common sense that we should safeguard this investment and make sure that it was not in vain.

The seeds of totalitarian regimes are nurtured by misery and want. They spread and grow in the evil soil of poverty and strife. They reach their full growth when the hope of a people [dies].

We must keep that hope alive.

The free peoples of the world look to us for support in maintaining their freedoms.

If we falter in our leadership, we may endanger the peace of the world — and we shall surely endanger the welfare of our own Nation.

Great responsibilities have been placed upon us by the swift movement of events.

I am confident that the Congress will face these responsibilities squarely.

80

Mao Tse-tung [Mao Zedong], "The People's Democratic Dictatorship"

Until his death in 1976, Mao Tse-tung was the supreme figure, reminiscent of the old Chinese emperor, in the People's Republic of China (PRC). He was one of the dozen who gave birth to the Communist Party of China in Shanghai in 1921. He emerged as the sole "survivor" among the original members of the party. The rest left the party for one reason or another, including purges, defections, resignations, or deaths. His rise to the leadership of the Chinese Communist Party, which was dominated in its early years by the Moscow-trained and urban-oriented Chinese Communists, was through a rather unorthodox means. He carefully built his power base in the countryside, believing that the peasants, rather than the urban proletariat, were the mainstay of the Communist revolution. He spent more than 20 years in rural China organizing and leading peasants and the peasant army, the forerunner of the People's Liberation Army. He presided over the Communist insurgent government (known as the Chinese Soviet Republic) in a mountainous region of south-central China from 1931 to 1934. After the collapse of this "Red Republic" in 1935, during the 6,000-mile Long March, harassed by pursuing Chiang Kai-shek's Nationalist troops, Mao emerged as the undisputed leader in the Communist Party by eclipsing the Moscow-oriented party leadership which had lost its urban base to Chiang Kai-shek. His leadership of the party was formalized in 1943 when he was elected chairman of the Central Committee and the Politburo of the Communist Party of China. In Yenan (Yan'an), the new hinterland base of operations of the Communists from 1936 to 1947,

Mao enjoyed not only unchallenged leadership in the Chinese Communist movement, but he also emerged as a Communist theoretician by adapting Marxism-Leninism to the unique socioeconomic and political conditions within China. He produced a number of theoretical works, including "On Practice," "On Contradiction," and "Problems of Strategy in China's Revolutionary War."

Following Japan's defeat in World War II in August 1945 and the subsequent Communist victory over Chiang Kai-shek's Nationalist forces in the bitterly fought four-year civil war, on October 1, 1949, 28 years after the formation of the Communist Party of China, Mao Tse-tung stood on the Gate of Heavenly Peace (Tienanmen) in Beijing (Peking) to proclaim the birth of the People's Republic of China. Mao, now as the leader of the world's most populous Communist state, gave the following speech on June 30, 1949, in commemoration of the Chinese Communist Party's 28th anniversary.

QUESTIONS TO CONSIDER

1. What meaning does Mao give to the term "democratic"? How does he make this term consistent with the term "dictatorship"?
2. What is Mao's attitude toward the Soviet Union? Did he remain constant in this attitude?

Communists the world over are wiser than the bourgeoisie, they understand the laws governing the existence and development of things, they understand dialectics and they can see farther. The bourgeoisie does not welcome this truth because it does not want to be overthrown.

As everyone knows, our Party passed through these twenty-eight years not in peace but amid hardships, for we had to fight enemies, both foreign and domestic, both inside and outside the Party. We thank Marx, Engels, Lenin and Stalin for giving us a weapon. This weapon is not a machine-gun, but Marxism-Leninism. . . .

The Russians made the October Revolution and created the world's first socialist state. Under the leadership of Lenin and Stalin, the revolutionary energy of the great proletariat and labouring people of Russia, hitherto latent and unseen by foreigners, suddenly erupted like a volcano, and the Chinese and all mankind began to see the Russians in a new light. Then, and only then, did the Chinese enter an entirely new era in their thinking and their life. They found Marxism-Leninism, the universally applicable truth, and the face of China began to change. . . .

There are bourgeois republics in foreign lands, but China cannot have a bourgeois republic because she is a country suffering under imperialist oppression. The only way is through a people's republic led by the working class. . . .

From Mao Tse-tung, Speech "In Commemoration of the 28th Anniversary of the Communist Party of China, June 30, 1949," in *Selected Works*, vol. 5 (New York: International Publishers, n.d.), pp. 411–423.

Twenty-four years have passed since Sun Yat-sen's death, and the Chinese revolution, led by the Communist Party of China, has made tremendous advances both in theory and practice and has radically changed the face of China. Up to now the principal and fundamental experience the Chinese people have gained is twofold :

1. Internally, arouse the masses of the people. That is, unite the working class, the peasantry, the urban petty bourgeoisie and the national bourgeoisie, form a domestic united front under the leadership of the working class, and advance from this to the establishment of a state which is a people's democratic dictatorship under the leadership of the working class and based on the alliance of workers and peasants.
2. Externally, unite in a common struggle with those nations of the world which treat us as equals and unite with the peoples of all countries. That is, ally ourselves with the Soviet Union, with the People's Democracies and with the proletariat and the broad masses of the people in all other countries, and form an international united front.

"You are leaning to one side." Exactly. The forty years' experience of Sun Yat-sen and the twenty-eight years' experience of the Communist Party have taught us to lean to one side, and we are firmly convinced that in order to win victory and consolidate it we must lean to one side. In the light of the experiences accumulated in these forty years and these twenty-eight years, all Chinese without exception must lean either to the side of imperialism or to the side of socialism. Sitting on the fence will not do, nor is there a third road. We oppose the Chiang Kai-shek reactionaries who lean to the side of imperialism, and we also oppose the illusions about a third road.

"You are too irritating." We are talking about how to deal with domestic and foreign reactionaries, the imperialists and their running dogs, not about how to deal with anyone else. With regard to such reactionaries, the question of irritating them or not does not arise. Irritated or not irritated, they will remain the same because they are reactionaries. Only if we draw a clear line between reactionaries and revolutionaries, expose the intrigues and plots of the reactionaries, arouse the vigilance and attention of the revolutionary ranks, heighten our will to fight and crush the enemy's arrogance can we isolate the reactionaries, vanquish them or supersede them. We must not show the slightest timidity before a wild beast.

"Victory is possible even without international help." This is a mistaken idea. In the epoch in which imperialism exists, it is impossible for a genuine people's revolution to win victory in any country without various forms of help from the international revolutionary forces, and even if victory were won, it could not be consolidated. This was the case with the victory and consolidation of the great October Revolution, as Lenin and Stalin told us long ago.

"We need help from the British and U.S. governments." This, too, is a naive idea in these times. Would the present rulers of Britain and the United States, who are imperialists, help a people's state ? Why do these countries do business with us and, supposing they might be willing to lend us money on terms of mutual benefit in the future, why would they do so ? Because their capitalists want to make money and their bankers want to earn interest to extricate themselves from their own crisis — it is not a matter of helping the Chinese people.

"You are dictatorial." My dear sirs, you are right, that is just what we are. All the experience the Chinese people have accumulated through several decades teaches us to enforce the people's democratic dictatorship, that is, to deprive the reactionaries of the right to speak and let the people alone have that right.

"Who are the people?" At the present stage in China, they are the working class, the peasantry, the urban petty bourgeoisie and the national bourgeoisie. These classes, led by the working class and the Communist Party, unite to form their own state and elect their own government; they enforce their dictatorship over the running dogs of imperialism — the landlord class and bureaucrat-bourgeoisie, as well as the representatives of those classes, the Kuomintang reactionaries and their accomplices — suppress them, allow them only to behave themselves and not to be unruly in word or deed. If they speak or act in an unruly way, they will be promptly stopped and punished. Democracy is practised within the ranks of the people, who enjoy the rights of freedom of speech, assembly, association and so on. The right to vote belongs only to the people, not to the reactionaries. The combination of these two aspects, democracy for the people and dictatorship over the reactionaries, is the people's democratic dictatorship.

"Why must things be done this way?" The reason is quite clear to everybody. If things were not done this way, the revolution would fail, the people would suffer, the country would be conquered.

"Don't you want to abolish state power?" Yes, we do, but not right now; we cannot do it yet. Why? Because imperialism still exists, because domestic reaction still exists, because classes still exist in our country. Our present task is to strengthen the people's state apparatus — mainly the people's army, the people's police and the people's courts — in order to consolidate national defence and protect the people's interests. Given this condition, China can develop steadily, under the leadership of the working class and the Communist Party, from an agricultural into an industrial country and from a new-democratic into a socialist and communist society, can abolish classes and realize the Great Harmony. The state apparatus, including the army, the police and the courts, is the instrument by which one class oppresses another. It is an instrument for the oppression of antagonistic classes; it is violence and not "benevolence". "You are not benevolent!" Quite so. We definitely do not apply a policy of benevolence to the reactionaries and towards the reactionary activities of the reactionary classes. Our policy of benevolence is applied only within the ranks of the people, not beyond them to the reactionaries or to the reactionary activities of reactionary classes. . . .

Here, the method we employ is democratic, the method of persuasion, not of compulsion. When anyone among the people breaks the law, he too should be punished, imprisoned or even sentenced to death; but this is a matter of a few individual cases, and it differs in principle from the dictatorship exercised over the reactionaries as a class.

As for the members of the reactionary classes and individual reactionaries, so long as they do not rebel, sabotage or create trouble after their political power has been overthrown, land and work will be given to them as well in order to allow them to live and remould themselves through labour into new people. If they are not willing to work, the people's state will compel them to work. . . .

Such remoulding of members of the reactionary classes can be accomplished only by a state of the people's democratic dictatorship under the leadership of the

Communist Party. When it is well done, China's major exploiting classes, the land-lord class and the bureaucrat-bourgeoisie (the monopoly capitalist class), will be eliminated for good. There remain the national bourgeoisie; at the present stage, we can already do a good deal of suitable educational work with many of them. When the time comes to realize socialism, that is, to nationalize private enterprise, we shall carry the work of educating and remoulding them a step further. The people have a powerful state apparatus in their hands — there is no need to fear rebellion by the national bourgeoisie. . . .

The people's democratic dictatorship is based on the alliance of the working class, the peasantry and the urban petty bourgeoisie, and mainly on the alliance of the workers and the peasants, because these two classes comprise 80 to 90 per cent of China's population. These two classes are the main force in overthrowing im-perialism and the Kuomintang reactionaries. The transition from New Democ-racy to socialism also depends mainly upon their alliance.

The people's democratic dictatorship needs the leadership of the working class. For it is only the working class that is most farsighted, most selfless and most thoroughly revolutionary. The entire history of revolution proves that without the leadership of the working class revolution fails. In the epoch of imperialism, in no country can any other class lead any genuine revolution to victory. This is clearly proved by the fact that the many revolutions led by China's petty bourgeoi-sie and national bourgeoisie all failed. . . .

To sum up our experience and concentrate it into one point, it is: the peo-ple's democratic dictatorship under the leadership of the working class (through the Communist Party) and based upon the alliance of workers and peasants. This dictatorship must unite as one with the international revolutionary forces. This is our formula, our principal experience, our main programme. . . .

The Communist Party of the Soviet Union is our best teacher and we must learn from it. The situation both at home and abroad is in our favour, we can rely fully on the weapon of the people's democratic dictatorship, unite the people throughout the country, the reactionaries excepted, and advance steadily to our goal.

81

Korea: The Thirty-Eighth Parallel

On August 9, 1945, the Soviet Union declared war on Japan, and soon after-wards the Soviet Red Army crossed into Manchuria and Korea. The United States, whose armed forces were hundreds of miles away from Korea, had to draw up a military demarcation line across the Korean peninsula to prevent the Russians from overrunning the entire region. On August 11, the State-War-Navy Coordinating Committee ordered two former Rhodes scholars, Colonels Dean Rusk and Charles H. Bonesteel III, to determine a line within 30 minutes. They recommended the thirty-eighth parallel as a division be-tween U.S. and Soviet occupation zones. By the time American troops entered Korea on September 8, the Russians were already entrenched along the thirty-eighth parallel. This line had been intended merely as a temporary military line to expedite the disarming of the Japanese troops in Korea. On August 14, Japan surrendered and Japanese rule in Korea ended; however, Korea found itself bisected and a focal point of intense rivalry between the United States and the Soviet Union. The following excerpt provides a detailed account of who actually drew the line and why.

QUESTIONS TO CONSIDER

1. How do you assess the behind-the-scenes decision for the containing of the Soviet advance in the Korean peninsula? Was the decision to divide Korea at the thirty-eighth parallel a wise one? Would another approach have been feasible?
2. How did the decision to divide Korea shape the course of Korean history and influence the cold war?

At Potsdam, the chief of the Russian General Staff told General Marshall that Russia would attack Korea after declaring war on Japan. He asked whether the Americans could operate against Korean shores in co-ordination with this offensive. General Marshall told him that the United States planned no amphibious operation against Korea until Japan had been brought under control and Japanese strength in South Korea was destroyed. Although the Chiefs of Staff developed ideas concerning the partition of Korea, Manchuria, and the Sea of Japan into U.S. and USSR zones, these had no connection with the later decisions that partitioned Korea into northern and southern areas.

Russian entry into the war against Japan on 9 August, and signs of imminent Japanese collapse on 10 August 1945 changed U.S. Army planning from defeating Japan to accepting its surrender. Military planners in the War Department Operations Division began to outline surrender procedures in General Order No. 1, which General MacArthur would transmit to the Japanese Government after its surrender. The first paragraph of the order specified the nations and commands that were to accept the surrender of Japanese forces throughout the Far East.

The Policy Section of the Strategy and Policy Group in the Operations Division drafted the initial version of the order.

Under pressure to produce a paper as quickly as possible, members of the Policy Section began work late at night on 10 August. They discussed possible surrender zones, the allocation of American, British, Chinese, and Russian occupation troops to accept the surrender in the zones most convenient to them, the means of actually taking the surrender of the widely scattered Japanese military forces, and the position of Russia in the Far East. They quickly decided to include both provisions for splitting up the entire Far East for the surrender and definitions of the geographical limits of those zones.

From James F. Schnabel, *United States Army in the Korean War. Policy and Direction: The First Year* (Washington, DC: Office of the Chief of Military History, United States Army, 1972), pp. 8–11.

The Chief of the Policy Section, Col. Charles H. Bonesteel, had thirty minutes in which to dictate Paragraph 1 to a secretary, for the Joint Staff Planners and the State-War-Navy Coordinating Committee were impatiently awaiting the result of his work. Colonel Bonesteel [along with Colonel Dean Rusk] thus somewhat hastily decided who would accept the Japanese surrender. His thoughts, with very slight revision, we incorporated into the final directive.

Bonesteel's prime consideration was to establish a surrender line as far north as he thought the Soviets would accept. He knew that Russian troops could reach the southern tip of Korea before American troops could arrive. He knew also that the Russians were on the verge of moving into Korea, or were already there. The nearest American troops to Korea were on Okinawa, 600 miles away. His problem therefore was to compose a surrender arrangement which, while acceptable to the Russians, would at the same time prevent them from seizing all of Korea. If they refused to confine their advance to North Korea, the United States would be unable to stop them.

At first Bonesteel had thought of surrender zones conforming to the provincial boundary lines. But the only map he had in his office, which was a small National Geographic map, a 1942 Gilbert Grosvenor Edition of "Asia and Adjacent Areas," was hardly adequate for this sort of distinction. The 38th Parallel, he noted, cut Korea approximately through the middle. If this line was agreeable to President Truman and to Generalissimo Stalin, it would place Seoul and a nearby prisoner of war camp in American hands. It would also leave enough land to be apportioned to the Chinese and British if some sort of quadripartite administration became necessary. Thus he decided to use the 38th Parallel as a hypothetical line dividing the zones within which Japanese forces in Korea would surrender to appointed American and Russian authorities. . . .

When Bonesteel's draft paper reached the Joint Planners in the predawn hours of 11 August, Admiral M. B. Gardner suggested moving the surrender line north to the 39th Parallel, a recommendation that the planners believed the Navy Secretary, James C. Forrestal, favored. Gardner pointed out that the 39th Parallel would place Dairen in the military zone to be occupied by the Americans. General Lincoln, however, felt that the Russians would hardly accept a surrender line that barred them from Dairen and other parts of the Liaotung Peninsula ; besides, American units would have great difficulty reaching the Manchurian port ahead of the Russians. Calling Assistant Secretary of State James Dunn, Lincoln ascertained that his opinion was shared. Mr. Dunn believed that Korea was more important politically to the United States than Dairen, and he felt this to be the view of Secretary of State James F. Byrnes. As a result, the 38th Parallel remained in the draft when the Joint Planners handed the general order to the State-War-Navy Coordinating Committee.

While General Lincoln was shepherding the document through the State-War-Navy Coordinating Committee on 11 and 12 August, the Russians invaded Korea, landing on the northeast coast near Rashin. Russian troops then poured out of the maritime provinces of Siberia, down the Korean peninsula, and into the Kaesong-Ch'unch'on area above Seoul, where they looted much equipment, including locomotives and rolling stock. Reports of the Russian troop movements reaching Washington underscored the need for concurrence in the proposed general order. Otherwise, the Russian advance would render academic the American acceptance of the Japanese surrender in southern Korea. At the same time, swift Russian troop movements into key areas of southern Manchuria eliminated the possibility of including Dairen in the American surrender zone.

Between 11 and 14 August, the State-War-Navy Coordinating Committee and the Joint Chiefs of Staff discussed the wording of the surrender instrument. Meanwhile, General MacArthur informed the Joint Chiefs of Staff that he would adhere to three priorities for the use of the forces under his command. After the Japanese surrender, the occupation of Japan would come first, Korea second, China third.

In Washington, the War Department Operations Division rephrased General Order No. 1 to the satisfaction of the Joint Chiefs of Staff and the heads of the State, War, and Navy Departments. On 15 August 1945, clean copies of the draft order were sent to Fleet Admiral William D. Leahy's White House office. Within a few hours President Truman gave his approval, directing at the same time that General Order No. 1 be sent also to the capitals of Great Britain and the USSR with requests for concurrence by the heads of those states. . . .

Among the items it specified, General Order No. 1 stated that Japanese forces north of the 38th Parallel in Korea would surrender to the Russian commander, while those south of the parallel would surrender to the commanding general of the U.S. expeditionary forces. As Washington waited for the Moscow reaction to President Truman's message, there was a short period of suspense. Russian troops had entered Korea three days before the President accepted the draft of General Order No. 1. If the Russians failed to accept the proposal, and if Russian troops occupied Seoul, General Lincoln suggested that American occupation forces move into Pusan.

Stalin replied to President Truman on 16 August 1945. He said nothing specifically about the 38th Parallel but offered no objection to the substance of the President's message.

82

Nikita S. Khrushchev, Address to the Twentieth Party Congress

On February 28, 1956, in an address to the Twentieth Congress of the Soviet Communist Party, Nikita Khrushchev provided a long list of the crimes of the late Joseph Stalin. Khrushchev's rough, earthy humor did not mask the fact that Stalin had perpetrated an immense reign of terror against the Russian people. The detailed indictment confirmed long-held Western views that between 1928 and 1953 Stalin imprisoned, deported, and killed millions of Russians (see Reading 68). Khrushchev's address to the Party Congress inadvertently raised the hope of reform in Eastern Europe.

QUESTIONS TO CONSIDER

1. What steps did Khrushchev propose to eradicate the "cult of the individual" in the Soviet Union?
2. How did Khrushchev employ the legacy of Lenin to attack his predecessor?
3. Are there any connections between Khrushchev's attacks on Stalin and Mikhail Gorbachev's policies of *Perestroika* (see Reading 98)?

When we analyze the practice of Stalin in regard to the direction of the party and of the country, when we pause to consider everything which Stalin perpetrated, we must be convinced that Lenin's fears were justified. The negative characteristics of Stalin, which, in Lenin's time, were only incipient, transformed themselves during the last years into a grave abuse of power by Stalin, which caused untold harm to our party.

We have to consider seriously and analyze correctly this matter in order that we may preclude any possibility of a repetition in any form whatever of what took place during the life of Stalin, who absolutely did not tolerate collegiality in leadership and in work, and who practiced brutal violence, not only toward everything which opposed him, but also toward that which seemed to his capricious and despotic character, contrary to his concepts.

Stalin acted not through persuasion, explanation, and patient cooperation with people, but by imposing his concepts and demanding absolute submission to his opinion. Whoever opposed this concept or tried to prove his viewpoint, and the correctness of his position — was doomed to removal from the leading collective and to subsequent moral and physical annihilation. This was especially true during the period following the 17th party congress, when many prominent party leaders and rank-and-file party workers, honest and dedicated to the cause of communism, fell victim to Stalin's despotism. . . .

. . . Lenin's traits — patient work with people; stubborn and painstaking education of them; the ability to induce people to follow him without using compulsion, but rather through the ideological influence on them of the whole collective — were entirely foreign to Stalin. He (Stalin) discarded the Leninist method of convincing and educating; he abandoned the method of ideological struggle for that of administrative violence, mass repressions, and terror. He acted on an increasingly larger scale and more stubbornly through punitive organs, at the same time often violating all existing norms of morality and of Soviet laws. . . .

During Lenin's life party congresses were convened regularly; always when a radical turn in the development of the party and the country took place Lenin considered it absolutely necessary that the party discuss at length all the basic matters pertaining to internal and foreign policy and to questions bearing on the development of party and government. . . .

Were our party's holy Leninist principles observed after the death of Vladimir Ilyich?

From U.S. Congress, *Congressional Record,* 84th Congress, 2nd Session, 1956, CII, pp. 9389–9403, passim.

Whereas during the first few years after Lenin's death party congresses and central committee plenums took place more or less regularly; later, when Stalin began increasingly to abuse his power, these principles were brutally violated. This was especially evident during the last 15 years of his life. Was it a normal situation when 13 years elapsed between the 18th and 19th party congresses, years during which our party and our country had experienced so many important events? These events demanded categorically that the party should have passed resolutions pertaining to the country's defense during the patriotic war and to peacetime construction after the war. Even after the end of the war a congress was not convened for over 7 years.

Central committee plenums were hardly ever called. It should be sufficient to mention that during all the years of the patriotic war not a single central committee plenum took place. . . .

In practice Stalin ignored the norms of party life and trampled on the Leninist principle of collective party leadership. . . .

Facts prove that many abuses were made on Stalin's orders without reckoning with any norms of party and Soviet legality. Stalin was a very distrustful man. . . . He could look at a man and say: "Why are your eyes so shifty today," or "Why are you turning so much today and avoiding to look me directly in the eyes?" The sickly suspicion created in him a general distrust even toward eminent party workers whom he had known for years. Everywhere and in everything he saw enemies, "two-facers" and spies.

Possessing unlimited power he indulged in great willfulness and choked a person morally and physically. A situation was created where one could not express one's own will. . . .

The willfulness of Stalin showed itself not only in decisions concerning the internal life of the country but also in the international relations of the Soviet Union.

The July plenum of the Central Committee studied in detail the reasons for the development of conflict with Yugoslavia. It was a shameful role which Stalin played here. The "Yugoslav affair" contained no problems which could not have been solved through party discussions among comrades. There was no significant basis for the development of this "affair"; it was completely possible to have prevented the rupture of relations with that country. This does not mean, however, that the Yugoslav leaders did not make mistakes or did not have shortcomings. But these mistakes and shortcomings were magnified in a monstrous manner by Stalin, which resulted in a break of relations with a friendly country.

I recall the first days when the conflict between the Soviet Union and Yugoslavia began artificially to be blown up. Once, when I came from Kiev to Moscow, I was invited to visit Stalin who, pointing to the copy of a letter lately sent to Tito, asked me, "Have you read this?"

Not waiting for my reply he answered, "I will shake my little finger and there will be no more Tito. He will fall."

We have dearly paid for this "shaking of the little finger." This statement reflected Stalin's mania for greatness, but he acted just that way: "I shall shake my little finger and there will be no Kossior"; "I will shake my little finger once more and Postyshev and Chubar will be no more"; "I will shake my little finger again and Voznesensky, Kuznetsov and many others will disappear."

But this did not happen to Tito. No matter how much or how little Stalin shook, not only his little finger but everything else that he could shake, Tito did not fall. Why? The reason was that, in this case of disagreement with the Yugoslav comrades, Tito had behind him a state and a people who had gone through a severe school of fighting for liberty and independence, a people which gave support to its leaders.

You see to what Stalin's mania for greatness led. He had completely lost consciousness of reality; he demonstrated his suspicion and haughtiness not only in relation to individuals in the U.S.S.R., but in relation to whole parties and nations.

We have carefully examined the case of Yugoslavia and have found a proper solution which is approved by the peoples of the Soviet Union and of Yugoslavia as well as by the working masses of all the people's democracies and by all progressive humanity. The liquidation of the abnormal relationship with Yugoslavia was done in the interest of the whole camp of socialism, in the interest of strengthening peace in the whole world. . . .

If we are to consider this matter as Marxists and as Leninists, then we have to state unequivocally that the leadership practice which came into being during the last years of Stalin's life became a serious obstacle in the path of Soviet social development.

Stalin often failed for months to take up some unusually important problems concerning the life of the party and of the state whose solution could not be postponed. During Stalin's leadership our peaceful relations with other nations were often threatened, because one-man decisions could cause and often did cause great complications.

In the last years, when we managed to free ourselves of the harmful practice of the cult of the individual and took several proper steps in the sphere of internal and external policies, everyone saw how activity grew before their very eyes, how the creative activity of the broad working masses developed, how favorably all this acted upon the development of economy and of culture. [Applause.]

Some comrades may ask us: Where were the members of the Political Bureau of the Central Committee? Why did they not assert themselves against the cult of the individual in time? And why is this being done only now?

First of all we have to consider the fact that the members of the Political Bureau viewed these matters in a different way at different times. Initially, many of them backed Stalin actively because Stalin was one of the strongest Marxists and his logic, his strength, and his will greatly influenced the cadres and party work. . . .

. . . Later, however, abusing his power more and more, [Stalin] began to fight eminent party and government leaders and to use terroristic methods against honest Soviet people. . . .

It is clear that such conditions put every member of the Political Bureau in a very difficult situation. And when we also consider the fact that in the last years the Central Committee plenary sessions were not convened, and that the sessions of the Political Bureau occurred only occasionally, from time to time, then we will understand how difficult it was for any member of the Political Bureau to take a stand against one or another unjust or improper procedure, against serious errors and shortcomings in the practices of leadership. . . .

Comrades, we must abolish the cult of the individual decisively, once and for all; we must draw the proper conclusions concerning both ideological-theoretical and practical work.

It is necessary for this purpose:

First, in a Bolshevik manner to condemn and to eradicate the cult of the individual as alien to Marxism-Leninism and not consonant with the principles of party leadership and the norms of party life, and to fight inexorably all attempts at bringing back this practice. . . .

Secondly, to continue systematically and consistently the work done by the party's central committee during the last years, a work characterized by minute observation in all party organizations, from the bottom to the top, of the Leninist principles of party leadership, characterized, above al., by the main principle of collective leadership, characterized by the observation of the norms of party life described in the statutes of our party, and, finally, characterized by the wide practice of criticism and self-criticism.

Thirdly, to restore completely the Leninist principles of Soviet Socialist democracy, expressed in the constitution of the Soviet Union, to fight willfulness of individuals abusing their power. The evil caused by acts violating revolutionary Socialist legality which have accumulated during a long time as a result of the negative influence of the cult of the individual has to be completely corrected. . . .

We are absolutely certain that our party, armed with the historical resolutions of the 20th Congress, will lead the Soviet people along the Leninist path to new successes, to new victories. [Tumultuous, prolonged applause.]

Long live the victorious banner of our party — Leninism. [Tumultuous, prolonged applause ending in ovation. All rise.]

83

The Brezhnev Doctrine

Early in 1968, under the leadership of Alexander Dubček, the Czechoslovakian Communist Party introduced a number of reforms, including the abolition of censorship. Dubček's "Prague Spring," though endorsed in Czechoslovakia, was considered heretical and threatening by Moscow and key allies. In a quick, well-planned invasion, Soviet, East German, Hungarian, Polish, and Bulgarian military units occupied Czechoslovakia on the night of August 21, 1968. Dubček was spirited out of the country and the "Prague Spring" was over. Later, in November 1968, speaking before Polish workers, Soviet leader Leonid Brezhnev (1906–1982) justified the invasion of Czechoslovakia and explained to the world why the Soviet Union had the right to invade any socialist country threatened by internal "anti-socialist forces."

QUESTIONS TO CONSIDER

1. Are there any parallels between the Brezhnev Doctrine and the Monroe Doctrine? Why? Why not? (See Reading 32.)
2. Václav Havel is in many ways Alexander Dubček's protégé (see Reading 99). Does Mr. Havel still take the Brezhnev Doctrine seriously?

In connection with the events in Czechoslovakia, the question of the correlation and interdependence of the national interests of the socialist countries and their international duties acquire particular topical and acute importance.

The measures taken by the Soviet Union, jointly with other socialist countries, in defending the socialist gains of the Czechoslovak people are of great significance for strengthening the socialist community, which is the main achievement of the international working class.

We cannot ignore the assertions, held in some places, that the actions of the five socialist countries run counter to the Marxist-Leninist principle of sovereignty and the rights of nations to self-determination.

The groundlessness of such reasoning consists primarily in that it is based on an abstract, nonclass approach to the question of sovereignty and the rights of nations to self-determination.

The peoples of the socialist countries and Communist parties certainly do have and should have freedom for determining the ways of advance of their respective countries.

However, none of their decisions should damage either socialism in their country or the fundamental interests of other socialist countries, and the whole working class movement, which is working for socialism.

This means that each Communist party is responsible not only to its own people, but also to all the socialist countries, to the entire Communist movement. Whoever forget this, in stressing only the independence of the Communist party, becomes one-sided. He deviates from his international duty.

Marxist dialectics are opposed to one-sidedness. They demand that each phenomenon be examined concretely, in general connection with other phenomena, with other processes.

Just as, in Lenin's words, a man living in a society cannot be free from the society, one or another socialist state, staying in a system of other states composing the socialist community, cannot be free from the common interests of that community.

The sovereignty of each socialist country cannot be opposed to the interests of the world of socialism, of the world revolutionary movement. Lenin demanded that all Communists fight against small-nation narrow-mindedness, seclusion and isolation, consider the whole and the general, subordinate the particular to the general interest.

From *Pravda*, September 25, 1968; translated by Novosti, Soviet press agency. Reprinted in L. S. Stavrianos, *The Epic of Man* (Englewood Cliffs, NJ: Prentice-Hall, 1971), pp. 465–466.

The socialist states respect the democratic norms of international law. They have proved this more than once in practice, by coming out resolutely against the attempts of imperialism to violate the sovereignty and independence of nations.

It is from these same positions that they reject the leftist, adventurist conception of "exporting revolution," of "bringing happiness" to other peoples.

However, from a Marxist point of view, the norms of law, including the norms of mutual relations of the socialist countries, cannot be interpreted narrowly, formally, and in isolation from the general context of class struggle in the modern world. The socialist countries resolutely come out against the exporting and importing of counterrevolution.

Each Communist party is free to apply the basic principles of Marxism-Leninism and of socialism in its country, but it cannot depart from these principles (assuming, naturally, that it remains a Communist party).

Concretely, this means, first of all, that, in its activity, each Communist party cannot but take into account such a decisive fact of our time as the struggle between two opposing social systems — capitalism and socialism.

This is an objective struggle, a fact not depending on the will of the people, and stipulated by the world's being split into two opposite social systems. Lenin said: "Each man must choose between joining our side or the other side. Any attempt to avoid taking sides in this issue must end in fiasco."

It has got to be emphasized that when a socialist country seems to adopt a "non-affiliated" stand, it retains its national independence, in effect, precisely because of the might of the socialist community, and above all the Soviet Union as a central force, which also includes the might of its armed forces. The weakening of any of the links in the world system of socialism directly affects all the socialist countries, which cannot look indifferently upon this.

The antisocialist elements in Czechoslovakia actually covered up the demand for so-called neutrality and Czechoslovakia's withdrawal from the socialist community with talking about the right of nations to self-determination.

However, the implementation of such "self-determination," in other words, Czechoslovakia's detachment from the socialist community, would have come into conflict with its own vital interests and would have been detrimental to the other socialist states.

Such "self-determination," as a result of which NATO troops would have been able to come up to the Soviet border, while the community of European socialist countries would have been split, in effect encroaches upon the vital interests of the peoples of these countries and conflicts, as the very root of it, with the right of these people to socialist self-determination.

Discharging their internationalist duty toward the fraternal peoples of Czechoslovakia and defending their own socialist gains, the U.S.S.R. and the other socialist states had to act decisively and they did act against the antisocialist forces in Czechoslovakia.

Decolonization: Africa

Changes in the developing countries of Africa, Latin America, and Asia have shaped much of the history of the second half of the twentieth century. In the first two decades following World War II, one-third of the world's population threw off colonial rule. Between 1945 and 1980, more than 90 new nations joined the ranks of independent countries. For some new nations, the transition was relatively easy; others found the process painful, deceptive, and fraught with bloodshed and economic failure.

For Algeria (1962), Egypt (1956), and India (1947), the quest for independence led to an assault on French or British colonial rule. During the same period, countries such as Mao Tse-tung's (Mao Zedong) China (1949) and Fidel Castro's Cuba (1959) were undergoing profound social and economic revolutions. In other cases, such as Uganda and Vietnam, the overthrow of colonial rule has been followed by revolution.

France and Great Britain, two Western powers that built huge colonial empires in the nineteenth century, saw their empires collapse in the decades following World War II. This was due in part to the costs of fighting the war. By 1945, Britain was nearly bankrupt and France, though nominally a victor, was afflicted with the psychological wounds of defeat and the stigma of having collaborated with German occupiers. The last day of the European War, May 8, 1945, marked the first day of French-controlled Algeria's struggle for independence — a struggle that continued for 17 years, at a cost of 750,000 lives. A year later, in 1946, Ho Chi Minh broke off negotiations with France, and for the next eight years he directed a guerrilla insurgency that won independence for North Vietnam in 1954 at a cost of hundreds of thousands of Vietnamese lives and over 90,000 soldiers of the French Indochina Army.

The following selections suggest some of the differing perspectives on decolonization, apartheid — a lingering effect of colonization — and Third World revolution, particularly during the critical decade of the 1960s.

84

A. L. Geyer, "The Case for Apartheid"

The policy of *apartheid* — separate development rather than decolonization — was the choice of the Republic of South Africa in dealing with its black, African-majority population. In the following document, a speech given before the Rotary Club of London on August 19, 1953, a supporter of apartheid explains why it is the best policy for all races in South Africa.

QUESTIONS TO CONSIDER

1. Can the case for *apartheid* be made using the historical and anthropological arguments presented in the speech?
2. If *apartheid* is but a variant form of African racism, why is it that the racial problems of South Africa are so widely reported and the racial problems of Uganda are not (see Reading 87)?

As one of the aftermaths of the last war, many people seem to suffer from a neurotic guilt-complex with regard to colonies. This has led to a strident denunciation of the Black African's wrongs, real or imaginary, under the white man's rule in Africa. It is a denunciation, so shrill and emotional, that the vast debt owed by Black Africa to those same white men is lost sight of (and, incidentally, the Black African is encouraged to forget that debt). Confining myself to that area of which I know at least a very little, Africa south of the Equator, I shall say this without fear of reasonable contradiction: every millimetre of progress in all that vast area is due entirely to the White Man.

You are familiar with the cry that came floating over the ocean from the West — a cry that "colonialism" is outmoded and pernicious, a cry that is being vociferously echoed by a certain gentleman in the East. (This refers to Jawaharlal Nehru, Prime Minister of India.)

May I point out that African colonies are of comparatively recent date. Before that time Black Africa did have independence for a thousand years and more — and what did she make of it? One problem, I admit, she did solve most effectively. There was no over-population. Interminable savage intertribal wars, witchcraft, disease, famine, and even cannibalism saw to that.

Let me turn to my subject, to that part of Africa south of the Sahara, which, historically, is not part of Black Africa at all — my own country. Its position is unique in Africa as its racial problem is unique in the world.

1. South Africa is no more the original home of its black Africans, the Bantu, than it is of its white Africans. Both races went there as colonists and, what is more, as practically contemporary colonists. In some parts the Bantu arrived first, in other parts the Europeans were the first comers.
2. South Africa contains the only independent white nation in all Africa — a South African nation which has no other homeland to which it could retreat; a nation which has created a highly developed modern state, and which occupies a position of inestimable importance.
3. South Africa is the only independent country in the world in which white people are outnumbered by black people. Including all coloured races or peoples, the proportion in Brazil is 20 to 1. In South Africa it is 1 to 4.

This brings me to the question of the future. To me there seems to be two possible lines of development: *Apartheid* or Partnership. Partnership means cooperation

From *Union of South Africa Government: Information Pamphlet* (New York, 1953), reprinted in Ruth E. Gordon and Clive Talbot, eds., *From Dias to Vorster: Source Material on South African History, 1488–1975* (Goodwood, S.A.: Nasou, n.d.), pp. 409–410. Reprinted by permission.

of the individual citizens within a single community, irrespective of race. . . . (It) demands that there shall be no discrimination whatsoever in trade and industry, in the professions and the Public Service. Therefore, whether a man is black or a white African, must according to this policy be as irrelevant as whether in London a man is a Scotsman or an Englishman. I take it that Partnership must also aim at the eventual disappearance of all social segregation based on race. This policy of Partnership admittedly does not envisage immediate adult suffrage. Obviously, however, the loading of the franchise in order to exclude the great majority of the Bantu could be no more than a temporary expedient. . . . (In effect) "there must one day be black domination, in the sense that power must pass to the immense African majority." Need I say more to show that this policy of Partnership could, in South Africa, only mean the eventual disappearance of the white South African nation? And will you be greatly surprised if I tell you that this white nation is not prepared to commit national suicide, not even by slow poisoning?

The only alternative is a policy of *apartheid*, the policy of separate development. The germ of this policy is inherent in almost all of our history, implanted there by the force of circumstances. . . . *Apartheid* is a policy of self-preservation. We make no apology for possessing that very natural urge. But it is more than that. It is an attempt at self-preservation in a manner that will also enable the Bantu to develop fully as a separate people.

We believe that, for a long time to come, political power will have to remain with the whites, also in the interest of our still very immature Bantu. But we believe also, in the words of a statement by the Dutch Reformed Church in 1950, a Church that favours *apartheid*, that "no people in the world worth their salt, would be content indefinitely with no say or only indirect say in the affairs of the State or in the country's socio-economic organisation in which decisions are taken about their interests and their future."

The immediate aim is, therefore, to keep the races outside the Bantu areas apart as far as possible, to continue the process of improving the conditions and standards of living of the Bantu, and to give them greater responsibility for their own local affairs. At the same time the long-range aim is to develop the Bantu areas both agriculturally and industrially, with the object of making these areas in every sense the national home of the Bantu — areas in which their interests are paramount, in which to an ever greater degree all professional and other positions are to be occupied by them, and in which they are to receive progressively more and more autonomy.

85

Desmond Tutu, "The Question of South Africa"

Desmond Tutu (1931 —) was elected the first black Archbishop of Cape Town in 1986. In recognition of his leadership in seeking racial justice in South Africa, he was awarded the Nobel Peace Prize in 1984. Shortly after receiving the Nobel Prize, Tutu gave the following speech, attacking South Africa's racial policies, to the United Nations Security Council. Although he commends South African President P. W. Botha for signing the non-aggression pact (the Nkomati Accords of 1984) between South Africa and Mozambique, he is not as sanguine about the future of race relations within South Africa. His reference to the "KTC squatter camps" probably indicates a transient camp that derives its name from a nearby KTC General Dealer Store.

QUESTIONS TO CONSIDER

1. What specific steps does Archbishop Tutu urge to overcome apartheid?
2. Do the apartheid laws apply only to black South Africans? What other groups are affected by these laws? Why?

I speak out of a full heart, for I am about to speak about a land that I love deeply and passionately; a beautiful land of rolling hills and gurgling streams, of clear starlit skies, of singing birds, and gamboling lambs; a land God has richly endowed with the good things of the earth, a land rich in mineral deposits of nearly every kind; a land of vast open spaces, enough to accommodate all its inhabitants comfortably; a land capable of feeding itself and other lands on the beleaguered continent of Africa, a veritable breadbasket; a land that could contribute wonderfully to the material and spiritual development and prosperity of all Africa and indeed of the whole world. It is endowed with enough to satisfy the material and spiritual needs of all its peoples.

And so we would expect that such a land, veritably flowing with milk and honey, should be a land where peace and harmony and contentment reigned supreme. Alas, the opposite is the case. For my beloved country is wracked by division, by alienation, by animosity, by separation, by injustice, by avoidable pain and suffering. It is a deeply fragmented society, ridden by fear and anxiety, covered by a pall of despondency and a sense of desperation, split up into hostile, warring factions.

It is a highly volatile land, and its inhabitants sit on a powder-keg with a very short fuse indeed, ready to blow us all up into kingdom-come. There is endemic unrest, like a festering sore that will not heal until not just the symptoms are treated but the root causes are removed.

South African society is deeply polarized. Nothing illustrates this more sharply than the events of the past week. While the black community was in the seventh heaven of delight because of the decision of that committee in Oslo, and while the world was congratulating the recipient of the Nobel Peace Prize, the white government and most white South Africans, very sadly, were seeking to devalue that prize. An event that should have been the occasion of uninhibited joy and thanksgiving revealed a sadly divided society.

Before I came to this country in early September to go on sabbatical, I visited one of the trouble-spots near Johannesburg. I went with members of the Executive Committee of the South African Council of Churches, which had met in emergency session after I had urged Mr. P. W. Botha to meet with church leaders

From Bishop Desmond Tutu, "The Question of South Africa," *Africa Report,* 30 (January–February 1985), pp. 50–52. Originally a statement to the United Nations Security Council, October 23, 1984.

to deal with a rapidly deteriorating situation. As a result of our peace initiative, we did get to meet with two cabinet ministers, demonstrating thereby our concern to carry out our call to be ministers of reconciliation and ambassadors of Christ.

In this black township, we met an old lady who told us that she was looking after her grandchildren and the children of neighbors while they were at work. On the day about which she was speaking, the police had been chasing black schoolchildren in that street, but the children had eluded the police, who then drove down the street past the old lady's house. Her wards were playing in front of the house, in the yard. She was sitting in the kitchen at the back, when her daughter burst in, calling agitatedly for her. She rushed out into the living room. A grandson had fallen just inside the door, dead. The police had shot him in the back. He was six years old. Recently a baby, a few weeks old, became the first white casualty of the current uprisings. Every death is one too many. Those whom the black community has identified as collaborators with a system that oppresses them and denies them the most elementary human rights have met cruel death, which we deplore as much as any others. They have rejected these people operating within the system, whom they have seen as lackies and stooges, despite their titles of town councilors, and so on, under an apparently new dispensation extending the right of local government to the blacks.

Over 100,000 black students are out of school, boycotting — as they did in 1976 — what they and the black community perceive as an inferior education designed deliberately for inferiority. An already highly volatile situation has been ignited several times and, as a result, over 80 persons have died. There has been industrial unrest, with the first official strike by black miners taking place, not without its toll of fatalities among the blacks.

Some may be inclined to ask : But why should all this unrest be taking place just when the South African government appears to have embarked on the road of reform, exemplified externally by the signing of the Nkomati accord and internally by the implementation of a new constitution which appears to depart radically from the one it replaces, for it makes room for three chambers : one for whites, one for Coloureds, and one for Indians ; a constitution described by many as a significant step forward ?

I wish to state here, as I have stated on other occasions, that Mr. P. W. Botha must be commended for his courage in declaring that the future of South Africa could no longer be determined by whites only. That was a very brave thing to do. The tragedy of South Africa is that something with such a considerable potential for resolving the burgeoning crisis of our land should have been vitiated by the exclusion of 73 percent of the population, the overwhelming majority in the land.

By no stretch of the imagination could that kind of constitution be considered to be democratic. The composition of the committees, in the ratio of four whites to two Coloureds to one Indian, demonstrates eloquently what most people had suspected all along — that it was intended to perpetuate the rule of a minority. The fact that the first qualification for membership in the chambers is racial says that this constitution was designed to entrench racism and ethnicity. The most obnoxious features of apartheid would remain untouched and unchanged. The Group Areas Act, the Population Registration Act, separate educational systems for the different race groups ; all this and more would remain quite unchanged.

This constitution was seen by the mainline English-speaking churches and the official white opposition as disastrously inadequate, and they called for its rejection in the whites-only referendum last November. The call was not heeded. The blacks overwhelmingly rejected what they regarded as a sham, an instrument in the politics of exclusion. Various groups campaigned for a boycott of the Coloured and Indian elections — campaigned, I might add, against very great odds, by and large peacefully. As we know, the authorities responded with their usual iron-fist tactics, detaining most of the leaders of the United Democratic Front (UDF) and other organizations that had organized the boycott — and we have some of them now holed up in the British Consulate in Durban, causing a diplomatic contretemps. . . .

As blacks we often run the gauntlet of roadblocks on roads leading into our townships, and these have been manned by the army in what are actually described as routine police operations. When you use the army in this fashion, who is the enemy?

The authorities have not stopped stripping blacks of their South African citizenship. Here I am, 53 years old, a bishop in the church, some would say reasonably responsible; I travel on a document that says of my nationality that it is "undeterminable at present." The South African government is turning us into aliens in the land of our birth. It continues unabated with its vicious policy of forced population removals. It is threatening to remove the people of Kwa Ngema. It treats carelessly the women in the KTC squatter camp near Cape Town whose flimsy plastic coverings are destroyed every day by the authorities; and the heinous crime of those women is that they want to be with their husbands, with the fathers of their children.

White South Africans are not demons; they are ordinary human beings, scared human beings, many of them; who would not be, if they were outnumbered five to one? Through this lofty body I wish to appeal to my white fellow South Africans to share in building a new society, for blacks are not intent on driving whites into the sea but on claiming only their rightful place in the sun in the land of their birth.

We deplore all forms of violence, the violence of an oppressive and unjust society and the violence of those seeking to overthrow that society, for we believe that violence is not the answer to the crisis of our land.

We dream of a new society that will be truly non-racial, truly democratic, in which people count because they are created in the image of God.

We are committed to work for justice, for peace, and for reconciliation. We ask you, please help us; urge the South African authorities to go to the conference table with the . . . representatives of all sections of our community. I appeal to this body to act. I appeal in the name of the ordinary, the little people of South Africa. I appeal in the name of the squatters in crossroads and in the KTC camp. I appeal on behalf of the father who has to live in a single-sex hostel as a migrant worker, separated from his family for 11 months of the year. I appeal on behalf of the students who have rejected this travesty of education made available only for blacks. I appeal on behalf of those who are banned arbitrarily, who are banished, who are detained without trial, those imprisoned because they have had a vision of this new South Africa. I appeal on behalf of those who have been exiled from their homes.

I say we will be free, and we ask you: Help us, that this freedom comes for all of us in South Africa, black and white, but that it comes with the least possible violence, that it comes peacefully, that it comes soon.

86

Kwame Nkrumah, Statement of African Unity

Kwame Nkrumah (1909–1972) led the former British colony of the Gold Coast to become the independent country of Ghana in 1957. Until he was overthrown by a coup d'état in 1966, Kwame Nkrumah was one of Africa's most influential leaders.

QUESTIONS TO CONSIDER

1. Why would Kwame Nkrumah's dreams of African unity have so little appeal for modern African political leaders?
2. Is the dream of African unity too idealistic? Why? Why not?

For centuries, Europeans dominated the African continent. The white man arrogated to himself the right to rule and to be obeyed by the non-white; his mission, he claimed was to 'civilise' Africa. Under this cloak, the Europeans robbed the continent of vast riches and inflicted unimaginable suffering on the African people.

All this makes a sad story, but now we must be prepared to bury the past with its unpleasant memories and look to the future. All we ask of the former colonial powers is their goodwill and co-operation to remedy past mistakes and injustices and to grant independence to the colonies in Africa. . . .

It is clear that we must find an African solution to our problems, and that this can only be found in African unity. Divided we are weak; united, Africa could become one of the greatest forces for good in the world.

Although most Africans are poor, our continent is potentially extremely rich. Our mineral resources, which are being exploited with foreign capital only to enrich foreign investors, range from gold and diamonds to uranium and petroleum. Our forests contain some of the finest woods to be grown anywhere. Our cash crops include cocoa, coffee, rubber, tobacco and cotton. As for power, which is an important factor in any economic development, Africa contains over 40% of the total potential water power of the world, as compared with about 10% in Europe and 13% in North America. Yet so far, less than 1% has been developed. This is one of the reasons why we have in Africa the paradox of poverty in the midst of plenty, and scarcity in the midst of abundance.

Never before have a people had within their grasp so great an opportunity for developing a continent endowed with so much wealth. Individually, the independent states of Africa, some of them potentially rich, others poor, can do little for their people. Together, by mutual help, they can achieve much. But the economic development of the continent must be planned and pursued as a whole. A loose confederation designed only for economic cooperation would not provide the necessary unity of purpose. Only a strong political union can bring about full and effective development of our natural resources for the benefit of our people.

The political situation in Africa today is heartening and at the same time disturbing. It is heartening to see so many new flags hoisted in place of the old ; it is disturbing to see so many countries of varying sizes and at different levels of development, weak and, in some cases, almost helpless. If this terrible state of fragmentation is allowed to continue it may well be disastrous for us all.

There are at present some 28 states in Africa, excluding the Union of South Africa, and those countries not yet free. No less than nine of these states have a population of less than three million. Can we seriously believe that the colonial powers meant these countries to be independent, viable states? The example of South America, which has as much wealth, if not more than North America, and yet remains weak and dependent on outside interests, is one which every African would do well to study.

Critics of African unity often refer to the wide differences in culture, language and ideas in various parts of Africa. This is true, but the essential fact remains that we are all Africans, and have a common interest in the independence of Africa. The difficulties presented by questions of language, culture and different political systems are not insuperable. If the need for political union is agreed by us all, then the will to create it is born ; and where there's a will there's a way.

The present leaders of Africa have already shown a remarkable willingness to consult and seek advice among themselves. Africans have, indeed, begun to think continentally. They realise that they have much in common, both in their past history, in their present problems and in their future hopes. To suggest that the time is not yet ripe for considering a political union of Africa is to evade the facts and ignore realities in Africa today.

The greatest contribution that Africa can make to the peace of the world is to avoid all the dangers inherent in disunity, by creating a political union which will also by its success, stand as an example to a divided world. A union of African states will project more effectively the African personality. It will command respect from a world that has regard only for size and influence. The scant attention paid to African opposition to the French atomic tests in the Sahara, and the ignominious spectacle of the U.N. in the Congo quibbling about constitutional niceties while the Republic was tottering into anarchy, are evidence of the callous disregard of African Independence by the Great Powers.

We have to prove that greatness is not to be measured in stock piles of atom bombs. I believe strongly and sincerely that with the deep-rooted wisdom and dignity, the innate respect for human lives, the intense humanity that is our heritage, the African race, united under one federal government, will emerge not as just another world bloc to flaunt its wealth and strength, but as a Great Power whose greatness is indestructible because it is built not on fear, envy and suspicion, nor won at the expense of others, but founded on hope, trust, friendship and directed to the good of all mankind.

The emergence of such a mighty stabilising force in this strife-worn world should be regarded not as the shadowy dream of a visionary, but as a practical proposition, which the peoples of Africa can, and should, translate into reality.

There is a tide in the affairs of every people when the moment strikes for political action. Such was the moment in the history of the United States of America when the Founding Fathers saw beyond the petty wranglings of the separate states and created a Union. This is our chance. We must act now. Tomorrow may be too late and the opportunity will have passed, and with it the hope of free Africa's survival.

87

Thomas and Margaret Melady, *Idi Amin Dada: Hitler in Africa*

In Africa, decolonization often brought a drive toward Africanization and unleashed a powerful sense of xenophobia. An extreme example of this occurred in Uganda after Idi Amin, an ex-sergeant, engineered a successful coup and seized power in January 1971. He installed an authoritarian military regime which initiated many years of terror and lawlessness. In August 1972, he announced that all Asians (many of whom had settled there during the colonial era and were Ugandan citizens) would be required to leave the country within three months. By the end of the year, 90 percent of the Asians had left the country. The following account, written by the U.S. Ambassador and his wife, provides a glimpse into the nature of Amin's Uganda.

QUESTIONS TO CONSIDER

1. What is the meaning of *kondoism,* and how did Amin use it as an effective instrument of control?
2. What were the causes of the tensions between Africans and Asians, and why did Amin focus on the Asians as scapegoats?
3. Discuss and consider the British response to Asian resettlement. Why did so few countries respond and offer resettlement to the Asian refugees?

Kondoism In Uganda

In 1972, the killings in the military barracks died down. The Acholi and Langi members had been virtually eliminated.[1] The civilian disappearances, however, continued sporadically. William Kalema, minister of commerce and industry

Thomas and Margaret Melady, *Idi Amin Dada : Hitler in Africa* (Kansas City, MO : Sheed & Ward, 1977), pp. 36–37 ; 80–84, passim. Thomas Melady was a specialist in African-Asian affairs and was appointed U.S. Ambassador to Uganda in 1972.

1. The Acholi and Langi are tribes of northern Uganda. In the year following Amin's coup, about two-thirds of the Langi and Acholi soldiers who made up 40 percent of the military force were killed.

under Obote,[2] who had been outside Uganda during the coup, decided to return believing that there would be no reprisals against those who had served in the Obote government. He was driving in his car when another car approached and forced him to stop. He was never seen again.

A district commissioner and a hotel manager were arrested after a dispute with army officers over the payment of a hotel bill for drinks. They both disappeared. Three employees of the Coffee Marketing Board disappeared. A prominent Asian lawyer was arrested by two men identified as members of the State Research Department. Another Coffee Marketing Board worker vanished. These and other disappearances, arrests, and killings were carried out by the military police, the Public Safety Unit (a special police force), and the State Research Bureau (an intelligence unit).

In June 1972, a month before we arrived, George Kamba, a former ambassador to India and West Germany who served in the Amin government as director of the East African Posts and Telecommunications Corporation, was arrested while attending an official cocktail party at the International Hotel in Kampala. A witness told that Kamba, after leaving the hotel at about 10 P.M., came running back screaming for help. Three men with dark glasses followed him in and dragged him off. Kamba pleaded for help, shouting that they were going to kill him. Many leading personalities, including ministers, witnessed the seizure, but none could help. The men were armed and were believed to be part of Amin's State Research Bureau.

The official reaction of the government to these murders followed a pattern. First the government acknowledged the disappearance and ordered an investigation. The investigations usually revealed nothing, concluding that the people involved were missing and their whereabouts were unknown. In the case of Kamba's arrest, the official statement indicated that he was arrested by "unknown persons" and that extensive investigations had revealed nothing. Many people, unfortunately, believed these government explanations. . . .

In Uganda, roving bands of robbers were called *kondos.* Many Ugandans and foreigners had been victims of their attacks. The Uganda government under Milton Obote had tried to crack down on these criminals. In 1968, the punishment for robbery with violence was raised to that of a capital offense. With this severe punishment, Ugandan officials hoped to frighten *kondos* into refraining from violence. Some claimed that the severity of the law encouraged hardened criminals to be even more violent since they would be more likely to kill any witnesses to a robbery.

The existence of bands of criminals in Uganda made the atmosphere ripe for the soldiers to carry on their arbitrary arrests and killings under the guise of *kondoism.* The government issued two decrees in March 1971 that gave the military wide powers in searching and arresting. The decrees were described as a method of stemming the rampant *kondoism.* In effect, it legalized the killer squads of Amin, and also transformed some soldiers into *kondos.* Realizing that they had become the law, many soldiers found this an easy way to amass a small fortune. The police were rendered ineffective. . . .

2. Milton Obote, former President of Uganda.

Expulsion of the Asians

Among the masses, the Africans did not understand the Asians nor did the Asians comprehend their African neighbors. Asians complained about the Africans being lazy. They did not understand why they could not produce more. Some ridiculed the African who received an education, mostly on scholarship, and then landed a plush government job that paid well and required little effort. Others became particularly incensed by the existence of corruption in government. Having been pressured into giving bribes and payoffs for licenses and permits, many Asians believed that African politicians could only be expected to exploit their people.

The African, on the other hand, saw the Asian — particularly those who had sought British protected status — as draining the economy of Africa. They saw Asians use devious methods of transferring money out of Uganda. In our travels throughout Africa, we would frequently be approached by an Asian asking us to facilitate the transfer of money. A favorite method was selling something to a European or American in exchange for a personal check in U.S. currency to be sent directly to the Asian's overseas bank account.

There was indeed deep alienation. The Asian small businessmen were no different from any other minority group involved in trade. It seems to be a worldwide phenomenon to distrust and dislike the small trader particularly when the trader is a member of a racial or ethnic minority. The Chinese in Southeast Asia, the Lebanese in parts of Africa and Asia, and the Armenians have all been accused of the same self-protecting attitudes. . . .

The weekend of Amin's announcement of the expulsion edict in August 1972, passed quietly. The Asians hoped that Amin was just bluffing, but as the next work week began, it became apparent that he was dead serious. The high commissioner from Great Britain, Richard Slater, was asked by Amin to facilitate the departure of all Asians entitled to British passports. As with many decisions of Amin, the expulsion order was not thoroughly thought out. Consequently, Amin issued a series of statements amending the order. On August 22, it was announced that Asians with Ugandan passports would be allowed to stay. However, the announcement was qualified by Amin's promise to "weed out all those who got their citizenship through corruption or forgery."

The British High Commission, which is equivalent to an embassy in commonwealth countries, brought extra staff to deal with the problems of the exodus. Preparations for departure were long and tedious. Every emigré had to fill out several forms, have the necessary doctor's certificates and the required inoculations, and finally arrange to pay the air fare. All properties and businesses were registered in the hope that someday their owners would be compensated for what they left behind. They were only permitted to take some personal belongings and a mere 50 pounds (almost $120). Long lines appeared in front of the British high commissioner's office. Asians waited, documents in hand, from early morning to late at night. "Why should we wait in line and fill out so many forms in order to be allowed to go to England?" many thought. "We have British passports. Why are not all British passport holders treated in the same way?" According to the official British attitude, Britain had a responsibility for its "colored" subjects, but it did not want to take them right away and all at once. Amin, however, demanded that the British take the responsibility for these people who claimed to be British and arrange for their departure immediately. It was a hard pill to swallow, but the British government had no choice.

We remember picking up the *Uganda Argus,* the daily newspaper, and reading advertisements placed by various English towns and communities. The message of these ads was, "Don't come here. We are already overcrowded."

As the weeks wore on, Asians who thought they were Ugandan citizens were asked to check on their status. Many were told that their papers were not in order or that they had made application for citizenship after the deadline. Some officials blithely tore up the papers in front of the desperate Asians.

The diplomatic community became alarmed. The right of citizenship was being arbitrarily taken from a group of people who happened to be of another race and culture. Protests were made, but it had no effect. Britain appealed to other countries for assistance in aiding these Asians that were rendered stateless. Canada was the first nation to come to their rescue. Other European and some Latin American countries followed. I sent a number of telegrams back to Washington requesting that a special immigration quota be opened for Ugandan Asians.

The situation had become even worse. Fear had spread among the Asian community and rightly so. Ugandan soldiers searched the departing Asians completely and repeatedly. If an Asian was found with more money than allowed, not only was the money taken by the soldiers but he was often beaten mercilessly. Jewelry with precious stones was confiscated. Some women were forced to remove all clothing during the searches, and there were several reports of rape. One woman was taken off the plane at Nairobi and hospitalized after having been raped five times on the road from Kampala to the airport in Entebbe.

When the British government brought the matter of maltreatment before the United Nations, the Ugandan representative assured the world body that Ugandan soldiers and police would be stationed on the airport road to prevent any mishandling of the departing Asians. This was ludicrous. The entire diplomatic community in Kampala knew that the soldiers were responsible for the mistreatment and abuse. They had taken advantage of the situation to loot and steal from the Asians who had no way to defend their rights.

Asians who were leaving for India and Pakistan took the train from Kampala to Mombasa, Kenya. The soldiers inspecting these trains were particularly harsh. Many people were beaten, stoned, and robbed of even the mere 1,000 shillings they were permitted to take. Some were stripped naked and made to crawl through the train.

Even Asians who were Ugandan citizens panicked. Many wished to leave and went from embassy to embassy hoping to find someone to take them. By the end of September, halfway through the ninety-day period for departure, the United States government had not acted on a special quota for Asians. Asians knocked desperately on the embassy doors; but I had to tell them that I could only take applications in certain preference categories, and these would not be guaranteed entry. A mere seventy-seven Asians were granted visas under the normal immigration regulations.

Third World Perspectives

After the assassination of Mohandas K. Gandhi in 1948, Jawaharlal Nehru (1889–1964), who had been a close associate of Gandhi and was serving as prime minister of the newly independent Union of India, became the dominant figure in Indian government and politics. He presided over a constitutional convention through which the status of India was changed from dominion to republic, and he continued as India's prime minister until his death. A graduate of Cambridge University in England, Nehru communicated effectively with the Western media and remained the most widely cited spokesman for Asian and African countries until his death in 1964.

Nehru first coined the terms "neutralism," "Third World," and "nonaligned countries," which are important for an understanding of international relations today. "Neutralism," as stressed by Nehru in the 1950s, meant creating a positive set of moral values from a country's neutral stance in international conflicts. "Third World," in Nehru's speeches and writings, originally meant those countries that belonged neither to the Western industrial world nor to the Communist world. In the 1960s, however, "Third World" came to signify *all* the underdeveloped countries of Asia, Africa, and Latin America. A more drastic shift in meaning occurred with the term "nonalignment." Nehru originally presented "nonalignment" as the rational stance for developing nations to take, supporting neither the Soviet bloc nor the Western industrial countries. However, by the 1970s, it was evident that "nonaligned" meant not aligned with the West, but possibly aligned with the Soviet bloc. For example, in 1979 Fidel Castro, whose Cuba had supported the Soviet Union and opposed the United States in international relations for nearly 20 years, hosted a conference of the 95-member "Organization of Non-Aligned Nations" in Havana and was its president until 1982.

In the first section of the following reading, Nehru recounts how and why he came to lean toward the Communist side in international relations during India's struggle for independence from Britain. The second section, describing his concept of nonalignment, also illustrates the apparent double standard used by Nehru and subsequent Third World spokespersons in judging imperialism. This portion of the reading is from a speech in 1956. By "tragedies in Egypt and Hungary," Nehru refers to two major events of that year — the Suez crisis and the Hungarian Revolution. British, French, and Israeli armed forces had attempted to re-internationalize the Suez Canal after Egypt had unilaterally nationalized it. The invasion was condemned by the United Nations and the forces were withdrawn with minimal damage to Egypt. At the same time as this crisis in Suez, a revolution was taking place in Hungary. The Hungarians attained independence for a brief period of time but were overwhelmed by the Soviet Army with much destruction and loss of life. Despite Nehru's reference to this as a tragedy, neither he nor other Third World leaders pressed the United Nations for a condemnation of the Soviet Union.

88

Jawaharlal Nehru on Marxism and Nonalignment

QUESTIONS TO CONSIDER

1. What made Nehru's sympathies go "increasingly toward the communist side" during India's struggle for independence?
2. What led Nehru to believe that "a measure of political liberty" is not always important as a standard for judging governments?
3. What appeal does Marxism as a philosophy have for Nehru?
4. What developments does Nehru point to in order to show democratic principles at work in India?
5. Why does Nehru believe that the outcome of simultaneous "tragedies in Egypt and Hungary" has at least "one hopeful aspect"?

Marxism, Capitalism, and India's Future

As our struggle toned down and established itself at a low level, there was little of excitement in it, except at long intervals. My thoughts traveled more to other countries, and I watched and studied, as far as I could in jail, the world situation in the grip of the great depression. I read as many books as I could find on the subject, and the more I read the more fascinated I grew. India with her problems and struggles became just a part of this mighty world drama, of the great struggle of political and economic forces that was going on everywhere, nationally and internationally. In that struggle my own sympathies went increasingly toward the communist side.

I had long been drawn to socialism and communism, and Russia had appealed to me. Much in Soviet Russia I dislike — the ruthless suppression of all contrary opinion, the wholesale regimentation, the unnecessary violence (as I thought) in carrying out various policies. But there was no lack of violence and suppression in the capitalist world, and I realized more and more how the very basis and foundation of our acquisitive society and property was violence. Without violence it could not continue for many days. A measure of political liberty meant little indeed when the fear of starvation was always compelling the vast majority of people everywhere to submit to the will of the few, to the greater glory and advantage of the latter.

Violence was common in both places, but the violence of the capitalist order seemed inherent in it; while the violence of Russia, bad though it was, aimed at a new order based on peace and co-operation and real freedom for the masses. With

The first section of this reading is from *Toward Freedom : The Autobiography of Jawaharlal Nehru* (New York : John Day Co., 1941), pp. 228–231 ; reprinted by permission of Shri Rajiv Gandhi, copyright holder. The second section is from a speech in Washington, DC, December 18, 1956, printed in the U.S. *Department of State Bulletin*, January 14, 1957, pp. 49–50.

all her blunders, Soviet Russia had triumphed over enormous difficulties and taken great strides toward this new order. While the rest of the world was in the grip of the depression and going backward in some ways, in the Soviet country a great new world was being built up before our eyes. Russia, following the great Lenin, looked into the future and thought only of what was to be, while other countries lay numbed under the dead hand of the past and spent their energy in preserving the useless relics of a bygone age. In particular, I was impressed by the reports of the great progress made by the backward regions of Central Asia under the Soviet regime. In the balance, therefore, I was all in favor of Russia, and the presence and example of the Soviets was a bright and heartening phenomenon in a dark and dismal world.

But Soviet Russia's success or failure, vastly important as it was as a practical experiment in establishing a communist state, did not affect the soundness of the theory of communism. The Bolsheviks may blunder or even fail because of national or international reasons, and yet the communist theory may be correct. On the basis of that very theory it was absurd to copy blindly what had taken place in Russia, for its application depended on the particular conditions prevailing in the country in question and the stage of its historical development. Besides, India, or any other country, could profit by the triumphs as well as the inevitable mistakes of the Bolsheviks. Perhaps the Bolsheviks had tried to go too fast because, surrounded as they were by a world of enemies, they feared external aggression. A slower tempo might avoid much of the misery caused in the rural areas. But then the question arose if really radical results could be obtained by slowing down the rate of change. Reformism was an impossible solution of any vital problem at a critical moment when the basic structure had to be changed, and, however slow the progress might be later on, the initial step must be a complete break with the existing order, which had fulfilled its purpose and was now only a drag on future progress.

In India, only a revolutionary plan could solve the two related questions of the land and industry as well as almost every other major problem before the country. . . .

Russia apart, the theory and philosophy of Marxism lightened up many a dark corner of my mind. History came to have a new meaning for me. The Marxist interpretation threw a flood of light on it, and it became an unfolding drama with some order and purpose, howsoever unconscious, behind it. In spite of the appalling waste and misery of the past and the present, the future was bright with hope, though many dangers intervened. It was the essential freedom from dogma and the scientific outlook of Marxism that appealed to me. It was true that there was plenty of dogma in official communism in Russia and elsewhere, and frequently heresy hunts were organized. That seemed to be deplorable, though it was not difficult to understand in view of the tremendous changes taking place rapidly in the Soviet countries when effective opposition might have resulted in catastrophic failure.

The great world crisis and slump seemed to justify the Marxist analysis. While all other systems and theories were groping about in the dark, Marxism alone explained it more or less satisfactorily and offered a real solution.

As this conviction grew upon me, I was filled with a new excitement, and my depression at the nonsuccess of civil disobedience grew much less. Was not the world marching rapidly toward the desired consummation? There were grave dangers of wars and catastrophes, but at any rate we were moving. There was no stagnation. Our national struggle became a stage in the longer journey, and it was as well that repression and suffering were tempering our people for future struggles and forcing them to consider the new ideas that were stirring the world. We would be the stronger and the more disciplined and hardened by the elimination of the weaker elements. Time was in our favor.

Economic Development and Nonalignment

We are now engaged in a gigantic and exciting task of achieving rapid and large-scale economic development of our country. Such development, in an ancient and underdeveloped country such as India, is only possible with purposive planning. True to our democratic principles and traditions, we seek, in free discussion and consultation as well as in implementation, the enthusiasm and the willing and active cooperation of our people. We completed our first Five-Year Plan 8 months ago, and now we have begun on a more ambitious scale our second Five-Year Plan, which seeks a planned development in agriculture and industry, town and country, and between factory and small-scale and cottage production. I speak of India because it is my country and I have some right to speak for her. But many other countries in Asia tell the same story, for Asia today is resurgent, and these countries which long lay under foreign yoke have won back their independence and are fired by a new spirit and strive toward new ideals. To them, as to us, independence is as vital as the breath they take to sustain life, and colonialism, in any form, or anywhere, is abhorrent. . . .

. . . Peace and freedom have become indivisible, and the world cannot continue for long partly free and partly subject. In this atomic age peace has also become a test of human survival.

Recently we have witnessed two tragedies which have powerfully affected men and women all over the world. These are the tragedies in Egypt and Hungary. Our deeply felt sympathies must go out to those who have suffered or are suffering, and all of us must do our utmost to help them and to assist in solving these problems in a peaceful and constructive way. But even these tragedies have one hopeful aspect, for they have demonstrated that the most powerful countries cannot revert to old colonial methods or impose their domination over weak countries. World opinion has shown that it can organize itself to resist such outrages. Perhaps, as an outcome of these tragedies, freedom will be enlarged and will have a more assured basis.

The preservation of peace forms the central aim of India's policy. It is in the pursuit of this policy that we have chosen the path of nonalinement [nonalignment] in any military or like pact of alliance. Nonalinement does not mean passivity of mind or action, lack of faith or conviction. It does not mean submission to what we consider evil. It is a positive and dynamic approach to such problems that confront us. We believe that each country has not only the right to freedom but also to decide its own policy and way of life. Only thus can true freedom flourish and a people grow according to their own genius.

We believe, therefore, in nonaggression and non-interference by one country in the affairs of another and the growth of tolerance between them and the capacity for peaceful coexistence. We think that by the free exchange of ideas and trade and other contacts between nations each will learn from the other and truth will prevail. We therefore endeavor to maintain friendly relations with all countries, even though we may disagree with them in their policies or structure of government. We think that by this approach we can serve not only our country but also the larger causes of peace and good fellowship in the world.

89

Fidel Castro, Second Declaration of Havana

The Cuban Revolution of 1959 was a broadly based nationalist revolution made possible by the island's revolutionary tradition. Since the mid-nineteenth century, each generation had participated in a struggle for change, only to produce disillusionment: The Ten Years' War (1868–1878) to break from Spain ended in failure; the war of independence that began in 1895 resulted in semi-independence under U.S. guardianship; and the revolution of 1933, which tried to restore constitutional order and democracy, saw the rise of Fulgencio Batista, an army sergeant who dominated the nation's affairs for many years. All of these major upheavals that ended in failure nurtured a frustrated, strident brand of Cuban nationalism. During the twentieth century, nationalists frequently perceived the United States as a menacing threat rather than as a protector of their sovereignty and independence (compare with Reading 50).

They placed the blame for many of their nation's problems on U.S. foreign policy and its support of unpopular regimes, and on U.S. sugar interests that dominated the economy. Cuban nationalists believed that their dependent relationship on their North American neighbor must be modified or broken if they were to gain true independence and freedom.

When Fidel Castro's "provisional" government assumed power in 1959, it drew from this legacy and had the support of most Cubans. But internal struggles quickly erupted as contending groups, including the Cuban Communist Party, attempted to gain influence and control the direction of the revolution. Castro drew support from Communist officials and began to reduce U.S. influence; this approach increased tensions with the Eisenhower administration, which became suspicious about the true nature of the new government.

In May 1960, President Eisenhower approved covert assistance to Cuban exiles who had fled the island and hoped to overthrow Castro. After the failure of the Bay of Pigs invasion ordered by President Kennedy in April 1961, Castro officially adopted Marxism-Leninism as the ideology of the Cuban Revolution. This is clearly evident in his Second Declaration of Havana, delivered on February 4, 1962.

QUESTIONS TO CONSIDER

1. Why would so many Cubans and others in the developing world find Fidel Castro's arguments so appealing?
2. Are there any connections between Dana Munro's definition of the objectives of U.S. policy in Latin America and Castro's criticisms of the United States (see Reading 49)?

What is Cuba's history but that of Latin America? What is the history of Latin America but the history of Asia, Africa, and Oceania? And what is the history of all these peoples but the history of the cruelest exploitation of the world by imperialism?

At the end of the last century and the beginning of the present, a handful of economically developed nations had divided the world among themselves, subjecting two thirds of humanity to their economic and political domination. Humanity was forced to work for the dominating classes of the group of nations which had a developed capitalist economy.

The historic circumstances which permitted certain European countries and the United States of North America to attain a high industrial development level put them in a position which enabled them to subject and exploit the rest of the world.

What motives lay behind this expansion of the industrial powers? Were they moral, "civilizing" reasons, as they claimed? No. Their motives were economic.

The discovery of America sent the European conquerors across the seas to occupy and to exploit the lands and peoples of other continents; the lust for riches was the basic motivation for their conduct. America's discovery took place in the search for shorter ways to the Orient, whose products Europe valued highly.

A new social class, the merchants and the producers of articles manufactured for commerce, arose from the feudal society of lords and serfs in the latter part of the Middle Ages.

The lust for gold promoted the efforts of the new class. The lust for profit was the incentive of their behavior throughout its history. As industry and trade developed, the social influence of the new class grew. The new productive forces maturing in the midst of the feudal society increasingly clashed with feudalism and its serfdom, its laws, its institutions, its philosophy, its morals, its art, and its political ideology. . . .

Since the end of the Second World War, the Latin American nations are becoming pauperized constantly. The value of their capita income falls. The dreadful percentages of child death rate do not decrease, the number of illiterates grows higher, the peoples lack employment, land, adequate housing, schools, hospitals, communication systems and the means of subsistence. On the other hand, North America investments exceed 10 billion dollars. Latin America, moreover, supplies cheap raw materials and pays high prices for manufactured articles. Like

From *Fidel Castro's Personal Revolution in Cuba : 1959–1973*, by James Nelson Goodsell (New York : Knopf, 1975), pp. 264–268. Copyright © 1974 by Alfred A. Knopf, Inc. Reprinted by permission of the publisher.

the first Spanish conquerors, who exchanged mirrors and trinkets with the Indians for silver and gold, so the United States trades with Latin America. To hold on to this torrent of wealth, to take greater possession of America's resources and to exploit its long-suffering peoples : this is what is hidden behind the military pacts, the military missions and Washington's diplomatic lobbying. . . .

Wherever roads are closed to the peoples, where repression of workers and peasants is fierce, where the domination of Yankee monopolies is strongest, the first and most important lesson is to understand that it is neither just nor correct to divert the peoples with the vain and fanciful illusion that the dominant classes can be uprooted by legal means which do not and will not exist. The ruling classes are entrenched in all positions of state power. They monopolize the teaching field. They dominate all means of mass communication. They have infinite financial resources. Theirs is a power which the monopolies and the ruling few will defend by blood and fire with the strength of their police and their armies.

The duty of every revolutionary is to make revolution. We know that in America and throughout the world the revolution will be victorious. But revolutionaries cannot sit in the doorways of their homes to watch the corpse of imperialism pass by. The role of Job does not behoove a revolutionary. Each year by which America's liberation may be hastened will mean millions of children rescued from death, millions of minds, freed for learning, infinitudes of sorrow spared the peoples. Even though the Yankee imperialists are preparing a bloodbath for America they will not succeed in drowning the people's struggle. They will evoke universal hatred against themselves. This will be the last act of their rapacious and cave-man system. . . .

90

Frantz Fanon, *The Wretched of the Earth*

One of the most articulate spokesmen for decolonization in the Third World was the French-educated Algerian psychiatrist Frantz Fanon (1925–1961). Fanon's writings, coupled with his struggle against French colonial rule in Algeria, ensured that he would become one of the most celebrated leaders of decolonization in the 1960s.

QUESTIONS TO CONSIDER

1. Are there any parallels between Frantz Fanon's diagnosis of colonialism and Fidel Castro's justification of revolution (see Reading 89)?
2. Fanon describes the colonial world as a "Manichean world." Would Rudyard Kipling agree (see Reading 43)? Why? Why not?

The colonial world is a world cut in two. The dividing line, the frontiers are shown by barracks and police stations. In the colonies it is the policeman and the soldier who are the official, instituted go-betweens, the spokesmen of the settler and his rule of oppression. . . . In the capitalist countries a multitude of moral teachers, counselors and "bewilderers" separate the exploited from those in power. In the colonial countries, on the contrary, the policeman and the soldier, by their immediate presence and their frequent and direct action maintain contact with the native and advise him by means of rifle butts and napalm not to budge. It is obvious here that the agents of government speak the language of pure force. The intermediary does not lighten the oppression, nor seek to hide the domination ; he shows them up and puts them into practice with the clear conscience of an upholder of the peace ; yet he is the bringer of violence into the home and into the mind of the native.

The zone where the natives live is not complementary to the zone inhabited by the settlers. The two zones are opposed, but not in the service of a higher unity. Obedient to the rules of pure Aristotelian logic, they both follow the principle of reciprocal exclusivity. No conciliation is possible, for of the two terms, one is superfluous. The settlers' town is a strongly built town, all made of stone and steel. It is a brightly lit town ; the streets are covered with asphalt, and the garbage cans swallow all the leavings, unseen, unknown and hardly thought about. The settler's feet are never visible, except perhaps in the sea ; but there you're never close enough to see them. His feet are protected by strong shoes although the streets of his town are clean and even, with no holes or stones. The settler's town is a well-fed town, an easygoing town ; its belly is always full of good things. The settlers' town is a town of white people, of foreigners.

The town belonging to the colonized people, or at least the native town, the Negro village, the medina, the reservation, is a place of ill fame, peopled by men of evil repute. They are born there, it matters little where or how ; they die there, it matters not where, nor how. It is a world without spaciousness ; men live there on top of each other, and their huts are built — one on top of the other. The native town is a hungry town, starved of bread, of meat, of shoes, of coal, of light. The native town is a crouching village, a town on its knees, a town wallowing in the mire. It is a town of niggers and dirty Arabs. The look that the native turns on the settler's town is a look of lust, a look of envy ; it expresses his dreams of possession — all manner of possession : to sit at the settler's table, to sleep in the settler's bed, with his wife if possible. The colonized man is an envious man. And this the settler knows very well ; when their glances meet he ascertains bitterly, always on the defensive, "They want to take our place." It is true, for there is no native who does not dream at least once a day of setting himself up in the settler's place. . . .

The violence which has ruled over the ordering of the colonial world, which has ceaselessly drummed the rhythm for the destruction of native social forms and broken up without reserve the systems of reference of the economy, and the customs of dress and external life, that same violence will be claimed and taken over by the native at the moment when, deciding to embody history in his own person, he surges into the forbidden quarters. To wreck the colonial world is hencefor-

From Frantz Fanon, *The Wretched of the Earth,* trans. Constance Farrington (New York : Grove Press, 1968), pp. 37–41, passim. Reprinted by permission.

ward a mental picture of action which is very clear, very easy to understand and which may be assumed by each one of the individuals which constitute the colonized people. To break up the colonial world does not mean that after the frontiers have been abolished lines of communication will be set up between the two zones. The destruction of the colonial world is no more and no less than the abolition of one zone, its burial in the depths of the earth or its expulsion from the country.

The natives' challenge to the colonial world is not a rational confrontation of points of view. It is not a treatise on the universal, but the untidy affirmation of an original idea propounded as an absolute. The colonial world is a Manichean world. It is not enough for the settler to delimit physically, that is to say with the help of the army and the police force, the place of the native. As if to show the totalitarian character of colonial exploitation the settler paints the native as a sort of quintessence of evil. Native society is not simply described as a society lacking in values. It is not enough for the colonist to affirm that those values have disappeared from, or still better never existed in, the colonial world. The native is declared insensible to ethics ; he represents not only the absence of values, but also the negation of values. He is, let us dare to admit, the enemy of values, and in this sense he is the absolute evil. He is the corrosive element, destroying all that comes near him ; he is the deforming element, disfiguring all that has to do with beauty or morality ; he is the depository of maleficent powers, the unconscious and irretrievable instrument of blind forces.

The Middle East:
Politics and Upheaval

In the second half of the twentieth century, the Middle East has been tormented by the agonies of war and the explosive politics of religious violence. Although the causes of these upheavals are deeply rooted and complex, three central, and intertwined, episodes have shaped the politics of this region : the birth of the state of Israel ; the quest for a Palestinian state ; and, in the wake of the Iranian Revolution (1979), the emergence of religious fundamentalism in Islamic politics.

Israel's Proclamation of Independence in 1948 placed the new state on a collision course with its Arab neighbors, resulting in four major wars and the displacement of more than one million Palestinians from their homeland. Despite the wars, four decades of guerrilla attacks and reprisals, active intervention by the United Nations, and diplomatic efforts such as the Camp David agreements aimed at a comprehensive peace, deep hostilities still exist between Israel, her Arab neighbors, and the Palestine Liberation Organization (PLO).

These hostilities — especially between the PLO and Israel — have been complicated by a destructive civil war in Lebanon (beginning in 1975), the Iranian Revolution (1979), the inconclusive war between Iran and Iraq

(1980–1988), and the Persian Gulf War (1991). The near-destruction of the state of Lebanon, coupled with the Israeli occupation of south Lebanon, have not only deepened Arab-Israeli hostility but have also signaled the emergence of Syria, Iraq and Iran as powers in the region, further complicating the search for peace. Well before Iranian revolutionaries toppled the government of Mohammed Reza Pahlavi, Islamic teachers such as Ali Shariati cited the dangers of Western culture — especially its materialism — and urged Arab intellectuals to cleanse Islamic society of Western corruption. After the fall of the Shah, Islamic fundamentalist leaders such as Ayatollah Ruhollah Khomeini, spiritual leader of Iran's Shiite Muslims, gained wide influence in shaping Iranian revolutionary politics. And, in Khomeini's case, his influence extended far beyond Iran because his writings and speeches commanded respect and interest in the disparate Shiite communities throughout the Middle East.

91

Israel's Proclamation of Independence

One day before the termination of the British mandate for Palestine, the Provisional State Council (a forerunner of the Israeli Parliament) declared the independence of Israel on May 14, 1948. The following selection is an excerpt from this official announcement.

QUESTIONS TO CONSIDER

1. Can the historic and religious ties of the Jewish people to Israel accommodate the fact that for nearly 2000 years Israel was also the dwelling place of Arabs and other non-Jewish populations?
2. How does Israel's Proclamation of Independence suggest the influence of European history in this area (see Readings 57, 58, and 60)?

The Land of Israel was the birthplace of the Jewish people. Here their spiritual, religious and national identity was formed. Here they achieved independence and created a culture of national and universal significance. Here they wrote and gave the Bible to the world.

Exiled from the Land of Israel the Jewish people remained faithful to it in all the countries of their dispersion, never ceasing to pray and hope for their return and the restoration of their national freedom.

Impelled by this historic association, Jews strove throughout the centuries to go back to the land of their fathers and regain their statehood. In recent decades they returned in their masses. They reclaimed the wilderness, revived their language, built cities and villages, and established a vigorous and ever-growing community, with its own economic and cultural life. They sought peace, yet were prepared to defend themselves. They brought the blessings of progress to all inhabitants of the country and looked forward to sovereign independence.

In the year 1897 the First Zionist Congress, inspired by Theodor Herzl's vision of the Jewish State, proclaimed the right of the Jewish people to national revival in their own country.

This right was acknowledged by the Balfour Declaration of November 2, 1917, and re-affirmed by the Mandate of the League of Nations, which gave explicit international recognition to the historic connection of the Jewish people with Palestine and their right to reconstitute their National Home.

The recent holocaust, which engulfed millions of Jews in Europe, proved anew the need to solve the problem of the homelessness and lack of independence of the Jewish people by means of the re-establishment of the Jewish State, which would open the gates to all Jews and endow the Jewish people with equality of status among the family of nations.

The survivors of the disastrous slaughter in Europe, and also Jews from other lands, have not desisted from their efforts to reach Eretz-Yisrael, in face of difficulties, obstacles and perils ; and have not ceased to urge their right to a life of dignity, freedom and honest toil in their ancestral land.

In the second World War the Jewish people in Palestine made their full contribution to the struggle of the freedom-loving nations against the Nazi evil. The sacrifices of their soldiers and their war effort gained them the right to rank with the nations which founded the United Nations.

On November 29, 1947, the General Assembly of the United Nations adopted a Resolution requiring the establishment of a Jewish State in Palestine. The General Assembly called upon the inhabitants of the country to take all the necessary steps on their part to put the plan into effect. This recognition by the United Nations of the right of the Jewish people to establish their independent State is unassailable.

It is the natural right of the Jewish people to lead, as do all other nations, an independent existence in its sovereign State.

ACCORDINGLY WE, the members of the National Council, representing the Jewish people in Palestine and the World Zionist Movement, are met together in solemn assembly today, the day of termination of the British Mandate for Palestine ; and by virtue of the natural and historic right of the Jewish people and of the Resolution of the General Assembly of the United Nations.

WE HEREBY PROCLAIM the establishment of the Jewish State in Palestine, to be called Medinath Yisrael (The State of Israel).

WE HEREBY DECLARE that, as from the termination of the Mandate at midnight, the 14th–15th May, 1948, and pending the setting up of the duly elected bodies of the State in accordance with a Constitution, to be drawn up by the Constituent Assembly not later than the 1st October, 1948, the National Council shall act as the Provisional State Council, and that the National Administration shall constitute the Provisional Government of the Jewish State, which shall be known as Israel.

THE STATE OF ISRAEL will be open to the immigration of Jews from all countries of their dispersion ; will promote the development of the country for the benefit of all its inhabitants ; will be based on the principles of liberty, justice and peace as conceived by the Prophets of Israel ; will uphold the full social and political equality of all its citizens, without distinction of religion, race, or sex ; will guarantee freedom of religion, conscience, education and culture ; will safeguard the Holy Places of all religions ; and will loyally uphold the principles of the United Nations Charter.

THE STATE OF ISRAEL will be ready to co-operate with the organs and representatives of the United Nations in the implementation of the Resolution of the Assembly of November 29, 1947, and will take steps to bring about the Economic Union over the whole of Palestine.

We appeal to the United Nations to assist the Jewish people in the building of its State and to admit Israel into the family of nations.

In the midst of wanton aggression, we yet call upon the Arab inhabitants of the State of Israel to preserve the ways of peace and play their part in the development of the State, on the basis of full and equal citizenship and due representation in all its bodies and institutions — provisional and permanent.

92

The Palestinian National Charter

In the wake of the Israeli victory in the Six-Day War between the Arabs and Israelis in June 1967, the PLO met in Cairo, Egypt, on July 17, 1968, to adopt a new version of its 1964 charter.

QUESTIONS TO CONSIDER

1. Can the resolutions of the Palestinian National Charter be reconciled with Israel's Proclamation of Independence ?
2. Why would the Palestinians insist upon using the terms "Zionist" and "Commando action" in this document ?

Article 1. Palestine, the homeland of the Palestinian Arab people, is an inseparable part of the greater Arab homeland, and the Palestinian people are a part of the Arab Nation.

Article 2. Palestine, within the frontiers that existed under the British Mandate, is an indivisible territorial unit.

Article 3. The Palestinian Arab people alone have legitimate rights to their homeland, and shall exercise the right of self-determination after the liberation of their homeland, in keeping with their wishes and entirely of their own accord.

From "The Palestine National Charter Adopted by the Fourth Palestine National Assembly, Cairo, July 17, 1968," in Zuhair Diab, ed., *International Documents on Palestine : 1968* (Beirut : The Institute for Palestine Studies, 1971), pp. 393–395.

Article 4. The Palestinian identity is an authentic, intrinsic and indissoluble quality that is transmitted from father to son. Neither the Zionist occupation nor the dispersal of the Palestinian Arab people as a result of the afflictions they have suffered can efface this Palestinian identity.

Article 5. Palestinians are Arab citizens who were normally resident in Palestine until 1947. This includes both those who were forced to leave or who stayed in Palestine. Anyone born to a Palestinian father after that date, whether inside or outside Palestine, is a Palestinian.

Article 6. Jews who were normally resident in Palestine up to the beginning of the Zionist invasion are Palestinians.

Article 7. Palestinian identity, and material, spiritual and historical links with Palestine are immutable realities. It is a national obligation to provide every Palestinian with a revolutionary Arab upbringing, and to instil in him a profound spiritual and material familiarity with his homeland and a readiness both for armed struggle and for the sacrifice of his material possessions and his life, for the recovery of his homeland. All available educational means and means of guidance must be enlisted to that end, until liberation is achieved. . . .

Article 9. Armed struggle is the only way of liberating Palestine, and is thus strategic, not tactical. The Palestinian Arab people hereby affirm their unwavering determination to carry on the armed struggle and to press on towards popular revolution for the liberation of and return to their homeland. They also affirm their right to a normal life in their homeland, to the exercise of their right of self-determination therein and to sovereignty over it.

Article 10. Commando action constitutes the nucleus of the Palestinian popular war of liberation. This requires that commando action should be escalated, expanded and protected and that all the resources of the Palestinian masses and all scientific potentials available to them should be mobilised and organised to play their part in the armed Palestinian revolution. It also requires solidarity in national struggle among the different groups within the Palestinian people and between that people and the Arab masses, to ensure the continuity of the escalation and victory of the revolution. . . .

Article 12. The Palestinian Arab people believe in Arab unity. To fulfil their role in the achievement of that objective, they must, at the present stage in their national struggle, retain their Palestinian identity and all that it involves, work for increased awareness of it and oppose all measures liable to weaken or dissolve it. . . .

Article 15. The liberation of Palestine is a national obligation for the Arabs. It is their duty to repel the Zionist and imperialist invasion of the greater Arab homeland and to liquidate the Zionist presence in Palestine. The full responsibility for this belongs to the peoples and governments of the Arab nation and to the Palestinian people first and foremost.

For this reason, the task of the Arab nation is to enlist all the military, human, moral and material resources at its command to play an effective part, along with the Palestinian people, in the liberation of Palestine. Moreover, it is the task of the Arab nation, particularly at the present stage of the Palestinian armed revolution, to offer the Palestinian armed revolution, to offer the Palestinian people all possible aid, material and manpower support, and to place at their disposal all the means and opportunities that will enable them to continue to perform their role as the vanguard of their armed revolution until the liberation of their homeland is achieved. . . .

Article 19. The partition of Palestine, which took place in 1947, and the establishment of Israel, are fundamentally invalid, however long they last, for they contravene the will of the people of Palestine and their natural right to their homeland and contradict the principles of the United Nations Charter, foremost among which is the right of self-determination.

Article 20. The Balfour Declaration, the Mandate Instrument, and all their consequences, are hereby declared null and void. The claim of historical or spiritual links between the Jews and Palestine is neither in conformity with historical fact nor does it satisfy the requirements for statehood. Judaism is a revealed religion; it is not a separate nationality, nor are the Jews a single people with a separate identity; they are citizens of their respective countries.

Article 21. The Palestinian Arab people, expressing themselves through the Palestinian armed revolution, reject all alternatives to the total liberation of Palestine. They also reject all proposals for the liquidation or internationalisation of the Palestine problem.

Article 22. Zionism is a political movement that is organically linked with world imperialism and is opposed to all liberation movements or movements for progress in the world. The Zionist movement is essentially fanatical and racialist; its objectives involve aggression, expansion and the establishment of colonial settlements, and its methods are those of the Fascists and the Nazis. Israel acts as cat's paw for the Zionist movement, a geographic and manpower base for world imperialism and a springboard for its thrust into the Arab homeland to frustrate the aspirations of the Arab nation to liberation, unity and progress. Israel is a constant threat to peace in the Middle East and the whole world. Inasmuch as the liberation of Palestine will eliminate the Zionist and imperialist presence in that country and bring peace to the Middle East, the Palestinian people look for support to all liberals and to all forces of good, peace and progress in the world, and call on them, whatever their political convictions, for all possible aid and support in their just and legitimate struggle to liberate their homeland.

93

Ali Shariati, *Reflections of Humanity*

Dr. Ali Shariati (1933–1977) was the ideologue of Iran's Islamic revolution. He enjoyed enormous influence among the students and intellectuals within Iranian universities during the 1970s and 1980s.

QUESTIONS TO CONSIDER

1. Why would "modernization" be a threat to Shariati's vision of Islam?
2. Have Shariati's views influenced the contemporary Middle East? Why? Why not?

But today, western societies have been able to impose their philosophy, their way of thinking, their desires, their ideas, their tastes and their manners upon non-European countries to the same extent that they have been able to force their symbols of civilization (technological innovations) into these countries which consume new products and gadgets ; countries which can never adjust themselves to European manners, longing, tastes and ways of thinking. . . .

Modernity was the best method of diverting the non-European world, from whatever form and mold of thinking, from their own mold, thought and personality. It became the sole task of Europeans to place the temptation of "modernization" before the non-European societies of any complexion. The Europeans realized that by tempting the inhabitant of the East with a compulsive desire for modernization, he would cooperate with them to deny his own past and desecrate and destroy with his own hands the constituents of his unique culture, religion and personality. So the temptation and longing for "modernization" prevailed all across the Far East, Middle East, Near East and in Islamic and Black countries — and to become modernized was regarded as becoming like the Europeans.

Strictly speaking, "modernized" means modernized in consumption. One who becomes modernized is one whose tastes now desire "modern" items to satisfy his wants. In other words, he imports from Europe new forms of living and modern products, and he does not use new types of products and a lifestyle developed from his own original and national past. Non-Europeans are modernized for the sake of consumption. Westerners, however, could not just tell others they were going to reshape their intellect, mind and personality for fear of awakening resistance. Therefore, the Europeans had to make non-European equate "modernization" with "civilization" to impose the new consumption pattern upon them, since everyone has a desire for civilization. "Modernization" was defined as "civilization" and thus people cooperated with the Europeans plans to modernize. Even more than the bourgeois and capitalist, the non-European intellectual labored mightily to change consumption patterns and life styles in their societies. Since the non-Europeans could not produce the new products, they became automatically dependent upon the technology which produces for them and expects them to buy whatever it produces.

94

Ayatollah Ruhollah Khomeini, "Message to the Pilgrims"

Ayatollah Ruhollah Khomeini (1900 ?–1989) was a religious leader who by 1960 had become the spokesman for Iran's Shiite Muslim community. Because of his opposition to Shah Reza Pahlavi, he was forced into exile in 1964. He returned to Iran on February 1, 1979, two weeks after the collapse of the Shah's government. The following selection is from a speech he gave

From Ali Shariati, *Reflections of Humanity : Two Views of Civilization and the Plight of Man* (Houston : Free Islamic Literatures Book Distribution Center, 1980), pp. 26, 30–31. Reprinted by permission.

in Tehran on September 13, 1980. This speech is a call for Muslim unity and a condemnation of the United States. Khomeini further suggests that Iraq is an agent of the United States and is fighting Iran at the behest of the United States.

QUESTIONS TO CONSIDER

1. Why would Khomeini's views appeal to Muslim youth in the Middle East?
2. What does Khomeini's message suggest about Shiite perceptions of Western culture, the United States, and the Soviet Union?

Muslims the world over who believe in the truth of Islam, arise and gather beneath the banner of tauhid [divine unity] and the teachings of Islam! Repel the treacherous superpowers from your countries and your abundant resources. Restore the glory of Islam, and abandon your selfish disputes and differences, for you possess everything! Rely on the culture of Islam, resist Western imitation, and stand on your own feet. Attack those intellectuals who are infatuated with the West and the East, and recover your true identity. Realize that intellectuals in the pay of foreigners have inflicted disaster upon their people and countries. As long as you remain disunited and fail to place your reliance in true Islam, you will continue to suffer what you have suffered already. We are now in an age when the masses act as the guides to the intellectuals and are rescuing them from abasement and humiliation by the East and the West. For today is the day that the masses of the people are on the move; they are the guides to those who previously sought to be the guides themselves.

Know that your moral power will overcome all other powers. With a population of almost one billion and with infinite sources of wealth, you can defeat all the powers. Aid God's cause so that He may aid you. Great ocean of Muslims, arise and defeat the enemies of humanity. If you turn to God and follow the heavenly teachings, God Almighty and His vast hosts will be with you.

The most important and painful problem confronting the subjugated nations of the world, both Muslim and non-Muslim, is the problem of America. In order to swallow up the material resources of the countries it has succeeded in dominating, America, the most powerful country in the world, will spare no effort.

America is the number-one enemy of the deprived and oppressed people of the world. There is no crime America will not commit in order to maintain its political, economic, cultural, and military domination of those parts of the world where it predominates. It exploits the oppressed people of the world by means of the large-scale propaganda campaigns that are coordinated for it by international Zionism. By means of its hidden and treacherous agents, it sucks the blood of the defenseless people as if it alone, together with its satellites, had the right to live in this world.

From Hamid Algar, ed. and trans., *Islam and Revolution: Writings and Declarations of Imam Khomeini* (Berkeley: Mizan Press, 1981), pp. 304–306, passim. Reprinted by permission.

Iran has tried to sever all its relations with this Great Satan and it is for this reason that it now finds wars imposed upon it. America has urged Iraq to spill the blood of our young men, and it has compelled the countries that are subject to its influence to boycott us economically in the hope of defeating us. Unfortunately, most Asian countries are also hostile to us. Let the Muslim nations be aware that Iran is a country effective at war with America, and that our martyrs — the brave young men of our army and the Revolutionary Guards — are defending Iran and the Islam we hold dear against America. Thus, it is necessary to point out, the clashes now occurring in the west of our beloved country are caused by America ; everyday we are forced to confront various godless and treacherous groups there. This is a result of the Islamic content of our Revolution, which has been established on the basis of true independence. Were we to compromise with America and the other superpowers, we would not suffer these misfortunes. But our nation is no longer ready to submit to humiliation and abjection ; it prefers a bloody death to a life of shame. We are ready to be killed and we have made a covenant with God to follow the path of our leader, the Lord of the Martyrs.

Muslims who are now sitting next to the House of God, engaged in prayer! Pray for those who are resisting America and the other superpowers, and understand that we are not fighting against Iraq. The people of Iraq support our Islamic Revolution ; our quarrel is with America, and it is America whose hand can be seen emerging from the sleeve of the Iraqi government. God willing, our struggle will continue until we have achieved real independence, for, as I have said repeatedly, we are warriors, and for Muslims surrender has no meaning.

Neutral countries, I call upon you to witness that America plans to destroy us, all of us. Come to your senses and help us achieve our common goal. We have turned our backs on the East and the West, on the Soviet Union and America, in order to run our country ourselves. Do we therefore deserve to be attacked by the East and the West ? The position we have attained is an historical exception, given the present conditions in the world, but our goal will certainly not be lost if we are to die, martyred and defeated.

I have said repeatedly that the taking of hostages by our militant, committed Muslim students was a natural reaction to the blows our nation suffered at the hands of America. They can be set free if the property of the dead Shah is returned, all claims of America against Iran are annulled, a guarantee of political and military non-interference in Iran is given by America, and all our capital is released. Of course, I have turned the affair over to the Islamic Assembly for it to settle in whatever way it deem best. The hostages have been well treated in Iran, but the propaganda of America and its satellites has left no lie untold in this respect. At the same time, our beloved young people in America and England have suffered the worst kind of indignity as well as physical and psychological torture. No official in any international organization had defended those dear friends of ours, and no one has condemned America and Britain for their barbaric behavior.

I ask God Almighty that He grant all captive people freedom, independence, and an Islamic republic.

And peace be upon the righteous servants of God.

America and the Second Indochina War

The Geneva Agreements of July 1954, which ended the First Indochina War (1946–1954) between France and Ho Chi Minh's Viet Minh, provided for (1) a temporary division of Vietnam into two parts at the seventeenth parallel; (2) general elections to be held no later than 1956 to decide upon Vietnamese reunification; (3) the creation of free and independent states of Laos and Cambodia; and (4) the end of the French empire in Indochina. Although the United States did not sign the Geneva Agreements, it did agree "to refrain from the threat of the use of force to disturb them" and that it "would view any renewal of the aggression . . . with grave concern and as seriously threatening international peace and security."[1]

The expected general elections of 1956 were never held, and Vietnam remained divided. Ho Chi Minh governed the Democratic Republic of Vietnam (North Vietnam) from Hanoi, while in 1955 Ngo Dinh Diem was elected president of the Republic of Vietnam (South Vietnam), which he governed from Saigon.

Between 1955 and 1975, the United States assisted South Vietnam in establishing its government and in attacking a political-military insurgency that in 1960 identified itself as the National Front for the Liberation of South Vietnam (NLF). The more familiar label for this insurgency was Viet Cong, a shorthand term for Vietnamese Communist. By the early 1960s, the NLF, organized and operating in South Vietnam, was receiving instructions and supplies from Ho Chi Minh's Communist government of North Vietnam. By the spring of 1963, the NLF insurgency in the countryside and the Buddhist-led antigovernment demonstrations in the key cities of Hue and Saigon posed severe military and political problems for President Diem. On November 1, 1963, three weeks before U.S. President John F. Kennedy's death, a South Vietnamese military junta seized power from Diem and killed him and his brother.

Diem's assassination ushered in a period of political instability and an acceleration of the NLF insurgency, prompting President Lyndon B. Johnson to increase America's role in fighting the Viet Cong. Although Congress never formally declared war, two million Americans served in Vietnam and U.S. combat troops remained there until 1973. During this Second Indochina War (c. 1957–1975), America spent over $239 billion fighting the war, suffered 296,000 casualties, and lost over 57,000 lives.

The sudden collapse of South Vietnam, followed by the rapid and unexpectedly easy North Vietnamese takeover of the South in May 1975, left a bewildering legacy of confusion, doubt, and frustration for many Americans and Vietnamese.

---

1. Quoted in Marvin E. Gettleman, ed., *Vietnam: History, Documents, and Opinions on a Major World Crisis* (New York: New American Library, 1970), pp. 184–185.

95

Marguerite Higgins, An Interview with Ngo Dinh Diem

On August 7, 1963, Marguerite Higgins (1920–1966), an American journalist in Saigon, interviewed President Diem.

QUESTIONS TO CONSIDER

1. In light of the Kennedy administration's policy vis-à-vis Vietnam, was Diem's characterization of American attitudes toward him correct?
2. What did Diem mean when he told Marguerite Higgins that "there are no George Washingtons among our military"?
3. Was the Kennedy administration correct in supporting the military junta that killed Diem in November 1963?

"It would help," said Diem, "if the people of the United States would try and understand the complexities of this country and the nature of the Communist war we are fighting. You, Miss Higgins, have been in the countryside. You have seen the Montagnards, with their spears and their superstitions. The Chams. The Cao Dia. The Hoa Hao. The primitive villages where the ancestors rule — as they do most places in Vietnam. Tell me, Miss Higgins, what can parliamentary democracy mean to a Montagnard when his language does not even have a term to express it. . . ."

Here Diem leaned forward in his chair, his voice growing tense. "The French did not leave us a pretty legacy," he said. "In the days before colonialism, people could read and write even in the villages. Now we have to rebuild, and the Viet Cong are doing their worst to prevent it. . . . But we must build slowly, beginning with the villages. There is a tradition of democracy and autonomy in the village. . . . It is part of the Confucian tradition . . . and Confucian customs and duties have survived illiteracy, for they are bound up in worship of the ancestor. . . . And we want to tap these deep roots of our Confucian traditions in rebuilding our society. I know that some Americans try to tarnish me by calling me a mandarin. . . . But I am proud of being a mandarin. . . . It may not be similar to anything that you Americans have experienced — this mandarin-Confucian system. But it has its merits and its own inner democracy. We are not going to adapt the best of our heritage to the modern situation. You Americans have a finished, polished society built on entirely different ideas of the priorities and values because your needs are totally different from ours. After the chaos of our recent history and the subversion by the Communists, Vietnam's priority is stability, central control, respect for authority, and law and order. Do you realize that when I took power, the central government had lost all control of the countryside? . . . What do Americans know of mandarins? . . . The Americans are breaking Vietnamese psychology and they don't even know what they are doing. Your press and radio mock the idea of discipline and respect for authority and glorify so-called civil liberties and the right to criticize and the need for political opposition, but this country is in a life-and-death struggle. Even Western democracies suspend civil liberties during war emergencies.". . .

"Your ambassador," Diem resumed, "comes and tells me that it enhances my 'liberal image' to permit demonstrations in the street by the Buddhists and the political opposition. . . . I cannot seem to convince the embassy that this is Vietnam — not the United States of America. We have had good reason to ban street demonstrations in the middle of a war, and the reason is that the Viet Cong are everywhere. . . . What would happen if the Viet Cong should infiltrate a demonstration here in Saigon, toss a bomb, kill dozens of persons, including some American press? What would 'liberal opinion' say of me then? Would they believe my government when it said that the Viet Cong were responsible for the killings because only the Communists could profit from such an event? Consider what happened at Hue. Those plastic bombs were thrown by the Viet Cong. . . .

At one point Diem startled me by suddenly changing the subject to ask me point blank: "What am I to think of the American government, Miss Higgins? Am I merely a puppet on Washington's string? Or — as I had hoped — are we partners in a common cause?"

"Why, exactly, do you ask?" I countered.

"Why?" said Diem, half smiling. "I ask because I am trying to be a loyal ally. Yet almost daily I hear of broadcasts over Voice of America or of inspired articles in the American press discussing whether Washington is going to retain my services or throw me out. We are a small power and America is a great power. But what would Mr. Kennedy think if our press were filled with inspired stories virtually urging the people of America to overthrow him? We admire America in many ways. But we cannot always take American advice, for many reasons. It is, much of it, often contradictory. Procedures applicable to one culture cannot be transplanted wholly to another culture. We appreciate American aid. But we would like to believe that it is not given as a favor or to serve as a lever for controlling this government. Surely there is only one justification for Americans to be in Vietnam — and that justification is that America's national interest requires you to help prevent Communism from conquering this country. If this were your attitude, then your aid would be offered as part of a wartime partnership to defeat the Viet Cong. But now I hear hints that this aid may be withdrawn if I do not do exactly what the Americans demand. Isn't there a certain arrogance in these demands? America has a magnificent economy and many good points. But does your strength at home automatically mean that the United States is entitled to dictate everything here in Vietnam, which is undergoing a type of war that your country has never experienced? If you order Vietnam around like a puppet on a string, how will you be different — except in degree — from the French? I am not unaware that some Americans are flirting with elements in my country that perennially plot against me. These elements cannot succeed without the Americans, and they know it."

"But do you really think the United States is plotting against you, President Diem?" I asked with some astonishment.

He hesitated. Then choosing his words deliberately and speaking slowly, as if making points in a debate, he replied: "I do not think Ambassador Nolting is plotting against me. I do not think Richardson [of the C.I.A.] is plotting against me. I know there are American officials who are preparing the way in the event the decision is taken to try and get rid of me. I cannot foresee the future. I cannot believe that America would turn against an ally under attack, engaged in a struggle for its very existence. But some people are crazy — and the world is crazy. Still, Miss Higgins, I hope that your government will take a realistic look at these young generals plotting to take my place. How much maturity or political understanding do they have — of their own country, let alone the world? I am afraid there are no George Washingtons among our military."

96

Views of a Viet Cong Official

Truong Nhu Tang was a founder of the National Liberation Front (NLF) and a Minister of Justice in the NLF's Provisional Revolutionary Government. In 1982 he gave the following account of the Viet Cong movement and the collapse of South Vietnam. The 1968 Tet offensive he refers to was a failed North Vietnamese and Viet Cong campaign against South Vietnamese cities. This occurred while General Thieu, Truong Nhu Tang's captor, was President of South Vietnam.

QUESTIONS TO CONSIDER

1. According to Truong Nhu Tang, was the Tet offensive a military victory for the insurgency? Why did the American public perceive Tet as an American defeat?
2. As a southerner in the NLF, what was Truong Nhu Tang's attitude toward the North Vietnamese? Did American policy take into account this division in the NLF ranks?

The North Vietnamese on their part never indicated that they wanted to impose communism on the South. On the contrary, they knew, they said, that the South must have a different program altogether, one that embodied our aspirations not just for independence but also for internal political freedom. I believe, in addi-

From Truong Nhu Tang, "Myth of a Liberation," *The New York Review of Books*, 39, no. 16 (October 21, 1982), pp. 31–36, passim. Reprinted with permission from *The New York Review of Books*. Copyright © 1982 Nyrev, Inc.

just for independence but also for internal political freedom. I believe, in addition, that the Northern leadership would have the wisdom to draw from the experiences — both good and bad — of other communist countries, and especially of North Vietnam, and that they could avoid the errors made elsewhere. North Vietnam was, as Ho Chi Minh often declared, a special situation in which nationalists and communists had combined their efforts. Clearly South Vietnam was no less special, and the newly constituted NLF Permanent Committee felt a certain amount of confidence in working with our Northern compatriots. . . .

The great majority of our troops then were Southern resistance fighters many of whom were veterans of the French colonial wars. Others were peasants who joined us when the NLF was formed. Almost all of this latter group still lived at home. During the day they were loyal citizens of South Vietnam ; at night they became Viet Cong.

For the most part these guerrillas cared nothing about Marxist-Leninism or any other ideology. But they despised the local officials who had been appointed over them by the Saigon dictatorship. Beyond this, joining the Viet Cong allowed them to stay clear of the ARVN draft and to remain near their families. They were treated as brothers by the NLF, and although Viet Cong pay was almost nonexistent, these peasant soldiers were loyal and determined fighters. Moreover, they had the support of much of the population : people in the countryside and even in the cities provided food and intelligence information and protected our cadres. Although South Vietnamese propaganda attacked us as communists and murderers, the peasants believed otherwise. To them we were not Marxist-Leninists but simply revolutionaries fighting against a hated dictatorship and foreign intervention.

Because it was a people's war, the Viet Cong cadres were trained carefully to exploit the peasants' sympathies. But our goals were in fact generally shared by the people. We were working for Southern self-determination and independence — from Hanoi as well as from Washington. While we in the Viet Cong were beholden to Hanoi for military supplies and diplomatic contacts, many of us still believed that the North Vietnamese leadership would respect and support the NLF political program, that it would be in their interest to do so.

As early as the 1968 Tet offensive, after I was released from Thieu's prisons, I protested to the communist leaders about the atrocities committed by North Vietnamese troops in Hue, where many innocent people were murdered and about a dozen American prisoners were shot. It was explained to me that these were political executions and also that a number of "errors" had been made. I managed to persuade myself then that no such "errors" would be necessary once the war was over.

Unfortunately the Tet offensive also proved catastrophic to our plans. It is a major irony of the Vietnamese war that our propaganda transformed this military debacle into a brilliant victory, giving us new leverage in our diplomatic efforts, inciting the American antiwar movement to even stronger and more optimistic resistance, and disheartening the Washington planners.

The truth was that Tet cost us half of our forces. Our losses were so immense that we were simply unable to replace them with new recruits. One consequence was that the Hanoi leadership began to move unprecedented numbers of troops into the South, giving them a new and much more dominant position in the NLF deliberations. The Tet failure also retarded the organization of the Alliance of

National, Democratic, and Peace Forces, an opposition coalition that had formed around thirty prominent South Vietnamese intellectuals and opinion makers. . . .

The Hanoi leadership knew all this and orchestrated their position toward us accordingly. They accepted and supported the NLF platform at every point, and gave the firmest assurances of respect for the principle of South Vietnamese self-determination. Later, of course we discovered that the North Vietnamese communists had engaged in a deliberate deception to achieve what had been their true goal from the start, the destruction of South Vietnam as a political or social entity in any way separate from the North. They succeeded in their deception by portraying themselves as brothers who had fought the same battles we were fighting and by exploiting our patriotism in the most cynical fashion. Nevertheless, the eventual denouement would not have taken place except for several wholly unpredictable developments.

After the Paris peace agreement was signed in 1973, most of us were preparing to create a neutralist government, balanced between Northern leftists and Southern rightists. We hoped that America and other signers would play an active role in protecting the agreement. Certainly no one expected Watergate and Nixon's resignation. No one expected America's easy and startlingly rapid abandonment of the country. I myself, the soon-to-be minister of justice, was preparing a reconciliation policy that specifically excluded reprisals. But the sudden collapse of the South Vietnamese regime (caused partly by the hasty departure of many top Saigon leaders) together with the abandonment by the Americans left me and other "independent socialists" with no counterweight to the huge influx of Northern communists.

It is important to note that our views were not based solely on naivete. During the Sixties neither the NLF leaders nor the Politburo ever hoped for total military victory against the Americans and their clients. Our entire strategy was formulated with the expectation that eventually we would be involved in some kind of coalition government. Such a government would have been immune to outright North Vietnamese domination and could have expected substantial international support. . . .

Unfortunately when the war did end, North Vietnamese vindictiveness and fanaticism blossomed into a ferocious exercise of power. Hundreds of thousands of former officials and army officers of the Saigon regime were imprisoned in "re-education camps." Literally millions of ordinary citizens were forced to leave their homes and settle in so called New Economic Zones. . . .

97

An American Prisoner of War

Congressional Medal of Honor winner and retired Vice Admiral James Bond Stockdale was a prisoner of war in Vietnam for eight years. In the following essay, he recounts some of his experiences in Vietnam and offers his views on the lessons to be learned from the war.

QUESTIONS TO CONSIDER

1. President Ronald Reagan described the Vietnam War as a "noble crusade." James B. Stockdale describes it "as a misguided experiment of the Harvard Business School crowd. . . ." Which description do you believe to be correct? Why?
2. What do the accounts of Ngo Dinh Diem, Truong Nhu Tang, and James B. Stockdale suggest about the ambiguities and frustrations of the Second Indochina War (see Readings 95 and 96)?

My viewpoint of the Vietnam War was that Eisenhower's domino theory was probably valid: that if North Vietnam took over the south, a chain reaction could be expected to proceed to the southwest. I also knew that South Vietnam was not really like the western democracy our government tried to pretend it was. I knew there was a formidable framework of a Communist infrastructure in the south that would have to be burned out. I also knew how militantly doctrinaire and disciplined the North Vietnamese were. Putting all this together, I thought, during the war, after it, and still today, that Barry Goldwater had the only sensible outlook: either move quickly against Hanoi with repeated high impact non-nuke hammer blows from the air or forget it. Vietnam was no place for the Army.

So how do I classify the tragedy of Vietnam, if not a crusade, a mistake, a crime or a conspiracy? I classify it as a misguided experiment of the Harvard Business School crowd — the "whiz kids" — in achieving foreign policy objectives by so-called rational game theory, while ignoring the reality and obstinacy of human nature.

These were some of the policy lessons of Vietnam: You can't finesse human nature, human will, or human obstinacy, with economic game theory. And you should never let those who think you can, call the shots in a war!

. . . The central strategy of the North Vietnamese prison system was extortion pressure — pressure to get us to contribute to what turned out to be their winning propaganda campaign beamed at the American man on the street, pressure to get us to inform on one another. These ideas were tied together as integral parts of the whole and were to be extracted by the imposition of loneliness, fear and guilt — fear of pain, guilt at having betrayed a fellow prisoner. . . .

Chivalry was dead in my prison. Its name was Hoa Lo, meaning "fiery furnace," located in downtown Hanoi, a prison the French built in 1895.

I arrived there, a prisoner of war in North Vietnam, in the late morning of a rainy Sunday in September 1965, a stretcher case. I had a broken leg (which my welcoming party, a street mob of civilians, had inflicted), a broken back (which I charge off to my carelessness in not having had the presence of mind to brace myself correctly before ejecting into low altitude, high-speed air from a tumbling air-

From James B. Stockdale, *A Vietnam Experience: Ten Years of Reflection* (Stanford, CA: Hoover Institution, 1984), pp. 109, 122–128. This material originally appeared in: "The Most Important Lesson of Vietnam: Power of the Human Spirit," *San Jose Mercury News*, January 3, 1982, copyright 1982 by *The San Diego Union*; and "Dignity and Honor in Vietnam," *The Wall Street Journal*, April 16, 1982. Reprinted by the kind permission of James Bond Stockdale, *The San Diego Union*, and *The Wall Street Journal*.

plane), and a gunshot wound in my good leg (which an irate farmer had pumped into my stretcher during my first night on the ground, an act I credit as morally neutral just to keep the score balanced). The North Vietnamese officer who presided over my arrival after three days in the back of a truck was about my age (42 at the time), also a career military man.

I asked him for medical attention for my broken bones and open wounds. "You have a medical problem and you have a political problem," he said. "In this country we handle political problems first, and if they are satisfactorily resolved, that is, if you demonstrate a proper understanding of the American war of imperialist aggression in Vietnam and take concrete actions to stop it, we will attend to your medical problems." That was the last time the subject of medical attention for me ever came up in my next eight years as a prisoner of war. . . .

These prisons are all the same ; the name of the game is to unstring their victims with fear and polarize them with guilt. There are always more rules than can practically be obeyed, always a tripwire system to snare you in a violation that the jailers can brand as moral turpitude — and there is always an escape valve, a way to make amends if you repent.

The tripwire in Hanoi was based on the "no communication" rule. As with all tripwires, the prisoner had a choice to make and he stood to lose either way. If he obeyed and did not communicate with his comrades, he accrued the conscience problems of betraying his fellows and at the same time sentenced himself to a desperate loneliness which would likely get to him after a year or two. If he communicated, and this was the only way to go for loyalty, for a feeling of self-worth, for dignity, he would periodically be caught and tortured under the charge of ingratitude for the "humane and lenient treatment" he was being given.

(Incidentally, communication grew to be a very refined, high-volume, high-speed, highly accurate though dangerous art. We used the same code Koestler's fictional Commissar N. S. Rubashov used during his Moscow trial and execution period in the late 1930's.)

By torture, I don't mean leg irons or handcuffs or isolation. We were always careful to remind ourselves that those were just inconveniences, not to panic. By torture we meant the intentional imposition of pain and claustrophobia over as short a time as necessary to get the victim to "submit."

In my experience this is best done by heavily slapping the prisoner, seating him on the brick floor, reeving his upper arms with ropes, and while standing barefoot on his back cinching up the elaborate bindings by jerks, pulling his shoulders together while stuffing his head down between his feet with the heel of your foot. Numb arms under contorted tension produce an excruciating pain and a gnawing but sure knowledge that a clock is ticking while your blood is stopped and that the longer you wait before submitting the longer useless arms will dangle at your sides (45 minutes of blood stoppage usually cost about six months of dangle). The claustrophobia also concentrates the mind wonderfully.

How long to submission for a good man ? About 30 minutes. Why not hold your silence and die? You can't just will yourself dead and have it happen — especially in that position. Why not just give them what they want and be done with it ? Reasons that come to mind include dignity, self-esteem, contempt for B-grade pageants. They can make you tell them most anything they know you know. The trick is, year in and year out, never to level with your captors, never let them really know what you know. . . .

The political prison experience is an emotional experience in that you learn that your naked, most inner self is in the spotlight, and that any detected shame or deep fear, any chink in your moral armor is a perfect opening for the manipulative crowbar. And once the manipulator gets it into you, he can put you out front working for him because he has something on you of which you are genuinely ashamed; he has the means to destroy your reputation if you fail him. Fates like that are what prison nightmares are made of, not the fear of pain. . . .

Americans in Hanoi learned fast. They made no deals. They learned that "meeting them half way" was the road to degradation. My hypothetical young prison mate soon learned that impulses, working against the grain, are very important in political prisons, that one learns to enjoy fighting city hall, to enjoy giving the enemy upside-down logic problems, that one soon finds himself taking his lumps with pride and not merely liking but loving that tapping guy next door, the man he never sees, the man he bares his soul to after each torture session, until he realizes he is thereby expiating all residual guilt. Then he realizes he can't be hurt and he can't be had as long as he tells the truth and clings to that forgiving band of brothers who are becoming his country, his family.

This is the power of comradeship and high mindedness that ultimately springs up among people of good will under pressure in mutual danger. It is a source of power as old as man, one we forget in times of freedom, of affluence, of fearful pessimism — like now.

Eight years in a Hanoi prison, survival and dignity. What does it all come down to? It does not come down to coping or supplication or hatred or strength beyond the grasp of any normal person. It comes down to unselfish comradeship, and it comes down to pride, dignity, an enduring sense of self-worth and to that enigmatic mixture of conscience and egoism called personal honor.

TOWARD THE TWENTY-FIRST CENTURY

Mikhail Gorbachev and *Perestroika*

Soon after Mikhail Gorbachev (1931 —) assumed leadership in the Soviet Union in 1985, he announced his policy of *perestroika* (restructuring), which initiated a powerful process of revolutionary renovation and presented a provocative challenge to many — both in the USSR and the West. Numerous changes, both internally and abroad, have generated great debate. Gorbachev's economic policies included an effort to reduce the role of central planning in the Soviet economy and have allowed greater authority for the managers of the nation's enterprises. An effort has also been made to encourage more autonomy for private businesses as well as cooperative ventures with Western firms. Politically, Gorbachev's reforms included a loosening of centralized controls both internally as well as in the satellite states of Eastern Europe. This permitted a resurgence of national consciousness which led to the liberation of Eastern Europe, the dismantling of the Berlin Wall, and the unification of Germany — historic events signifying the end of the cold war. Some of Gorbachev's reforms have been met with suspicion, cynicism, and strong opposition within Soviet officialdom. Although he appears to have consolidated his power, it is extremely precarious and there is considerable debate and uncertainty about the nature of the reforms, how long-lasting they may be, or where they may lead.

The first selection, taken from Gorbachev's book *Perestroika: New Thinking for Our Country and the World* explains his reasons and thoughts behind the urgent need for reforms. The second reading consists of excerpts from an address to the U.S. Congress by Václav Havel (1936 —), the dissident playwright and intellectual who became president of Czechoslovakia. The final selection contains excerpts from a speech by Richard von Weizsäcker, president of the Federal Republic of Germany.

98

Perestroika

QUESTIONS TO CONSIDER

1. What is the meaning of *perestroika,* and what prompted the idea? What domestic and international examples of *perestroika* have occurred under Gorbachev's leadership?
2. What does "restructuring" mean for the history of socialism? Are there dangers in encouraging economic but not political reforms? What historic examples are there to illustrate the implications of such "unequal" changes?
3. How do the changes Gorbachev advocates indicate a greater openness to Western-style democracy and market capitalism, a break from the isolation of the Soviet Union, and a return to a policy of co-existence if not an end to the cold war?
4. In what ways do Gorbachev's initiatives represent a response to some of the issues raised in the Sakharov reading (see Reading 77)?
5. Compare Gorbachev's reforms with those initiated by Peter the Great (see Reading 12) and Catherine the Great (see Reading 22).

What is perestroika? What prompted the idea of restructuring? What does it mean in the history of socialism? What does it augur for the peoples of the Soviet Union? How might it influence the outside world? All these questions concern the world public and are being actively discussed. Let me begin with the first one.

Perestroika — An Urgent Necessity

I think one thing should be borne in mind when studying the origins and essence of perestroika in the USSR. Perestroika is no whim on the part of some ambitious individuals or a group of leaders. If it were, no exhortations, plenary meetings or even a party congress could have rallied the people to the work which we are now doing and which involves more and more Soviet people each day.

Perestroika is an urgent necessity arising from the profound processes of development in our socialist society. This society is ripe for change. It has long been yearning for it. Any delay in beginning perestroika could have led to an exacerbated internal situation in the near future, which, to put it bluntly, would have been fraught with serious social, economic and political crises.

We have drawn these conclusions from a broad and frank analysis of the situation that has developed in our society by the middle of the eighties. This situation and the problems arising from it presently confront the country's leadership, in

From Mikhail Gorbachev, *Perestroika : New Thinking for Our Country and the World* (New York : Harper & Row, 1987), pp. 17–25, passim. Reprinted by permission of Harper & Row, Publishers, Inc.

which new people have gradually appeared in the last few years. I would like to discuss here the main results of this analysis, in the course of which we had to reassess many things and look back at our history, both recent and not so recent.

Russia, where a great Revolution took place seventy years ago, is an ancient country with a unique history filled with searchings, accomplishments and tragic events. It has given the world many discoveries and outstanding personalities.

However, the Soviet Union is a young state without analogues in history or in the modern world. Over the past seven decades — a short span in the history of human civilization — our country has traveled a path equal to centuries. One of the mightiest powers in the world rose up to replace the backward semi-colonial and semi-feudal Russian Empire. Huge productive forces, a powerful intellectual potential, a highly advanced culture, a unique community of over one hundred nations and nationalities, and firm social protection for 280 million people on a territory forming one-sixth of the Earth — such are our great and indisputable achievements and Soviet people are justly proud of them.

I am not saying this to make my land appear better than it was or is. I do not want to sound like an apologist for whom "mine" means best and unquestionably superior. What I have just said is actual reality, authentic fact, the visible product of the work of several generations of our people. And it is equally clear that my country's progress became possible thanks to the Revolution. It is the product of the Revolution. It is the fruit of socialism, the new social system, and the result of the historical choice made by our people. Behind them are the feats of our fathers and grandfathers and millions of working people — workers, farmers and intellectuals — who seventy years ago assumed direct responsibility for the future of their country.

I would like the reader to contemplate all this : otherwise it would be hard to see what had happened and is happening in our society. I shall return to the historical aspects of our development later. Let me first explain the far-from-simple situation which had developed in the country by the eighties and which made perestroika necessary and inevitable.

At some stage — this became particularly clear in the latter half of the seventies — something happened that was at first sight inexplicable. The country began to lose momentum. Economic failures became more frequent. Difficulties began to accumulate and deteriorate, and unresolved problems to multiply. Elements of what we call stagnation and other phenomena alien to socialism began to appear in the life of society. A kind of "braking mechanism" affecting social and economic development formed. And all this happened at a time when a scientific and technological revolution opened up new prospects for economic and social progress.

Something strange was taking place : the huge fly-wheel of a powerful machine was revolving, while either transmission from it to work places was skidding or drive belts were too loose.

Analyzing the situation, we first discovered a slowing economic growth. In the last fifteen years the national income growth rates had declined by more than a half and by the beginning of the eighties had fallen to a level close to economic stagnation. A country that was once quickly closing on the world's advanced nations began to lose one position after another. Moreover, the gap in the efficiency of production, quality of products, scientific and technological development, the production of advanced technology and the use of advanced techniques began to widen, and not to our advantage.

The gross output drive, particularly in heavy industry, turned out to be a "top-priority" task, just an end in itself. The same happened in capital construction, where a sizable portion of the national wealth became idle capital.

There were costly projects that never lived up to the highest scientific and technological standards. The worker or the enterprise that had expended the greatest amount of labor, material and money was considered the best. It is natural for the producer to "please" the consumer, if I may put it that way. With us, however, the consumer found himself totally at the mercy of the producer and had to make do with what the latter chose to give him. This was again a result of the gross output drive.

It became typical of many of our economic executives to think not of how to build up the national asset, but of how to put more material, labor and working time into an item to sell it at a higher price. Consequently, for all "gross output," there was a shortage of goods. We spent, in fact we are still spending, far more on raw materials, energy and other resources per unit of output than other developed nations. Our country's wealth in terms of natural and manpower resources has spoilt, one may even say corrupted, us. That, in fact, is chiefly the reason why it was possible for our economy to develop extensively for decades.

Accustomed to giving priority to quantitative growth in production, we tried to check the falling rates of growth, but did so mainly by continually increasing expenditures: we built up the fuel and energy industries and increased the use of natural resources in production.

As time went on, material resources became harder to get and more expensive. On the other hand, the extensive methods of fixed capital expansion resulted in an artificial shortage of manpower. In an attempt to rectify the situation somehow, large, unjustified, i.e., in fact unearned, bonuses began to be paid and all kinds of undeserved incentives introduced under the pressure of this shortage, and that led, at a later stage, to the practice of padding reports merely for gain. Parasitical attitudes were on the rise, the prestige of conscientious and high-quality labor began to diminish and a "wage-leveling" mentality was becoming widespread. The imbalance between the measure of work and the measure of consumption, which had become something like the linchpin of the braking mechanism, not only obstructed the growth of labor productivity, but led to the distortion of the principle of social justice.

So the inertia of extensive economic development was leading to an economic deadlock and stagnation.

The economy was increasingly squeezed financially. The sale of large quantities of oil and other fuel and energy resources and raw materials on the world market did not help. It only aggravated the situation. Currency earnings thus made were predominantly used for tackling problems of the moment rather than on economic modernization or on catching up technologically.

Declining rates of growth and economic stagnation were bound to affect other aspects of the life of Soviet society. Negative trends seriously affected the social sphere. This led to the appearance of the so-called "residual principle" in accordance with which social and cultural programs received what remained in the budget after allocations to production. A "deaf ear" sometimes seemed to be turned to social problems. The social sphere began to lag behind other spheres in terms of technological development, personnel, know-how and most importantly, quality of work.

Here we have more paradoxes. Our society has ensured full employment and provided fundamental social guarantees. At the same time, we failed to use the full potential of socialism to meet the growing requirements in housing, in quality and sometimes quantity of foodstuffs, in the proper organization of the work of transport, in health services, in education and in tackling other problems which, naturally, arose in the course of society's development.

An absurd situation was developing. The Soviet Union, the world's biggest producer of steel, raw materials, fuel and energy, has shortfalls in them due to wasteful or inefficient use. One of the biggest producers of grain for food, it nevertheless has to buy millions of tons of grain a year for fodder. We have the largest number of doctors and hospital beds per thousand of the population and, at the same time, there are shortcomings in our health services. Our rockets can find Halley's comet and fly to Venus with amazing accuracy, but side by side with these scientific and technological triumphs is an obvious lack of efficiency in using scientific achievements for economic needs, and many Soviet household appliances are of poor quality.

This, unfortunately, is not all. A gradual erosion of the ideological and moral values of our people began.

It was obvious to everyone that the growth rates were sharply dropping and that the entire mechanism of quality control was not working properly ; there was a lack of receptivity to the advances in science and technology ; the improvement in living standards was slowing down and there were difficulties in the supply of foodstuffs, housing, consumer goods and services.

On the ideological plane as well, the braking mechanism brought about ever greater resistance to the attempts to constructively scrutinize the problems that were emerging and to the new ideas. Propaganda of success — real or imagined — was gaining the upper hand. Eulogizing and servility were encouraged ; the needs and opinions of ordinary working people, of the public at large, were ignored. In the social sciences scholastic theorization was encouraged and developed, but creative thinking was driven out from the social sciences, and superfluous and voluntarist assessments and judgments were declared indisputable truths. Scientific, theoretical and other discussions, which are indispensable for the development of thought and for creative endeavor, were emasculated. Similar negative tendencies also affected culture, the arts and journalism, as well as the teaching process and medicine, where mediocrity, formalism and loud eulogizing surfaces, too.

The presentation of a "problem-free" reality backfired : a breach had formed between word and deed, which bred public passivity and disbelief in the slogans being proclaimed. It was only natural that this situation resulted in a credibility gap : everything that was proclaimed from the rostrums and printed in newspapers and textbooks was put in question. Decay began in public morals ; the great feeling of solidarity with each other that was forged during the heroic times of the Revolution, the first five-year plans, the Great Patriotic War and postwar rehabilitation was weakening; alcoholism, drug addiction and crime were growing; and the penetration of the stereotypes of mass culture alien to us, which bred vulgarity and low tastes and brought about ideological barrenness increased.

Party guidance was relaxed, and initiative lost in some of the vital social processes. Everybody started noticing the stagnation among the leadership and the violation of the natural process of change there. At a certain stage this made for a poorer performance by the Politburo[1] and the Secretariat[2] of the CPSU Central Committee, by the government and throughout the entire Central Committee and the Party apparatus, for that matter.

Political flirtation and mass distribution of awards, titles and bonuses often replaces genuine concern for the people, for their living and working conditions, for a favorable social atmosphere. An atmosphere emerged of "everything goes," and fewer and fewer demands were made on discipline and responsibility. Attempts were made to cover it all up with pompous campaigns and undertakings and celebrations of numerous anniversaries centrally and locally. The world of day-to-day realities and the world of feigned prosperity were diverging more and more.

The need for change was brewing not only in the material sphere of life but also in public consciousness. People who had practical experience, a sense of justice and commitment to the ideals of Bolshevism criticized the established practice of doing things and noted with anxiety the symptoms of moral degradation and erosion of revolutionary ideals and socialist values.

Workers, farmers and intellectuals, Party functionaries centrally and locally, came to ponder the situation in the country. There was a growing awareness that things could not go on like this much longer. Perplexity and indignation welled up that the great values born of the October Revolution and the heroic struggle for socialism were being trampled underfoot.

All honest people saw with bitterness that people were losing interest in social affairs, that labor no longer had its respectable status, that people, especially the young, were after profit at all cost. Our people have always had an intrinsic ability to discern the gap between word and deed. No wonder Russian folk tales are full of mockery aimed against people who like pomp and trappings; and literature, which had always played a great role in our country's spiritual life, is merciless to every manifestation of injustice and abuse of power. In their best works writers, film-makers, theater producers and actors tried to boost people's belief in the ideological achievements of socialism and hope for a spiritual revival of society and, despite bureaucratic bans and even persecution, prepared people morally for perestroika.

By saying all this I want to make the reader understand that the energy for revolutionary change has been accumulating amid our people and in the Party for some time. And the ideas of perestroika have been prompted not just by prag-

1. *Politburo of the CPSU Central Committee* — the collective leadership body of the CPSU Central Committee, which is elected at a plenary meeting of the Central Committee to guide the Party work between the plenary meetings of the CPSU Central Committee.
2. *Secretariat of the CPSU Central Committee* — a body of the CPSU Central Committee which is elected at a plenary meeting of the Central Committee to supervise the Party's day-to-day work, mainly in selecting the cadres and organizing the verification of the fulfillment of the decisions adopted.

matic interests and considerations but also by our troubled conscience, by the indomitable commitment to ideals which we inherited from the Revolution and as a result of a theoretical quest which gave us a better knowledge of society and reinforced our determination to go ahead.

99

Václav Havel, Address to Congress

Václav Havel (1936 —) refused to be silenced after the 1968 Soviet suppression of the "Prague Spring" and courageously continued writing plays. He emerged as one of Czechoslovakia's leading dissidents and spent many years in prison. His most recent arrest occurred on October 27, 1989, but he was quickly released as a result of Moscow's new policy allowing greater autonomy in Eastern Europe. On December 18, 1989, the Czechoslovakian Parliament unanimously elected him president of the nation. The excerpts that follow are from a speech he delivered to the U.S. Congress in Washington, DC, on February 21, 1990.

QUESTIONS TO CONSIDER

1. Why does Havel express gratitude toward President Woodrow Wilson (see Reading 59) and toward Thomas Jefferson?
2. According to Havel, how has the United States helped Czechoslovakia survive?
3. Why does Havel urge that everyone must "... enter at last into an era of multipolarity"? What does he mean?
4. What is the meaning of Havel's statement: "Consciousness precedes Being, and not the other way around, as the Marxists claim"? (Compare with Reading 36, *The Communist Manifesto*.)
5. What examples could you cite to support Havel's declaration that "... we still don't know how to put morality ahead of politics, science and economics"? How could we learn to do that?

When they arrested me on October 27, I was living in a country ruled by the most conservative Communist government in Europe, and our society slumbered beneath the pall of a totalitarian system. Today, less than 4 months later, I am speak-

From an address entitled "Help the Soviet Union on its Road to Democracy" in *Vital Speeches of the Day* (Mount Pleasant, SC : City News Publishing Co.), Vol. LVI, No. 11 (March 15, 1990), pp. 327–330, passim.

ing to you as the representative of a country that has set out on the road to democracy, a country where there is complete freedom of speech, which is getting ready for free elections, and which wants to create a prosperous market economy and its own foreign policy.

It is all very extraordinary.

But I have not come here to speak for myself or my feelings, or merely to talk about my own country. I have used this small example of something I know well, to illustrate something general and important.

We are living in very extraordinary times. The human face of the world is changing so rapidly that none of the familiar political speedometers are adequate.

We playwrights, who have to cram a whole human life or an entire historical era in a 2-hour play, can scarcely understand this rapidity ourselves. And if it gives us trouble, think of the trouble it must give to political scientists, who spend their whole lives studying the realm of the probable. And have even less experience with the realm of the improbable than us, the playwrights.

Let me try to explain why I think the velocity of the changes in my country, in Central and Eastern Europe, and of course in the Soviet Union itself, has made such a significant impression on the face of the world today, and why it concerns the fate of us all, including you Americans. I would like to look at this, first from the political point of view, and then from a point of view that we might call philosophical.

Twice in this century, the world has been threatened by a catastrophe ; twice this catastrophe was born in Europe, and twice you Americans, along with others, were called upon to save Europe, the whole world and yourselves. The first rescue mission — among other things — provided significant help to us Czechs and Slovaks.

Thanks to the great support of your President Wilson, our first President, Tomas Garrigue Masaryk, could found our modern independent state. He founded it, as you know, on the same principles on which the United States of America has been founded, as Masaryk's manuscripts held by the Library of Congress testify.

In the meantime, the United States made enormous strides. It became the most powerful nation on Earth, and it understood the responsibility that flowed from this. Proof of this are the hundreds of thousands of your young citizens who gave their lives for the liberation of Europe, and the graves of American airmen and soldiers on Czechoslovak soil.

But something else was happening as well : the Soviet Union appeared, grew, and transformed the enormous sacrifices of its people suffering under totalitarian rule, into a strength that, after World War II, made it the second most powerful nation in the world. It was a country that rightly gave people nightmares, because no one knew what would occur to its rulers next and what country they would decide to conquer and drag into their sphere of influence, as it is called in political language.

All of this taught us to see the world in bipolar terms, as two enormous forces, one a defender of freedom, the other a source of nightmares. Europe became the point of friction between these two powers and thus it turned into a single enormous arsenal divided into two parts. In this process, one half of the arsenal became part of that nightmarish power, while the other — the free part —

bordering on the ocean and having no wish to be driven into it, was compelled, together with you, to build a complicated security system, to which we probably owe the fact that we still exist.

So you may have contributed to the salvation of us Europeans, of the world and thus of yourselves for a third time: you have helped us to survive until today — without a hot war this time — but merely a cold one.

And now what is happening is happening: the totalitarian system in the Soviet Union and in most of its satellites is breaking down and our nations are looking for a way to democracy and independence. The first act in this remarkable drama began when Mr. Gorbachev and those around him, faced with the sad reality of their country, initiated their policy of "perestroika." Obviously they had no idea either what they were setting in motion or how rapidly events would unfold. We knew a lot about the enormous number of growing problems that slumbered beneath the honeyed, unchanging mask of socialism. But I don't think any of us knew how little it would take for these problems to manifest themselves in all their enormity, and for the longings of these nations to emerge in all their strength. The mask fell away so rapidly that, in the flood of work, we have literally no time even to be astonished.

What does all this mean for the world in the long run? Obviously a number of things. This is, I am firmly convinced, a historically irreversible process, and as a result Europe will begin again to seek its own identity without being compelled to be a divided armory any longer. Perhaps this will create the hope that sooner or later your boys will no longer have to stand on guard for freedom in Europe, or come to our rescue, because Europe will at last be able to stand guard over itself. But that is still not the most important thing: the main thing is, it seems to me, that these revolutionary changes will enable us to escape from the rather antiquated straitjacket of this bipolar view of the world, and to enter at last into an era of multipolarity. That is, into an era in which all of us — large and small — former slaves and former masters — will be able to create what your great President Lincoln called the family of man. Can you imagine what a relief this would be to that part of the world which for some reason is called the Third World, even though it is the largest?...

... I have already said this in our parliament, and I would like to repeat it here, in this Congress, which is architecturally far more attractive: for many years, Czechoslovakia — as someone's meaningless satellite — has refused to face up honestly to its co-responsibility for the world. It has a lot to make up for. If I dwell on this and so many important things, it is only because I feel — along with my fellow citizens — a sense of culpability for our former reprehensible passivity, and a rather ordinary sense of indebtedness.

... [W]e are of course delighted that your country is so readily lending its support to our fresh efforts to renew democracy. Both our peoples were deeply moved by the generous offers made a few days ago in Prague at the Charles University, one of the oldest in Europe, by your Secretary of State, Mr. James Baker. We are ready to sit down and talk about them.

Ladies and gentlemen, I've only been president for 2 months and I haven't attended any schools for presidents. My only school was life itself. Therefore I don't want to burden you any longer with my political thoughts, but instead I will move on to an area that is more familiar to me, to what I would call the philosophical aspect of those changes that still concern everyone, although they are taking place in our corner of the world.

As long as people are people, democracy in the full sense of the word will always be no more than an ideal; one may approach it as one would a horizon, in ways that may be better or worse, but it can never be fully attained. In this sense you too are merely approaching democracy. You have thousands of problems of all kinds, as other countries do. But you have one great advantage: You have been approaching democracy uninterruptedly for more than 200 years, and your journey toward the horizon has never been disrupted by a totalitarian system. Czechs and Slovaks, despite their humanistic traditions that go back to the first millennium, have approached democracy for a mere 20 years, between the two world wars, and now for the 3½ months since the 17th of November of last year.

The advantage that you have over us is obvious at once.

The Communist type of totalitarian system has left both our nations, Czechs and Slovaks — as it has all the nations of the Soviet Union and the other countries the Soviet Union subjugated in its time — a legacy of countless dead, an infinite spectrum of human suffering, profound economic decline, and above all enormous human humiliation. It has brought us horrors that fortunately you have not known.

At the same time, however — unintentionally, of course — it has given us something positive: a special capacity to look, from time to time, somewhat further than someone who has not undergone this bitter experience. A person who cannot move and live a somewhat normal life because he is pinned under a boulder has more time to think about his hopes than someone who is not trapped that way.

What I am trying to say is this: we must all learn many things from you, from how to educate our offspring, how to elect our representatives, all the way to how to organize our economic life so that it will lead to prosperity and not to poverty. But it doesn't have to be merely assistance from the well-educated, the powerful and the wealthy to someone who has nothing and therefore has nothing to offer in return.

We too can offer something to you: our experience and the knowledge that has come from it.

This is a subject for books, many of which have already been written and many of which have yet to be written. I shall therefore limit myself to a single idea.

The specific experience I'm talking about has given me one great certainty: Consciousness precedes Being, and not the other way around, as the Marxists claim.

For this reason, the salvation of this human world lies nowhere else than in the human heart, in the human power to reflect, in human meekness and in human responsibility.

Without a global revolution in the sphere of human consciousness, nothing will change for the better in the sphere of our Being as humans, and the catastrophe toward which this world is headed, be it ecological, social, demographic or a general breakdown of civilization, will be unavoidable. If we are no longer threatened by world war, or by the danger that the absurd mountains of accumulated nuclear weapons might blow up the world, this does not mean that we have definitively won. We are in fact far from the final victory.

We are still a long way from that "family of man"; in fact, we seem to be receding from the ideal rather than drawing closer to it. Interests of all kinds: personal, selfish, state, national, group and, if you like, company interests still considerably outweigh genuinely common and global interests. We are still under the sway of the destructive and vain belief that man is the pinnacle of creation, and not just a part of it, and that therefore everything is permitted. There are still many who say they are concerned not for themselves, but for the cause, while they are demonstrably out for themselves and not for the cause at all. We are still destroying the planet that was entrusted to us, and its environment. We still close our eyes to the growing social, ethnic and cultural conflicts in the world. From time to time we say that the anonymous megamachinery we have created for ourselves no longer serves us, but rather has enslaved us, yet we still fail to do anything about it.

In other words, we still don't know how to put morality ahead of politics, science and economics. We are still incapable of understanding that the only genuine backbone of all our actions — if they are to be moral — is responsibility. Responsibility to something higher than my family, my country, my company, my success. Responsibility to the order of Being, where all our actions are indelibly recorded and where, and only where, they will be properly judged.

The interpreter or mediator between us and this higher authority is what is traditionally referred to as human conscience.

If I subordinate my political behavior to this imperative mediated to me by my conscience, I can't go far wrong. If on the contrary I were not guided by this voice, not even 10 presidential schools with 2,000 of the best political scientists in the world could help me.

This is why I ultimately decided — after resisting for a long time — to accept the burden of political responsibility.

I am not the first, nor will I be the last, intellectual to do this. On the contrary, my feeling is that there will be more and more of them all the time. If the hope of the world lies in human consciousness, then it is obvious that intellectuals cannot go on forever avoiding their share of responsibility for the world and hiding their distaste for politics under an alleged need to be independent.

It is easy to have independence in your program and then leave others to carry that program out. If everyone thought that way, pretty soon no one would be independent.

I think that you Americans should understand this way of thinking. Wasn't it the best minds of your country, people you could call intellectuals, who wrote your famous Declaration of Independence, your Bill of Human Rights and your Constitution and who — above all — took upon themselves the practical responsibility for putting them into practice? The worker from Branik in Prague that your President referred to in his State of the Union message this year is far from being the only person in Czechoslovakia, let alone in the world, to be inspired by those great documents. They inspire us all. They inspire us despite the fact that they are over 200 years old. They inspire us to be citizens.

When Thomas Jefferson wrote that, "Governments are instituted among Men deriving their just Powers from the Consent of the Governed," it was a simple and important act of the human spirit.

What gave meaning to that act, however, was the fact that the author backed it up with his life. It was not just his words, it was his deeds as well.

I will end where I began : history has accelerated. I believe that once again it will be the human mind that will notice this acceleration, give it a name, and transform those words into deeds.

Thank you.

100

Richard von Weizsäcker, "The Day of German Unity"

Certainly one of the key events signifying the thaw in East-West tensions, the end of the cold war, and the new opportunities that provided was the unification of Germany which formally occurred on October 3, 1990. To mark the significance of the historic event Richard von Weizsäcker (1920 —), the president of the Federal Republic of Germany, delivered an address in Berlin. The following reading is an excerpt from his speech.

QUESTIONS TO CONSIDER

1. According to von Weizsäcker, what was the relationship between Gorbachev's policies and the unification of Germany?
2. What may have been von Weizsäcker's purpose in stating that ". . . anyone who believes we can cope with the future with the nation state alone is living in a bygone era"?
3. What are von Weizsäcker's views concerning Germany's role in the European Community? What other global responsibilities does he envision for Germany?
4. Compare and contrast the division of Germany with that of Korea (see Reading 81). What are the prospects for the unification of Korea? Might the Koreans learn something from the German experience?

After the Second World War the division of Germany epitomized the division of Europe. It was not the result of the joint will of the victors but rather of their disagreement. The growing East-West confrontation cemented that division. But we will not use that as an excuse. No one in our country will forget that there would have been no division if the war started by Hitler had not happened.

Against the background of the Cold War and under the protective shield of the nuclear stalemate, the social systems in East and West competed with one another for over forty years. That phase is now drawing to a close.

From Federal Republic of Germany, *Statements & Speeches*, Vol. XIII, No. 20 (New York : German Information Center), Nov. 14, 1990, pp. 1–6 passim. Reprinted by permission.

The Soviet leadership under President Gorbachev has realized that reforms leading to democracy and a market economy have become inevitable. But without freedom such reforms would be doomed to failure. As a result, courageous decisions were taken. The Soviet Union ceased dominating its allies and respected their right to decide their own political future. This led to the unprecedented peaceful revolutions in Central, Eastern and South-Eastern Europe. It led to the acceptance of the German people's free decision in favour of national unity.

The success of the reform course pursued by the Soviet leadership is still in considerable jeopardy, but it has already gone down in history as a worthy endeavour. And many people, including we Germans, have reason to be grateful.

We are grateful to the civil rights movements and peoples in Hungary, Poland and Czechoslovakia. The citizens of Warsaw, Budapest and Prague have set examples. They saw the path leading to freedom in the German Democratic Republic as part of a common historical process and gave it their encouragement.

Nor will we forget the help they gave to refugees, which was a very direct contribution toward overcoming the wall and the barbed wire. In future the united Germany will seek an open, a close neighborly relationship with them.

The defence of freedom and human rights is fundamental to the commitment of our Western allies and friends, above all the Americans, the French and the British. Their protection, their resolve and cooperation, have been of crucial assistance to us. Most important of all, they place their confidence in us. For this we are deeply grateful.

The nation-state has not ceased to exist, but anyone who believes we can cope with the future with the nation-state alone is living in a bygone era. No nation in the world can solve the world's major problems by itself. Modern systems do not think and function nationally. This applies to security and the environment, to industry and energy, to transport and telecommunications. In our age sovereignty means playing our part within the community of states.

The European Community has created a convincing model for such cooperation. It has fused national powers — and precisely those which are crucial for peaceful neighborly relations — into a supranational framework. In the contest between the systems of East and West it has been the source of powerful impulses for reform in Eastern Europe.

The Cold War is over. Freedom and democracy have prevailed in nearly every country. Not through coercion by the countries that dominated them but of their own free will they can now intensify and institutionalize their relations in order to create, for the first time, a common peaceful order. This marks the beginning of a completely new chapter in the history of the nations of Europe. The goal is pan-European unification.

It is an ambitious goal. We can achieve it, but we can also fall short. There is no time to lose. We face the clear alternative of uniting Europe or relapsing into the sorrowful nationalistic confrontations of the past.

Tangible prospects for the economic and social development of the countries of Central, Eastern and South-Eastern Europe must now be given priority. The newly acquired freedom must take root. It must not be allowed to wither for lack of nourishment. The European Community can provide crucial assistance. It will above all depend on the Community how the situation in the whole of Europe develops.

We Germans have a key role to play. We speak out in support of a common, constructive Eastern policy by the West as a whole. Now that all Germans have become direct neighbors of the Poles, who are so important to us, it is our duty to urge that the Community conclude an association agreement with them, not in the distant future but very soon. The same applies to Czechoslovakia and Hungary.

The Soviet Union, to mention another extremely important example, needs close European cooperation on its incomparably difficult course. The Soviet Union wishes to close the traditional gap between itself and the rest of Europe. It has realized that German unification is not an obstacle but rather a condition for that step. This is the principal message of the highly significant Two-plus-Four conference.[1] As we all know that Europe's future stability depends to a large extent on Moscow's contribution. The Soviet Union's western frontier must not become Europe's eastern frontier.

When we Germans send such messages to the whole of Europe we do so as an integral part of the Western community. This firm integration has shaped life in the Federal Republic; it has mobilized our resources and generated fresh energy. We will on no account jeopardize our Atlantic and European partnership. That is our very own interest — and it is shared by our countrymen in the new federal states. They know how important friendship, especially with France, will continue to be and are themselves glad to have this direct neighbourly relationship.

We will only make headway if we proceed together with our western partners, especially within and through the European Community. Everything the member countries do for the whole of Europe through the Community strengthens both the Community itself and its individual member.

We Germans can best look after our interests and dispel our partners' doubts by not allowing ourselves to be outdone in our efforts to strengthen the Community, and by continuing without any hesitation along the road to economic and monetary union leading to political union, as we have promised.

To remain fully integrated within the West and oriented to the whole of Europe, that is the task of the united Germany. We will have accomplished it if, at some time in the future, it is said : The crucial chapter leading to the unification of the whole of Europe began with the termination of Germany's division.

The faster we Europeans settle our own conflicts, the better will we be able to meet our global responsibilities. During the Cold War Europeans time and again exported tension and weapons to the southern hemisphere. Our duty now is to promote the CSCE[2] process, to reduce armaments and to boost assistance for the South.

Swords into ploughshares — this wonderful biblical picture from the days of the peaceful revolution does not imply that we should forego a sensible, adequate defence capability. It means satisfying hunger and alleviating want around the world. We are encouraged in this aim by the many young voices from all parts of Germany. . . .

---

1. A conference of representatives from (1) the Federal Republic of Germany (West Germany), (2) the German Democratic Republic (East Germany), (3) France, (4) Great Britain, (5) the Soviet Union, and (6) the United States.
2. European Conference on Security and Cooperation.

Today, fellow countrymen, we have founded our common state. What we make of unity in human terms will not be decided by any government treaty, constitution, or law. It depends on the attitude adopted by each one of us, on our own openness and our care for one another. It is the "plebiscite of each single day" (Renan)[3] which will determine the character of our community.

I am confident we shall succeed in filling existing and newly emerging gulfs. We can fuse the constitutional patriotism of the one side with human solidarity experienced by the other into a powerful whole. We share the will to carry out our great responsibilities as expected by our neighbors.

We realize how much harder life is for other nations at present. History has given us a chance. We must seize it, with confidence and trust.

And joy — we heard it last night — the joy we feel, is a divine spark.

Human Rights and American Foreign Policy

After World War II, the establishment of the United Nations' Commission on Human Rights reflected the international concern over the violation of human rights, defined in part as the right to life, liberty, and the integrity of the individual. Although the U.S. government appeared ready to make the protection of human rights an important aspect of its foreign policy immediately after World War II, the issue became increasingly politicized as ideological disagreements over defining human rights were reinforced by cold war tensions. Throughout the 1950s and most of the 1960s, the relatively small numbers of human-rights activists were generally viewed as naive and unrealistic.

By the 1970s however, the human rights movement began to revive. Representatives from 35 nations met in Helsinki, Finland, for a two-year conference that focused on issues of security, human rights, and cooperation in Europe. The Helsinki Accords was an agreement signed on August 1, 1975. In the United States, the human rights movement began to revive and pressure mounted to make it an important component of American foreign policy, especially in dealing with Third World nations. The U.S. Congress passed legislation requiring the State Department to assess the status of human rights in various nations. The law also called for the possible curtailment of U.S. foreign aid if a nation was found to be in gross violation of those rights or if insufficient progress had occurred to reflect improvement.

After Jimmy Carter's inauguration in 1977, the issue of human rights quickly became a high priority in foreign policy decisions, especially in U.S. relations toward Latin America. As a result, the administration withheld economic and military aid to the military regimes of Guatemala, Argentina, and Chile, and in early 1979, to the government of Anastasio Somoza in Nicaragua.

3. Ernest Renan (1823–1892), French historian of religion and European nationalism.

Critics of Carter's methods of attempting to foster human rights improvements in other nations viewed his approach as simplistic, inconsistent, and, most of all, dangerous to the U.S. national interest. The debate intensified as the nation approached the 1980 presidential elections. One of the leading spokesmen for American conservatives, William F. Buckley, Jr. (1925 —), attacked Carter's policies in the *National Review,* the journal he edited, through his syndicated column, and in numerous public appearances. The second reading in this section is an excerpt from one of his essays, which was written after the victory of the Sandinistas in Nicaragua and after the Muslim revolutionaries expelled the Shah from Iran and seized American hostages.

101

Jimmy Carter, Notre Dame Address

Shortly after his inauguration, President Carter delivered an important foreign policy speech at the University of Notre Dame. In the following excerpt, he outlines the fundamental principles that must shape the U.S. role in international affairs.

QUESTIONS TO CONSIDER

1. Why did Carter declare that previous foreign policies were flawed? What examples does he use to illustrate his argument?
2. What did Carter mean by his statement that ". . . we have now found our way back to our own principles and values, and we have regained our lost confidence"? How was he attempting to redefine the U.S. national interest?
3. Compare Carter's approach in foreign policy with that of Woodrow Wilson (see Reading 59) and Harry Truman (see Reading 79).

I want to speak to you today about the strands that connect our actions overseas with our essential character as a nation. I believe we can have a foreign policy that is democratic, that is based on fundamental values, and that uses power and influence, which we have, for humane purposes. We can also have a foreign policy that the American people both support and, for a change, know about and understand.

I have a quiet confidence in our own political system. Because we know that democracy works, we can reject the arguments of those rulers who deny human rights to their people.

From *The Review of Politics* (University of Notre Dame), 39, no. 3 (July 1977), pp. 229–297.

We are confident that democracy's example will be compelling, and so we seek to bring that example closer to those from whom in the past few years we have been separated and who are not yet convinced about the advantages of our kind of life.

We are confident that democratic methods are the most effective and so we are not tempted to employ improper tactics here at home or abroad.

We are confident of our own strength, so we can seek substantial mutual reductions in the nuclear arms race.

And we are confident of the good sense of American people, and so we let them share in the process of making foreign policy decisions. We can thus speak with the voices of 215 million, and not just of an isolated handful.

Democracy's great recent successes — in India, Portugal, Spain, Greece — show that our confidence in this system is not misplaced. Being confident of our own future, we are now free of that inordinate fear of communism which once led us to embrace any dictator who joined us in that fear. I'm glad that that's being changed.

For too many years, we've been willing to adopt the flawed and erroneous principles and tactics of our adversaries, sometimes abandoning our own values for theirs. We've fought fire with fire, never thinking that fire is better quenched with water. This approach failed, with Vietnam the best example of its intellectual and moral poverty. But through failure, we have now found our way back to our own principles and values, and we have regained our lost confidence.

By the measure of history, our Nation's 200 years are very brief, and our rise to world eminence is briefer still. It dates from 1945 when Europe and the old international order lay in ruins. Before then America was largely on the periphery of world affairs, but since then we have inescapably been at the center of world affairs.

Our policy during this period was guided by two principles: a belief that Soviet expansion was almost inevitable but that it must be contained, and the corresponding belief in the importance of an almost exclusive alliance among non-Communist nations on both sides of the Atlantic. That system could not last forever unchanged. Historical trends have weakened its foundation. The unifying threat of conflict with the Soviet Union has become less intensive even though the competition has become more extensive.

The Vietnamese war produced a profound moral crisis sapping worldwide faith in our own policy and our system of life, a crisis of confidence made even more grave by the covert pessimism of some of our leaders.

In less than a generation, we've seen the world change dramatically. The daily lives and aspirations of most human beings have been transformed. Colonialism is nearly gone. A new sense of national identity now exists in almost 100 new countries that have been formed in the last generation. Knowledge has become more widespread; aspirations are higher. As more people have been freed from traditional constraints, more have been determined to achieve for the first time in their lives social justice.

The world is still divided by ideological disputes, dominated by regional conflicts, and threatened by danger that we will not resolve the differences of race and wealth without violence or without drawing into combat the major military powers. We can no longer separate the traditional issues of war and peace from the new global questions of justice, equity, and human rights.

It is a new world — but America should not fear it. It is a new world — and we should help to shape it. It is a new world that calls for a new American foreign policy — a policy based on constant decency in its values and on optimism in our historical vision.

We can no longer have a policy solely for the industrial nations as the foundation of global stability, but we must respond to the new reality of a politically awakening world.

We can no longer expect that the other 150 nations will follow the dictates of the powerful, but we must continue — confidently — our efforts to inspire, to persuade, and to lead.

Our policy must reflect our belief that the world can hope for more than simple survival and our belief that dignity and freedom are fundamental spiritual requirements. Our policy must shape an international system that will last longer than secret deals.

President Carter went on to discuss the need for U.S. foreign policy to be conducted openly and constructively on the following principles: (1) a strong commitment to human rights as a fundamental tenet of U.S. foreign policy; (2) a reinforcement of the bonds among the world's democracies; (3) a firm commitment to engage the Soviet Union in a joint effort to halt the strategic arms race; (4) attempts to improve chances for peace in the Middle East; and (5) efforts to reduce the danger of nuclear proliferation and the spread of conventional weapons.

But all of this that I've described is just the beginning. It's a beginning aimed towards a clear goal: to create a wider framework of international cooperation suited to the new and rapidly changing historical circumstances.

We will cooperate more closely with the newly influential countries in Latin America, Africa, and Asia. We need their friendship and cooperation in a common effort as the structure of world power changes.

More than 100 years ago, Abraham Lincoln said that our Nation could not exist half slave and half free. We know a peaceful world cannot long exist one-third rich and two-thirds hungry.

Most nations share our faith that in the long run, expanded and equitable trade will best help the developing countries to help themselves. But the immediate problems of hunger, disease, illiteracy, and repression are here now.

The Western democracies, the OPEC nations, and the developed Communist countries can cooperate through existing international institutions in providing more effective aid. This is an excellent alternative to war.

We have a special need for cooperation and consultation with other nations in this hemisphere — to the north and to the south. We do not need another slogan. Although these are our close friends and neighbors, our links with them are the same links of equality that we forge for the rest of the world. We will be dealing with them as part of a new, worldwide mosaic of global, regional, and bilateral relations.

It's important that we make progress toward normalizing relations with the People's Republic of China. We see the American and Chinese relationship as a central element of our global policy, and China as a key force for global peace. We wish to cooperate closely with the creative Chinese people on the problems that confront all mankind, and we hope to find a formula which can bridge some of the difficulties that still separate us.

Finally, let me say that we are committed to a peaceful resolution of the crisis in southern Africa. The time has come for the principle of majority rule to be the basis for political order, recognizing that in a democratic system the rights of the minority must also be protected.

To be peaceful, change must come promptly. The United States is determined to work together with our European allies and with the concerned African States to shape a congenial international framework for the rapid and progressive transformation of southern African society and to help protect it from unwarranted outside interference.

Let me conclude by summarizing: Our policy is based on an historical vision of America's role. Our policy is derived from a larger view of global change. Our policy is rooted in our moral values, which never change. Our policy is reinforced by our material wealth and by our military power. Our policy is designed to serve mankind. And it is a policy that I hope will make you proud to be Americans.

102

William F. Buckley, Jr., "Human Rights and Foreign Policy: A Proposal"

Since the early 1950s, William F. Buckley's ideas and writings have consistently expressed conservative viewpoints on many domestic and foreign policy issues. He also became familiar to many Americans as host of "Firing Line," a weekly television program, and through his syndicated column appearing in many newspapers. The excerpt that follows is from an essay published in 1980 as President Carter's foreign policies came under increasing attack and the domestic political debate increased preceding the presidential elections.

QUESTIONS TO CONSIDER

1. Why does Buckley view Carter's approach in foreign affairs and emphasis on human rights as a potentially dangerous shift in U.S. foreign policy? Do you agree with his argument?
2. What examples does Buckley use to demonstrate the "unparalleled state of confusion" engendered by the Carter administration?
3. Why does Buckley view Carter's rhetoric as incompatible with specific actions?

Although President Carter, as we have seen, had been generally bland on the subject of human rights, he was a tiger by the time of his inaugural address : "Our commitment to human rights must be absolute." The real problem, of course, is where to fix our commitment to human rights on this side of absoluteness. President Carter's inaugural address presaged the ensuing chaos. For a while there was great excitement. However short-lived, it was breathcatching. In a few days Jimmy Carter actually answered a letter addressed to him by Andrei Sakharov. A few weeks after that he contrived to meet and shake hands (no photographs) with the valiant Vladimir Bukovsky, among the most illustrious of Soviet dissidents. The Soviet Union exploded. Within a year, the United States ambassador to the United Nations Human Rights Commission in Geneva was being privately instructed by President Carter's Secretary of State *under no circumstances* even to mention the name of Yuri Orlov, who had just been packed off to jail for the crime of monitoring Soviet non-compliance with the provisions of the Helsinki Accords' Basket Three,[1] which Candidate Carter had castigated the Soviet Union for failure to live up to. Jimmy Carter was crestfallen, the great Human Rights Band laid down its instruments, and everyone has been struggling ever since plausibly to give the theme of our policy on human rights.

An attempt to say what is operative U.S. policy in respect of human rights requires a survey of the behavior of the principal Executive of U.S. foreign policy. President Carter's position is best attempted not by reasoning a priori from his general commitment ("absolute") to human rights, but a posteriori from his actions. Almost immediately it transpired that the State Department bureaucracy was apprehensive about the impact of Carter's human rights declarations on concrete questions being negotiated or prospectively in negotiation. The military, in pursuit of its own concerns for U.S. security, was similarly troubled. The State Department and the disarmament folk feared that an antagonized Soviet Union would behave more militantly at the bargaining table. The military was quite unwilling to trade Subic Bay in the Philippines for a moral boycott of President Marcos. An opportunity arose for President Carter to begin to make critical distinctions. Fogbound, he did not do so.

In a speech delivered March 25, 1964 in the Senate, Senator William Fulbright, at the time Chairman of the Senate Foreign Relations Committee, made a useful distinction, even if he went too far with it : "Insofar as a nation is content to practice its doctrines within its own frontiers, that nation, however repugnant its ideology, is one with which we have no proper quarrel." That distinction is geopolitically appealing. Thus in 1965, to guard against what President Johnson perceived as the threat of a communization of the Dominican Republic (it is immaterial whether the threat was real or fancied), we landed armed forces in the Dominican Republic. The western half of Hispaniola had been for eight years under the domination of a murderous Haitian doctor who routinely practiced all the conventional barbarities on his people, and not a few unconventional ones. It

William F. Buckley, Jr., "Human Rights and Foreign Policy : A Proposal," *Foreign Affairs*, 58(4), Spring 1980, 788–792, passim. Reprinted by permission of Foreign Affairs (Spring 1980). Copyright © 1980 by the Council on Foreign Relations, Inc.

1. The document produced at the conference was divided into four sections or "baskets" reflecting the way negotiations had been organized. "Basket Three" dealt with the human rights issue and has attracted the most attention.

did not occur to us to send the marines (as once we had done during this century, though our motives were eclectic) to put down Papa Doc[2] — tacit recognition of the intuitive cogency of Fulbright's doctrine. At its most menacing, Franco's Spain threatened nothing more than Gibraltar, which was in any event a nostalgic fantasy in irredentism, and excusable, if you like, under the various anti-colonialist covenants, save for the disconcerting fact that inhabitants of Gibraltar preferred to remain a crown colony. As it happened, Franco satisfied himself to lay economic siege to Gibraltar, and however persistent the criticism of his regime from its inception at the end of the civil war, no U.S. administration — from Roosevelt's forward — ever proposed collective action against Spain. By contrast, we very nearly went to war to protest the communization of Cuba, less because Castro's doctrines were inherently repugnant than because a Soviet salient deep within the womb of territory putatively protected by the Monroe Doctrine was deemed intolerable.

But President Carter not only failed to make Fulbright's distinction, he agitated to blur it. "I have never had an inclination to single out the Soviet Union as the only place where human rights are being abridged," he said at his press conference of February 23, 1977. And again on March 24 at a press conference, "I've tried to make sure that the world knows that we're not singling out the Soviet Union for abuse or criticism." By June, he was sounding defensive. Not only had the phrase become formulaic ("We've not singled out the Soviet Union for criticism"), he went on to say exactly the opposite of what all his rhetoric required: "and I've never tried to inject myself into the internal affairs of the Soviet Union. I've never made the first comment that personally criticized General Secretary Brezhnev."

Human rights everywhere was the President's Theoretical Objective. And so it remained, even if there were to be no more letters to Sakharovs, or visits with Bukovskys. He clung tenaciously to his theoretical position: "I've worked day and night to make sure that a concern for human rights is woven through everything our Government does, both at home and abroad," he said at a press conference at the end of his first year in office (December 15, 1977); and one year later, commemorating the 30th anniversary of the adoption of the Universal Declaration of Human Rights (December 6, 1978), he pronounced, "As long as I am President, the Government of the United States will continue, throughout the world, to enhance human rights. No force on Earth can separate us from that commitment."

It became clear, as time went on, that specific as distinguished from omnidirectional, censorious presidential declarations would become scarce, indeed might end altogether, leaving to the State Department the clerical duties Congress had legislated before Carter came to office. In due course, Chile, Argentina, Brazil and Paraguay were singled out for criticism, based on the annual reports by the State Department required in the 1976 law: economic credits and military assistance, in varying forms, were withheld. In other countries, notably South Korea and the Philippines, the President invoked the authority given him by Congress to subordinate the concern for human rights to a concern for security interests, and aid continued uninterrupted.

2. Nickname of François Duvalier, a physician who became president of Haiti in 1957 and created a brutal dictatorship. He manipulated elections to become president for life and ruled until his death in 1971.

But the President, although he summoned the necessary discipline to restrain himself from criticism, found it difficult to avoid diplomatic hyperbole. Arriving in Warsaw on December 30, 1977, he greeted the communist proconsul Gierek with the astonishing news that Poland was a "partner in a common effort against war and deprivation." He recalled that at the end of World War I Herbert Hoover ("a great American") "came to Poland to help you ease the suffering of an independent Poland. Circumstances were different and the struggle was long, but Hoover said, and I quote, 'If history teaches us anything, it is that from the unquenchable vitality of the Polish race, Poland will rise again from these ashes.' And," said Carter — jubilantly? — "his prediction came true." These words were perfectly congruent with the picture of Poland described during the famous debate by Gerald Ford. They would not have needed changing if it had happened that during the week before Carter's touchdown in Warsaw, Poland had suddenly wrested its independence from the Soviet Union. The press did not have long to wait. Later in the day:

Q. During the Presidential debates, in a celebrated exchange, President Ford claimed that Eastern Europe was not under Soviet domination. And you replied, 'Tell it to the Poles.' Well, now that you're here, is it your view that this domination will continue almost into perpetuity, or do you see a day when Poland may be actually free?

The President replied that "our nation is committed to the proposition that all countries would be autonomous . . . and . . . free of unwanted interference and entanglements with other nations. . . . I think . . . it's a deep commitment of the vast majority of the Polish people, a desire and a commitment not to be dominated."

Q. You don't deny that they are dominated here?
A. I think I've commented all I wish on that subject.

Four months later, on April 12, 1978, President Carter welcomed President Ceausescu of Romania to the White House. At the ceremony, Carter announced that "the people of the United States are honored by having as our guest a great leader of a great country." And he went on to say, "Our goals are also the same, to have a just system of economics and politics, to let the people of the world share in growth, in peace, in personal freedom." In Civil Liberties, Freedom House gives a rating of six to Romania (seven is the lowest rating). In its Ranking of Nations by Political Rights, it gives Romania a seven.

In greeting Yugoslav President Tito (March 7, 1978), Carter said: "Perhaps as much as any other person, he exemplifies in Yugoslavia the eagerness for freedom, independence, and liberty that exists throughout Eastern Europe and indeed throughout the world." Freedom House on Yugoslavia: Civil Liberties, five; Political Rights, six.

It was not until April 21, 1978 that Carter got around to criticizing Cambodia. When he did, he called it the world's "worst" violator of human rights. "America," he said, "cannot avoid the responsibility to speak out in condemnation of the Cambodian Government, the worst violator of human rights in the world today." America, through its President, precisely *had* avoided the responsibility to speak out in condemnation of the Cambodian government about whose practices as much was known by the end of 1975 as by the spring of 1978.

In brief: by his own example as President, and by the letdown that followed his exalted rhetoric on the subject, Mr. Carter, with some help from the 93rd Congress, has reduced the claims of human rights in U.S. foreign policy to an almost unparalleled state of confusion.

The Catholic Church in Latin America

An important development in Latin America since the 1960s has been the changing nature and role of the Catholic Church. Since the sixteenth-century conquest of the Indian civilizations, the Latin American Church frequently identified with the interests of large land owners and the military in an effort to maintain a traditional and stable society. This coalition began to fragment when concerned and sometimes radicalized clergy assumed activist roles on behalf of the poor. A Peruvian priest, Gustavo Gutiérrez, had an important effect on this movement. His work and his ideas provided the basis for discussion and analysis in subsequent years.

The Vatican's Second Ecumenical Council (1962–1965) also opened the door for change. In 1968, meeting in Medellín, Colombia, the bishops of Latin America drew from Gutiérrez ideas concerning the causes of poverty and injustice and recommended the re-evaluation of all facets of Christian life and practice. The bishops' position on the Church's role in society, known as the Medellín Conclusions, incorporated the ideas and principles that became known as liberation theology.

In Brazil, the Archbishop of Recife, Dom Hélder Câmara, strongly condemned the repressive policies of the Brazilian military regime, which had staged a coup in 1964, suspended constitutional guarantees, and governed by military decree. A Colombian priest and sociologist, Camilo Torres, concluded that his nation's political system offered no hope in dealing with the nation's socioeconomic problems and committed himself to the guerrilla movement in Colombia. He was killed in a battle between the military and the guerrillas in 1966.

In many Latin American countries, priests, nuns, and thousands of others, charged with aiding dissidents and participating in subversive activities, have been imprisoned and often tortured. The following readings reflect some of the issues and tensions faced by the Church in Latin America.

103

Gustavo Gutiérrez, *A Theology of Liberation*

After returning from studying in Europe and while ministering to the poor in the slums of Lima, Gustavo Gutiérrez (1928 —) began writing about the causes of poverty and injustice in Latin America and argued that faith also meant a commitment to work for social justice and reform. Some of his key ideas are revealed in the following excerpts from his book, *A Theology of Liberation,* originally published in the Spanish edition in 1971.

QUESTIONS TO CONSIDER

1. According to Gutiérrez, what are the chief causes of poverty and social injustice? What is one's Christian duty and what might be the consequences of the Church attempting to break its ties with an unjust social order?
2. Why might some of Gutiérrez's ideas appeal to many in Latin America and other Third World countries? Where has this appeal led to collaboration with revolutionary guerrilla groups in recent years? Have their efforts been successful? Why? Why not?

To characterize Latin America as a dominated and oppressed continent naturally leads one to speak of liberation and above all to participate in the process. Indeed, *liberation* is a term which expresses a new posture of Latin Americans.

The failure of reformist efforts has strengthened this attitude. Among more alert groups today, what we have called a new awareness of Latin American reality is making headway. They believe that there can be authentic development for Latin America only if there is liberation from the domination exercised by the great capitalist countries, and especially by the most powerful, the United States of America. This liberation also implies a confrontation with these groups' natural allies, their compatriots who control the national power structure. It is becoming more evident that the Latin American peoples will not emerge from their present status except by means of a profound transformation, *a social revolution,* which will radically and qualitatively change the conditions in which they now live. The oppressed sectors within each country are becoming aware — slowly, it is true — of their class interests and of the painful road which must be followed to accomplish the breakup of the status quo. Even more slowly they are becoming aware of all that the building of a new society implies.

Because of urbanization and increased industrialization, the Latin American popular movement grew from 1930 on, demanding greater participation in the

From Gustavo Gutiérrez, *A Theology of Liberation : History, Politics, and Salvation,* trans. and ed. Sister Caridad Inda and John Eagleson, revised edition (Maryknoll, NY: Orbis Books, 1988), pp. 54–55, 174.

economic and political life of its respective countries. Political parties of a populist bent capitalized on this basically urban movement. But the crisis of developmentalist policies to which we have referred, the rise of multinational businesses and their growing control of the economy of Latin America, and the appearance of militant peasant masses on the political scene — all these were responsible for the loss of political leadership, at different times in different countries, which the different forms of populism held up to that point. After a period of disorientation, an intense process of political radicalization began. In this regard, the Cuban revolution has played a catalytic role. With certain qualifications, this revolution serves as a dividing point for the recent political history of Latin America. One final factor in all this is the Sino-Soviet split,[1] which among other things has accelerated the internal breakup of the classical Communist parties and precipitated the birth of new and more radical revolutionary groups.

Guerrilla groups appeared, intending quickly to mobilize the masses: they did this by urging them to follow a radical line more than through an organization really representing their interests. Military defeats followed each other. The political lessons are nevertheless important. Revolutionary political action has diversified in recent years. It has gone from outbreaks of a leftist nationalism in search of definite options — under the pressure of radicalized groups and the masses — through in-depth connections with the popular masses and even the much-discussed "electoral path," to subversion under new forms of armed struggles. Moreover, it is becoming more obvious that the revolutionary process ought to embrace the whole continent. There is little chance of success for attempts limited to a national scope.

This radicalization has brought about a reaction — both domestically and overseas — on the part of the defenders of the established order. This has in turn frequently led to working outside existing institutions and legal norms and to clandestine, even violent political activity. The reaction becomes even more belligerent and in many cases resorts to severe and brutal forms of repression. The effect is what Dom Helder Camara refers to graphically as "the spiral of violence."

In Latin America we are in the midst of a full-blown process of revolutionary ferment. This is a complex and changing situation which resists schematic interpretations and demands a continuous revision of the postures adopted. Be that as it may, the untenable circumstances of poverty, alienation, and exploitation in which the greater part of the people of Latin America live urgently demand that we find a path toward economic, social, and political liberation. This is the first step towards a new society. . . . The theology of liberation attempts to reflect on the experience and meaning of the faith based on the commitment to abolish injustice and to build a new society; this theology must be verified by the practice of that commitment, by active, effective participation in the struggle which the exploited social classes have undertaken against their oppressors. Liberation from every form of exploitation, the possibility of a more human and more dignified life, the creation of a new man — all pass through this struggle.

1. Following Stalin's death, Mao Tse-tung (Mao Zedong) viewed himself as the foremost theoretician and exponent of world communism. By the 1960s, tensions between the two Communist states developed from deep ideological differences and border disputes which led to a deterioration in their relationship.

But in the last instance we will have an authentic theology of liberation only when the oppressed themselves can freely raise their voice and express themselves directly and creatively in society and in the heart of the People of God, when they themselves "account for the hope," which they bear, when they are the protagonists of their own liberation. For now we must limit ourselves to efforts which ought to deepen and support that process, which has barely begun. If theological reflection does not vitalize the action of the Christian community in the world by making its commitment to charity fuller and more radical, if — more concretely — in Latin America it does not lead the Church to be on the side of the oppressed classes and dominated peoples, clearly and without qualifications, then this theological reflection will have been of little value. Worse yet, it will have served only to justify half-measures and ineffective approaches and to rationalize a departure from the Gospel.

We must be careful not to fall into an intellectual self-satisfaction, into a kind of triumphalism of erudite and advanced "new" visions of Christianity. The only thing that is really new is to accept day by day the gift of the Spirit, who makes us love — in our concrete options to build a true human brotherhood, in our historical initiatives to subvert an order of injustice — with the fullness with which Christ loved us. To paraphrase a well-known text of Pascal, we can say that all the political theologies, the theologies of hope, of revolution, and of liberation, are not worth one act of genuine solidarity with exploited social classes. They are not worth one act of faith, love, and hope, committed — in one way or another — in active participation to liberate man from everything that dehumanizes him and prevents him from living according to the will of the Father.

104

Camilo Torres, "Why I Am Not Anti-Communist"

As a revolutionary priest, Camilo Torres (1929–1966) became a symbol for many Christians and Marxists in their struggle for change in Latin America. He explained his views in this message written in September 1965, after he had joined the guerrillas.

QUESTIONS TO CONSIDER

1. How does Torres reconcile Christian concepts with revolutionary Marxism?
2. Evaluate Torres's comments concerning socialism in Poland with reference to the worker's movement there in recent years.

Because of the traditional relations between Christians and Marxists, and between the Church and the Communist Party, it is quite likely that erroneous suspicions and suppositions will arise regarding the relations of Christians and Marxists within the United Front, and of a priest and the Communist Party.

This is why I want to clarify to the Colombian people my relations with the Communist Party and its position within the United Front.

I have said that I am a revolutionary as a Colombian, as a sociologist, as a Christian, and as a priest. I believe that there are elements within the Communist Party which are genuinely revolutionary. Consequently, I cannot be anti-Communist either as a Colombian, as a sociologist, as a Christian, or as a priest.

I am not anti-Communist as a Colombian because anti-Communism in my country is bent on persecuting the dissatisfied, whether they be Communists or not, who in the main are poor people.

I am not anti-Communist as a sociologist because the Communist proposals to combat poverty, hunger, illiteracy, and lack of housing and public services are effective and scientific.

I am not anti-Communist as a Christian, because I believe that anti-Communism condemns the whole of Communism, without acknowledging that there is some justice in its cause, as well as injustice. By condemning the whole we condemn the just and the unjust, and this is anti-Christian.

I am not anti-Communist as a priest because, whether the Communists realize it or not, there are within their ranks some authentic Christians. If they are working in good faith, they might well be the recipients of sanctifying grace. Should this be true, and should they love their neighbor, they would be saved. My role as a priest, even though I am not exercising its prerogatives externally, is to lead all men to God. The most effective way to do this is to get men to serve the people in keeping with their conscience.

I do not intend to proselytize among the Communists and to try to get them to accept the dogma and teachings of the Catholic Church. I do want all men to act in accordance with their conscience, to look in earnest for the truth, and to love their neighbor effectively.

The Communists must be fully aware of the fact that I will not join their ranks, that I am not nor will I ever be a Communist, either as a Colombian, as a sociologist, as a Christian, or as a priest.

Yet I am disposed to fight with them for common objectives: against the oligarchy and the domination of the United States, and for the takeover of power by the popular class.

I do not want public opinion to identify me with the Communists. This is why in all my public appearances I have wanted to be surrounded not only by the Communists but by all revolutionaries, be they independent or followers of other movements. . . .

Once the popular class assumes power, with the help of all revolutionaries, then our people will be ready to discuss the religious orientation they should give their lives.

From John Alvarez Garcia and Christian Restrepo Calle, eds., *Camilo Torres : His Life and His Message,* trans. Virginia M. O'Grady (Springfield, IL : Templegate, 1968), pp. 74–78. Reprinted by permission.

Poland is an example of how socialism can be established without destroying what is essential in Christianity. As a Polish priest once said: "As Christians we have the obligation of contributing to the construction of a socialist state so long as we are allowed to adore God as we wish."

105

Dom Hélder Câmara, *Revolution Through Peace*

Dom Hélder Câmara (1909 —) was born in Fortaleza, Brazil, and ordained a priest in 1931. He spent his lifetime trying to improve the economic and social conditions of the poor. For his work and his writings, he received a Martin Luther King International Peace Prize and was nominated for the Nobel Peace Prize in 1970.

QUESTIONS TO CONSIDER

1. What is Câmara's interpretation of freedom with reference to the fishermen of the Brazilian Northeast?
2. In addition to making profits, do foreign investors have other responsibilities when they operate in underdeveloped nations?
3. Why does Câmara see democracy losing ground in Brazil?

Once in my diocese, a thousand fishermen and their families, who were already poor, were on the point of sliding into a state of utter misery. In the developing Brazilian Northeast, a synthetic rubber plant and a vegetable protein factory, among others, had been installed on the bank of a river. The chemical waste flowing into the stream from these two factories was killing the fish and therefore gravely jeopardizing the already precarious situation of those fishermen.

I arranged a meeting between the managers of the two factories and the distressed fishermen. The managers explained that in about two and a half years their factories would be in a position to recycle the wastes; the fishermen would have to be patient until then. In vain the fishermen cried out that in two and a half years they would be living on the verge of starvation if they were not already dead.

We were face to face with one chapter in the universal balance sheet of investments. Unless I am much mistaken, the golden rule is still the same: invest

From Dom Hélder Câmara, *Revolution Through Peace* (New York: Harper & Row, 1971), pp. 57–60. Translated from the Portuguese by Amparo McLean. English translation copyright © 1971 by Harper & Row, Publishers, Inc. Reprinted by permission of HarperCollins Publishers.

where profits are highest, quickest, and safest. If that means crushing a few, or many, or numerous human beings, it is regrettable, but, the reasoning goes, that is the inevitable price of progress.

And thus we see that Communism has no monopoly on crushing human beings. Apropos of this subject, another important observation should be made. It is touching to see that the West does not hesitate to sacrifice the finest flower of its youth to fight and die to safeguard the free world.

When will the countries of the West become fully conscious of the fact that misery, too, crushes human beings and reduces them to a vile subhuman state?

When will we fully understand that "freedom" is a word without meaning to someone who does not have a house fit to live in, or food fit to eat, or clothes fit to wear, or a minimum of education and decent work?

It isn't easy to be rich and go on being human. It isn't easy to deprive oneself voluntarily of goods which may not be worth much today but will certainly be worth more tomorrow, or to think of others, or to listen to the Church when she reminds us that the right to property is never absolute and unconditional, or to make up our minds not to keep what is a luxury to us but a necessity to others.

Democracy must come to the aid of human frailty. If it does not lead to bringing about unions of free workers, free cooperatives, and free adult elementary education, there will be a serious lack of these democratic instruments of human advancement and community organization.

Some fear the possible abuses of liberty and foresee all kinds of pressure, threats, violence, a climate of uncertainty and uneasiness, all harbingers of social convulsion.

The government has the right and duty to insist that adult education, unions, and cooperatives be organized within the limits of the law and be restricted to the democratic process. But as long as they act within the law and the democratic process, they should not be subjected to the least constraint, they should be entirely free to act. Otherwise they will turn into caricatures of what they ought to be.

Is there anyone who does not know that on our continent the number of those who no longer believe in democracy and are ready to turn to violence is growing by leaps and bounds, precisely because they judge democracy to be timid and indecisive? They consider it to be without the courage to go to the root of our evils because out of fear it walks with such excessive caution that it ends by being inoperative and useless?

If we love democracy and believe in its methods, we must demand much of it. Democracy has no right to be blind and deaf, no right to be naïve. There are grave wrongs to be righted, above all in the rural areas. Mere pathetic appeals to the heartstrings, laws on paper, and bureaus with pompous names are not enough.

If we are sincere in our desire for human advancement and truly want to organize our communities — the initial step in authentic development — we should be overjoyed to see the workers struggling to get a basic education and running their own unions and their own cooperatives, without constraint or paternalism, without fear and without puppet leaders imposed from above.

So that the calumny of Communist sympathies on my part will not be repeated, this may be a good time to remind you that the selfish attitude of the United States during the first United Nations Conference on Trade and

Development — a conference of vital importance to the underdeveloped world — was equaled only by that of Soviet Russia. So that it will not be alleged that my attitude is anti-American, let me point out one example, among many, in which we might profitably imitate the United States : it would be greatly to our advantage to adopt an antitrust law like that adopted, for domestic use, by the North Americans.

This is a good time to remind the three branches of government of this Republic, a good time to remind this democracy of Brazil, that they must urgently seek ways and means of enforcing the laws passed by the legislature and promulgated by the executive branch. It is perilous in the extreme, it is an evil of unforeseeable consequences, to allow the laws to be discredited.

It grieves me to see that not only in Brazil, but to a greater or lesser degree in all of Latin America, many of the best of our young people find it harder and harder to trust in democracy ; to have faith in its validity, in its forthrightness in moving from theory to practice, in its courage to go straight to the heart of our socioeconomic ills and find a remedy for them.

Time is running out against democracy. Greater and greater numbers have become disenchanted with it and are in danger of falling either into a skeptical, even cynical attitude or into one of violence and despair.

It would be a grave error to take the scornful, superior stand of one who trusts public authority to break up any manifestations of violence. The solution this country needs is quite different : it is that the government and the people, the nation's vital forces, in a common love of freedom and democracy, join forces to transform fundamental laws which have heretofore existed only on paper into living laws for a living people who have a rendezvous with their own destiny.

Surely it is not so hard to sense the love concealed behind slogans which may sometimes sound harsh to the ear. If I demand much of democracy, it is because I believe in it. And it grieves me to see the democracies losing ground because their rich are getting richer and their poor are getting poorer.

My harshness toward certain countries may be a quixotic effort — but who does not love and respect Don Quixote, who is so much more a realist than he seems, very much worth listening to by politicians who call themselves practical and yet topple over into the most incredible lack of realism ? My harshness toward certain countries, I repeat, is what may be a quixotic effort to help them understand that in the middle run, for I cannot say in the long run, it is suicidal to persist in widening the growing gulf between the developed and the developing worlds.

The Pacific Rim

As the present century draws to a close, the Pacific Rim nations, particularly those newly industrializing countries (NICs) such as South Korea, Taiwan, Hong Kong, and Singapore among others are rapidly emerging as the world's fastest growing economies and are playing an increasingly important role in the world economic order. Such a phenomenal economic development in the Pacific Rim was spearheaded by Japan, which has already achieved the status of the world's second largest economy after the United States. What is amazing about the economic achievement of the Pacific Rim nations is that only less than three decades ago most of them were poor, technologically dependent, and politically unstable countries. Also, these East Asian NICs are small in area with high population density and are generally poorly endowed with natural resources. Hong Kong[1] and Singapore are merely city states with a combined population of 8 million people. In area, Hong Kong is a third of the size of the state of Rhode Island ; however, in population, it has more than five times that of Rhode Island. It has long been a busy trading port and has become a major financial and manufacturing center in the world. Its per capita gross national product (GNP) has reached $9600 (1988), the second highest in the Pacific Rim after Japan. It is said that this British colony has more Rolls Royce cars per square mile than any other place in the world. Singapore is about half the size of Hong Kong in both area and population, but it enjoys the third highest per capita GNP in the Pacific Rim — $8000 (1987). South Korea was a desperately poor and war-torn nation less than four decades ago and is still facing a very hostile Communist regime in the northern half of the Korean peninsula. Even so, Korea, often called "little Japan," has been enjoying impressive economic growth for the past two decades. Its manufactured goods such as automobiles and some high technology goods have been penetrating deep into the markets of North America, Western Europe, Southeast Asia, and recently Eastern Europe, the Soviet Union, and China. It felt secure enough to host the summer Olympic games in Seoul in 1988.

Despite its small size in area, which is about a third of that of the state of Virginia with four times Virginia's population, the economic growth of Taiwan, which is sometimes known as the Republic of China, is the envy of many less developed countries, including the People's Republic of China. Taiwan's per capita GNP is more than $6000 (1988) in sharp contrast with that of the other China which is less than $400.

For the past two decades, the Pacific Rim has been the most dynamic region of the world, especially in contrast with most of the Latin American and African countries, and those of North America to some extent, which have been going through painful economic stagnation, high inflation, and high unemployment. The awesome economic growth, trade expansion, and

---

1. Hong Kong has been a British Crown Colony ever since China's defeat in the Opium War in 1842 ; however, this colony is scheduled to revert back to China in 1997.

the staggering trade surplus of the Pacific Rim nations pose a major challenge to the rest of the world. Such a situation must inevitably cause strain between the Pacific Rim nations and other parts of the world, particularly North America and Western Europe. Such a strain has been well reflected in U.S.-Japan trade relations.

106

The Second "Maekawa" Report

Japan's economic recovery and development since the end of the Second World War have been phenomenal. Less than a half century after the utter destruction of the country by the war, Japan has emerged as the second largest economy in the world just behind the United States. The impressive economic success of Japan is often described as a national Cinderella story of modern times. In 1986, Japan's per capita gross national product which reached $17,000 finally surpassed that of the United States, which was $16,000. Boosted largely by the continuous trade surpluses with nearly all of her trading partners for more than two decades, Japan is today the largest creditor nation. (The United States is the largest debtor nation.) Such trade imbalances were, rightly or wrongly, attributed to the reluctance on the part of Japan to opening her market. Trade barriers were built, including even such nontariff barriers as the Japanese language, consumer habits, and the saving-minded "workaholic" life-styles of the Japanese people. Partly from the mounting pressure from without and partly from the genuine interest in reforming the Japanese economic system from within, in 1985, Prime Minister Yasuhiro Nakasone appointed a special commission, chaired by Haruo Maekawa, a former governor of the Bank of Japan, to explore ways to restructure the Japanese economy. This commission is commonly known as the Maekawa Commission. After a long study, this commission came up with two sweeping recommendations, one on April 7, 1986, and the other on April 23, 1987. These recommendations dealt with a number of very basic problem areas such as the expansion of domestic demand, market opening, shorter working hours, and international harmony, among others. The following is an excerpt from the second recommendation of the Maekawa Commission.

QUESTIONS TO CONSIDER

1. Would these recommended policies, if implemented by the Tokyo government, solve the problem of ongoing trade frictions between Japan and her trading partners, including the United States? How?

2. Why has the Japanese government been slow to implement these recommendations? What are the difficulties?
3. Are there any connections between Ito Hirobumi's "Reminiscences on the Drafting of the New Constitution" (see Reading 47), "Tojo Makes Plea of Self Defense" (see Reading 73), and the Maekawa Report? How do you explain Japan's quick rise to an economic superpower?

Japan is today posting large current account surpluses, and there are signs of intensifying economic friction with other countries. This imbalance cannot be allowed to continue, either for the Japanese economy itself or for the harmonious development of the world economy. This situation having arisen in an interdependent world economy, Japanese policy responses alone cannot rectify this imbalance. International policy coordination is also needed, including reductions in the United States fiscal deficit. Nevertheless, as a country largely dependent upon free trade, a country accounting for one-tenth of the world GNP, and the world's largest creditor nation, Japan must take the initiative in rolling back protectionism and defending the free trade system by seeking to achieve an internationally harmonious external balance and to make a positive contribution to the international community.

Looking inward, it is questionable whether or not Japan's economic growth is reflected in the quality of Japanese life: housing standards are low, the cost of living high, and working hours long. With the yen's recent appreciation, a yawning gap has developed between our personal perceptions of the yen's value in everyday life and its value on exchange markets. The people have thus begun to wonder whether the yen's strength is reflected in their own standard of living. As the yen has appreciated since September 1985, this has generated friction in a number of areas and this friction has in turn given rise to popular anxiety about Japan's economic future. The promotion of economic restructuring must be premised upon popular understanding that this restructuring will contribute to the quality of their lives.

Since the announcement of the Report of the Advisory Group on Economic Restructuring for the International Harmony in April 1986, the government has sought to flush out the specifics of the Report's recommendations. The government announced its Outline of Procedures for the Promotion of Economic Restructuring in May and the Government-Ruling Party Joint Headquarters for the Promotion of Economic Restructuring was established, headed by the Prime Minister. As a result, specific policies are being formulated for revising the preferential tax treatment for savings, improving the tax treatment for housing acquisition, reducing legal limits on working hours, cutting back on domestic coal output, establishing an offshore financial market, and more. Efforts have also been made to respond with flexible fiscal and monetary policies under the Comprehensive Economic Measures and other initiatives. However, we have just begun on the long

John K. T. Choy, *Japan, Exploring New Path* (Washington, DC: Japan Economic Institute, 1988), pp. 14–18.

road to economic restructuring and promoting economic restructuring which ensures both international harmony and better-quality Japanese living simultaneously is increasingly imperative and increasingly urgent.

Given this situation, this Committee was requested by the Economic Council on September 5, 1986, to conduct a study of the policies needed for medium- and long-term economic restructuring. Having held a total of 43 meetings since receiving its mandate eight months ago, the Committee is pleased to be able to present its final report. We call upon the government to work to promptly study and implement specific policies for the promotion of economic restructuring.

Chapter 1. Basic Approach to Restructuring

(1) Japanese restructuring is intended to simultaneously attain external harmony and domestic-demand-led economic growth. This will ultimately improve the quality of Japanese life.

(2) In order to rectify the major multilateral imbalances, it is necessary to have policy coordination including reductions in the United States fiscal deficit and a regaining of American industrial competitiveness. Japan should move to take the initiative in achieving restructuring and domestic-demand-led economic growth. The period of the mid-1990s will be a time of restructuring worldwide.

(3) Japan should seek to reduce its current account surplus as a percentage of GNP as quickly as possible within this context of international policy coordination.

(4) The process of economic restructuring should be based upon market mechanisms. Thus Japan

should seek to promote thorough deregulation, both for domestic industrial activity and for improved market access for imports. There is an urgent need for a thorough regulatory review by new organization.

(5) Fiscal monetary policy has an important role to play in stimulating domestic demand. It is especially important that fiscal policy's resource redistributive functions be utilized. While observing the basic spirit of administrative and fiscal reform and reaping the benefits of the progress made, extraordinary and urgent fiscal measures should be taken to stimulate domestic demand in light of the current economic situation. Efforts will continue to be made for appropriate and flexible fiscal and monetary policy management.

Chapter 2. Policies for Restructuring

I. Expansion of Domestic Demand

1. Housing

(1) The qualitative improving of housing is a mainstay of the effort to expand domestic demand, and policy resources should be allocated with a special priority on this field. Housing policy should be promoted with attention to economic policy considerations as well as social policy concerns.

(2) Instituting radically preferential tax treatment for housing acquisition and the like, an effort should also be made to further enhance and improve home financing and other incentives.

(3) On the supply side, there is a need to institute creative competition-promotion policies including en-

couraging more firms to enter the housing market.

2. Improving Social Capital

(1) Looking ahead to the twenty-first century, it is important that we work steadily and systematically to raise the quality of the Japanese social capital commensurate with Japan's international status.

(2) Achieving balanced enhancement of social capital demands that the public and private sectors work with an appropriate sharing of financing and that the necessary public moneys be secured.

(3) In enhancing social capital, it is imperative that the tradition allocation be reassessed and priority allocation promoted.

(4) In drawing on private-sector vitality, it is important that dramatic incentives be provided.

3. Land Policy

(1) The enhancement of housing and social assets hinges upon finding a solution to the land problem.

(2) It is thus fundamentally important that efficient use be made of national land resources through promoting the broader dispersion of industrial and other facilities for balanced national development.

(3) Land policy issues are inexorably linked to urban policy issues, and it is imperative that reform of large cities be actively promoted via redevelopment of urban areas.

(4) An effort should be made to promote the conversion from agricultural to residential land by taxing agricultural land in urbanization promotion areas to more closely approximate the taxation of residential land.

(5) Efforts should be made to expand the supply of residential land with rezoning and an ambitious effort to landfill public waters.

4. Consumption

(1) There is a considerable gap between Japan's per-capita GNP and popular perceptions from everyday life. An effort will thus be made to reduce the differential between Japanese and international prices and hence to close this gap.

(2) The benefits of the yen's appreciation should be used to spur domestic demand. This is especially important in sectors subject to public regulation.

(3) Stimulating consumption basically demands steady growth in real disposable income under conditions of sustained economic growth and price stability.

(4) Economic growth should be reflected in increased wage rates and shorter working hours.

II. Shorter Working Hours

(1) The shortening of working hours is important for enhancing national standards of living, for stimulating consumption, and for maintaining employment.

(2) An effort should be made to reduce Japanese working hours to about 1,800 hours per year as soon as possible and no later than the end of the century (as with five-day workweeks and 20 paid days off per year).

(3) It is important to ambitiously promote the five-day workweek by, for example, having government offices and financial institutions close on Saturdays.

III. Internationally Harmonious Industrial Structure

1. Efforts for Industrial Restructuring

(1) Industrial restructuring must be premised upon market mechanisms, and the government's re-

sponse must not entail involvement in specific industries, but must be restricted to easing the pain of restructuring.

(2) This process of industrial restructuring is a process of increasing industrial sophistication. While working to create a climate conducive to the full exercise of public and corporate vitality, we should facilitate this restructuring.

(3) Rather than see the present as a time of "hollowization" and seek to forestall it, we should push ahead with forward-looking responses.

2. Direct Overseas Investment

(1) Japanese direct overseas investment will contribute to increased horizontal division of labor and expand both production and employment in the host countries.

(2) This will also contribute to reducing Japan's current account surplus.

3. Enhancing Competitive Conditions

(1) In such fields as distribution, financial services, construction, agriculture, transportation, and telecommunications, it is necessary to work for greater efficiency and productivity through promoting far-reaching deregulation, further improved market access for import expansion, the use of investment in Japan, and other means.

(2) Some regulations in distribution have outlived their justification, and there is a need to fundamentally review the licensing regulations.

(3) Positive efforts should be made to ensure that foreign companies do business in the Japanese construction market.

(4) Efforts should be made to make the petroleum industry more rational and more efficient with step-by-step deregulation.

4. Expanding Imports and Improving Market Access

(1) Achieving an internationally harmonious import-export structure is prerequisite to rectifying the external imbalance.

(2) Further efforts should be made to reduce the number of products subject to the standards and certification systems, and to reduce the number of standards themselves, to promote improved market access.

(3) An effort should be made to promote the abolition of the tariffs on manufacturers in the GATT Uruguay Round.

(4) An effort should be made to improve the government procurement system and to promote governmental imports of manufactured goods.

(5) Japan will take an active role in promoting the GATT Uruguay Round, including services, agricultural products, and other fields.

5. Agriculture Policies Befitting an Era of Internationalization

(1) Efforts to promote agricultural policy must give full consideration not only to producers, but also to consumers and the food industry.

(2) An effort should be made to reduce the differential between Japanese and overseas prices and to achieve stable foodstuff supplies at popularly acceptable prices by improving productivity and promoting imports as appropriate.

(3) Efforts should be made to expand operational scale and improve productivity for greater value-added production to establish agriculture as a viable industry.

(4) Responsive to the diversification of consumer requirements, efforts should be made to improve government controls so as to expand trading in independent-market rice, to

introduce competitive principles in all stages from collecting to marketing.

(5) While seeking to make Japanese production more rational and more efficient, an effort should be made to hold border adjustment measures to a minimum for non-rice agricultural products.

IV. Responses to Unemployment

(1) Employment is the most important issue in industrial restructuring.

(2) The process of industrial restructuring may well generate unemployment arising from the supply-demand imbalance among industries, occupations, age groups, geographic locations, etc. Comprehensive employment policies are needed to facilitate labor mobility and develop expanded employment opportunities.

(3) In the longer term, we should work to become a vigorous long-lived society through Japanese-style work-sharing involving shorter work hours and the redistribution of employment across generational and other lines.

V. Responses for Regional Economics

(1) It is imperative that structurally depressed regions receive priority allocation of public works projects to alleviate occupational changes and other pains of restructuring.

(2) Efforts should be made to promote the creation of employment and other regional employment policies through encouraging the shift to new industries.

(3) In light of the fact that information- and service-oriented industries and other urban industries will be the mainstay of development, there is a need to promote the creation of attractive regional urban centers.

(4) As part of this effort, information and telecommunications infrastructures should be improved, heliports and other high-speed transport network facilities created, and the amenities of life provided in full.

VI. Contributions to a Better World

(1) Japan will make a positive effort to roll back protectionist pressures and to preserve and strengthen the existing free trade system by actively promoting the Uruguay Round.

(2) It is imperative that Japan respond positively to resolving the problems of excessive external indebtedness within the framework of international cooperation, including responding to the debtor countries' capital needs and working to lighten their interest burden.

(3) Every effort should be made to promptly attain the Medium-Term Target for Official Development Assistance (ODA) at an early stage so as to raise the ratio of ODA to GNP and to work for ODA's quantitative enhancement. Efforts will also be made to involve private-sector capital and personnel more in economic cooperation through a variety of means.

(4) Japan will contribute actively to international cooperation in basic research and international public works projects.

(5) Japan will work to revitalize and internationalize Japanese education with expanded acceptance of foreign educators and educational and research institutions.

Chapter 3. Immediate
Action for Restructuring

Although restructuring is a long-term national goal, it is imperative that efforts be concentrated in the next few years to achieve restructuring in view of the existing situation in Japan and overseas. In this context, the following recommendations should be implemented immediately and the expected results achieved within a certain period.

I. Deregulation

(1) Fundamental review of regulations by a new organization with a view to pursuing thorough economic deregulation in the domestic economy and market access.

(2) Relaxation of regulations in the distribution and finance sectors and in petroleum and other industries.

(3) Positive efforts to ensure that foreign companies do business in Japan's construction market.

II. Active Use of Fiscal Policy

Implementation of extraordinary and urgent fiscal measures to cope with the current economic situation while observing the basic spirit of administrative and fiscal reform and reaping the benefits of the progress made.

III. Housing Policy, Land Policy, and Improving Social Capital

(1) Priority allocation of public funds for housing.

(2) Reform of large cities via redevelopment of urban areas, etc.

(3) Promoting the conversion of land from agricultural to residential purposes by taxing agricultural land in urbanization promotion areas to more closely approximate the taxation of residential land, positively reviewing rezoning, and other means.

(4) Improvement and expansion of the residential environment, the infrastructure in such areas as telecommunications and information, and high-speed transportation networks in regional urban centers.

(5) Priority allocation of public works projects.

IV. Stepped-up Imports of Manufactured Goods

(1) Promoting the abolition of tariffs on manufactured products in the GATT Uruguay Round.

(2) Improving the government procurement system and promoting governmental imports of manufactured goods.

V. Agriculture

(1) Reducing the differential between Japanese and overseas foodstuff prices by raising productivity and promoting imports.

(2) Improving the existing food supply and demand system under government control by introducing competitive principles in all stages from collection to marketing.

VI. Shorter Working Hours

(1) Moving to reduce total working hours to 1,800 per year.

(2) Promotion of the five-day week for civil servants and personnel in financial institutions (including closing their offices on Saturdays).

VII. Economic Cooperation

Prompt attainment of the Medium Term Target for ODA and raising the ratio of ODA to GNP (including advancing the target for doubling ODA from seven years by two years).

In promoting these policy measures, it is imperative that all due consideration be paid to the impact on employment and local economies.

Translation provided by the Japanese Embassy, Washington, D.C.

M6 70